KT-403-491

DISPOSED OF
BY LIBRARY
HOUSE OF LORDS

The Chinese Legal System

The legal system of the People's Republic of China has seen significant changes since reforms were begun in 1978. By 2001, after the second decade of legal reform, law making and institution building have reached impressive levels. The achievements of legal reform in China are many and varied, but the imperative of maintaining supremacy for the Party-state remains a salient feature in the process. This book analyses the major features of the Chinese legal system on the eve of China's accession to the World Trade Organization, in light of tensions between international legal norms and local legal culture.

An introductory chapter establishes the conceptual foundations for the discussion of globalization and legal culture. The book then goes on to discuss:

* *Legal institutions*: examines the ways in which the Chinese legal system embodies tensions between imported legal norms and local legal culture.
* *Contracts and property*: reveals the ways in which the Chinese legal system embodies tensions between the imperative of state control associated with local legal culture and values about private property rights and freedom of contract.
* *Human rights*: examines how the legal system reflects tensions between the goals of social welfare and social control, while also being subject to pressure from abroad to improve human rights conduct.
* *Foreign economic relations*: examines the process and implications of China's accession to the World Trade Organization.

Essential reading for students and academics in the field of Chinese law, this book will also prove extremely valuable for those interested in comparative law, Chinese politics, international relations and the Chinese economy.

Pitman B. Potter is Director of the Institute of Asian Research at the University of British Columbia. He is also Professor of Law and Director of Chinese Legal Studies at the UBC Law Faculty. Dr Potter's publications include *Legitimation and Contract Autonomy in the PRC* (1992), *Domestic Law Reforms in Post-Mao China* (1994), and *Foreign Business Law in China* (1995).

Routledge Studies on China in Transition
Series editor: David S.G. Goodman

The Chinese Legal System

Globalization and local legal culture

Pitman B. Potter

London and New York

First published 2001
by Routledge
11 New Fetter Lane, London EC4P 4EE

Simultaneously published in the USA and Canada
by Routledge
29 West 35th Street, New York, NY 10001

Routledge is an imprint of the Taylor & Francis Group

© 2001 Pitman B. Potter

Typeset in Garamond by Taylor & Francis Books Ltd
Printed and bound in Great Britain by TJ International Ltd,
Padstow, Cornwall

All rights reserved. No part of this book may be reprinted or
reproduced or utilized in any form or by any electronic, mechanical,
or other means, now known or hereafter invented, including
photocopying and recording, or in any information storage or
retrieval system, without permission in writing from the publishers.

British Library Cataloguing in Publication Data
A catalogue record for this book is available from the British Library

Library of Congress Cataloging-in-Publication Data
Potter, Pitman B.
The Chinese legal system: globalization and local legal
culture/Pitman B. Potter.
Includes bibliographical references and index.
1. Law–China. 2. China–foreign economic relations. I. Title.
KNQ68 .P68 2001
349.51–dc21   2001019969

ISBN 0–415–23674–6

For Vicki, Kathleen and Jessie

Contents

Preface

Funding for the research resulting in this volume was provided by the Social Sciences and Humanities Research Council of Canada, for which I am deeply grateful.

Many people have assisted over the years in the research and analysis that have led to this book. First, I would like to thank Rick Edmonds, David Shambaugh, and the other participants at the *China Quarterly*'s special conference on "The PRC at 50," who encouraged me to expand my short article "The Chinese Legal System: Continuing Commitment to the Primacy of State Power" (*The China Quarterly* No. 159, 1999, pp. 673–83) into a book-length manuscript. I would also like to thank my graduate students at the Faculty of Law and the Institute of Asian Research at UBC, including in particular James Shi-Kuan Chen, Chi Yubin, Dong Shuguang, Daniel Freeman, Huang Xianfeng, Mark Kremzner, Li Jianyong, Li Yuguo, Song Longmei, Jennifer MacGregor-Greer, Jennifer Miller, Jan Oosterhuis, Xin Jianhong, Yin Li, Yun Zhu, and Zhang Yulin, who have over the years provided invaluable research assistance and insight. Paul Cowsill, a law student at UBC, has provided invaluable assistance in preparing the final manuscript. I owe a significant intellectual debt to colleagues in the China law field, whose comments and suggestions have improved my under-standing of the issues discussed in this book, including in particular William C. Alford, Albert H.Y. Chen, Donald C. Clarke, Anthony R. Dicks, R. Randle Edwards, James V. Feinerman, William C. Jones, and Stanley B. Lubman. I would also like to thank my colleagues and friends at the Vancouver office of Borden Ladner Gervais LLP (formerly Ladner Downs) for their ongoing support for my work on this project.

I am profoundly grateful to various colleagues at Beijing University Law Faculty, the Chinese University of Politics and Law, the Law Institute of the Chinese Academy of Social Sciences, the Law Institute of the Shanghai Academy of Social Sciences, the People's University of China Law Faculty, Shanghai University Law Faculty; Sichuan University Law Faculty, and Qinghua University Law Faculty for taking the time to provide me valuable counsel and advice on the development of the Chinese legal system. Several visiting scholars at UBC Law Faculty provided valuable insights to improve my understanding of Chinese law and society, including Hu Liling (Chinese University of Politics and Law), Liu Hainian (CASS Law Institute), Liu Yigong (Lanzhou University), Lu Guoqiang (Shanghai Higher Level People's Court), Qian Mingxing (Peking University), Wang Jianming (Sichuan University), Wang Weiguo (China University of Politics and Law), and Wu Zhipan (Peking University). Many individual lawyers, law professors, and judges in China have given generously of their time and knowledge about the workings of the Chinese legal system – wishing to remain anonymous, these individuals know who they are and to them I express my sincere thanks. Despite the sage advice and generous assistance received from the individuals mentioned above and from many others whom I have most grievously neglected to mention, I remain responsible for the errors and deficiencies in this book.

My sincere thanks go to Joe Whiting, Annabel Watson, Barbara Duke and Dennis Hodgson at Routledge for their assistance, steadfast support and encouragement in bringing the book to press.

Finally, I would like to thank my wife Vicki and daughters Kathleen and Jessie for putting up with the many extended absences and other instances of familial neglect that accompanied my work on this project. Without their support, this book would not have been possible and it is to them that the volume is dedicated.

Vancouver
January 10, 2001

Acknowledgements

Portions of Chapter 1 were adapted from Pitman B. Potter, "The Chinese Legal System: Continuing Commitment to the Primacy of State Power," in *The China Quarterly* No. 159 (1999), pp. 673–83.

Portions of Chapter 2 were adapted from Pitman B. Potter, "The Administrative Litigation Law of the PRC: Judicial Review and Bureaucratic Reform," in Pitman B. Potter (ed.), *Domestic Law Reforms in Post-Mao China*, Armonk, NY: M.E. Sharpe (1994).

Portions of Chapter 3 were adapted from Pitman B. Potter, "Contract Law," in Freshfields (eds), *Doing Business in China*, New York: Interjura (2000).

Portions of Chapter 4 were adapted from Pitman B. Potter, "Globalization and Local Legal Culture: Dilemmas of China's Use of Liberal Ideas of Private Property Rights," *Asian Law* vol. 2 (2000) and Mark Gillen and Pitman Potter, "The Convergence of Securities Laws in Asia: Case Studies of Malaysia, Singapore, Japan and China," in Gerald Ferguson (ed.), *Asia-Pacific Comparative Law*, Vancouver: UBC Press (1998).

Portions of Chapter 5 were adapted from Pitman B. Potter, "The Right to Development: Philosophical Differences and Political Implications," in E.P. Mendes and A.-M. Traeholt (eds), *Human Rights: Chinese and Canadian Perspectives*, Ottawa: Human Rights Research and Education Centre (1997).

Portions of Chapter 6 were adapted from Pitman B. Potter, "Foreign Investment Law in the PRC: Dilemmas of State Control," in *The China Quarterly*, No. 141 (1995), pp. 155–85.

Introduction

The legal system of the People's Republic of China is the product of policy decisions by the Party/state to build an institutional framework to support economic growth. The decision to pursue legal reform, first articulated at the Third Plenum of the 11th Central Committee Congress in late 1978, was the result of a tentative consensus among the top leadership that paralleled a similarly tentative commitment to introducing market mechanisms to the state-planned economy.[1] As a result, the legal reform effort has been marked by political and policy disagreements over broader issues of economic reform. Legal reform in China has also been complicated by issues of political reform and by ambivalence about the introduction of ideals of governance associated with the West. The linkage between economic and legal reform has become even more evident in the context of China's entry into the World Trade Organization, where commitment to liberal legal institutions is presented as the price of admission to a market-oriented world trading system.

Foreign perspectives on China's legal system often presume that the legal reforms of the Deng Xiaoping era are more or less natural complements to economic and social reform – and possibly a harbinger to political reform. Foreign observers are invited to conclude that Chinese legal reforms express an evolving willingness to approach governance in ways that are roughly comparable to or at least compatible with those of the industrialized democracies. These presumptions appear to be supported by the use in China of institutional forms described in the familiar nomenclature of the liberal legal tradition. Foreign observers are given to understand that Chinese courts, lawyers, and judges are categorically comparable with those of liberal legal systems, and that various categories of substantive and procedural law in China parallel their liberal legal counterparts.

However, the legal system of the PRC offers students of law a signal lesson in the dangers in uncritical acceptance of such easy comparisons. The record of foreign involvement in China's post-Mao legal and economic reforms suggests the very real costs that ensue from the failure to understand the ways in which legal institutions and processes borrowed from abroad are driven by local conditions to operate in unexpected ways. Business deals continue to go awry as assumptions about the performance of legal actors and institutions are proved unreliable. Diplomatic negotiations, ranging from trade relations to cultural exchanges, are often jeopardized by failed expectations about the content and performance of law and regulation. While the challenge of managing relations between China and the world extends far beyond the legal realm, attention to the local contexts for the operation of law in China can contribute in important ways to avoiding the costs of failed expectations.

This book is an attempt to explain the operation of the Chinese legal system by reference to the interplay of foreign legal norms and local legal culture. Legal norms refer to the values that underlie forms of law and legal institutions. Much of the story of the PRC's legal reform effort concerns the struggle to adapt international norms to local conditions. Local legal culture refers to the system of Chinese values and practices that informs legally significant behavior. Despite the influences exerted by foreign legal norms, Chinese law remains dominated by local legal culture. The development of the Chinese legal system over the past twenty years has reflected a process of selective adaptation, by which borrowed foreign norms about law and legal institutions have been mediated by local legal culture. This process is particularly evident in the areas of legal institutions, contract, property, human rights, and foreign economic relations, which are the focus of the chapters following the conceptual overview on globalization and local legal culture set forth in Chapter 1.

Legal institutions reflect much about the process of selective adaptation. The notion of popular sovereignty that informs liberal legal institutions and the accompanying norms restraining state action is largely absent in Chinese tradition. Upon taking power in 1949, the Chinese communists used their control of political and legal institutions to impose state control over virtually all social, economic, and political activities. The subservience of society to the revolutionary state was justified by reference to discourses of permanent revolution and class struggle. Economic relations were subject to the dictates of an administrative planning system that reserved all property rights to the state, imposed state supervision over virtually all economic transactions, and brought business actors under the regulation of party committees whose leaders were subject only to the controls of an obtuse system of Party discipline. The post-Mao economic reform policies granted limited autonomy to economic actors and their transactions. With this came recognition of the need for relatively formal and predictable legal institutions. However, as discussed in Chapter 2, legal reforms in the areas of legislation, administration, and dispute resolution remain heavily influenced by local legal culture.

In the regulation of property and contracts, the Chinese legal system reflects tensions between imperatives of state control and local autonomy. Building on a tradition where the notions of sanctity of private property rights and the autonomy of contract transactions, which are at the heart of the liberal legal systems of Europe and North America, were largely absent, the Maoist regime marginalized and restricted private contract and property rights. Under the post-Mao legal reforms, contract and property systems underwent significant changes as principles of autonomy, which appeared increasingly comparable with liberal norms, were gradually accepted. However, as discussed in Chapters 3 and 4, the limits to expansion of these concepts are also evident, as primary authority remains with regulatory bureaucracies.

In the area of human rights discussed in Chapter 5, the Chinese legal system reflects tensions between imperatives of social welfare and social control. Reliance on the doctrine of the right to development has permitted the government to retain nearly absolute authority in defining and protecting social welfare. Thus, provisions on labor law for example subordinate the interests of workers to those of the Party/state. In the area of social control, the Party/state retains its dominance despite reforms in criminal law and procedure.

Chapter 6 addresses foreign economic relations, where the discourse of *she-wai/dui-wai* (foreign-related) law suggests the extent to which China's foreign trade and investment regimes have reflected the same apprehensions and ambivalence about the outside world that affect China's foreign relations generally. However, during the 1990s, China's application to resume its seat at the GATT and to join the WTO drove reforms in law and regulation in foreign economic relations, encouraging greater stability and also gradual harmonization of the rules governing foreign business with those governing the domestic economy.

The Chinese legal system is constantly changing, in response to domestic conditions as government policies respond to socio-economic and political change, and in reaction to external factors such as WTO membership. Changing local conditions caused by rapid economic growth will drive new legislation and amendments of existing laws and regulations, while China's accession to the WTO will require far-reaching reforms that will affect virtually all the areas of law examined in this volume. This dynamic process can be understood more easily by reference to the process of selective adaptation by which conditions of local legal culture continue to mediate the application of legal norms associated with forms of law borrowed from abroad. I would hope that this volume might be of some limited assistance in furthering this process of understanding the ongoing evolution of the Chinese legal system.

1 Influences on the legal system

Norms and context

The legal reforms undertaken by the Chinese government since 1978 reflect the interplay of foreign legal norms with a local context. At the very outset of the legal reform process, legal reformers were admonished to learn from China's past and from the experience of foreign countries.[1] In light of the limitations on the development of law and legal institutions during the early period of the PRC, the past was of limited assistance. As a result, the post-Mao law reforms placed heavy reliance on imported legal norms. Even where China's legal reformers looked to prior PRC experience, this was strongly colored by foreign (mostly Soviet) ideals. Thus, the drafting of the 1978 Criminal Law and Criminal Procedure Law and the organizational laws for the People's Courts and the People's Procuracies relied primarily on prior drafts and enactments from the 1950s, which had been based largely on Soviet models.[2] The 1981 Economic Contract Law was influenced significantly by prior contract regulations, which were derived largely from the Soviet and Eastern European experience.[3] The General Principles of Civil Law (1986) were based on relatively well-developed drafts begun during the 1950s and continued during the post-Mao period, which themselves were derived from the European and Soviet experience.[4] Civil Procedure Law too was drawn largely from European models.[5]

As the economic reforms accelerated, China's legal specialists looked increasingly to Europe and North America for inspiration. During the 1980s, legislation on such matters as environmental protection, regulation of foreign and domestic business, intellectual property, and civil procedure and arbitration, and a host of other areas drew increasingly on European and North American models.[6] International agencies such as the UN Development Program and the Ford Foundation, as well as bilateral development programs with the USA, Canada, Japan and the EU, played a significant role in facilitating access to law models from abroad by Chinese legal specialists.[7] The process of borrowing from abroad accelerated during the second decade of legal reform as a wider array of legal scholars and officials recognized that China's economic reforms required the Chinese legal system to conform more fully with the international system.[8] Securities regulation, tax reform, company law, and a range of other measures aimed particularly at regulating the domestic economy and China's foreign economic reflected norms and terminology drawn from Europe and North America. As well, foreign influences in areas such as human rights, criminal law and procedure, and administrative law set the context and many of the parameters within which Chinese laws on these subjects were enacted and enforced. Increased attention to individual rights permitted development of tort law inspired by foreign models.[9] Taiwan civil law also served as an important reference point for legal reform in China, as the writings of Taiwanese jurists and the publication of Taiwanese law books in China increased.[10]

The content of international norms: globalization and the spread of Liberalism

China's efforts to borrow from foreign law models have coincided with the spread of liberal norms of private law and the rising discourse of unification of private international law and globalization.[11] The term "globalization" has been used to describe the contemporary spread of liberal ideals of free markets and private law relations around the world.[12] While globalization of private law is often juxtaposed against public law regimes aimed at a collectivist approach to social welfare,[13] it is also proposed as an antidote to "crony capitalism" and other perceived ills in the economies of East and Southeast Asia.[14] While the capacity of the liberal industrial economies to promote visions of globalization derives as much from political and economic power as from the inherent wisdom of the ideas themselves,[15] there is little doubt that the influence of liberal ideals of private property have spread dramatically in the past decade. The circumstances of the CISG convention and the WTO agreements on intellectual property rights (TRIPs Agreement), trade-related investment measures (TRIMs Agreement), trade in services (GATS Agreement) and dispute resolution (the "Dispute Resolution Understanding") are particularly noteworthy examples of the globalization of private law and private property regimes.[16] The CISG convention establishes uniform default rules for international sales contracts that impose norms drawn from the liberal market systems. The WTO reflects *inter alia* the export of liberal notions of private property rights, particularly in the areas of intellectual property rights enforcement and protection of investment rights. The WTO's Dispute Resolution Understanding, particularly its provisions for binding decisions by dispute resolution panels, reflects liberal norms of legal institutionalism.

The liberal legal norms associated with globalization constitute a belief system driven by changing historical conditions of socio-economic and political relations in Europe and North America. The essentially one-way direction by which these norms are disseminated around the world reflects the imbalances in political and economic power between developed and developing economies that characterize the current dynamic of globalization.

In the case of China, however, the effects of globalized legal norms are confronted by powerful forces of local culture.

Local norms and conditions: the role of legal culture

The influence of local norms and conditions is expressed in part through local legal culture. The efforts of numerous scholars to apply definitional precision to the concept of legal culture have succeeded mainly in underscoring its elusiveness. Drawing on the interplay of sociology and political science, Friedman defined legal culture in terms of customs and opinions, and ways of thinking and doing about the law.[17] Ehrmann's review of Friedman's initial explorations views legal culture as essentially a variant on political culture but in the realm of law.[18] Lubman has applied the Friedman approach more specifically to the study of law and legal culture in the PRC and juxtaposed it with functional approaches,[19] while Glendon takes Ehrmann and Friedman a step farther still in an effort to identify specific bases for comparison between different legal systems.[20] More recently, Varga has explored the term by reference to a challenge/response paradigm in the context of comparative perspectives ranging from the legal anthropology of Gluckman and Diamond to the civil/common law dichotomy and ultimately the Marxist revolutionary rejection of legal culture.[21] Each of these approaches underscores the importance of local values and norms in the development of the belief system that informs local systems of law.

The application of international liberal models of law and legal institutions to China's circumstances is affected by local contexts, particularly political imperatives and the reception of legal norms by individual specialists and by groups in society.[22] Mao Zedong's suggestions to the contrary notwithstanding, China is not a blank slate upon which can be written the normative preferences of the regime, imported or otherwise. Rather, the effect of imported law norms on local behavior and attitudes in China depends in part on the extent to which the norms of the legal regime resonate with existing values. The survival of customary norms despite new institutional arrangements is a salient factor in political culture of modernizing societies, and it no less evident in the area of Chinese legal culture.[23] Whereas indigenous legal norms may emerge gradually through a process of formalization of customary norms,[24] where law norms are imported, compliance requires that these imported norms accommodate local norms and practices.

The reception of imported law norms may also depend on the extent to which these respond to social and economic needs. Where traditional relational norms are ineffective to manage changing social and economic conditions, new norms may emerge as an alternative.[25] Thus, local acceptance of imported law norms may depend on a process by which traditional norms that are unresponsive to new realities are discarded ("delegitimization") and replaced by new norms as part of an evolving belief system ("transvaluation").[26] As increased complexity in social and economic relations permits creation of increasingly diverse and broad relationships beyond those of kinship and community, informal and subjective relational norms may give way to norms of formality and objectivity.[27] Thus, in China, compliance with imported law norms may depend not only on their accommodation of traditional norms and practices but also, paradoxically, on their displacing traditional relational norms with norms of formality and objectivity in response to new socio-economic conditions and the perceived needs of members of society that result.

The reception in China of largely imported legal norms entails necessarily an interaction of international and local values. In this regard, it is useful to recall first that the liberal notion of restraining state power conflicts strongly with the views of many in the post-Mao period (and earlier) that a strong state is essential to China's development.[28] Chinese legal scholars and officials today remain apprehensive about the applicability of Western legal norms to China.[29] Official statements about the proper role of law in contemporary China suggest that Chinese legal culture draws on a reservoir of Chinese tradition derived from Confucianism and its assumptions about authority and hierarchy in social organization.[30] While Confucianism and the collectivist norms that it has engendered have been severely criticized by many contemporary Chinese thinkers as overly authoritarian and repressive,[31] these remain powerful restraints on the penetration of foreign legal norms associated with liberalism. The traditional supremacy of familial and personal ties over institutional obligations remains strong, and the general absence of social ideals of individualism affects the selection and application of foreign legal norms.

Local norms in China derive from traditional values on social, economic, and political relations, and also from local conditions. Accepting that Chinese society is intersected by divisions of political and economic status as well as gender, age, education, etc., we may expect differences of world view and legal culture among disparate groups in society.[32] While legal reform was seen early on in the reform process as inseparable from the political system,[33] local social and economic conditions have gradually come to take on greater importance. Legal reform is presented as a political consequence of changing socio-economic conditions.[34] While it is the Party/state that determines China's progress in the march toward socialism,[35] recognition of this progress nonetheless requires that the discretionary political power exercised by the state under conditions of class struggle must yield to more formal processes associated with law. By the mid-1990s, the discourse of legal reform recognized changing socio-economic conditions and posited a civil legal culture that suggested limits to intrusion by the state.[36] While the specific effects on local value systems stemming from the transformation from the planned economy to a market economy remain uncertain, Chinese scholars have noted the importance of building social values grounded in morality and civility and expressed in part through law.[37] While official views that China's conditions justify distortions and denials of human rights often reflect hackneyed arguments aimed at protecting the regime from criticism for denying to Chinese people basic human rights widely considered to be universal, local conditions are still seen as the foundation for rights and other legal norms.[38] Indeed, it is perceived that changes in local conditions, namely the transition to a market economy, justify enforcement and equality of rights.[39] Recognizing the limits imposed by China's public law tradition on the use of law to support economic growth, Chinese scholars have called for a new approach that might reconcile private and public law paradigms.[40]

Components of legal culture in contemporary China: tradition, governance and society

Legal culture in contemporary China reflects intersecting influences of tradition, governance, and society. Traditional norms provide a context against which operate the norms of contemporary legal culture. Governance provides the context for official legal culture, while society provides the context for popular legal culture. As I have suggested elsewhere, significant tensions exist between official and popular legal culture in China,[41] although each of these elements influences the processes and outcomes of borrowing from abroad that characterize the legal reform effort.

Traditional norms: hierarchy and the denial of private law

Much has been made of the extremely hierarchical nature of society in traditional China. Although elements of the legalist tradition were retained in imperial China after the Han, these tended to focus on the severity of criminal punishment rather than the objectivity and universality that the legalist concept of *fa* extolled.[42] Rather, the Confucian concept of *li* (propriety) dominated the regulation of social relationships and held that these were inherently unequal. Inequality between men and women was also inherently a part of Chinese traditional culture, not only under doctrines of Confucianism but also in Daoism.[43] Such inequality, and the hierarchical social structures that resulted, were deemed essential to the orderly existence of society.[44]

However, the inherent inequality of social relationships proceeded from an assumption of the basic natural equality of men.[45] This did not extend natural equality to women and differed in both content and consequences from the concepts of natural law that derived from Greco-Roman ideas and were used as the basis for challenging the authority of European royalty, contributing to the fragmentation of European feudal society and the emergence of civil law traditions.[46] In China, the belief that man was born with equal natural abilities and characteristics meant that achievement of status was deemed to be the result of superiority in acquired virtue. Inequalities in social standing, economic wealth and/or political power were tolerated as the natural and just result of varying degrees of attained virtue. Consequently, there did not emerge a natural rights tradition that might have served as a basis for demands for equality.[47]

The dominance of social hierarchy was incorporated into legal norms that permitted law to be applied subjectively based on social standing. Thus, criminal sanctions were conceived and enforced differently based on the identity of the parties involved and their position in the social hierarchy.[48] Family and property relations were dictated by the primacy given male domination.[49] Commercial law also reflected the ethic of social inequality through emphasis on the role of custom in the formation and enforcement of obligations, and the role of informal mediation through guild and clan organizations in dispute resolution.[50] Social and economic relations in traditional China were enforced largely through reliance on informal norms that were consistent with regime norms about hierarchy yet were wholly separate from the regime's public law system. Thus, in the context of rural life, rent payments were considered a private obligation between peasant lessees and gentry lessors based on a reciprocal sense of obligation by which the lessee's payment of rent brought with it the lessor's extension of protection against encroachment by the power of the emperor and his officials.[51] Although coercion employed by local state officials was in theory available to ensure performance, it was generally avoided in favor of reliance on private relationships.[52]

Despite the predominance of private enforcement of obligations in traditional China, there did not emerge a system of private law. This was due to the co-optation of local gentry by the state and to the fact that the state's legal regime provided few rules for creating and enforcing private obligations. In contrast to Europe, where local power holders (economic as well as ecclesiastical) sought greater autonomy from the crown, in China no such fractionalization of the local society emerged.[53] Rather, the local gentry upheld and enforced the authority of the empire, largely because their autonomy and power were supported by the official Confucian norms of the state. Local power holders had little incentive to create formal rules for the regulation of social and economic relations, since these would limit their discretionary power and potentially conflict with the authority of the state, upon whose grace local power holders depended. Thus, the norms of hierarchy in traditional China marginalized the possibilities for private law and entrenched the authority of local power holders, who remained largely outside the reach of law.

In contrast, popular attitudes often challenged inequalities in social relations and revealed concerns with fairness. The plays "Injustice to Dou O," "Liang Tianlai," and "Yang Naiwu Yu Xiaobaicai" challenged rigid compliance with the hierarchical order where it resulted in corruption and the persecution and punishment of individuals who acted in accordance with principles of Confucian virtue even while enjoying a lowly social status.[54]

The novels *Hong Lou Meng* (Dream of the Red Chamber) and *Jin Ping Mei* (Golden Lily) offered parables of inevitable retribution for abusive behavior by persons with privileged status.[55] These and other works suggest that there were tensions in traditional Chinese society between official norms of hierarchy and popular norms of fairness. This dichotomy continues to influence Chinese legal culture today.

Governance and society: continued tensions between official and popular legal culture

If we conceive of legal culture as entailing a pattern of reciprocal influences between parallel phenomena of law and society,[56] the concept offers a vehicle for examining the responses to law reform in China and the interplay with traditional social practices such as *guanxi*. Official legal culture reflects norms of instrumentalism and formalism, each of which privilege the state's authoritarian role. Popular norms tend instead to prize informal relationships and autonomy from the state.

Norms of rule: instrumentalism and formalism

The Chinese government's approach to law is fundamentally instrumentalist.[57] This means that laws and regulations are intended to be instruments of policy enforcement. Legislative and regulatory enactments are not intended as expressions of immutable general norms that apply consistently in a variety of human endeavors, and neither are they constrained by such norms. Rather, laws and regulations are enacted explicitly to achieve the immediate policy objectives of the regime.[58] Law is not a limit on state power; rather, it is a mechanism by which state power is exercised, as the legal forms and institutions that comprise the Chinese legal system are established and operate to protect the Party/state's political power. In part as a result but also as a justification, Chinese constitutional and legal arrangements must conform to China's special circumstances, which set the conditions for policy enforcement and the justification for Chinese law's departure from international or Western norms.[59]

This approach to the role of law derives from a long tradition in Chinese history where law has been aimed primarily to achieve social control but also in pursuit of economic goals.[60] This approach has been incorporated in ideologies of rule through recent Chinese history, whether derived from the Confucianism of imperial China, the republicanism of China under the Kuomintang, or the Marxism–Leninism of China after 1949, which have emphasized law as an instrument of rule. Throughout the 1950s in the PRC, law and regulation were used to transform the economy and society to achieve the revolutionary goals of the Maoist regime.[61] The instrumentalism of the Maoist regime was amply illustrated during the Anti-Rightist Campaign, when, at a time that law had begun to be taken seriously as a source of norms and principles of general applicability that might give rise to rights and protections for the populace, it was subjected to criticism for obstructing the policy goals of the Party and state.[62]

In the post-Mao era, efforts at legal reform have been couched mainly in the language of instrumentalism – in part to enlist the support of conservative members of the regime who question the benefits of a legal system that intrudes on the Party's monopoly on power.[63] While the "rule of law" (*fazhi*) was to be preferred over the "rule of man" (*renzhi*), this was not to imply that the Party/state should not use law for its political ends.[64] In the words of Supreme Court President Xiao Yang:

> To ensure that the basic plan for running the country will be adhered to for a long time to come, it is necessary not only to emphasize the basic plan in Party documents but to have it stipulated in the constitution of the country.[65]

Legal reform remains confined to the discourse of "political-legal work" in which Party leadership continues as a dominant theme.[66] While Party members are subject to Party discipline for violating the law, the Party retains its authority to determine the content of law and the scope of its application.[67]

The resilience of the instrumentalist notion of rule by law was underscored during the course of debates over including a reference to the "rule of law" in the 1999 amendments to the Chinese constitution. Ultimately, the phraseology that was agreed upon (*yifa zhiguo*) was itself a rather instrumentalist approach to the role of law in governance and society. This meaning was reinforced by the insistence that the phrase "country ruled law" (*fazhi guojia*) be qualified by a reference to socialism (*shehuizhuyi fazhi guojia*), thus ensuring that the legal system would remain subject to the panoply of state and Party controls associated with socialism.[68]

Legal instrumentalism ensures that legal debate is confined within existing policy frameworks – calls for economic rights of citizens, for example, must be couched in terms of constitutionally mandated imperatives to promote state and social interests.[69] This draws on the discourse of "economic law," a legacy of the Soviet theorist Pashukanis, who held that economic law could operate as a non-bourgeois instrument by which the state regulates the economy.[70] The dominance of public law ideologies has remained strong, despite the enactment of the General Principles of Civil Law in 1986 and despite the efforts of legal intellectuals to articulate a legitimate space for private law relations.[71] One consequence of legal instrumentalism as practiced in China is that laws and regulations are intentionally ambiguous so as to give policy makers and implementing officials alike significant flexibility in interpretation and implementation.[72] Many Chinese laws and regulations are replete with vague passages that do not lend predictability or transparency to the regulatory process. While this does free the hands of political leaders to modify the policy foundations for these measures and permits local implementing officials to use broad discretion in ensuring that regulatory enforcement satisfies policy objectives, it also makes uniform interpretation and enforcement difficult if not impossible to obtain.

The instrumentalist bent of current policies of legal reform is complemented by the role of formalism in the assessment of the effects of law. Formalism in this sense means that the content of law is assumed to represent reality, with little if any inquiry permitted into gaps between the content and operation of law.[73] Law is not only seen as a tool by which desired social, economic, and political goals can be attained but is also presumed to be an *effective* tool. Where a policy is agreed upon and then expressed through law or regulation, the law or regulation serves as a conclusive indicator that the policy is being enforced. To a large extent, this formalism is a predictable consequence of the instrumentalism that drives the enactment of law and regulation. While consensus is difficult enough to achieve concerning the legislative and regulatory enactments that are expressions of policy ideals, it is nearly impossible to achieve in the area of implementation due to the numerous political trade-offs that accompany policy enforcement.[74] As a result, policies and the laws and regulations that express them are replete with thinly veiled compromises that represent programmatic ideals rather than implementational details. Where elaborate inquiry into implementation is likely to raise issues that may threaten the political consensus or even the policy ideals, such inquiry is not pursued. Rather, the content of law is seen as coterminous with its operational effects. In China's contentious policy environment, the ideal and its implementation become one.

Popular norms: informal relationships and autonomy

In contrast to the instrumentalism and formalism of official law norms, popular legal culture seems wedded to more informal mechanisms that insulate the parties from state intrusion. While surveys of popular attitudes about law suggest that economic actors have gradually come to recognize that formal law provides an element of predictability that can enhance business success, the dynamics of informal relationships continue to operate in juxtaposition to reliance on formal rules.[75] As significant as public hopes may be for the development of an effective legal system, however, expectations appear to remain relatively low, and preference is still given to extra-legal mechanisms for achieving goals.

The importance of informal *guanxi* relationships remains significant in the operation of the PRC legal system.[76] The role of informal relational ties operates alongside law and legal institutions,[77] reflecting in part the weakness of institutions for managing social, economic and political relations and allocating resources.[78] Informal relations represent a coping mechanism that substitutes for the norms and processes associated with formal institutions. The continued dominance of the state in Chinese society and the relative absence of formal institutional limits on state power continue to militate in favor of informal relationships. As the state takes on the attributes of the industrial firm,[79] *guanxi* relations become increasingly important in economic relationships. The prevalence of clientalism in market relations is another aspect of this phenomenon,[80] while the importance of building *guanxi* relations as a strategy for pursuing group interests in the absence of formal institutional structures is evident in the emergence of "civil associations" (*minjian xiehui*).[81]

In the context of the effort to build a legal system in China, informal personal relations and formal institutional relations can be seen to work together. The traditional *guanxi* system retains its importance but must operate alongside an increasingly formal set of largely imported rules and processes made necessary by the increased complexity of social, economic, and political relations. Thus, *guanxi* becomes an asset that can be banked or deployed as needed to serve the interests of the holder in the context of a larger institutional system.[82] As an expression of social capital, *guanxi* operates along with other mechanisms, economic or symbolic capital for regulating social, economic, and political relationships.[83] In the course of China's ongoing legal reforms, the role of *guanxi* may increasingly be seen as a complement to rather than a substitute for the formal institutions. But it is a necessary complement, which permits economic actors to conduct their affairs with some degree of insulation from state intrusion.

Legal authorities: interpreters of local norms

Interaction with foreign legal models and forms is also mediated by legal specialists in China, who by and large reflect the views of the state and the elite.[84] These actors are important because they are directly involved in the selection and application of legal norms, and thus they operate at the intersection between local traditional viewpoints and newly available legal norms. At the outset of legal reform, the regime depended on a surviving cadre of legal specialists who had withstood the persecutions of the Anti-Rightist Campaign and the Cultural Revolution. This community of legal intellectuals extended to judges, lawyers, legal scholars and others, who developed specialized legal knowledge in response to the legal reform effort. Although their main role initially was to generate the terminology and normative structures for the legal reforms that accompanied broader economic and political reform policies and policy proposals, members of this community also used their specialized knowledge to protect and expand their influence. While they are divided by policy preferences, institutional loyalties, family and personal ties, and all the other cleavages that rend Chinese society, commonalities in occupational outlook and professional training permit this community of legal intellectuals to unite in their support for expanded reliance on specialized knowledge about the law.[85] This serves as a major stimulus, bringing the discourse of law and legal institutions to the center of the political and policy realm.

However, the influence of China's legal intellectuals is colored significantly by several factors. First, many law specialists who are now in relatively senior positions were enlisted to the law reform effort initially on the basis of their knowledge of English and had little if any formal legal training. Those who do receive formal legal training are often driven to formalized rote learning of the content of rules, to the neglect of legal analysis of rules and their application based on varying factual situations.[86] And, as is the case with other elite sectors, selection for legal research and teaching posts, as well as judicial positions, continues to give significant weight to political loyalty and Party membership. Beset by the tension between political criteria and legal scholarship, a few courageous and innovative scholars have endeavored to rely on Chinese socialist ideological principles to give legitimacy to theories about the rule of law.[87] Thus, despite their potential to act as a community with a specific interest in promoting reliance on legal knowledge, China's legal intellectuals often lack academic training, career exposure, and intellectual commitment to the liberal ideals that are embodied in the legal norms they are charged with selecting and interpreting. As a result, a few notable individual exceptions notwithstanding, the legal intellectual community often has neither the capacity nor the temperament to resist the regime's instrumentalist approach to law reform.

In addition to the influence of legal intellectuals, an expanding range of bureaucratic officials associated with various legal institutions has developed bureaucratic interests that mandate their support for the institutions to which they were attached. This is a product of institutional and political incentives, however, rather than of legal education or world view, as many officials in legal departments have little formal training in law but nonetheless promote reliance upon the legal discourse that identifies and legitimates their offices. Yet, while their influence is significant, in many cases more so than that of the legal intellectual community, legal bureaucrats remain essentially bureaucratic-political actors. To the extent that they employ legal norms primarily in pursuit of bureaucratic-political goals, legal bureaucrats tend to reinforce the subordination of law to state power.

Summary

While most of the legal forms, structure, and terminology currently used in China derive from concepts of European and North American liberalism, their operation still reflects the influences of local legal culture. The influences of tradition, governance, and society suggest diverse perspectives on the role of law that will affect reception of globalized legal norms. Expectations about the performance of the institutions and rules of PRC law should proceed with due recognition that what is at work in the Chinese legal reform effort is a process of selective adaptation, by which the forms of law borrowed from abroad are given meaning based on the norms of local legal culture.

2 Legal institutions

Informed by the interaction of legal norms and local context, the Chinese legal system has seen significant changes in its institutional framework. Of particular importance are institutions of law making, administration, and dispute resolution. As with other aspects of the Chinese legal system, institutional developments are influenced by international and foreign norms. However, in contrast to the substantive law areas of contract, property, human rights, and foreign economic relations, where doctrinal content was often a reaction to foreign norms, in the institutions area international influences did not come into play until after the institutions had already been established.

Legislative reform

Among the significant achievements of the legal reform era has been the development of the National People's Congress and its legislative functions. Under the PRC Constitution, the NPC's legislative duties extend to enacting basic statutes of national application, as well as passing amendments to the Constitution and reviewing decisions by the State Council and the NPC's own Standing Committee (NPC-SC).[1] Legislative work is subject to general oversight by the NPC's Legislative Affairs Work Committee (*Falu gongzuo weiyuanhui* or *Fagongwei*), which coordinates the work of various specialized committees responsible for such areas as finance, education and science, foreign affairs, and culture. Communication with bureaucratic departments of government is handled through liaison between the *Fagongwei* and the Legislative Bureau (*Fazhiju*) of the State Council, which coordinates legislative proposals and drafting for the various administrative ministries. While the record of consultation is uneven, the links between the *Fagongwei* and the *Fazhiju* represent a potentially useful mechanism for coordinating legislation with administrative rule making.

Delegates to the National People's Congress are elected from lower-level people's congresses, although many deputies are appointed. Deputies to local people's congresses are generally selected through an increasingly competitive election system governed by the dictum that the number of candidates should exceed the number of positions (*houxianren de ming'e duoyu yingxuanren de ming'e*).[2] This does not mean that elections to local people's congresses are fully democratic affairs, however, as many "honorary" deputies are appointed, and the selection of Party-approved candidates is frequently a foregone conclusion regardless of nominal opposition on the candidate roles. Nonetheless, NPC deputies are increasingly active in representing the interests of their local constituencies.[3] Deputies are also increasingly active in proposing legislation, although broader data suggests that the Party and state bureaucracies continue to dominate most legislative proposals.[4]

Strengthening the NPC: conflicts over the Party's role

While the role of the NPC was traditionally circumscribed by Party prerogatives, during the early 1980s NPC-SC chairman Peng Zhen began to use the institution to build a political power base. Peng oversaw revisions to the 1982 Constitution that expanded the legislative and administrative powers of the Standing Committee.[5] Whereas previously the NPC-SC had served mainly to relay agenda items already decided by the Party Politburo and to organize full meetings of the NPC, the 1982 Constitution authorized the Standing Committee to enact laws and also to supervise the work of the State Council and other administrative bodies.[6] Throughout the period of his tenure as chairman of the NPC-SC, Peng Zhen consistently argued in favor of a stronger role for the NPC and the lower-level people's congresses.[7] Peng also suggested that the Constitution had increased the powers and authority of the local people's congresses to enact local laws and regulations and to handle economic legislation.[8] Peng asserted that the NPC-SC must work according to the expanded legal authority given it, even if this caused conflicts with other state organs.[9]

Peng Zhen's efforts to strengthen the role of the NPC-SC were continued by his successor as chairman, Qiao Shi. For example, Qiao's speech to the closing session of the Eighth NPC in March 1993 emphasized the importance of legislative institutions lending a degree of permanence to law making to insulate it from the whims of particular leaders.[10] Qiao's apparent approval of the notion of legislative superiority over the Party signaled further support for the NPC and its Standing Committee.[11] Qiao's speech to the Fourth Session of the Eighth NPC in March 1996 reiterated the theme:

> Running the country according to law is an important guarantee for strengthening the Party's leadership. Party organizations at all levels and the broad masses of party members, especially leading cadres, should conscientiously observe and safeguard the Constitution and laws, carry out their activities within the constitutional and legal framework in accordance with the provisions of the party constitution; act in strict accordance with the law and set an example for all sectors of society. We

should resolutely oppose the practices of substituting laws with one's words and overriding laws with one's power.[12]

Aside from emphasizing doctrinal matters such as equality before the law, Qiao also stressed the role of the NPC-SC not only in originating and passing legislation (by implication downplaying the Party's controlling role), but also in enforcement through "earnestly perform[ing] its important functions of supervising enforcement of the Constitution and laws, and the work of the state's administration, judiciary and procurate."[13]

By adopting expansive interpretations of the NPC's legislative and broader supervisory roles, Qiao seemed to use his NPC-SC position, as did Peng Zhen before him, as an institutional power base in the context of elite political struggle. In the end, however, differences between Qiao Shi and Jiang Zemin on questions over Party leadership of the law-making and law enforcement processes led to Qiao's loss of his Politburo seat and his chairmanship of the NPC Standing Committee.[14] His successor, Li Peng, has continued to champion the NPC's legislative activities, although with greater public attention to Party prerogatives. Speaking to the Ninth NPC Standing Committee in March 1998, Li emphasized that legislative activities derived from the directives of the Party:

The 15th CPC National Congress put forward that it is necessary to "strengthen legislation work, improve the quality of legislation, and form a socialist legal system with Chinese characteristics by the year 2010." In order to attain this goal, the Ninth NPC and its Standing Committee are facing a very heavy and formidable task in legislation work.[15]

Qiao Xiaoyang, vice-chairman of the NPC Law Committee and *Fagongwei*, put it more directly:

We uphold that the Party's leadership over the state also requires that the national legal system is unified because one of the ways the Party leads the government is to upgrade Party proposals into laws through legal procedures. Only through a united national legal system can we guarantee the Party's centralized and unified leadership over the state.[16]

The increased importance of the NPC as a resource in elite politics has worked to elevate the stature of China's legislative apparatus. The increased prominence of the NPC-SC, and by extension the NPC itself, has already given new significance to debates over legislation. An increased vigor has attended legislative debates, as contending institutions and individuals have engaged in bargaining and the manipulation of political resources in order to ensure favorable legislative outcomes. In a sense, the use of the NPC as a tool of political struggle and the increase in meaningful debate within its legislative chambers signifies the increased importance of the NPC as a source of political authority. It is this dynamic that raises the possibility for the NPC to serve also as a source of legal authority, as the bureaucratic-political aspects of the NPC lend the institution a degree of importance that traditional and Maoist Chinese legal culture would not.

Legislation law

Authoritative discourse on legislation has changed but slowly over the past twenty years. In the early 1980s, law was referred to explicitly as a "reflection of the will of the dominant class" (*fanying tongzhi jieji de yizhi*) that is set or approved by the state (*you guojia zhiding huo pizhun de*), such that the principle of Party leadership is mandated by the Constitution (*Zhonghua renmin gongheguo guiding: Gongmin bixu yonghu Zhongguo gongchandang de lingdao*).[17] In the late 1980s, the socialist legislative system remained an expression of Mao Zedong's thought with its emphasis on proletarian dictatorship and Party leadership.[18] In the early 1990s, legislation was authoritatively referred to as "a process by which the will of the dominant class is expressed as the will of the state" (*lifa shi tongzhi jieji yizhi tixian wei guojia yizhi de guocheng*), such that the socialist legislative system required adherence to Maoist principles of Party leadership.[19] While some legal scholars were calling for these instrumentalist norms to give way to normative standards of justice, change was slow in coming.[20]

By the end of the 1990s, however, efforts were underway to draft a Legislation Law. A "specialists' draft" of the proposed legislation prepared mainly by legal academics called for greater democracy and scientific-ness (*kexuehua*) in order to improve the quality of legislation.[21] In contrast to the instrumentalist purposes of furthering social and economic order and socialist development that characterize the bulk of PRC law and regulation, the "specialists' draft" emphasized protection of people's interests, principles of fairness and equality, legislative procedure and clear lines of jurisdiction and authority, adherence to democracy and openness, consistency within the legal system, and objectivity and investigation as the basis for legislation.

The Legislation Law of the PRC was enacted at the Third Session of the Ninth National People's Congress, March 15, 2000, and came into effect on July 1.[22] While the law carries forward many of the recommendations of the "specialists' draft" in areas such as clarification of jurisdiction and lines of authority,[23] the final legislation drew back significantly from the principles of democracy and openness proposed by the specialists. NPC Standing Committee discussions on the statute focused on compliance with the Constitution (and by implication the imperative of Party control); the central tasks of the Party and state on reform, development and stability, democracy, and the mass line; and perhaps most importantly, the principle that "strengthening Party leadership is the fundamental guarantee for making a success of legislation."[24] The Party's central role would remain. In the words of NPC vice-chairman Wang Guangying: "the People's Congress has consciously accepted CPC leadership in its work. This view has been seconded by vice-chairman Cao Zhi: "In performing the work of the People's Congress, we should uphold CPC leadership."[25] By qualifying references to democratic participation with provisions on the mass line and participation by the "whole people," the discourse of legislation law emphasized *pro forma* representatives of particular organizations, classes and groups that are carefully screened and selected by the Party.[26] Indeed, the Legislation Law's preamble reiterates the familiar litanies of the socialist legal system with Chinese characteristics (*you Zhongguo tese de shehui zhuyi fazhi*) and the country being governed by socialist law (*shehuizhuyi fazhi de guojia*) that have served as the basis for continued Party authority over the legal system.

The Legislation Law reflected ongoing policy tensions over law-making institutions and processes. While the NPC gained increased authority and independence, the imperative of Party control remained ever-present. Ironically, it is the National People's Congress formal monopoly on legislative action that works to perpetuate its subservience to Party power. For just as law remains an instrument of policy generally, so too must legislation reflect the policy goals of the regime. While nuanced analyses of the need for well-drafted legislation emerge with greater frequency from the legal academy in China, many proponents of careful legislation also argue that legislation must be aimed at managing social relationships successfully without hampering production and development.[27] Legislation remains an exercise in policy formulation and enforcement that is the province of the state exercising its mandate to govern. Legislation that is the product of initiative by autonomous social groups is rarely if ever considered a legitimate part of the exercise. While references to national conditions as a required referent for civil legislation can be taken as suggesting that the state's law-making activities must defer to local needs, the parallel assertion that the state retains the legitimate monopoly to determine the status and direction of China's development project means that local conditions will be determined in the light of state priorities.[28] As a result, legislative bodies must reflect the policy priorities of the state and the Party. Indeed, the possibilities for law reform generally remain subject to conclusions by the Party as to China's progress toward socialism.[29] Legislation is seen as proceeding necessarily from assessments about national conditions, which remain subject to determination and assessment by the Party state. Thus, it is the policy determinism that pervades legislation that at once lends power and authority to the NPC and also ensures its subservience to the Party.

Administrative reform: restraining the bureaucracy

Administrative bureaucracies in China have long dominated the process of governance, to the extent that administrative decision making virtually eclipsed the law-making authority of the NPC system. The most recent decade of legal reform saw efforts to curtail the power of bureaucratic agencies through administrative law. While international influences have been evident, they have been muted by the political imperatives that drive bureaucratic behavior and reform.[30]

Judicial review and the Administrative Litigation Law

The Administrative Litigation Law (ALL) formalized the authority of the People's Courts to review administrative agency decisions.[31] The enactment of the ALL was part of a broad effort by the Party to make decisions by administrative agencies more accountable and to provide remedies for administrative misconduct.[32] Administrative law was viewed as essential to the effective control of the bureaucracy.[33] The need for administrative law was also viewed as useful for promoting managerial autonomy in the context of the economic reform program.[34]

The ALL was formally enacted at the Second Session of the Seventh National People's Congress in March 1989. Legal Affairs Commission Director Wang Hanbin's explanatory speech focused on the importance of the legislation in ensuring legal restraint on bureaucratic action.[35] Although originally the law was to take effect on April 1, 1990, the date was delayed until October 1, 1990, in order to permit further consensus building in preparation for the law's coming into effect.[36]

The ALL (Article 5) authorizes the People's Courts to determine whether a challenged administrative decision is lawful and in accord with relevant laws and regulations. Under ALL Article 54, the People's Courts have the power to quash illegal administrative orders; to compel administrative action and to revise unfair administrative sanctions. Administrative cases are to be heard before specialized "Administrative Adjudication Chambers" (*xingzheng shenpan ting*) established in the People's Courts.[37] By the date the law came into effect, 2,600 tribunals under the provincial and local courts, staffed by 8,000 judges, had been established to handle ALL cases.[38]

The ALL's provisions supporting judicial review

The basic tenet of the ALL supports judicial supervision over administrative action, as the courts are empowered to quash illegal administrative decisions and to revise administrative penalties that are obviously unfair. The ALL supports expanded judicial review through provisions on the scope of cases accepted; the types of party that may bring suit or that may be compelled to appear as defendants; trial procedures and enforcement provisions; and provisions for tort damage remedies. Under Article 11 of the ALL, the People's Courts have authority to hear suits brought by citizens and juridical persons[39] (including foreign businesses[40]) regarding challenges to administrative decisions imposing punishments and fines; restricting or infringing on property rights; intervening in business operations; denying licenses; and a number of other matters.

The scope of cases subject to judicial review is extensive and permits challenges to a wide range of administrative conduct. The broad scope of administrative conduct subject to review under the ALL is intended to curb bureaucratism and prevent abuses of power by administrative officials who impose their will without reference to or support from regulatory rules.[41] This has significance not only to encourage administrative regulation but also as an anti-corruption measure, discouraging officials from enforcing regulations inconsistently based on favoritism and patronage.

Procedural rules

The ALL (Article 25) permits any administrative organ to be brought before the court as a defendant and allows a wide range of tangible and testimonial evidence to be admitted in the course of administrative litigation proceedings (ALL Article 31).[42] The burden of proof is on the defendant organization to show that the administrative act complained of was lawful (ALL Article 32).[43] Mediation is not available in proceedings under the ALL.[44] Plaintiffs who suffer harm as a result of improper administrative action may claim compensation in tort (*qinchuan*).[45] Prior to the ALL coming into effect, a meeting of the State Council was held at which each ministry was directed to set aside budgetary allocations for use in paying possible tort claims under the ALL, and indeed the issue of how to fund such payments has not yet been fully resolved.[46]

EXHAUSTION OF ADMINISTRATIVE REMEDIES

Article 37 of the ALL allows plaintiffs to seek judicial review of administrative decisions directly, without first seeking administrative reconsideration (*fu yi*), a procedure that entails review of lower-level decisions by supervisory administrative bodies.[47] In an effort to prevent delays by administrative organs in responding to requests for reconsideration, the law provides that in the event that an administrative organ fails to respond to an application for reconsideration within two months from the date of receipt, the applicant may bring the case directly to the People's Court for review (ALL Article 38).[48] This was a very hotly debated issue, as administrative agencies repeatedly urged that all administrative remedies be exhausted before the courts would hear a case.[49]

After the ALL was promulgated, calls were made for further restriction of the *fu yi* process by imposing procedural limits on reconsideration organs.[50] Regulations on reconsideration were enacted in 1990, which formalized the role of reconsideration offices in state administrative agencies and raised a significant barrier to judicial review under the ALL.[51] The regulations impose deadlines on administrative agencies for conducting the reconsideration process that are consistent with the two-month deadline specified in the ALL, but administrative plaintiffs are also required to satisfy substantive and procedural criteria before administrative reconsideration (and ultimately review under the ALL) is available.[52] Sensitive to the possibility that administrative agencies will use the *fu yi* process to thwart review under the ALL, some legal scholars have urged that *fu yi* decisions be based explicitly on laws and regulations, thus permitting a court to make a determination more easily as to whether the administrative decision under review was lawful under the referenced provisions.[53]

While the regulations were revised in 1994, obstacles to judicial review remain.[54] The Law on Administrative Reconsideration (1999) imposes procedural requirements on administrative agencies in handling *fu yi* appeals but also limits access to judicial remedies.[55] While the new law (Article 19) permits applicants to file complaints with the People's Courts where the administrative agency from which reconsideration was sought fails to act properly, the statute also emphasizes (Article 20) the authority of higher-level administrative organs to compel performance at lower levels, thus potentially extending the process of administrative reconsideration and denying effective judicial oversight.

ENFORCEMENT PROVISIONS

While the courts have authority under the ALL (Article 54) to quash (or, in limited instances, modify) administrative decisions and to compel administrative action, the practical effectiveness of this authority depends on enforcement. One of the widely recognized problems with the legal reforms and the rebuilding of the court system after 1978 concerned the refusal of state and Party officials to obey court judgments.[56] The ALL acknowledges this problem and gives courts power to order banks where administrative units have accounts to transfer funds directly to the aggrieved party in cases where refunds of fines or awards of damages are appropriate (ALL Article 65(i)).

The courts may also refer enforcement to the next highest administrative level over the administrative defendant or to the criminal authorities (ALL Arts. 65 (iii) and (iv)). These provisions parallel the use of fines and mandatory bank transfers as enforcement measures under the PRC Civil Procedure Law[57] and the PRC Economic Contract Law[58] and strengthen the power of the courts to enforce their decisions. Nonetheless, concerns over enforcement were raised shortly after the enactment of the ALL.[59]

Obstacles to effective judicial review

Despite its provisions supporting judicial review of administrative conduct, the ALL contains a number of problematic provisions that dilute its effectiveness. In particular, the courts hearing ALL cases are authorized to review only the legality and not the propriety of administrative decisions (ALL Article 5).[60] Since Chinese regulations are drafted to give officials maximum discretionary authority and so are often intentionally vague and ambiguous, it is difficult, if not impossible, to establish that any but the most egregious conduct was actually in violation of existing regulations. And since the courts have expressly been denied power to pass judgment on the propriety of administrative decisions that are not in violation of specific laws and regulations, administrative decisions that represent abuses of discretion but are technically within the law may not be overturned under the ALL.

The ALL also places significant limits on the range of decisions that the People's Courts are authorized to review. Judicial review does not extend to Party decisions or to:

- state acts involving national defense or diplomacy;
- the inherent validity of administrative laws and regulations or of administrative decisions or orders of universal application;
- the validity of administrative personnel decisions; and
- specific administrative acts that the law provides are subject only to final decision by administrative authorities (ALL Article 12).

The ALL's provision that the courts may not review the inherent validity of administrative regulations (Article 12(ii)) indicates that the political system retains ultimate authority to determine the validity of laws and regulations. The reluctance to permit the courts to substitute themselves for the legislative organs of government was at the root of this restriction.[61] At issue was the matter of legislative authority, and the view that the power to determine the essential validity of laws should remain solely with the NPC legislature or the delegated administrative departments of the State Council.[62] The contradiction was recognized that the courts could not adjudicate administrative cases effectively without ruling on the validity of underlying administrative regulations.[63] Nonetheless, the courts were barred from making such judgments. As a result, a decision by an administrative agency can be overturned by a court only if the decision is in violation of the agency's own rules, while the legality and interpretation of these rules remain the province of the agency, not the court. In response, the point has forcefully been made that the State Council should enact special rules permitting judicial interpretation of administrative laws and regulations.[64]

The ALL also limits the authority of the courts to substitute their own judgment for that of the administrative agency.[65] Although arguments were raised in favor of limited powers of the courts to amend administrative decisions,[66] resistance by administrative organs was sufficiently strong to prevent inclusion of such powers in the ALL. The final text permitted judicial amendment of administrative decisions only in cases of administrative penalties that are deemed manifestly unfair (ALL Article 54(iv)). Generally, however, courts were not to be substitutes for the administrative organs themselves and were thus limited in their authority to revise administrative decisions.[67]

Notwithstanding suggestions that the courts will be granted broader review authority as the system is perfected,[68] the limits on the scope of the judicial review continued to undermine the capacity of courts to exercise external supervision over administrative action. Ten years of practice under the Administrative Litigation Law suggest that protection against administrative abuses through effective judicial review remains an elusive goal.[69] In part, this is due to the intent and limited reach of the statute,[70] but popular confidence in the law's effectiveness is limited – a study published in 1998 suggested that less than 20% of potential claimants would be willing to file actions under the Administrative Litigation Law.[71]

Administrative remedies and supervision

The judicial review provisions of the ALL were augmented by those of the State Compensation Law (SCL), which permitted awards of compensation to individuals and organizations harmed physically or financially by unlawful bureaucratic action.[72] However, like the ALL, the SCL remains relatively weak as a basis for challenging misdeeds by high officials. The statute excludes the possibility of compensation for harm by officials acting outside the scope of their duties, where the complainant has caused harm through their own acts, or "under other circumstances prescribed by law." The law also requires that aggrieved parties file their claims first directly with the administrative agency charged with wrongdoing, an exhaustion of remedies requirement that may deter potential claimants. The empirical record suggests considerable weakness in implementation of administrative rules on compensation. A study published in 1998 indicated that of the 1,646 cases filed with the Beijing People's Courts at all levels during 1990–96, only seven resulted in compensation to the complainant.[73] In 1999, the People's Courts throughout the country handled only 6,788 cases involving claims for state and administrative compensation.[74]

Efforts to restrain bureaucratic power have also been extended to administrative rule making, although the impetus once again turns on compliance with higher-level directives rather than accountability to the subjects of rule. Measures to rein in the rule-making powers of the bureaucracy were attempted during the first decade of legal reform, exemplified by the "Provisional Regulations on the Procedure for Enacting Administrative Laws and Regulations,"[75] which purported to establish limits on the rule-making authority of administrative offices and departments based on their relative ranking in the bureaucratic hierarchy. However, supervision of the rule-making practices of bureaucratic agencies was confined to the authority of superior-level departments. This process was formalized in the Administrative Supervision Law (1997), which authorized superior-level agencies to require subordinate units to amend or annul their regulations where inconsistent with superior laws and regulations.[76] However, due to its limits on the rights of affected parties to bring legal action against errant officials, the statute offers little support for the subjects of administrative action to challenge bureaucratic rule making. The statute does permit higher-level administrative organs to monitor activities by lower-level officials to ensure compliance with valid laws and regulations and to curb corruption.[77] Ongoing efforts to draft a law on administrative procedure may help to strengthen this process, although it remains uncertain whether these will extend to judicial review of decisions and behavior by Party organs.[78]

Institutions for dispute resolution

China's dispute resolution system has undergone substantial changes over the past twenty years of legal reform. The transition from a planned to a market economy has required new structures and processes for resolving disputes between increasingly autonomous economic actors. The dispute resolution system that has emerged over the past decade in particular also operates in the context of China's participation in the international economic system.

Development of dispute resolution institutions

The first decade of legal reform in the 1980s saw revitalization of judicial institutions under the tripartite arrangement known under the rubric of *gong-jian-fa*. The triumvirate of public security (*gong an*); procuracy (*jian cha*) and the courts (*fayuan*) were viewed primarily as instruments for maintaining social order and public security, and confirmed the continued influence of a public law paradigm. However, with the expansion of economic reform, and particularly the expansion of market-oriented policies in the 1990s, the courts were called upon to play a stronger role in private commercial litigation, acting independently of the public security and procuracy organs.[79]

The courts' overall jurisdictional structure is set forth in the Organic Law of the PRC for the People's Courts.[80] The Supreme People's Court, which administers the court system as a whole, also acts as a trial court at the national level and as a court of final appeal. At the provincial and prefecture levels, respectively, the Higher- and Intermediate-Level People's Courts hear appellate and trial cases. The Basic-Level People's Courts hear trial cases at the county level. While special rules exist by which litigants can request a deciding court to review its own decision, litigants are discouraged from pursuing unreasonable and troublesome applications.[81] On the other hand, the Supreme Court's record of reviewing appeals suggests that it is quite prepared to overrule lower court decisions made in error.[82]

The People's Courts were initially subdivided into specialized criminal, economic, and civil trial divisions (*shenpanting*), but in the late 1980s new divisions were added for intellectual property, foreign economic matters, and administrative law.[83] Reflecting the increased importance of China's foreign ties, a renewed effort was made beginning in 1990 to set up specialized tribunals for handling civil cases involving foreigners.[84] This differentiation between economic and civil tribunals reflected tensions between the conventional (and still dominant) public law paradigm, which espoused Party/state leadership of social and economic relations under the rubric of economic law, and an emerging private law discourse that contemplated greater autonomy for civil law relations in the economy and society.[85]

Judicial practice is subject to the Civil Procedure Law of the PRC (1991). The legislation significantly revised the 1982 draft and signaled an effort to give the courts greater authority to resolve an increasingly large and complex array of private disputes. Whereas the original 1982 draft had imposed mediation as a process required at several instances in the course of civil court proceedings, the revised text of the statute all but abolished mediation as a requirement. Instead, courts were given increased authority to resolve disputes authoritatively rather than through party consensus. As well, the law clarified the responsibility of the People's Courts to enforce foreign arbitral awards under the New York Convention on the Recognition and Enforcement of Foreign Arbitral Awards, to which China acceded with effect from 1987.[86]

Arbitration of disputes has emerged as a workable alternative to reliance on the judicial system.[87] Arbitration of disputes involving Chinese domestic enterprises is handled by various administrative departments with jurisdiction over the subject matter: for example, labor disputes are handled by the local labor administration, while contract disputes are under the authority of the State Administration for Industry and Commerce (SAIC).[88] Under both the revised Economic Contract Law (1993) and the Unified Contract Law (1999), significant encouragement was given to arbitration of contract disputes. Chinese courts have actively engaged in arbitration as a more flexible alternative to the litigation process required by the Civil Procedure Law. Maritime disputes are subject to the China Maritime Arbitration Commission. Under the Arbitration Law of the PRC (1995), arbitration of domestic commercial disputes has devolved from administrative agencies such as SAIC to local chambers of commerce and other quasi-civil organizations.

Arbitration and conciliation between Chinese and foreign parties in economic and trade matters were traditionally under the exclusive jurisdiction of the China International Economic and Trade Arbitration Commission (CIETAC) under the China Council for the Promotion of International Trade (CCPIT) in Beijing and its sub-councils in Shanghai and Shenzhen. The CIETAC Arbitration Rules have been amended several times to accommodate the concerns of foreign parties and to accord with the requirements of the PRC Arbitration Law (1995).[89] Unlike the situation in the People's Courts, at CIETAC foreign lawyers are permitted to represent their clients directly before the arbitration tribunal. Pursuant to the

Arbitration Law, local arbitration committees linked to local people's governments are authorized to handle foreign-related disputes.[90] While this has the potential to expand and diversify the venues available for foreign dispute settlement, concerns have been raised about the effectiveness and impartiality of the new provincial arbitration bodies.[91]

Legal culture and dispute resolution

China's legal system for dispute settlement reflects the conflicting outlines of Chinese legal culture. The structures and processes of the dispute resolution system reflect features of instrumentalism and formalism in Chinese official legal culture, while the conduct of disputants and officials popularly reflect a conflicting mix of official and popular legal culture norms.

Official legal culture enshrined in legislation and doctrine

The 1982 draft of the Civil Procedure Law was aimed primarily at ensuring social and economic stability during a time of rapid change.[92] At a time when the initial economic reform policies were creating the possibility for conflict between and outside existing administrative structures, civil procedure was viewed as a process for empowering the courts as state institutions to resolve disputes and prevent conflicts undermining the reform effort. The Supreme Court's general interpretation of the draft clarified issues of jurisdiction, proper parties to litigation, the mandatory role of meditation, and the application of the draft to foreign-related disputes.[93] Despite its draft status, the law served as the basis for judicial proceedings in civil cases until 1992, often resulting in additional Supreme People's Court general opinions on such matters as economic disputes and intellectual property, as well as directions in specific cases.[94] The draft was revised and enacted as a statute in the early 1990s, a time of relative stability between the upheavals of 1989 and the Deng-led resurgence of economic liberalization policies beginning in 1992.

During this period of retrenchment, official commentaries on dispute resolution gave primary attention to the need to carry out state policies. The legislative drafting effort was driven specifically by policy goals aimed at safeguarding social stability and economic order, and to "meet the needs of China's commodity economy" and "fulfill the needs of reform."[95] As well, dispute settlement institutions and officials involved in mediation, arbitration, and litigation were instructed that their activities were to comply strictly with enacted legislation such as the General Principles of Civil Law (1986),[96] which enshrined the principle that all civil relations must serve state and social interests.[97] While civil disputes were seen as private in nature and dispensing with notions about working classes and the broad masses, their judicial resolution was still to accord with state and collective interests, including the preservation of social and economic order.[98] Even as they were charged with adjudicating economic disputes fairly according to law, the courts handling economic disputes were to follow the Party's basic line, upholding socialist economic construction and safeguarding the order of the socialist commodity economy.[99] Under the rubric of "using facts as the basis and using law as the criterion," courts were directed to ensure that their resolution of disputes accorded with the policies of the Party and state that were formalized into law.[100] This approach encapsulates the features of instrumentalism and formalism that characterize Chinese law and that drive the interpretation and application of the foreign law models and influences upon which Chinese dispute resolution rules draw.

By the late 1990s, several important changes were evident. Foreign-related litigation in the Chinese courts was increasing and with it the need to resolve lingering uncertainties on such issues as jurisdiction over foreign-invested Chinese companies and the implications for civil litigation stemming from contract arbitration clauses. The Supreme People's Court's 1992 opinion helped to clarify some of these issues.[101] The Supreme Court also enacted formal measures on open trials in 1999, purportedly to satisfy constitutional requirements.[102]

Increased attention has also been paid to training judges, first under the Supreme Court's Senior Judges Training Centre and later at the PRC Judicial Institute. Concerns aside over the patronage and resource impera-tives fueling the proliferation of specialized training institutes, these signal an important commitment to building the cohort of jurists that will be required for the long-term viability of the legal system. Efforts were also underway to strengthen consistency in judicial decision making through the publication of casebooks.[103] However, these compendia of court judgments promote officially sanctioned interpretations of law that limit judicial discretion and require rigid application of statutory provisions.[104]

As well, official norms adopted by the senior leadership of the court system retain an instrumentalist character. The president of the Supreme People's Court has identified social stability and economic construction as the most important tasks facing the courts and has urged that efforts to develop good courts and good judges should proceed by "closely centering on the overall interests of the Party and the country."[105] These comments suggest that despite calls from the NPC for increased supervision by the representative congresses over the court system,[106] the real supervision still comes from the Party. The vast majority of judges are Party members, thus entrenching Party dominance.[107] The Supreme People's Court has directed that courts throughout the system are to provide services in support of economic modernization, such that the courts' handling of such matters as intellectual property rights, unfair competition, and state-owned enterprise reform is to "ensure sound implementation of both the economic develop-ment strategy and the major policy decisions of the central authorities."[108] The Party's dominance is also exercised through the "adjudication commit-tees" that are attached to each court and that in effect review and approve

judicial decisions notwithstanding official directives ordering that the intervention of adjudication committees be curtailed. The Party's "political-legal
system" (*zheng fa xitong*) retains its overall authority to direct training and
supervision over judicial personnel.[109]

Legal culture and judicial behavior

The structure and role of judicial institutions reflects the influence of official
legal culture and contributes to the influence of popular legal culture in
judicial behavior.[110] The exclusion of foreign lawyers from direct participation in court proceedings and the limits against their obtaining membership
in the Chinese bar association have been seen as entrenching the subordination of judicial processes to government controls. Reflecting the influence of
instrumentalist norms aimed at ensuring that law serves the policy aims of
the state, courts have relatively low political status and are viewed essentially as but another government department commanding little attention
from other units.[111] This has impeded the capacity and willingness of judicial officials to compel production of evidence and enforce awards.

The influence of local legal culture, and particularly the influence of
informal relationships (*guanxi*) are increasingly evident in the behavior of
lawyers and legal officials. On one hand, widespread statistical and anecdotal
evidence of corruption among the judiciary suggests that the requirements
of formal law and legal institutions remain contingent on political arrangements and personal relations, while the commonplace offence of taking
bribes suggests that the requirements of formal law and institutions may be
disregarded altogether for monetary reward.[112] In a comment reflecting
both the problem of judicial abuse and the Party's expectations about judicial compliance with its mandates, Supreme Court president Xiao Yang
noted that "a minority of procuratorial leaders and judges do not have a
strong sense of working in the service of the Party and all of China."[113]
However, many instances of alleged judicial misconduct involve not bribery
but the use of *guanxi* to influence judicial and regulatory decision making
and conversely the willingness of judges and administrative regulators to
base decisions on the requirements of personal networks rather than the
requirements of law.[114] *Guanxi* thus permits litigants and their counsel to
make best use of the limited requirements of formal law.

The increased number of commercial disputes brought on by the market
reforms has created a certain degree of institutional competition for a share
of what is emerging as a dispute resolution "market." However, so far there
is little to indicate that this competition has motivated dispute settlement
organs to increase their autonomy and/or procedural rigor. Instead, institutional competition seems to be taking the form mainly of increased efforts to
strengthen ties with government departments.[115] Thus, competition for
influence in the context of local social and economic relations does not
necessarily require further adoption of foreign models. Rather, the process of

selective adaptation already underway in China's dispute settlement project is likely to see more selectivity rather than less.

The dilemma of corruption in the judiciary and in the administrative bureaucracy is not merely a matter of suspending moral or legal values. Rather, it reflects uncertainties and tensions as to the permissible parameters for *guanxi* behavior and the parameters for formal institutional behavior – in other words, where legal requirements and processes end and where informal relations may legitimately be permitted to have influence. Whereas effective formal rules provide officials with legitimate justification for denying requests for favoritism based on *guanxi* ties, thus protecting officials from the demands of *guanxi* networks, the absence of official rules permits *guanxi* relations to drive official decision making. Thus, where judges are expected to investigate personally the circumstances of disputes before them, this is generally seen to require judges to meet with litigants and their counsel to collect evidence and hear argument – not necessarily in the presence of the opposing party or their counsel. In the context of Chinese social practices, this investigation process is very likely to involve banquets, individual meetings, and other part social, part professional encounters.[116] During the course of such investigations, the temptation for one party or another to attempt to influence judicial decision making through improper inducements is high. Yet there is a fine line, and one that is not well understood, between a litigant hosting an investigating judge or judicial official to a series of banquets and meetings at which the litigant puts their case in a most favorable light, and the direct offering of economic inducements.

The uncertainty in the relationship between the permitted scope of investigatory behavior and the prohibited scope of taking bribes and engaging in corrupt conduct is heightened by the formalism that pervades official legal culture. Official legal cultural norms of formalism have led to rigid reliance on the content of rules and the requirements of procedure with little regard for substantive justice. Judicial decisions in the area of economic regulation have reflected norms of legal formalism, such that attention to formal rules and procedures has taken precedence over concern with resulting fairness.[117] Such an approach permits judges and legal and administrative officials to confine their decision-making processes to formalistic references to statutory provisions without the requirement of detailed fact *cum* law analysis. Such a circumstance then permits decisions to be made with little explanation and insulates them from challenge. Whether driven by improper economic inducements or skilled persuasion, the legal or administrative decision need not be explained in detail and the decision maker need not address how the balance of interest and argument between the disputants was handled. This in effect insulates from scrutiny the judicial investigatory and analytical processes, and it expands the possibilities for favoritism and possible corruption.[118]

This can have the effect of entrenching decisions based on relational norms of popular legal culture. The often parochial view taken by local

judges toward enforcement of judicial awards by courts outside the immediate area of jurisdiction reflects ingrained traditions of localism and the
centrality of personal relations as the basis for behavior. Judicial processes of
internal and informal fact finding and decision making often operate in
contradiction to formal requirements of civil procedure, leaving disputants
vulnerable to abuses of power and political connections by their adversaries.
Thus judges make subjective assessments of the relationships between the
parties and their needs and conditions without regard to formal legal
requirements.[119] This can also result in the application of formal regulatory
requirements based on subjective assessments by judges of the "real" intent
of the parties, such as when a compensation trade contract was considered by
the trial judge in Fujian to be a loan contract because there appeared to be
inadequate sharing of management and risk.[120]

Anecdotal discussions with Chinese and foreign lawyers involved in litigation and arbitration in China suggest that the inadequacy of formal rules
controlling the behavior of counsel and their clients permits *guanxi* relations
with judicial and arbitral decision makers to distort dispute settlement
processes.[121] The general absence in Chinese civil procedure law of provisions on abuse of process has been seen to permit Chinese counsel to delay or
derail dispute settlement processes through use of extremely aggressive
procedural tactics such as repeated requests for delay, refusals to produce
evidence based on claims of confidentiality that are not substantiated, broad
requests for evidence going far beyond the confines of a particular dispute,
and inflated damage estimates. Disregard for professional courtesy is also
evident in failures to answer correspondence or requests for cooperation in
organizing case files or the presentation of evidence, in personal attacks on
the character of witnesses and attorneys, and in demands for security bonds
aimed at crippling opposing parties financially. In many instances, this
behavior, while perhaps a natural outgrowth of zealous advocacy, becomes
what lawyers with experience in Europe and North America would consider
an abuse of process.

The absence of effective controlling rules has also been seen as
contributing to questionable conduct by disputing parties, such as obtaining
delays through repeated but unsubstantiated requests to change attorneys,
intimidation of witnesses, and what appear to be fraudulent conveyances of
assets to avoid paying damage awards. In the absence of formal rules or
informal norms controlling the conduct of attorneys and their clients, lawyer
tactics and client behavior are regulated at the discretion of judges and arbitrators. This in turn allows *guanxi* relations between counsel and/or their
clients with presiding judges or arbitral officers to determine how a court or
tribunal will respond to complaints about abusive conduct. Thus, abusive
behavior by clients and counsel becomes the product of formalistic reliance
on rules that either permit the behavior or fail effectively to manage it,
together with the use of *guanxi* relations to ensure compliant oversight by
judicial officers.

This process is justified, in theory at least, by presumptions about the virtue of judicial decision makers. In a manner reminiscent of the Confucian system, judges are appointed largely on the basis of Communist Party loyalty and military service rather than legal education. The premise that upstanding and loyal Party members will be immune from blandishments of corruption rings somewhat hollow in the face of actual practice,[122] as there is increased recognition of the need to provide clearer rules governing the conduct of judges and lawyers.[123]

Arbitration: efforts to incorporate international norms

The performance of Chinese arbitration institutions has reflected a conflicting mix of official and popular legal culture norms.[124] As with the courts, the instrumentalist bent of official legal culture contributes to the relative political weakness of arbitration institutions. As a result, their interaction with other institutions is often ineffective, as requests for cooperation in the collection of evidence, protection and sequestration of assets, production of witnesses, and other matters often go unheeded.

Relational norms of popular legal culture are also at work in the interaction between arbitrators and disputing parties and their counsel. Arbitrators have been known to engage in what are essentially *ex parte* contacts with the disputants, either during the course of the mediation process that was previously intertwined with arbitration, or during the course of preparing the matter for hearing.[125] Such contact, while seemingly odd to foreign litigators, is generally consistent with Chinese traditional norms regarding the judge/arbitrator, who is expected to meet regularly with disputants and personally investigate facts.[126] Since the disputants are seen to be in a subordinate position to the judge/arbitrator, not merely in the context of the dispute at hand but socially and morally as well, personal contacts are not expected to affect the ultimate judgment. Nonetheless, CIETAC's efforts to draft a code of ethics reflect a recognition that in practice such idealized notions of the relations between disputants and judge/arbitrators are often not realized, and that legal regulation not moral norms should be the basis for governing decision makers.[127]

Chinese arbitration decisions reflect a more conflicting set of influences. The influence of formalism is evident in decisions emphasizing the role of bureaucratic approvals and requirements over the subjective circumstances of the transaction.[128] On the other hand, some CIETAC arbitration panels have been willing to overlook formal approval requirements on issues such as mutually agreed but not officially approved contract amendments where international practice permits it.[129] Reliance on international practice in these cases parallels an increased willingness to follow international legal norms in other cases where the specific provisions of Chinese law are either unavailable or unclear.[130]

To a large extent, CIETAC practices reflect the conflicting position in which that organization finds itself. On one hand, it is organized under the Chinese government and is staffed and led by government-appointed officials whose education and training draw almost exclusively on the Chinese experience. Therefore, it is hardly surprising that the influence of official legal culture should be evident. On the other hand, by virtue of its hearing process in which foreign lawyers can participate and at which foreign and international law can be pleaded as governing law, and through the inclusion of foreign specialists on its panel of arbitrators, CIETAC is constantly exposed to international norms. Moreover, CIETAC's audience includes foreign firms, which have the opportunity to select or reject CIETAC as an arbitration venue. These factors exercise a powerful influence, drawing CIETAC arbitral decisions increasingly under the ambit of international norms.

The long-term effect of this remains uncertain, however, as local legal cultural norms affect practices and commentaries on international commercial disputes and the judicial enforcement of arbitral awards. Cultural precepts about the centrality and uniqueness of China and historically derived imperatives about separating Chinese and foreign matters are evident in Chinese teaching case books, which present disputes involving foreign and Chinese parties by reference to an "us and them" dichotomy.[131] This combines with norms of instrumentalism in discussions about whether CIETAC jurisdiction and international commercial arbitration in general should be limited to "foreign-related" matters.[132] Bureaucratic politics have also played a role, as Chinese courts have long insisted that arbitral decisions that are not "foreign-related" may fall outside the jurisdiction of CIETAC and in any event are subject to full judicial review (including review of facts and the application of law) prior to enforcement. Some commentators have urged that judicial involvement is warranted throughout the process of international commercial arbitration in many cases, even to the extent of adopting a rather liberal reading of the limited conditions for refusing enforcement set out in the New York Convention on Recognition and Enforcement of Foreign Arbitral Awards.[133] Court officials have suggested that the nationality of the parties determines whether or not a matter is "foreign-related" – such that a Chinese arbitration involving foreign investment enterprises registered in China or involving international contracts by Chinese-registered parties would be subject to full judicial scrutiny rather than the limited recognition and enforcement procedures required by the New York convention and reiterated in China's Civil Procedure Law.

Perhaps the most notable example of the failure of Chinese courts to recognize and enforce foreign arbitral awards was the case involving Revpower, where enforcement of a foreign arbitral award was refused, apparently in violation of the New York convention.[134] This refusal was compounded by the local Chinese court's willingness to take jurisdiction over the dispute despite the existence of a valid arbitration clause – a practice that has been repeated by other courts in similar circumstances.[135]

Other cases have had similar results, to the dismay of the prevailing party and the muted chagrin of Chinese academic commentators.[136] This creates disturbing problems of reciprocity in light of the apparent readiness of the courts of signatory states party to the New York convention to enforce Chinese arbitral awards.[137]

International influences on China's legal institutional reforms

China's legal institutions have been influenced to varying degrees by international legal norms and institutions. In the legislative area, foreign influences have been largely limited to exchanges and dialog with legislators and academics. Constitutional norms mandating Party domination over the legislative process through the principle of the Four Basic Principles limit the applicability of liberal democratic principles. However, in practical operational matters such as record keeping, communications, and staffing, international exchanges have been influential. The NPC maintains regular contacts with foreign legislative organs through exchange vehicles such as the Canada–China Legislative Association. Foreign academics are increasingly welcome as resident scholars, able to interview NPC officials and obtain public documentation on the NPC's activities. Similarly, NPC officials have been hosted as resident scholars and visitors at legislative organs in Europe and North America. These information exchange processes lead naturally to better mutual understanding and in particular expose NPC officials and staffers to democratic legislative processes and their attendant political climates and cultures. To a certain extent, these exchanges permit senior Chinese officials to develop the confidence that quasi-democratic processes within the legislative arena need not threaten the Chinese Communist Party's overall monopoly on power. And, indeed, there have been signs of increased acceptance of democratic behavior in NPC committees and even in the Standing Committee and the NPC itself. Legislative models from the USA, Europe, and Japan have been influential in the preparation of the PRC Legislation Law.[138] In the main, however, foreign influences have been limited to internal procedures and the organization of legislative organs and have not extended to the broader questions of Party dominance.

In the administrative law area, foreign influences were somewhat more extensive. Foreign practices in administrative law informed discussion in China on such matters as resolution of administrative disputes, enforcement of administrative orders, and judicial review.[139] The Administrative Litigation Law was heavily influenced by the US Federal Administrative Procedure Act, a somewhat ironic situation in light of the contradictions between China's civil law governance system and the separation of powers principles that inform the US APA. As well, American academics frequently lecture at Chinese law schools on administrative law, imparting broad norms that could be adapted to China's conditions.[140] Administrative law systems in Germany and Japan were also referenced in the course of drafting the ALL.[141]

As has been the case with Chinese legislative institutions, foreign influences have largely been limited to issues of structure and organization. The administrative law system in China is intended primarily to ensure that subordinate institutions comply with directives from their superiors. This extends to the issue of corruption, where administrative law measures have been particularly evident.[142] However, foreign influences have had little effect on the basic normative premise underlying China's administrative law system, namely that administrative law remains an instrument in the service of Party-led governance. The unhappy experiences of dissidents such as Guo Luoji, who attempted to utilize administrative law to challenge Party domination, underscore the limitations of foreign liberal principles on government accountability.[143] While the State Compensation Law promises remedies for harm caused by venal officials acting outside their mandate, even this measure does not permit challenges to Party dominance *per se*. On the other hand, administrative law has provided remedies against the improper behavior of regulators in areas such as land regulation, where there is less direct political challenge to the Party's dominance.[144]

Foreign influences have been more pronounced in the area of dispute resolution. The 1981 Civil Procedure Law (Draft) was influenced significantly by the need to support economic exchanges with foreign countries.[145] While obligatory recognition was given to China's special experience, explanations of the law noted the importance of the experience of other countries (which was a significant point in 1982).[146] The drafters relied in part on the experience of the continental systems of France and Germany, as well as the US and UK common law systems.[147] International agencies such as the UN Development Program and the Ford Foundation, as well as bilateral development programs with the USA, Canada, Japan, and the EU, played a significant role in facilitating Chinese legal specialists gaining access to law models from abroad. Foreign models on evidence law are increasingly influential.[148] In the arbitration area, international norms of private law are increasingly seen by Chinese commentators as necessary components of China's transition to a market economy.[149] Thus, notions about free will and contract theory as the basis for commercial arbitration suggest a respect for individual autonomy that would have been unheard of in China even during the 1980s.[150]

Remarkably however, the amendments that resulted in the 1993 Civil Procedure Law were somewhat silent on the influence of foreign law models. Unstructured interviews with Chinese legal officials suggest that since foreign civil procedure models had already influenced the 1982 draft, the main task of subsequent amendments was to accommodate the practical needs of local conditions. Also, the early 1990s were a time of significant political repression in the aftermath of the 1989 student movement and the retreat from uncritical open-door policies. Nonetheless, the dispute settlement structure, with its reliance on lawyers, judges, arbitrators, and their affiliate institutions, reflected the importance of influences from international liberal models of judicial and arbitral institutions. By the late 1990s, more open reference was made to foreign models in such areas as alternative dispute resolution.[151]

China's accession to several international conventions, including the New York Convention on Recognition and Enforcement of Foreign Arbitral Awards,[152] the UN Convention on Service Abroad of Judicial and Extrajudicial Documents in Civil or Commercial Matters, the UN Convention on Collection of Evidence Abroad, and the Convention on the Settlement of Disputes Between State and the Nationals of Other States (ICSID Treaty),[153] has brought into the Chinese dispute resolution discourse norms drawn from the liberal paradigm. Also influential has been the "Understanding on Rules and Procedures Governing the Settlement of Disputes" appended to the Marrakech Agreement establishing the World Trade Organization, which also reflects liberal norms extolling the binding character of legal institutions and rejecting negotiated relational approaches to trade disputes.[154] To the extent that China continues to seek membership in the WTO, it is expected increasingly to conform to a paradigm that privileges the notion of relative autonomy of law, which in turn supports the panoply of Western liberal political and economic institutions.

Summary

To a large extent, the development of Chinese legal institutions and practices has reflected the dynamics of local legal culture, and particularly the imperatives of political control for the Chinese Communist Party. While the structures of legislative, administrative and dispute resolution institutions appear quite recognizable to foreign-trained lawyers, the norms and practices of these institutions often depart quite significantly from the expectations of those familiar with liberal legal systems. This reflects the influence of local legal culture, which acts as a normative filter through which flow the influences of foreign and international legal models. Both the instrumentalism and formalism of official legal culture and the relational and autonomous features of popular legal culture affect the performance of Chinese legal institutions. This suggests the ways in which the process of selective adaptation affects the introduction into China of international norms on legal institutions.

3 Contract law

Perhaps no single area of Chinese law encapsulates so thoroughly as does contract law the interplay between legal and economic reform. The enactment of the Unified Contract Law (UCL) in 1999 represented a culmination of nearly twenty years of contract law development and reflected a combination of local economic policy issues and a process by which international legal forms were adapted to Chinese conditions. This chapter will examine the tensions inherent in the Unified Contract Law of the PRC, which to a large extent was the product of borrowing the form and structure of foreign contract laws but which operates in the context of a vibrant local legal culture.

Contract law in the PRC: legislation in pursuit of policy goals

Contract law stands at the intersection of legal and economic reform in China, embodying the policy conflicts and tensions inherent in both. Issues of contract formation go to the heart of the transition from the state-planned economy to one where economic actors have a greater degree of autonomy. Contract enforcement reflects conflicting views on the role of state supervision in economic transactions and the extent to which these might be subject to the interpretation and enforcement of institutions not linked to the state's economic planning process. The extent to which economic actors and their transactions may be subject to the requirements of formal legislation also has important implications for the role of Party policy. Not surprisingly, therefore, debates over contract law throughout the past twenty years have reflected debates over economic policy and over the supremacy of Party rule. While legislation has reflected the broad contours of national policy debate, interpretation of contract rights and obligations has reflected local concerns.

China's first contract law was enacted in 1981. The Economic Contract Law (ECL, 1991, revised 1993) governed Chinese domestic contracts. The law was a major component of the post-Mao economic reform policies and represented a compromise between the policies of central planning and the recognition that economic reform required increased autonomy for economic actors and their transactions.[1] The ECL contained basic provisions for ten different types of contract, including sales contracts, construction contracts, lease contracts and contracts for storage of goods. Of particular importance in the original ECL were provisions recognizing the rights of the parties and authorizing strict contract enforcement. Proceeding from assertions about the legal equality of contracting parties, the Economic Contract Law granted to all juridical persons equal capacity to enter into contracts.[2] Key to understanding the policy role of the ECL was its classification as "economic law," thus underscoring its basic function as an instrument for economic policy enforcement.[3] While the economic reform policies enacted beginning in 1978 granted enterprises greater autonomy in decision making and permitted increased diversity of economic actors and transactions,[4] the role of law remained one of policy enforcement. Thus, the ECL required contracts to remain in compliance with the state plan.[5] In keeping with economic policy changes and a major amendment to the PRC constitution made in 1992, revisions were made in 1993 to the ECL to replace references to the state plan with references to state policies.

Complementing the ECL, the 1985 Foreign Economic Contract Law (FECL) of the PRC was enacted to govern contracts between Chinese and foreign firms in areas of foreign trade, foreign investment, and technology transfer transactions. The effect of the FECL was qualified by China's accession in 1998 to the UN Convention on Contracts for the International Sales of Goods. This convention augments and in some instances displaces FECL provisions in instances where the foreign contracting party is from a signatory state. The FECL offered contracting parties significant autonomy to select governing law, dispute resolution rules, and determine commercial terms and conditions, although in keeping with the "economic law" character of the FECL the validity of contracts remained subject to state approval.[6]

The "economic law" character of Chinese contract legislation was qualified significantly by the enactment of the General Principles of Civil Law (GPCL) in 1986.[7] The law contained important provisions on party capacity, formation and enforcement. Notions of legal equality were extended to a broad array of civil relations under the GPCL through references to natural and legal persons as legal actors.[8] The GPCL permitted all natural and legal persons to participate in civil obligations of contract without regard to subjective characteristics such as class background, social or political status, or degree of state or private ownership.[9] The introduction of the GPCL raised significant doctrinal and policy issues as to whether contracts should remain a creature of state economic policy, or rather should reflect relatively autonomous civil relationships operating outside the state's policy mandate. While the GPCL required that contract transactions not conflict with state policies,[10] nonetheless the characterization of contracts as "civil law" relations implied a reduction in state intrusion.

Revisions to the ECL passed in 1993 suggested continued conflict over the "economic" and "civil" law character of contracts.[11] The revised ECL acknowledged the official policy of the "socialist market economy," enshrined as well in the 1993 revisions to the PRC Constitution,[12] and the concomitant support for further reductions in the state's control over economic life. Nonetheless, the fact that revisions to the ECL could not break out of the bounds imposed by presumptions about the economic law character of contracts signaled that opposition to unfettered markets remained strong. Despite the revisions, Chinese jurists recognized the problems of adapting contract legislation borne of the state planning era to the needs of a market economy, and called for further revisions – particularly in the area of autonomy on contract formation through an offer and acceptance model.[13]

Drafting the Unified Contract Law

Efforts to draft a unified contract law reflected a recognition in some quarters at least that the system of specialized laws for different types of contract was problematic. The drafting process began, ironically enough, shortly after approval of the revisions to the ECL. In September 1993, the Legal Affairs Work Committee (*fagongwei*) of the National People's Congress began debating a unified contract law.[14] The small drafting group comprising Liang Huixing (CASS Law Institute), Jiang Ping (China University of Politics and Law), Wang Liming (People's University), Cui Jianyuan (Jilin University), Guo Mingrui (Yantai University), Li Fan (Supreme People's Court); He Xi (Beijing High Court), and Zhang Guangxing (editorial department of the CASS Law Institute Journal *Faxue yanjiu*) issued a " Legislative Proposal" for China's new contract law.[15]

This proposal contained several principles to guide the drafting process.[16] First, the law was to reflect common principles of the objective laws of the current market economy, as well as international treaties and agreements. Second, the draft was to give adequate attention to the autonomy of the parties. Third, the new law was to suit the needs of the socialist market economy while also meeting the circumstances of the transition from the planned economy. The new law was also to attend to needs of economic efficiency and public well-being and the facility and security of transactions. Finally, the law needed to be enforceable in practice. A generalized statute was the clear objective of the next round of revisions – aimed particularly at joining the Economic Contract Law, the Foreign Economic Contract Law and the Technology Contract Law into a single statute.[17]

After a review of the proposal, the *fagongwei* appointed a small drafting group comprising Liang Huixing, Zhang Guangying and Fu Jingshen to prepare a proposed draft contract law based on input from a broader committee of specialists from across China. The "Provisional Draft of the Contract Law of the PRC" (also referred to as the "contract academics' proposal draft" – *hetong faxuezhe jianyi gao*) was presented to the *fagongwei* in January 1995 and incorporated the bulk of the provisions in the "Legislative Proposal."[18] Preparation of a second draft began in May 1995, and it was issued in October.[19] The central issue of freedom of contract was much discussed – especially the dilemma of balancing autonomy with the need to preserve public welfare.[20] Issues of fundamental justice and fairness in contract relations were raised largely in response to the general imperative of promoting party autonomy.

The third UCL draft was issued and discussed under the auspices of the *fagongwei* in May–June 1996.[21] The discussions in 1995–96 leading up to the third draft saw the influence of legal academics at its height.[22] The influence of academic specialists began to wane, however, as the process proceeded to the fourth draft of April 1997, which was based on input from state ministries and related companies and enterprises.[23] With the agreement of NPC Standing Committee vice-chairman Wang Hanbin, this draft was formalized into the "Draft for Soliciting Opinions" (*zhengqiu yijian gao*) and distributed to provinces, autonomous regions, and centrally administered cities as well as to relevant central departments and legal teaching and research units. The period following the release of the "draft for soliciting opinions" saw considerable debate, not least because this draft was the first to contain a provision on basic principles.[24] Debate centered on broad issues of equality and autonomy, as well as more detailed questions about contract form, required contents, compliance with state mandatory plans, and avoiding fraud and oppression. Provisions were added for technology contracts.

Based on these discussions, a formal "Draft" (*cao an*) of the UCL was released publicly on September 7, 1998.[25] Reports on opinions were to be submitted to the NPC Standing Committee by October 15, 1998, whereupon meetings were held virtually continuously from September 1998 to March 1999, when the draft was submitted to the NPC for consideration.[26] The draft faced continued debate at the Fifth, Sixth and Seventh Sessions of the Ninth NPC Standing Committee and in the Second Session of the Ninth NPC.[27] Substantive revisions continued to be made, based on opinions submitted from specialists and related units.[28] The identity of parties to contracts was clarified (the term "citizens" was changed to "natural persons" in keeping with the provisions of the General Principles of Civil Law). The contract relationship came to be described as entailing one of "civil rights and obligations" (*minshi quanli yiwu guanxi*) rather than a creditor–debtor relationship (*zhaiquan zhaiwu guanxi*), a critical step toward moving contracts away from the state-dominated realm of "economic law."[29] This debate dated back to discussions of the GPCL and continued during the drafting process.[30] The debate was not closed entirely, however, as indicated by subtle disagreements among legal academics as to the influence that "economic law" doctrine should have on the interpretation and application of the Unified Contract Law.[31] Additional provisions were made for engineering and technology contracts, incorporating provisions from the Technology Contracts Law and ancillary regulations and decisions on dissemination of innovation and resolution of technology-related disputes.[32]

The final text of the law was passed by the Second Session of the Ninth NPC on March 15, 1999, and came into effect on October 1 of the same year.[33] The importance of the statute was recognized in part through the decision for NPC chairman Li Peng to give an explanatory speech to the Congress, when typically explanations of new legislation are given by a representative of the Legislative Affairs Work Committee.[34] Nearly a year following enactment of the UCL, the Supreme People's Court issued an official interpretation of the legislation.[35] In keeping with a long tradition of Supreme Court interpretations of legislation,[36] the edict provides relatively detailed interpretation of issues including contract effect, applicable law, assignment, and nullification.

Salient provisions of the Unified Contract Law

The UCL entails policy compromises between proponents of conflicting principles of contract autonomy and state control. These compromises in turn reflect the differing preferences of the legal academics who first proposed the new law and prepared the early drafts, and the administrative and state enterprise sectors that saw their status and power challenged by the grants of equality and autonomy that characterized the early drafts. While the law contains provisions for fifteen specific types of contract, the sections containing general provisions, ancillary provisions and governing formation, performance and remedies are of particular interest for the purposes of this book.

General and ancillary provisions

The general provisions of the UCL state that the law aims to protect the "lawful (*hefa*) rights and interests of contract parties, preserve social and economic order and promote socialist modernization" (UCL Article 1). The bifurcation of "rights" and "interests" reflects longstanding Chinese doctrine distinguishing between the legal rights and the social/class interests of legal actors, and it suggests that legal rights are not the only basis or criterion for protecting contract parties.[37] As well, the reference to preserving social and economic order indicates that the rights and interests of contract parties are qualified by pursuit of this somewhat ambiguous and elusive goal – a point underscored by the provisions of UCL Article 7 prohibiting contract parties from disrupting social and economic order and undermining the public interests of society. The longstanding debate over whether contracts represent an economic or civil law relationship is apparently resolved through the provision (UCL Article 2) that contracts are agreements that establish, modify, and terminate civil rights (*minshi quanli*).[38] This is reiterated by provisions on equality of contracting parties (UCL Article 3) and non-interference by "units or individuals" (UCL Article 4). However, the principles of equality and non-interference are not absolute, as contract parties must also adhere to laws and administrative regulations that may, and often do, privilege domestic parties and permit state agencies to intervene in contract formation and performance.[39]

Policy compromises are also prominent in the section on ancillary matters, which addresses administration, choice of law, dispute resolution and various gap-filling measures. The UCL operates in the context of the broader PRC legal regime and specifically declines to challenge provisions of law and regulation that conflict with those of the UCL. Thus, where other laws contain provisions on contracts, these are to be observed (UCL Article 123). While the implication is clear that the provisions of other laws will govern even where they are in conflict with those of the UCL, official interpretations of the UCL go to great lengths to harmonize the statute with the provisions of existing laws and regulations.[40] The Supreme People's Court has clarified that this requires interpretation of national legislation from the NPC or its Standing Committee and national administrative regulations of the State Council, rather than local laws and regulations.[41] The UCL's general provisions apply only where its separate rules on fifteen enumerated types of contract and where specific rules of other laws lack express provisions. In the absence of specific UCL rules, reference is to be made to the most similar provisions contained in the specific provisions of the UCL and other laws. The UCL's provisions for resolving conflicts with other legislation were added following the September 1998 draft – reflecting the influence of the regulatory bureaucracies, which wished to protect their authority and jurisdiction from being eroded by the UCL's liberal provisions on contract formation and enforcement. Thus, the UCL operates as a default regime, to apply when not in conflict with existing law.

The ancillary provisions section also contains gap-filling provisions, requiring interpretation of contract provisions to be made in light of (in descending order of importance) expressed language of the contract, pertinent contract terms, purposes of the contract, business practice, and the principles of honesty and good faith (UCL Article 125). This expands on the gap-filling provisions of the CISG Convention that focus on incorporating party practices and usage of trade in the parties' intent regarding the meaning of their agreements. The expanded approach of the UCL suggests a hierarchy of factors to be relied upon specifically in interpreting contract provisions. However, the UCL's references to business practices and to honesty and good faith leave open the possibility that these terms will be interpreted by Chinese courts in ways that may be unfamiliar to foreigners. Naturally, specific application and interpretation of these terms will require reference to existing Chinese practices and law, raising the prospect of interpretations that vary from those applied to the CISG Convention.

The ancillary provisions section modifies existing provisions on choice of law (UCL Article 126). Under the FECL, the parties to foreign-related contracts had the right to select the law governing the contract, except in cases of equity and cooperative joint venture contracts and contracts for the exploration and exploitation of natural resources. This exception is narrowed somewhat by the provision that Chinese law must be selected to govern these contracts only where performed within the territory of the PRC. This permits foreign law to govern joint venture and natural resource contracts performed outside China. On the other hand, there is a further provision not contained in the FECL that the parties' choice of law may also otherwise be restricted by Chinese law. While the FECL required compliance with the general laws and regulations of the PRC, the new UCL explicitly raises the possibility that laws may be enacted or interpreted so as to preclude or limit choice of law by the contracting parties. For example, a 1988 Supreme Court interpretation of the FECL[42] mandated that contracts between foreign investment enterprises and local Chinese units were in essence domestic contracts subject to the Economic Contract Law rather than the FECL.

The ancillary provisions section specifies that the State Administration of Industry and Commerce (SAIC) shall have responsibility for administration and supervision of contracts, along with other responsible administrative departments (UCL Article 127). This reflects the arrangement by which SAIC had primary authority to supervise domestic contract activity under the ECL but raises the possibility of bureaucratic conflict between SAIC and MOFTEC over the supervision of foreign-related contracts. The supervision provisions also contain reminders of the policy conflict over contract autonomy and national interest, as supervisory organs are empowered to deal with (*chuli*) violations of national interest and public welfare. The final text omits the reference contained in the September 1998 draft requiring the supervisory and sanctioning processes to comply with laws and administrative regulations, thus muting the previous suggestion that the Administrative Litigation Law, the Administrative Supervision Law and other legal restraints on administrative authority would govern contract supervision matters.

The statute permits contract parties to foreign-related contracts to select the method and forum for resolving disputes (UCL Article 128). As was the case under the FECL, disputing parties can still pursue arbitration outside as well as within China. The new law also provides that the parties may pursue litigation before the Chinese courts, where there is no arbitration agreement or where the arbitration agreement is invalid. This expands on the provisions of the FECL and the Civil Procedure Law, which prohibited litigation where the parties had entered into an arbitration agreement. The rationale behind the old rule was that by concluding an arbitration agreement, the parties indicated their intent to resolve disputes through arbitration and so should be barred from filing suit. By including a new requirement that the arbitration agreement be valid, the UCL raises uncertainties as to how far a party can presume the inherent validity of an arbitration agreement.

The policy conflicts evident in the general principles and the ancillary provisions are less obvious but still detectable in other sections of the law. The statute is structured similarly to the former ECL and FECL, such that the section on general principles is followed by sections on formation, validity, performance, modification, transfer termination, and liability. As well, specific provisions are added for fifteen types of contract.

Contract formation and effect

Provisions on conclusion of contract require contract parties to have civil capacity (UCL Article 9), which in turn is governed by the General Principles of Civil Law (GPCL, 1986). Individuals are considered to be "natural persons" and are now permitted to form contracts with foreign parties – a right not offered under the 1985 FECL. However, in most cases, contract parties will be "legal persons" (*faren*), including companies, partnerships and other organizations. While use of the civil law-derived concept of the "legal person" suggests an objectification of contract actors that might transcend ideological limits on what entities will be permitted to participate in economic activity, the state retains control over the registration and approval requirements upon which the status of "legal person" is based. Contracts may take oral, written or other forms (UCL Article 10), including "data text format" (*shuju dianwen xingshi*). However, the UCL requires a written form in some instances, such as loan contracts (UCL Article 197), rental contracts for a term in excess of six months (UCL Article 215), financed rental contracts (UCL Article 238), construction contracts (UCL Article 270), and technology transfer contracts (UCL Article 342). The Technology Contract Law had previously required a written form for technology transfer agreements.[43] In other instances, such as trade and investment contracts, guarantee agreements and certain contracts of carriage, the use of a written form will be required by substantive law and regulation.[44] In a departure from past practice, the new law does not impose content requirements. Instead, in keeping with the general theme of party autonomy, the statute allows the parties to determine content, but indicates that contracts generally include provisions on such matters as identity of the parties, nature of goods, quantity, quality, method of payment, liability for breach, and methods for dispute resolution (UCL Article 12).

Offer and acceptance

Formation of contracts is based on offer and acceptance by the parties (UCL Article 13), an offer being defined as an expression of interest that is detailed, clearly stated and to which the offeror is bound upon acceptance by the offeree. No consideration is required, suggesting that despite the borrowing of foreign legal language Chinese conceptual approaches to offer and acceptance still differ considerably from those of the common law world. Offers are effective when received but may expire or be withdrawn or revoked with proper notice and absent prohibitions imposed by the offeror or offeree (UCL Articles 17–20). Offers may be rendered invalid through substantial modification such as changes in signature, quantity, quality, method of payment, performance terms (including location and form), liability for breach, and dispute resolution provisions, and will be treated as a new offer (UCL Article 30).[45] Acceptance of an offer requires an expression of interest by the offeree, without the requirements for detail and clarity required of offers (UCL Article 21). Once acceptance is made, the contract is formed. Acceptance is effective generally upon receipt by the offeror.

The statute provides that lawfully concluded contracts are effective upon conclusion. In a modification of past practice (see FECL Article 7) conclusion of contracts is not delayed until completion of formalities of approval and registration where required by law and administrative regulations.[46] Instead, the new law simply provides that such formalities should be followed. Thus, the absence of contract approval will not necessarily relieve the parties of their contractual obligations unless and until the contract is declared invalid. This was confirmed by the Supreme People's Court's "Interpretation on Several Questions Concerning the Application of the Contract Law of the PRC," which clarified that absent a specific statutory or regulatory provision that a contract is not valid until registered and/or approved the contract remains valid when formed even if registration and approval have not yet been completed.[47] Under the former FECL, approval of foreign business contracts was a requirement for the contract to be formed, and as a result the parties were often unsure of their legal rights and obligations during the approval process, which often extended to considerable lengths of time. The new text may lend greater certainty to the contract relationship prior to formal approval by the administrative agencies.

The UCL also includes provisions on agency, which are much needed in view of the prevalence of agent-driven transactions and in light of the underdeveloped state of this area of PRC law at present.[48] Recognizing a longstanding problem of protecting proprietary information disclosed during the course of contract negotiations, the statute requires protection of commercial secrets learned by a party in the course of concluding a contract, whether or not the contract is ultimately formed and provides for compensation of loss caused by unlawful disclosure or use of such information (UCL Article 43).

Limits on contract autonomy

While the provisions in the new law on contract formation and effect give significant attention to the wishes of the parties, there are a number of exceptions. First, specific allowance is made for contracts that formalize the terms of state directives or mandated procurement transactions issued to legal persons or other organizations (UCL Article 38). In effect, this provision permits administrative edicts to take on the appearance of voluntary contracts. In the absence of specific interpretation and enforcement rules that acknowledge the adhesive character of these agreements, parties to contracts formed under this provision may well face the contradiction of having their behavior interpreted in the light of a statute derived largely from principles of voluntariness, when in fact the conduct is ordered by the state.

The principles of freedom of contract are also limited by the provisions of the new law governing the effectiveness of contracts. Provisions requiring that contracts satisfy the requirements of "good faith" (UCL Article 6) and "social public morality" (UCL Article 7) permit government officials wide discretion in determining which contracts are lawful and which are not. A key issue is the question of information disclosure and deceit. Liability for compensation of resulting losses may be imposed on parties who conclude bogus (*jiajie*) contracts or negotiate in bad faith, for intentionally concealing key facts or providing false information, or for other conduct that violates principles of honesty and trust (UCL Article 42). These limits on contract autonomy suggest a recognition that China's transition to a market economy has not yet progressed to the stage where contracting parties can be imputed with relatively equal access to information and negotiating position. Even in liberal market systems, where pursuit of commercial advantage is often based on building superior knowledge and access to information, difficult issues arise about disclosure of information. In China, the problems are compounded. For example, it is unclear to what extent contract parties will be required to disclose market information, potential profit margins, or other information that drives their price negotiations in production and export contracts, in order to avoid liability. As well, under the following circumstances, contracts will be invalid (UCL Article 52):

- one party has concluded a contract through fraud or coercion, which damages state interests;
- malicious collusion, which damages state, collective, or third party interests;
- a legal means is used to conceal an illegal purpose;
- the public welfare of society is violated; or
- mandatory provisions of law or administrative regulations have been violated.

While the factors of illegal purpose, public welfare, and violation of law and regulation are unqualified grounds for invalidity of contract, the remaining factors reveal a curious combination of attention to action and consequence. Fraud and coercion must apparently result in harm to state interests before the contract can be invalid. This approach was apparently adopted in order to avoid the problems of the previous FECL regime, where foreign business contracts deemed too advantageous to the foreign party could be rendered invalid for violation of state interests. Similarly, damage to state, collective, or third party interest must be the result of "malicious collusion" (*eyi chuantong*) before the relevant contract may be deemed invalid. Interpretations of the new law will need to make clear that invalidation of contract requires a finding of *both* the improper conduct and the resulting harm in order to avoid bootstrapping approaches that invalidate contracts under circumstances where perceived damage to state, collective, or third party interests is considered on its own to be sufficient evidence of fraud, coercion, or malicious collusion.

Limits to transactional autonomy in the Contract Law complement provisions in legislation on such issues as financial guarantees and pricing that limit the freedom of contract parties. The Secured Interests Law (1995), for example, imposes significant approval requirements and absolute restrictions on financing arrangements such as liens and mortgages. This has enabled the government to control finance flows regardless of the will and capacity of economic actors. The Price Law (1998) recognizes the principle of market-based pricing but reserves for the state significant authority to intervene in pricing matters. Thus, the efforts to expand notions of freedom of contract in the contract law operate in a context of general limits on party and transactional autonomy.

Performance, modification, termination

The new contract law imposes a general duty of full performance of agreed commitments and requires compliance with commitments for notification, assistance, and security (UCL Article 60).[49] Third party performance of contracts is a common practice in China, and the new law aims to clarify the governing rules by adopting a primary and secondary liability approach. An obligor who fails to perform for the benefit of a third party is liable to the obligee for the failure (UCL Article 64). An obligor whose performance is promised from a third party remains liable to the obligee when the third party fails to perform (UCL Article 35). Also common is the so-called "triangular debt" (*sanjiao zhai*) problem, where contract performance by a party obligor is dependent on its receipt of performance of ancillary contracts by one or more third parties.[50] The new contract law attempts to address this issue by permitting the obligee to file suit in the People's Court to compel the obligor/obligee to enforce their rights against a non-performing third party(ies) (UCL Article 73). Also, where an obligor has improperly renounced or transferred rights or property in which the obligee has an interest, judicial intervention to revoke the transfer may be sought (UCL Article 74).

In light of the principle of simultaneous performance of contract obligations (which are seen as mutually dependent), the law allows for anticipatory breach when one party has precise evidence proving that the other party has (1) seriously deteriorating operating conditions; (2) moved property or withdrawn funds to evade the obligation; (3) lost its business reputation; or (4) has otherwise lost or might lose its capacity to perform (UCL Article 68). This extends the provisions of the FECL to domestic contracts, in part allowing domestic contracts signed by foreign investment enterprises to benefit from protections previously available only to foreign-related contracts.

As was the case under the previous FECL regime, parties may modify contracts by agreement. In a departure from past practice, mutual agreement is not necessary for a transfer of one party's rights to another, except where the nature of the contract prohibits a transfer, where the parties prohibit it, or where transfer is prohibited by law (UCL Article 79). Notice of assignment is required, and the requirements of law and regulation on approval and registration must be observed. Upon merger or dissolution of a contract party, the rights and obligations follow and attach to the legal persons created by the merger or dissolution.

Termination of contract rights occurs where (1) the underlying obligation is performed; (2) the contract is terminated; (3) the obligations are mutually terminated; (4) the obligor lawfully appropriates the contract goods; (5) the obligee absolves the obligation; (6) the rights and obligations are merged; and (7) other circumstances provided by law (UCL Article 91). Upon termination, parties must perform commitments of notification, assistance and security in accordance with business customs. Where a contract is terminated prior to completion of performance, a party who has given partial performance may seek restitution, damages, or other remedies (UCL Article 97). Termination may also be by agreement. Other circumstances of termination include (1) *force majeur* (*bu ke kang li*, defined in UCL Article 117 as "objective circumstances that cannot be foreseen, avoided or overcome"); (2) one party clearly states or shows that it will not perform; (3) delay by a party; (4) delay or violation by a party that make it impossible for the contract aims to be met; (5) other circumstances provided by law. The formalities of approval and registration must be complied with.

Liability for breach

Liability for breach of contract can take the form of continued performance, remedial measures and compensation (UCL Article 107 *et seq.*). Continued performance is generally made in response to a demand from the obligor issued when the required performance is not forthcoming. Remedial measures (*bujiu cuoshi*) include repair, exchange, redo, return, and reduction of payment and are usefully made in response to a disagreement over quality of goods (UCL Article 111). Compensation is calculated by the loss caused by the non-performance, including lost profits but not extending to unforeseen damages (UCL Article 113).

Non-performance fees (*weiyue jin*) may be agreed by the parties, which may be adjusted to match the actual damages caused by the non-performance (UCL Article 114). The parties may agree on earnest money payments, pursuant to the Secured Interests Law of the PRC. Upon non-performance by the payor, the earnest money is not returnable, whereas return of double the amount is required of a payee who fails to perform (UCL Article 115). Earnest money payments and violation fees may be used to compensate for losses caused by non-performance.

Liability may be excused by *force majeur*, except when the *force majeur* event occurs after a party has delayed performance. A party claiming *force majeur* must give proper notice and proof of the *force majeur* event. The aggrieved party must attempt to minimize its losses resulting from non-performance by the other party. Where both parties violate the contract, liability is shared (UCL Article 120). In yet another effort to address the "triangular debt" problem, the law provides that where non-performance is the result of the actions of a third party, the non-performing party must bear liability and seek recovery separately from the third party (UCL Article 121).

Contending influences on Chinese contract law

Chinese contract law exhibits a number of contradictory influences. Many of the basic structures and rules of Chinese contract law are borrowed from foreign models, yet these structures operate in the context of a local legal culture that exerts a powerful influence over the interpretation and application of contract law.

International models of liberal contract relations

China's increased participation in the international economic system has brought with it increased pressures to conform to the norms of liberal market capitalism. In the area of contract relations, the Convention on Contracts for the International Sales of Goods (CISG Convention) emphasizes the importance of the autonomy of contracting parties from state interference in economic relations. The CISG Convention purports to establish uniform standards for international sales contracts.[51] Work on the agreement was done under the auspices of the UN Commission on International Trade Law (UNCITRAL), which includes the United States and other major industrialized countries as founding and more or less permanent members. The final version drew heavily on liberal contract principles. As a result, the contract interests of capital equipment exporters (generally identified with the industrialized economies of the West) receive privileged treatment through limitations on the time frames and processes for acceptance or rejection of goods.[52] The convention promotes the liberal private law paradigm more generally by limiting the extent to which contracting parties can bar oral modification of contracts – a common practice in developing economies.[53] Thus, the liberal norms associated with Europe and North America are privileged, while the informal and collectivist norms most often associated with non-Western economies are marginalized. While the CISG Convention is presented as being intended simply to bring uniformity to international contracts, it is a uniformity that entrenches liberal norms of private law relations.

China's participation in the international economy has also brought with it bilateral pressures to conform to liberal ideals of contract regulation. Thus, the record of China's "open-door" policy of encouraging foreign investment has also been a record of ongoing efforts by foreign businesses and their respective government representatives to encourage reforms in the Chinese contract system that would increase transactional autonomy for economic actors while reducing the role of the state.[54] In some respects, Chinese policy has been responsive to these entreaties. By portraying itself as a regime that accepts the rule of law, the Chinese government has hoped to encourage foreign business interests to downplay the political risks of participating in China's economic growth. By offering specific legal regimes to govern its foreign economic relations, China has hoped to establish clear and predictable frameworks for foreign business. By providing specific preferences in its laws, the government has hoped to induce foreign business activities in various targeted geographical areas and commercial sectors. Most recently, efforts have been made to remove disparities in the legal treatment of foreign and Chinese businesses. The drafting of a unified contract law is part of this effort.

The influence of liberal legal forms on Chinese contract law

The influence of foreign legal forms on Chinese contract law has been evident from an early stage. Much of the emphasis on transactional autonomy has come from abroad. For example, at the time of the drafting and enactment of the 1981 Economic Contract Law, the Chinese Academy of Social Sciences (CASS) scholar who currently heads the drafting committee for the unified contract law wrote extensively on the principles of freedom of contract, drawing heavily albeit not uncritically on foreign sources and ideas.[55] During the process of revising the ECL in the early 1990s, explicit reference was made to principles drawn from the US Uniform Commercial Code.[56] China's contract law doctrine was also influenced by norms in such areas as international contract practices in the areas of jurisdiction, party agreement, and dispute resolution.[57]

During the process of drafting the Unified Contract Law, specific attention was paid to foreign contract law models.[58] Indeed, much of the scholarly debate centered not on whether to rely on foreign models but rather on whether the continental or the common law model of contract was most suited to the drafting agenda.[59] Many of the academics involved in the early drafting process relied heavily on foreign legal discourses in putting forward proposals on the general aims and principles of contract law reform.[60] Academic discussion of specific contract principles drew heavily on principles of foreign law – both European civil law and common law.[61]

The second draft of the UCL took significant account of international treaties as well as views from abroad and from Taiwan.[62] Reports on contract law in the United States and Canada were reviewed by the drafting group, and interviews were held with legislative counsel of the US Senate, the Canadian Ministries of Justice and Foreign Affairs, the Ontario Law Reform Commission, and several US and Canadian courts, universities and research institutes as well as the World Bank.[63] Discussion of references to international and foreign models focused principally on European and Anglo-American approaches, as well as the norms of international treaties – especially the CISG Convention. During the discussions over the statute draft in 1997–98, consultations were held with members of the committee to revise the US Unified Commercial Code and with US representatives to UNCITRAL specializing in international sales matters, as well as scholars from universities in the USA, Germany, the UK, Europe and Australia.[64]

The influence of local legal culture

Despite the effects of influences from abroad, Chinese contract law continues to reflect the influences of local legal culture. Official legal cultural norms were often couched in terms of Chinese conditions, the state appropriating constructions of tradition to suit its governance imperatives. Throughout the drafting process, the point was frequently made that the new law must comply with China's actual conditions and experience.[65] When the section on general principles was added to the 1997 "draft for soliciting opinions," complaints were raised that this gave too much weight to international approaches and contradicted domestic contract practices.[66]

Official legal cultural norms were evident in the commentaries that accompanied the drafting process. Even in the early stages of drafting during 1993–94, opinions on the aims and scope of contract law supported a qualified approach to market-driven contract autonomy. While striving to meet the needs of the modern market economy, drafting efforts should not harm the security of transactions (*you bu ke yin ce sunji jiaoyi anquan*).[67] Efforts to improve efficiency and productivity should not override state and social interests, the need for economic order, and the rights and interests of consumers and workers.

Elements of instrumentalism and formalism in Chinese official legal culture became evident in efforts to limit draft language on such issues as party equality and autonomy. For example, whereas the 1997 "draft for soliciting opinions" contained general provisions to the effect that contracting parties were to have equal status and enjoy the right to enter into contracts freely, the subsequent formal draft issued in 1998 specified only that whatever rights to quality and autonomy the parties might have will be respected.[68] Thus the formal draft reinforced the principle that any rights contracting parties might have are those conferred by the legislation rather than inherent rights of general enjoyment. In light of the state's continued control over the legislative process, this allows rights to be interpreted subject to the state's policy priorities.

Perhaps the most telling example of the influence of official legal culture on the drafting process lay in the debates that led ultimately to discarding provisions entrenching a principle of freedom of contract (*hetong ziyou*) in favor of a more limited prohibition against interference in the voluntariness of contracts (*hetong ziyuan*).[69] Throughout the process, influential legal academics lent strong support for broad principles of contract autonomy.[70] However, challenges to contract autonomy were raised by reference to general principles of justice.[71] Provisions on contract autonomy were also limited through emphasis on principles of fairness.[72] Assertions about the need to limit contract autonomy called for greater reliance on supervision by state agencies, extolling the need for stability in the socialist market economy.[73] Thus, consistent with the instrumentalism that informs much of Chinese law, priority was given to public law expressions of justice over private law principles of autonomy.

Consistent with this, the formal draft also added provisions on contract supervision, yet a further diminution of party autonomy. Contract supervision has long been a point of contention between proponents of state planning and supporters of market reform. Beset by irreconcilable policy differences, the drafters of the 1981 Economic Contract Law opted to avoid a strict requirement of contract supervision while holding to the principle that contract validity depended on compliance with the state plan.[74] Debate over the final draft of the law saw attempts to expand the provisions for state-mandated contracts to include state procurement contracts, thus reflecting debate on the extent of state planning intrusion in increasingly autonomous market transactions.[75] Despite the intervening reforms in economic policy, the bureaucratic imperatives of control through law remain evident in ongoing provisions for contract supervision.

Popular legal culture plays a role in contract practice, as the attitude of economic actors affects their willingness to rely on formal law in arranging their commercial relations.[76] Popular resistance to the requirements of formal law was common in the early years of reform and was not unexpected in light of the dramatic changes brought on by legal reform.[77] Efforts to avoid the restrictions of the regulatory system remain in evidence, as indicated, for example, by the plethora of court cases in which parties attempted to avoid regulatory restrictions on loan contracts by entering into what were later termed "sham joint enterprises."[78]

Many of the case reports emerging from China in the mid- and late 1990s reveal popular ambivalence to formal legal and regulatory requirements in the conduct of business relations.[79] One common example of contracting parties disregarding regulatory requirements centers on the failure to conform to the requirements of the "legal person" and the resulting lack of capacity to form contracts.[80] Disregard of registration requirements appears in reporting on cases involving real estate transfers[81] and contracts for the importing and sale of manufactured goods.[82] Other examples of contracting parties engaging in commercial pursuits without regulatory compliance include instances of improper delegation of agency powers in sales of goods contracts;[83] exceeding the scope of authority delegated to an agent;[84] forming contracts that extend beyond the permitted scope of business of one of the parties;[85] disregarding the requirements for contracting party signatures;[86] and disregarding requirements as to contract form.[87] Contracting parties also appear relatively amenable to compromise and settlement of contract disputes, even to the point of revising the content of agreements.[88]

Reflecting in part a determination to bring contract practice into compliance with the requirements of law and regulation, the formalism evident in Chinese official legal culture remains a dominant characteristic of judicial decision making.[89] Collections of judicial decisions to be used in judicial training programs give primary emphasis to uniformity and consistency in judicial decisions.[90] As well, the process of case analysis begins with a review of statutory provisions, which themselves reflect the instrumentalist character of state law and regulation. Little attention is paid to close analysis of pertinent facts, or to the subtleties of fact *cum* law analysis. Thus the importance of formalistic compliance with state law is instilled into judicial decision makers early on. The bulk of judicial decisions contained in various case reporting volumes suggest a rigid and somewhat mechanical assessment process addressing, in sequence, issues of (1) contract validity based on compliance with law and regulation; (2) contract content; and (3) party performance, or the lack thereof. In a typical example, the judge faced with a case involving a failure to register an interest in real estate disregarded the parties' attempt to resolve the problem of ownership on their own and awarded restitution.[91]

However, the effects of popular legal culture are also evident in judicial decisions, particularly where judges show resistance to official legal norms of formalism and instrumentalism.[92] Recently published compendia of judicial decisions support more flexible judgments based on subjective assessment of the relationships between the parties and their needs and conditions.[93] In one example, the court permitted a party to terminate a contract prior to completion (anticipatory breach) when it became clear that the other party could not or would not perform.[94] This decision, dating back to 1993, foreshadowed the subsequent provisions on anticipatory breach in the Uniform Contract Law and suggested an important element of flexibility to an otherwise rigid insistence on complete performance regardless of subjective circumstances. In another example, the court allowed non-performance to be excused on the grounds of *force majeur*, where the foreign seller-defendant was unable to complete performance due to a government termination of economic cooperation with China – an unsubtle suggestion that undue intervention in contract practice by Chinese bureaucrats would bring about similar results.[95]

Conclusion: tensions in China's contract law

The development of contract law and practice in the PRC illustrates the process of selective adaptation evident in other aspects of the Chinese legal system. Considerable effort has been made to draw on foreign models of contract doctrine, and in many instances foreign legal forms, such as the offer and acceptance model of contract formation, are being adapted rather closely into the UCL. Particularly where legal academics drive the process, reliance on international legal forms seems strong. As the drafting process moves toward broader consultation with local interests, including government interests, the influence of local legal culture becomes stronger.

Finally, the interpretation of contract law remains heavily influenced by local cultural norms. This creates a tension between the international legal forms and local legal culture. Resolution of this tension lies not in slavish emulation of foreign legal models. Nor does it lie in cynical reliance on apocryphal notions of Chinese traditional values that entrench state power. Rather, the resolution of the tension lies in recognizing the validity and resilience of the process of selective adaptation that characterizes contract law in China.

4 Property[1]

Unlike contract law, where China had significant policy and legal antecedents to guide legal reform, property law reform had little in the way of precedent.[2] Property rights in traditional China provided some guidance, but in the main Chinese legal specialists working on property rights were compelled to look abroad for guidance. The adoption of foreign law norms, however, is moderated by local tradition and norms of political and legal culture. In particular, the individualist orientation of liberal property rights regimes conflicts with the collectivist norms in China, while private rights discourses of liberalism conflict with the public law norms of Chinese tradition and PRC policy. The development of property rights in the PRC is largely a process of mediating these conflicts.

International influences on China's property rights regimes

The development of property rights in China stands against a background of reference to the discourse of property rights in the Western liberal tradition.[3] Indeed, under the rubric of internationalization of property rights, Chinese jurists have called for greater reference to be made to foreign law from Japan, Europe and the Anglo-North American tradition as precedents for property rights reforms in China.[4] Chinese civil law notions of property behavior (*wuquan xingwei*) have been influenced by German law in particular (either directly or in the forms adopted in Japan and Taiwan).[5] Taiwan law scholars such as Wang Zejian have been particularly influential in the transmission of German civil law concepts to China.[6]

Classical approaches to private property

Although contemporary doctrines about private property rights often begin with Locke, the classical tradition of theorizing about these issues began long before. Continental scholars such as Bartolus (1313–57) and Grotius (1583–1645) were examining and commenting on property law doctrines derived from Roman law and articulating views about tenancy, enforceable rights to property, and the natural law foundations for private property realms independent of the state.[7] Responding to the feudal legacy of limited property rights, Enlightenment theorists began to articulate a vision of private property that would insulate the emerging bourgeoisie from the reach of the crown.[8] The classical theorists pursued different approaches, which addressed issues of economic and political utility in terms of economism, republicanism, and collectivism.

Locke addressed property rights as having economic utility within a broader theory of governance. He also viewed property as an appropriate mechanism for recognizing the value of labor.[9] Thus, he contemplated private property as a basis for establishing production and labor incentives, and promoting economic accumulation. He considered it a duty of the state to protect property rights as part of its responsibility to build economic and social wealth. The political utility of private property rights was addressed more explicitly by Madison. Drawing on Locke's focus on the property rights of individuals, but less concerned with the purely economic utility of the approach, Madison viewed property rights as an essential element of insulating society from intrusion by the state.[10] While he recognized that differential access to property and the disparities of rights that might result would contribute to contention between "factions" in society, Madison insisted on government protection of the rights of the minority of property holders. These views were particularly influential in the drafting of restraints on government control of private property in the US Constitution.[11]

Political utility also informed Hegel's thinking, albeit with different results. Hegel began with an assessment of property rights of the individual as an "abstract right,"[12] but then he examined the resulting implications for social relations. In the context of the "ethical life" (*Sittlichkeit*), the property rights derived from the inalienability of the individual and their labor should in Hegel's view be qualified by the relations of community and civil society. Thus, Hegel called for attention to be paid to the material realities of social and economic life as a basis for restraining the unfettered application of abstract concepts of absolute rights to private property.

While the various strands of thought articulated by these classical theorists of property are by no means uniform in their approach to the nature, situs, and conditions for private property and private property rights, a common theme is the importance of the state. For Locke, the state's interest in economic accumulation presented a utilitarian basis for property rights. For Madison, the interests of republican justice demanded that the state protect property owners against the demands of factional majorities. For Hegel, the state was a component of the community that served to qualify the abstract right of property. Contemporary scholars continue to debate the role of the state in ways that reveal the continued effects of economism, republicanism, and collectivism in the views of the classical thinkers.

Contemporary approaches to private property

Notions of private property rights in the industrialized democracies of Europe and North America have centered on notions of economic and political utility.[13] The themes of economic and political utility are also useful to describe the approaches taken by many contemporary property thinkers, although not necessarily in the same ways as characterized the work of Locke, Madison, and Hegel. The centrality of economic utility is evident in the work of law and economics scholars such as Richard Epstein[14] and Richard Posner,[15] whose support for largely undiminished private property rights stems from assessments of the greater economic benefits to be derived therefrom. Broadly speaking, this approach suggests that the protection of property owners against most kinds of interference promotes freedom of exchange and hence advances the economic well-being of society as a whole.[16]

Economic utility approaches often cross over into the territory of political utility, through assertions that private property's implications for protection of individual liberty constitute a utilitarian political benefit.[17] The republicanism of Madison is taken up most obviously by proponents of strict protection of traditional private property, who argue that the individual liberties associated with private property are the best reason for its protection.[18] Madisonian republicanism is also raised by those who argue for limits on political regulation of private property,[19] although this view is rebutted by critical scholars, who note the fundamentally political character of all property regimes.[20]

The dilemmas of economic and political utility are also evident in contrasting perspectives of political philosophers, such as John Rawls and Robert Nozick, who address the utility of various property regimes for the distribution of wealth.[21] In contrast to Rawls' approach calling for relative protection of property rights in light of the need to redress social and economic inequalities, Nozick adopts a more absolute standard. He treats justly acquired property as an entitlement, which can be appropriated only with the consent of the owner. While these conflicting approaches obviously have different consequences for government policies on the protection of private property, they remain at root utilitarian, albeit with a conflicting view of the common good.[22] Natural rights theorists, on the other hand, challenge approaches based on economic or political utility and suggest that the balancing analysis attendant on determinations of common good should give way to absolutist views on the rights of the individual.[23]

The communitarian views associated with Hegel also appear in the contemporary discourse, primarily in the form of critiques of absolutist doctrines of private property rights. Some writers call for a comprehensive approach to property rights that accounts for collective interests to a greater degree than is possible under a more traditional approach.[24] Communitarian views are also evident in calls that property rights not be considered exclusively the province of the individual but must intersect with principles of democracy.[25] Collective approaches to property rights have also been raised by comparative scholars looking to the legal traditions outside the bounds of the West.[26]

The importance of public welfare as a component of economic utility has been noted by some economists and law and society scholars.[27] Louis Kelso's "Binary Economics" offers an approach that aims to empower all members of society to acquire an adequate holding of capital.[28] Such an approach does not depart significantly from the traditional utilitarian approach to property but rather suggests that the problem with achieving full economic utility is mainly one of distribution of opportunity.

A nuanced consideration of private property rights in the context of political utility is advanced by theorists of the "New Property," who suggest that social entitlement policies empower individuals to participate more fully in society and therefore promote goals of individual liberty.[29] Despite conservative rhetoric that government-sponsored programs recognizing and protecting property interests in employment, housing, health care, and so on represent a paternalistic diminution of individual liberty, the New Property proposals are aimed at promoting individual liberty by redressing the inequalities between individuals and the organized units of political (governmental) and economic (corporate) actors that have come to dominate contemporary life and that undermine the meaningful exercise of individual liberties.[30] In contrast to property rights discourses aimed at the protection of corporate interests,[31] the New Property approach aims at promoting public well-being in order to preserve the republican ideals of individual liberty articulated by Madison.

The bulk of contemporary scholarship on private property rights tends to rely on variations of economic and political utility as the basis for argument. While debates emerge as to how best to achieve economic and political utility, there remains a broad, if unrecognized, consensus that private property rights remain the most effective mechanism for achieving economic and political well-being.

Internationalization of private property regimes

The completion of the Uruguay Round of the GATT, the finalizing of the Marrakech Agreement and the formation of the World Trade Organization reflect the liberal market paradigm associated with the Western capital and technology-exporting economies.[32] The TRIPs Agreement extends GATT and WTO protection to intellectual property rights and provides standards for enforcement that complement existing international regimes set forth under the World Intellectual Property Association Treaty, the Berne Convention on copyrights, and the Universal Copyright Convention.[33] This expanded regime for private property rights in technology is of particular benefit to the technology-exporting economies, which dominate the newly protected business sectors such as integrated circuits and computer software, biotechnology, unregistered trade secrets, and entertainment.[34] As well, the TRIPs provisions limiting the capacity of governments to impose compulsory licensing to combat anti-competitive behavior by technology licensors undermine the role of the state as an agent for development and work against the interests of technology-importing economies. While Article 40 of the agreement appears to permit states to enact legislation to limit anti-competitive practices by technology licensors, the conditions attached are more severe than previous provisions on compulsory licensing associated with the WIPO, Berne and Universal Copyright Conventions. Thus, the TRIPs Agreement operates to protect private property rights of technology licensors while undermining the role of the technology-importing states in attempting to ensure that the uses and distribution of technology serve the goals of social and economic development.

The TRIMs Agreement appended to the WTO extends GATT disciplines of transparency and national treatment to investment activities,[35] while the General Agreement on Trade in Services (GATS) extends the GATT's "most-favored nation" (MFN) and transparency disciplines to services, with significant implications for investment.[36] The TRIMs Agreement restricts the capacity of host countries to limit trade in goods produced through foreign investment in order to protect local firms, while the GATS focuses on removing local regulatory obstacles to free trade in services. These agreements also impose transparency principles on government decision making related to foreign investment and trade in services. While both agreements provide compliance grace periods and other concessions for developing countries, these are not unlimited but are intended merely to ease the process of bringing developing country economies and political systems into line. Just as the TRIPs Agreement extends GATT rules to intellectual property rights protection, so too do the TRIMs Agreement and GATS extend the GATT doctrines on free trade in goods to the investment sector.

The Multilateral Agreement on Investment, while it was limited by its terms to the OECD economies, stands as a model for a global investment protection treaty.[37] A comparison of the MAI with the various model bilateral investment treaties suggests that the policy preferences of capital-exporting states have been particularly influential.[38] Following an absolutist approach to private property rights, the MAI treats foreign direct investment as a right that should not be limited except with the consent of the investor. This is supported by provisions for private rights of action by corporate actors against states, which expand on the provisions of the treaty governing arbitration under the International Center for the Settlement of Investment Disputes (ICSID).[39] Whereas the ICSID treaty requires that a state named as a respondent in an arbitration brought by a private entity must consent to the process, under MAI, state consent is granted presumptively upon ratification of the agreement. Expansive concepts of market access requirements permit MAI signatories to transcend even the relatively minimal market protection provisions of the WTO.

The dominance of the private property ideals associated with liberal capitalism is facilitated by the extent to which the themes of efficiency and liberty operate to constrain discussion and debate about the appropriate place for private property in contemporary society. Economic utility theorists emphasize the importance of efficiency and acknowledge the side benefits of individual liberty that stem from an absolute (or near absolute) private property regime. Political utilitarians emphasize the importance of private property rights for protection of individual liberties, while also noting the efficiency gains to be had from the system. Taken together, efficiency and individual liberty work to legitimate and protect the private property discourse of economism and republicanism from challenge and result in the entrenchment of private property into law and popular culture.[40] The expansion of these regimes through the international trading system and the process of globalization invites assimilation of liberal norms of law by developing economies. While the property regime in China reveals the effects of the global spread of liberal ideology, important factors of local legal culture are also at work, and these limit the operation of the liberal paradigm.

Property rights in China: mediating private rights and public obligations

In China, property rights operate against a backdrop of a legal culture that emphasizes collective interests over individual identity. The role ascribed to private property rights in the West, as a source of economic utility and protector of individual liberty, was not generally evident in the discourse of property in traditional China. More recently, the socialist ideology of Maoism directly and explicitly repudiated the notion of private property rights and entrenched the Party/state as the guardian of public welfare. The early post-Mao period saw a gradual introduction of imported notions of private autonomy in the acquisition and management of property, but subject always to the overarching political imperative of collective and public interests.[41] In the absence of relatively autonomous norms and effective institutions to restrain state action, China's adoption of the liberal private property rights regime remains incomplete.

In traditional China, the interests of the individual were subordinate to those of the collective. The interests of the extended family–clan structure took precedence over those of each individual member, while the state's relation to society was viewed as an extension of the collective dynamic of the family. The subordination of the individual to collective interests has been driven largely by social and historical traditions derived from Confucianism and its assumptions about authority and hierarchy in social organization.[42] While there is significant evidence to suggest that the role of the individual was once highly prized,[43] and later came gradually to be suppressed as a result of the political and ideological imperatives of the Chinese state,[44] the collective tradition remains a dominant feature of Chinese legal culture.[45] Thus, while private property rights were recognized, the situs of these rights was the collective rather than the individual. For example, the *dian* contracts permitting use of land title as security prohibited the creditor from selling the mortgaged property, thus creating a relationship of mutual obligation between the creditor and debtor and underscoring their collective interest in the debt and the underlying land.[46] In traditional China, commercial contracts and property relations were generally guaranteed and enforced through community organizations such as clan and guild.[47]

While much has been made of the tensions between Mao's vision of socialist China and the imperatives of local norms supporting greater private property rights, using as examples the resiliency of peasant preferences for private agriculture,[48] at issue was not a tension between individuals and the collective but rather a conflict between competing collectives. Thus, the Maoist state found itself in conflict with the parochial interests of family and village collectivities. The role of the Party/state as a revolutionary vanguard meant that the state was central to virtually all economic and political relationships, including those involving property rights.

Property relations and the post-Mao economic reforms

The economic reform policies begun in 1978 raised the prospect of greater managerial autonomy in state-owned enterprises and increased diversity of economic actors and transactions.[49] However, during the post-Mao period of economic reform, the state remained a key player in property relations – state property rights remained dominant, albeit purportedly in the service of social interests.[50] The 1982 Constitution extended protection to property, but only to the extent that it is "lawful property," the definition of which remains the exclusive province of the state.[51] Constitutional requirements that the exercise of citizens' rights, including the right to own property, not conflict with the state or social interest effectively grant the state a monopoly on interpreting that interest and on determining the extent to which private property rights that might possibly conflict with it will be recognized and enforced.[52]

The General Principles of Civil Law (GPCL, 1986) codified broad principles of property rights, albeit subject to provisions that these not conflict with state policies and public and social interests.[53] The GPCL reflected CPC policies that at once had begun to limit the intrusion of the state into social and economic relationships while still asserting the basic provisions of state control. Thus the GPCL emphasized notions of party equality, voluntariness, and the protection of citizens' lawful rights and interests (thus diminishing the arbitrary authority of state organs and officials to intrude upon civil law relations in property), the law also recognized the fundamental principle of socialist legal order and the still central role of state planning.[54]

Despite the changes brought on by economic reform, the state's responsibility to harmonize different economic and social interests remained, despite the formal equality provided by civil law.[55] Judicial decisions in property cases during the mid-1980s relied heavily on interpretations of the General Principles of Civil Law (1986), which enshrined the centrality of state interests.[56] Decisions on such matters as unjust enrichment (*budang deli*) cited with favor GPCL provisions emphasizing the importance of state and collective property.[57] The policy implications about the diminution of class struggle, stemming from the 13th CPC Congress (October 1987) consensus on China being in the early stage of socialism, supported broader social and economic autonomy and stronger protection for property rights based on civil law.[58] As the exploitative possibilities of property relations received less concern, limited efforts were made subsequently to recognize the rights of privately operated enterprises[59] and individuals.[60]

However, throughout the 1980s and early 1990s, law and regulation on property matters focused mainly on state-owned property and the extent of managerial autonomy granted to (generally state-owned) enterprise managers. The General Principles of Civil Law recognized the rights of enterprise managers to administer enterprise property.[61] These provisions were expanded in the Law on Industrial Enterprises Owned by the Whole People (1988), otherwise referred to as the "State-Owned Enterprise Law."[62] The rights of enterprise managers were grounded in the policies of the socialist commodity economy and the rights of persons in possession of property (*zhanyouquan*).[63] By distinguishing ownership from rights to managerial autonomy, reform policies attempted to stimulate enterprise performance without compromising orthodox views on public ownership.[64] Regulations were issued in 1988 covering private enterprises, including individually operated businesses.[65] However, the "provisional" nature of the regulations and explicit provisions subordinating the private economy to the socialist publicly owned economy underscored that private enterprises were still viewed as policy concessions to the needs of economic growth and were subject to the will and the dispensation of the state. Despite continued challenges to conventional limits on private property rights, further constitutional protection was not forthcoming.[66]

Deepening property reform in the 1990s

During the period of accelerated reform following Deng Xiaoping's 1992 Southern Tour, property policy and legislation emerged as an important agenda item for both academics and government officials. While conventional norms of public ownership and protection of public interest remained well represented,[67] increased attention was paid to reforming the system of state ownership. Existing discourses on management rights were expanded to address not only issues of managerial autonomy but also managerial responsibility to conserve state property.[68] Problems of corruption and mismanagement of state property (particularly in state-owned enterprises) gave rise to calls for tighter regulation.[69] However, policy changes supporting the transition to a market economy meant that state ownership rights must also evolve and in some instances give way to diverse alternatives.[70]

The PRC Constitution was amended in 1993 to affirm the socialist market economy as the foundation for economic policy.[71] The transition from the socialist commodity economy meant that increased market autonomy for economic actors (including individuals as well as enterprises) could extend beyond the realm of commodities. This was supported by a property rights regime that could extend beyond immovable property such as land and movables such as personal property to include intangibles such as intellectual property.[72] A semi-official proposal on property legislation suggested that conventional boundaries for property rights as set forth in the General Principles of Civil Law should be re-examined.[73]

A key issue has been whether property rights are abstract (*wuyinxing*) or the result of causation (i.e. transactional – *youyinxing*). Influenced by principles of German law (drawn from the Roman law tradition), proponents of inherency argue that rights in property transcend the transactions by which they are transferred.[74] The implications of inherency suggest a diminution of the state's authority to control the content and scope of property rights, as the state's regulatory authority over transactions would not extend to the underlying property rights themselves. A contrary approach suggests that property rights are transactional.[75] Thus, the character and scope of property rights are dependent upon the terms and conditions of the transactions by which they are transferred. Land use rights or ownership rights to building and improvements may depend on the validity of the agreements through which these rights are transferred.[76] Under the transactional approach to property rights, the state's power to determine the effectiveness of transactions also extends to the character of the underlying property rights that are the subject of those transactions.[77] The issue of whether civil law rights (including property rights) derive from and are thus dependent upon transactional conditions remained a major issue in the drafting of a civil code in the late 1990s, reflecting along with continued debates about the public and private character of civil law the continued difficulty of bringing full autonomy to civil law relations under China's socialist system.[78] In inheritance, for example, property rights have been conditional on the conduct of legatees in such areas as parental support.[79]

The question is complicated by the increased recognition of multiple rights bound up in the same item of property. Calling for a departure from the tradition notion of "one thing, one right" (*yi wu yi quan*), Chinese jurists have begun to assert the importance of a more flexible property rights regime that can account for intersecting and overlapping property claims. Property rights reform in China also intersects other policy issues such as family relations, where greater recognition of the rights of women has driven broader recognition of common marital property.[80] These efforts call attention to the processes for registration and recognition of property rights, raising again the question of whether the property rights derive from the transactions to which they are bound or exist independently.

In an effort to expand upon Party policies suggesting greater tolerance for private property rights, formal legal protection was sought for private property rights of corporations[81] as well as individuals.[82] The influence of foreign property regimes also emboldened efforts to expand the scope of private property rights.[83] Recognizing the centrality of public ownership orthodoxy, proponents of expanded private property rights focused on changing the terms governing standards of public ownership by distinguishing between public ownership of natural resources from collective ownership of land by economic entities such as companies.[84] Building on these discussions, formal proposals for constitutional revisions were couched in the language of the market economy. No longer could property rights remain within the confines of civil law – constitutional provisions would be unavoidable.[85] The market economy required diversity in the means of distributing wealth and thus should permit expanded private property rights.[86] Broader civil law autonomy for individuals need not displace the collective imperative of state-centric economic law – rather than operate in conflict, the two paradigms could be mutually sustaining.[87]

Limits to private property rights

Efforts to draft a code of property law in 1998 under the aegis of a Civil Code drafting team suggested continued limits to the discourse of private property rights. On the one hand, the draft property law contained a principle that property rights could not be interfered with by third parties (including government organs).[88] On the other hand, the draft retains the basic principles of protecting lawful rights and interests and safeguarding social and economic order and socialist modernization, as well as a prohibition against property rights harming the public interest.[89] Explanations of this section make specific reference to the constitutional provisions on the market economy – and by extension the limits on marketization imposed by the Party's policy imperatives on socio-economic order.[90] Thus, even as renewed efforts are made to enshrine property rights in legal codes, the rights that result will unavoidably remain subject to the general tenor of the Constitution, which currently favors socialist public ownership over private property rights.

Confronting those who argued for more expansive private property rights protections in the Constitution, opponents of expanded constitutional protection suggested that this would contribute to problems of corruption and misuse of state property.[91] This reflected more fundamentally the extent to which the system of public ownership remains deeply ingrained in the normative and institutional framework of China's property law regime.[92] Indeed, the importance of conforming to China's particular conditions (*tedian*) remains a powerful orthodoxy governing the scope and terms of property rights reform.[93] Doctrinal norms continue to emphasize the importance of state interests in the enforcement of private law relations.[94] The centrality of public ownership is part of this orthodoxy, and it inhibits the emergence of private property rights.[95]

The 1999 revisions to the Constitution did not ultimately include a provision on the sanctity of private property rights – instead, the language provided that the self-employed, private, and other non-public sectors constituted an important component of the socialist market economy whose lawful rights and interests would be protected by the state.[96] While this was touted as a major step forward in China's reform process, the reference to state protection of lawful rights and interests signals that the private sector will remain subject to significant state control.[97] Parallel provisions can be found in the Unified Contract Law of the PRC, which confines contracts to notions of "lawful rights and interests of the parties" and to the imperative to protect "state and social interests."[98] The limits of the constitutional revision reflect the fundamental position that China's socialist system privileges socialist public property, and while it might tolerate or even encourage private property, this was still dependent on the policy direction and dispensation of the Party/state.[99] Indeed, complaints about the phenomenon of "unit crimes" (*danwei zui*) such as bribery and tax evasion committed by enterprises suggest further limits to official tolerance of private businesses.[100] The constitutional amendment originated with the CPC Central Committee[101] and confirmed that while the policy of the socialist market economy would permit individual enterprises and private firms to play an important role, ultimately property rights remained subject to the policy priorities of the Party/state and were not to receive absolute constitutional sanction.

In the legal and policy discourse of property law, property relations remain a creation of the state and are subject to the limitations of positive public law enacted by the state.[102] Chinese jurists point to foreign precedents, such as Japan's Civil Code, as support for this approach: "The civil laws of most modern countries adopt legal positivism [*fading zhuyi*] over *laissez-faire* [*fangren zhuyi*]" to address property rights.[103] Thus, procedural requirements that the formation of private law relations depends on establishing the requisite capacity and authority of the parties permit state licensing and approval agencies to play a central role in determining what kinds of legal right will be recognized.[104] Public notice requirements on property transfers, for example, are intended primarily to meet the needs of economic stability and security and remain subject to the controls imposed by state registries.[105]

Changing perspectives on the nature of property rights and the continuing role of the state are evident in many areas, but the examples of land, intellectual property, and securities regulation are particularly noteworthy. Rights to land are often considered the most fundamental of property rights and in the case of China's agricultural society are tied closely to traditional power relations. Rights to intellectual property are emblematic of changing ideas about property rights in knowledge. Rights in securities combine elements of intangible property with financial management and corporate governance.

Traditional property relations: the case of land-use rights

The transformation of property rights in land has been a key element in Chinese Communist Party policy since the CCP was formed in 1921. Not surprisingly, this gave rise to significant policy and political discord. During the revolutionary period, both in the Jiangxi Soviet, where the communist movement was limited to the rugged Jinggangshan area, and in the northern border areas of Jin Cha Ji and Shen Gan Ning, land ownership rights were a critical issue.[106] Departing from the Soviet model, the Chinese communists pursued policies of land redistribution rather than collectivization. After the revolution, the party was split initially on the issue of whether full collectivization was desirable. Collectivization policies began in earnest in 1955 and culminated in the establishment of the communes during the Great Leap Forward (1958–1960).[107] Despite the resulting famine, which killed upwards of 30 million peasants, collectivization remained the centerpiece of CCP land policies until 1978, although allowances were occasionally made for small private farming arrangements in times of need.

The post-Mao reforms associated with Deng Xiaoping saw far-reaching changes in PRC land policy. While under the PRC Constitution and the PRC's General Principles of Civil Law ownership of land remained the exclusive province of the state and the collective, land-use rights were increasingly granted to private farming and business operations. In the rural areas, this often conflicted initially with local collectivist sentiments, leading to violence in some cases.[108] The acceleration of agricultural reform, based in part on the appearance of private family farming, has not apparently diminished the importance of collective ideals about land use, leading one prominent observer to describe the result as "redistributive corporatism."[109]

The Land Administration Law enacted in 1986 reiterated the constitutional principles of public ownership of land and clarified the jurisdictional arrangements for land administration.[110] Reforms continued, however, with revisions to the Constitution and the Land Administration Law of the PRC in 1988 to permit broader land-use rights to be conveyed to private entities; land registration rules were enacted shortly thereafter.[111] In 1990, China enacted regulations permitting businesses to take long-term interests in land for the purpose of subdivision and development.[112] As a result, investment in real property for residential and industrial purposes soared, although speculation and flipping of property leases was common.[113] Judicial decisions in disputes before the People's Courts reflected confusion over such issues as the rights of lessor and lessee regarding leased property.[114] The Law of the PRC on Urban Real Estate was enacted in 1994 in an effort both to expand the possibilities of private acquisition and management of land-use rights and to tighten state control over perceived abuses.[115] Local governments began enacting implementing regulations for their own real estate markets,[116] giving rise to concerns over jurisdictional conflicts and administrative problems in the system of land administration.[117] Nonetheless, problems continued. For example, litigation in the Shanghai People's Courts over real estate transactions tended to reflect problems with real estate valuation,[118] unauthorized sale and leasing of real estate where the seller lacked a proper legal interest,[119] disregard for licensing requirements,[120] and disputes over building quality.[121] Rights to inherit real estate also arose,[122] as did questions concerning cooperation between agencies and compatibility across regulatory regimes on such issues as resolving real estate issues for firms in bankruptcy.[123]

However, Chinese legislation has yet to recognize private ownership rights in land. Reflecting the policies of the Politburo committee from which it emerged, the revised Land Administration Law (enacted August 29, 1998; in effect from January 1, 1999) reiterated the importance of safeguarding socialist public ownership of land – particularly arable land.[124] This had particular implications for mining enterprises and other activities where ownership rights affect the value of land and operating licenses.[125] Since real estate transactions involve transfers of two kinds of property interest – ownership of buildings and fixtures, and use rights to the underlying land – the regulatory system must be able to deal effectively with each of these transfers and the rights that underlie them.[126] The focus of law and regulation is increasingly moving beyond the traditional focus of clarifying the scope of state and collective ownership, respectively, to manage transfers and registration of land-use rights.[127] While obligatory recitation of principles of socialist public ownership is unavoidable, increased attention is being paid to the problem of legal protection for land-use rights as a property right.[128] With land-use rights recognized as enforceable and transferable, mortgages and other ancillary relationships can proceed more easily.[129]

Although the increased flexibility of land-use rights and the more recent discussions of the possibility of establishing an actual land ownership system reveal a transition toward a private property regime of sorts, the state continues to play a critical role. Registration agencies permit state intrusion in the transfer of property interests in land.[130] The state's Land Administration Bureau (*tudi guanli ju*) remains firmly in control of the approval of land use and the creation and assignment of leases in land. As well, ancillary administrative organs have direct interests in land management. The Environmental Protection Bureau, for example, oversees environmental management on all urban and rural land. The Ministry of Civil Affairs oversees the relocation of families and individuals resulting from changes in land use. Moreover, the residual ownership rights held by the state and the collective mean in effect that all rights to land exist at the discretion and with the consent of the state. Rather than beginning with a presumption of individual rights to private ownership of property in land, the Chinese system proceeds from the assumption that the state holds the basic rights of ownership and that all subsequent uses, transfers, and so on depend on state approval. Thus, individualized notions of liberty and economic utility yield to the Chinese state's conception of public responsibility and collective interest.

Rights to knowledge: the case of intellectual property rights

China's intellectual property rights regime reflects a dynamic interaction between international norms and local legal and political culture.[131] On the one hand, China has been subjected to direct and ongoing pressure for the content and operation of its IPR system to conform to the expectations of the United States and other trading partners.[132] On the other hand, local factors of traditionalism and economic interest have played a significant role in diluting the influence of foreign norms.[133] Perhaps most importantly, China's transition toward a market economy and the increased acceptance of the importance of a knowledge economy have created interests favoring stronger protection of intellectual property.[134]

The role of international IPR norms

Since the beginning of its reform program, China has also been subjected to bilateral pressures to adapt foreign property norms in its IPR system.[135] Bilateral memoranda of understanding (MOU) concluded with the United States in 1989, 1992, and 1995 imposed specific obligations on China to improve its IPR regime. These agreements grew out of the 1979 US–China Trade Agreement and reflected US efforts to use formal agreements to bind China to comply with the general provisions of multilateral treaties.[136] The three Sino-US MOUs also reflected the ongoing tensions between China's emphasis on legislation and rule making in IPR enforcement[137] and the attention given by the USA and many of China's other trading partners to practical implementation.

US–China bilateral memoranda of understanding

Under the 1979 trade agreement with the United States, China agreed that patent, trademark, and copyright protection for US firms and individuals should be commensurate with US protections in these areas offered to Chinese parties. Ten years later, the US government and many US companies believed that China's IPR system remained inadequate. China was one of nine nations and regions (including Taiwan) placed on the "priority watch list" in 1989 when the Special Section 301 provisions of the US Trade Act became effective. In May 1989, in order to avoid the imposition of trade sanctions, China agreed to a memorandum of understanding with the USA that contained broad language about improving IPR protection. In the agreement, China stated that it was actively studying the possibility of joining various international IPR conventions, but it also agreed to a number of specific steps. The 1989 MOU committed China to introducing copyright legislation by the end of the year, which would include computer software as a category of protected work. China also agreed to revise its patent law by the end of 1989 to extend the duration of patent protection and expand its scope in accord with international practice.

In January 1992, a second MOU was entered into between the USA and China by which China agreed to accede to the Berne Convention on Protection of Literary and Artistic Works by October 1992[138] and to amend its newly enacted Copyright Law and issue new regulations in order to implement the convention. In furtherance of this agreement, China proceeded to join the Berne Convention and to adjust its existing laws and regulations to comply with international treaty requirements.[139]

While the 1989 and 1993 MOUs were aimed primarily at encouraging China to step up its law-making efforts, the third MOU signed in 1995 focused primarily on enforcement. By mid-1994, the USTR determined that China was not enforcing its intellectual property and again placed China on the Special Section 301 "priority watch list." One day before retaliatory 100 per cent tariffs on $1.08 billion worth of Chinese imports were to go into effect, China signed another MOU with the USA containing two major components:

1   an exchange of letters between PRC Minister of Foreign Trade and Economic Cooperation (MOFTEC) Wu Yi and United States Trade Representative Ambassador Mickey Cantor; and
2   an action plan for better protection of intellectual property rights.

The action plan contemplated three–five years of sustained enforcement effort by the Chinese State Council's IPR Working Conference (*Bangong huiyi*) to improve the enforcement of intellectual property rights and to strengthen dissemination of information and training.[140] The action plan's enforcement system also envisioned the creation of task forces responsible for intellectual property protection and enforcement. While the conference is an attempt at inter-agency cooperation, the enforcement task forces are aimed at pursuing enforcement in specific spheres of jurisdiction. In compliance with the requirements of the MOU and the action plan, the State Council's Intellectual Property Working Conference began issuing annual reports on the status of intellectual property enforcement in

China, and became active in issuing periodic calls for increased IPR enforcement.[141]

International IPR treaties

China is also increasingly subject to international treaties on IPR protection. It has joined various international conventions on intellectual property, including the World Intellectual Property Organization Convention (1980), the Paris Convention for the Protection of Industrial Property (1984), the Berne Convention for the Protection of Literary and Artistic Works (1992), and the Universal Copyright Convention (1992).[142] China's legislation on protection of Patents, Trademarks and Copyrights reflects generally the requirements of these conventions.

Upon its entry to the WTO, China will be subject to the Agreement on Trade-Related Aspects of Intellectual Property Rights (TRIPs Agreement) appended to the Marrakech Agreement establishing the WTO.[143] The TRIPs Agreement incorporates the provisions of the 1967 Paris Convention on Industrial Property, the 1971 Berne Convention on Copyrights and a number of other agreements into the WTO system. The TRIPs Agreement extends to seven categories of rights:

1 copyrights
2 trademarks
3 geographical indications
4 industrial designs
5 patents
6 integrated circuit designs
7 trade secrets.

The agreement incorporates principles of nation treatment and most favored nation treatment, because these are already enshrined in the WTO and GATT and are provided for in the Paris and Berne Conventions. The TRIPs Agreement also contains provisions against unfair competition and particularly protects against the disclosure of privileged information.

Of particular importance in the TRIPs Agreement is the section on enforcement of intellectual property rights. This section requires that signatory states ensure that enforcement procedures are available to permit affective action against the infringement of intellectual property rights. This includes civil and administrative procedures and remedies through the use of judicial and administrative tribunals. Particular emphasis is given to the role of injunctions and the payment of compensation as remedies. As well, the TRIPs Agreement incorporates GATT principles of transparency and requires signatories to publish laws and regulations as well as final judicial decisions and administrative rulings of general application, and also provide for the release of judicial and administrative decisions and rulings to interested parties whose rights may be affected by them. In sum, the TRIPs Agreement establishes substantive standards for the protection of intellectual property rights consistent with the international treaty regimes, principles for enforcement, and principles of transparency.

Driven in part by a practical recognition that mastery of the international system will strengthen China's ability to develop an intellectual property system that suits its national interest, Chinese specialists have actively publicized foreign and international norms and discourses of intellectual property. The prestigious journal *Intellectual Property Studies* (*Zhishi chanquan yanjiu*), edited by CASS scholar Zheng Chengsi, blends reports on foreign and international IP developments with studies on China's regulatory framework and case decisions. Sponsored by the Wang Family Foundation and encouraged by the Asia Foundation headquartered in San Francisco, the journal offers both English- and Chinese-language content – reflecting its aim to reach both Chinese and international audiences. Teaching materials used in Chinese law schools also give prominent coverage to the international IP regime,[144] while increased attention is paid in practice and teaching to international copyright law and the IP aspects of international technology transfers.[145] Both the World Intellectual Property Organization (WIPO) and the World Intellectual Property Rights Organization have provided technical assistance to China on IPR legislation and enforcement.[146] However, as discussed below, implementation of these provisions with regard to China's intellectual property protection system faces significant challenges.

Ideals of intellectual property protection – the legal regime

China has promulgated an impressive array of laws and regulations on intellectual property, including a Trademark Law (1982, revised 1993), Patent Law (1984, revised 1992 and 2000), Copyright Law (1991), and a Law Against Unfair Competition protecting trade secrets (1993).[147] In addition, the General Principles of Civil Law (1986) recognizes the rights of individuals and legal persons to hold copyrights, patents, and trademarks. Specialized regulations on such matters as protection of computer software and customs procedures for IPR protection are also in place.

Trademark protection

The first area of intellectual property rights (IPR) protection in China after reform involved trademarks. In 1983, China replaced its 1963 Regulations Governing Trademarks with the Trademark Law of the People's Republic of China.[148] The Trademark Law differs from the earlier rules by establishing a new administrative structure, detailing the rights associated with a registered trademark, clarifying the actions that constitute infringement, and providing additional remedies and sanctions.[149] Implementing Regulations for the Trademark Law further refined the procedures for trademark protection and enforcement.[150]

Under the Trademark Law and its Implementing Regulations, foreign businesses seeking to obtain protection for their trademarks must retain an agent authorized by the State Administration for Industry and Commerce. The Trademark Implementing Rules have provided greater flexibility for foreign businesses in selecting an authorized agent. Although China operates under a first-to-register system, the difficulties that this approach presented to foreign registrants were lessened when China became a signatory to the Paris Convention, thus permitting an applicant registered in any other Paris Convention signatory country to claim a six-month priority for its filings.

The application for trademark protection must specify the product or products to which the mark applies: protection is limited to the product specifically listed by the applicant.[151] After an application (including a copy of the requested trademark) is submitted to the Trademark Office of the SAIC, this body conducts a preliminary examination.[152] Upon obtaining preliminary approval, the proposed trademark is published for public review and comment. If there is no justifiable opposition to the published trademark, a registration certificate is issued. While there are some specific guidelines on allowable trademarks,[153] the Trademark Office has broad discretion in ruling upon trademark applications. Originally, the decision of the Trademark Review and Adjudication Board of the Trademark Office was final, although with the enactment of the Administrative Litigation Law[154] judicial review of the Board's decisions may be available.

Certain benefits and duties accrue to the owners of trademarks in China. Of particular significance is the requirement that the owners of trademarks bear responsibility for the quality of the goods on which the trademark is used.[155] In its role as a consumer protection agency, the Trademark Office may order unsafe or poorly manufactured goods to be remedied, otherwise the trademark holder may face the imposition of fines and cancellation of his or her trademark. The holders of trademarks may amend their marks and license or assign their rights after obtaining the approval of the Trademark Office.

Trademark owners are protected against acts of infringement, which is defined under the Trademark Law to be the use of an identical or similar mark on similar or identical goods; making or selling of representations of a registered mark on other goods; or causing prejudice to the exclusive rights of a trademark holder.[156] Intent to confuse is also a factor, as when a defendant producer of electric irons labeled its products with the "*jiang xin*" brandname, knowing that the Chinese character for *jiang* was very similar to the character for *hong* in a competitor's "hong xin" brand.[157] Intent to engage in unfair competition has also influenced judicial thinking on trademark infringement, as where a repair facility receiving a limited license to use the "Shanghai Da Zhong" trademark registered to a large taxi firm expanded its use of the trademark beyond the limits of the license.[158] The Trademark Law and Implementing Rules provide for administrative sanctions against trademark violators and compensation for the economic losses incurred by the trademark owner. Both the Trademark Office and the People's Court have original jurisdiction to hear infringement matters, many of which are mediated by the court.[159] If proceedings are initiated at the Trademark Office, as most cases are, an appeal may be brought before the People's Court.

In response to the 1992 MOU with the United States, the Trademark Law was amended in February 1993 (effective July 1, 1993) to provide additional protection for registered trademarks.[160] The 1993 Trademark Amendments have extended the definition of infringement to include the knowing sale of counterfeit goods. The amendments also provide for criminal penalties for infringers. Additionally, trademarks that were obtained by deceptive or improper means may be cancelled by the Trademark Office. Finally, the 1993 Trademark Amendments extended coverage of the Trademark Law to service marks. Administrative provisions were issued by MOFTEC and the SAIC, effective from 1995, governing trademark protection in international trade to complement China's 1994 Foreign Trade Law.[161] Further revisions to the Trademark Law are expected in 2001, to accommodate China's access to the West.

Patent legislation

Prior to enacting its own patent legislation, China joined the World Intellectual Property Organization (WIPO) in March 1983 and signed the Paris Convention for the Protection of Industrial Property in December 1984.[162] The Patent Law of the People's Republic of China and its implementation regulations both came into effect on April 1, 1985.[163] Amendments to the Patent Law and the Patent Implementing Regulations were made in 1992.[164] Further amendments are underway to bring the legislation into compliance with WTO requirements and to meet constitutional revisions on the socialist market economy.[165]

The Patent Law offers protection to inventions, utility models and designs that possess novelty, inventiveness or practical applicability. The Patent Implementing Regulations define an invention to be any new technical solution relating to a product or process, a utility model to be any new technical solution relating to the shape or structure of a product, and a design to be any new shape, pattern or color of a product.[166] The terms "novelty," "inventiveness," and "practical applicability" are sometimes applied in China in a different way to the US patent law system: although China adopts different standards for different types of patent, the USA adheres to a single standard.[167] Thus, an invention will not lose its novelty if it is publicly disclosed or used outside China so long as the prospective patent holder files an application within six months of such disclosure.[168]

The Patent Law grants protection to foreign persons and enterprises to the extent that their home country has concluded an agreement with China or is a party to any international agreements entered into by both countries. Foreigners are defined to be those persons or enterprises that do not have a residence or business office in China. Depending upon one's status as a foreigner or Chinese entity or person, there are differing application procedures. Foreign companies registering patents as part of a technology transfer arrangement are required to provide evidence of patent registration in another country.

After receiving an application for an invention, the Patent Office conducts a substantive examination at the request of the applicant. Failure to submit such a request within three years of the filing date results in the rejection of the application. For utility models or design patents, the Patent Office conducts a preliminary review and then publishes the application in the *Patent Gazette*. In the event that there is no justified opposition, patent approval is granted. Procedures for internal reviews by the Patent Re-examination Board and appeals to the People's Court for review of decisions granting or refusing invention patent protection are available. However, no judicial review is available for decisions on utility models or design patents.[169]

Upon approval, patent protection dates back to the time of filing. Under the original Patent Law, invention patents were protected for a term of fifteen years, while utility models or design patents had a five-year term with a renewal period of three years. The patentee has an obligation to bring the patent into effect by using or producing the patented item, or by authorizing others to do so, within three years, otherwise the Patent Office may grant a compulsory license to exploit the patent.[170] The extent of patent protection for an invention or utility model is determined by the content of the patent claims, while for designs reference is made to the drawings and photographs.

Patent infringement is generally defined under the Patent Law as any act exploiting the patent, including manufacture, sale or use of the patented item, without the authorization of the patent owner. A central issue, and one where there is significant room for uncertainty, is whether the infringing patent duplicates one already lawfully registered.[171] There are a number of activities that do not constitute infringement, such as "use without knowledge" and "use for scientific research."[172] In disputes over patent rights to inventions developed through joint research or where multiple parties claim an interest in the same patent, courts have tended to focus on the patent registration documents to determine the rightful owner.[173] Civil and criminal sanctions are available for parties found guilty of patent infringement.

In March 1988, the municipal governments of Beijing and Shanghai each promulgated procedures providing for the resolution of patent disputes through mediation conducted by the municipal patent administration bureaux.[174] Both sets of rules were an attempt to provide additional remedies and forums for disputes involving patents beyond the relief set forth in the Patent Law and Implementing Regulations. Based on these models, procedures with national application were issued by the Patent Bureau in 1990.[175]

Under both the 1989 and 1992 MOUs, China had agreed to amend its Patent Law to extend the scope and duration of patent protection. In January 1993, China did amend its Patent Law, extending the duration of patents to twenty years for inventions and ten years for utility models and industrial designs.[176] The revised law also extended patent protection to chemical formulas, permitting patents to be issued for pharmaceuticals and agricultural chemicals for example, and foods and beverages. The Regulations for the Administrative Protection of Pharmaceuticals expanded on the protection regime applicable to these products.[177] Further draft amendments to the Patent Law completed in April 2000 contemplated additional punishments for patent violations (particularly passing off) and simplified registration and administration provisions.[178] The new revisions also strengthen the rights of state-owned enterprises over inventions created by their employees, while also providing for compensation of inventor-employees.[179]

Copyright legislation

China enacted its Copyright Law in 1990 and the implementing regulations for the law the following year.[180] The drafting of revisions to the Copyright Law and its implementing regulations is currently underway.[181] Draft revisions to the Copyright Law were adopted by the State Council in November 1998, ostensibly so that the statute conforms with constitutional revision on the "socialist market economy" and to ensure consistency of copyright protection between foreign and Chinese authors.[182]

The Copyright Law defines a copyright as including both "economic" and "moral" rights, which are the rights to publish, revise, protect the work, and use it for monetary gain. Limits are placed on these rights, thereby allowing others to use a work without providing remuneration for private use, study, research, or entertainment purposes; quoting or publishing a work for circulation in the media; and translating or copying limited quantities of a work for use in teaching or cultural and governmental activities.[183] Uses that are generally beyond the scope of these limitations require an authorization contract entered into between the copyright owner and user.

Copyrightable works include printed, video, and audio material, as well as diagrams, designs and computer software. Translated works can be copyrighted by the translator.[184] While copyrights generally belong to the creator of a work, they may attach to an employer or other legal entity if the work is created in the course of employment or completed primarily with material support from an employer. The right of a creator to publish, use, and receive compensation for a work lasts for the lifetime of the creator plus fifty years if a natural person and fifty years if a legal person, such as a business association. For natural or legal persons in China, a copyright comes into existence upon the date of the creation of the work. For foreigners, a copyright begins on the date that the work is first published in China, or for works published outside China, within thirty days after initial foreign publication.[185] The Copyright Law does not specifically protect the works of foreigners first published outside China but leaves this to multilateral or bilateral agreements to which China is a party. In January 1992, a second MOU was entered into between the USA and China by which China agreed to accede to the Berne Convention on Protection of Literary and Artistic Works by October 1992.[186] The convention permits foreign copyright owners to obtain rights of priority for copyrighted property first registered outside China.[187] China enacted provisions on implementing international copyright treaties in 1992, thus bringing domestic law into line with its international obligations.[188]

Infringement is defined under the Copyright Law to be publication or reproduction of another's work without permission, or using the work without providing compensation. Infringers may be required to discontinue the infringement, eliminate the damage to the creator, pay compensation, or make a public apology. The NPC Standing Committee issued a draft decision approving the application of criminal penalties for copyright violations in February 1994.[189] Amendments to the Copyright Law approved in April 2001 provide for more effective civil remedies in the areas of injunctive relief and damages.

While the Copyright Law included software as a protected item, it stated that software would be addressed in a separate set of rules.[190] China promulgated the Computer Software Protection Regulations, which came into effect on October 1, 1991[191] and provide protection for computer software that is either first published in China or created by the nationals of countries that have entered into bilateral agreements with China or multilateral agreements to which China is a party. The landmark Juren Computer copyright case stands as a leading case on protection of foreign copyright.[192] In another major decision on copyright protection of foreign software, the Shanghai court departed from the customary pattern of formalistic decision making evident elsewhere and determined that the foreign owner's failure to register their AEDK software did not preclude it from receiving protection under Chinese law.[193] While concerns remain over the provision for registration of software as a condition for receiving protection, the regulations were seen as a major first step toward effective protection of foreign software.

IPR enforcement: the role of local culture and interests

Enforcement of intellectual property rights can be pursued through a variety of channels. The People's Courts have specialized "Intellectual Property Chambers" (*zhishi chanquan shenpanting*),[194] although these may soon be merged with the general Civil Law Chambers. The Supreme People's Court has taken an active role in publicizing the importance of IPR protection and has directed the lower courts to intensify their activities in this area.[195] In the six years prior to 1998, these tribunals handled 22,860 intellectual property disputes.[196] In 1998, the People's Courts decided 3,953 cases.[197] Mediation services are also available through the government departments responsible for the various sectors of the intellectual property regime. The Public Security Bureau has cooperated with foreign firms to raid suspected IP violators, although a significant amount of independent investigation is often necessary before the matter can be brought to the PSB's attention. Criminal penalties are available for IPR piracy under the revised Criminal Law of the PRC (1997), and there is evidence that the law is being implemented, at least in selected circumstances.[198] Among the more famous copyright cases were those involving copyright violations in the passing off of a painting by Wu Guanzhong, and a record judgment of RMB13 million and conviction for piracy of Microsoft's Windows 95 and Office 97 software by two software development companies in Beijing with links to Peking University.[199] Provincial-level campaigns to crack down on CD and VCD piracy have been publicized widely in the Chinese press.[200] However, many of these efforts seem aimed at issues of pornography and other content that is offensive to the regime, rather than IPR issues.[201]

Throughout most of the 1980s and 1990s, IPR enforcement in China was scandalously ineffective. Experts suggest that up to 95 percent of software in use in China is pirated, while annual losses to US companies from copyright piracy ranged from $2.39 billion in 1996 to $2.59 billion in 1998.[202] Software has been a particular problem, largely because piracy is so easy.[203] Losses to US companies from software piracy in 1998 totaled $1.4 billion.[204] Pirated films on digital video discs (DVDs) are seen as out of control, with little enforcement effort by the government.[205] Prior to a formal prohibition being issued in May 1999, Chinese government agencies were among the most active users of pirated software.[206] As a result of pressure from the United States, China has made some improvements in intellectual property protection in recent years.[207] However, it remains uncertain whether these improvements are sustainable.[208] Realizing the limits of the formal legal system, foreign intellectual property owners are recognizing the benefits of alliances with Chinese firms to protect IPR.[209]

China's enactment of a legal regime for the protection of intellectual property rights has been driven by policy goals of economic development and the need to attract foreign capital and technology. Moreover, the legal norms underlying China's IPR system are drawn largely from the Western tradition emphasizing private property rights and private causes of action to enforce such rights. Indeed, in many cases, the texts of Chinese laws have been copied from models borrowed from Europe and North America.

Yet the relevant rules and institutions often contradict local cultural norms born of the Confucian tradition, which did not generally consider knowledge to be a form of property.[210] In the culture and society of traditional China, copying was not viewed with disdain. Whether copying the masters in the realm of painting or poetry or in the repetition of Confucian classics during the official examinations, emulation was seen as an exercise in deference as well as a socialization exercise.[211] Thus, there is not the social opprobrium attached to copying that serves as the cultural foundation for Western notions about intellectual property. These views have been closely held at both the governmental and popular levels despite the introduction of Western concepts of private intellectual property rights in the early twentieth century and the drafting of some IPR laws by the Qing (until 1911) and republican (since 1911) governments. During the Maoist period, the Communist Party specifically denied protection to private intellectual property, because it was deemed to have been produced from the exploitation of labor. This contributes to problems with enforcement of intellectual property rules, since these rules are not consonant with the underlying cultural views on the autonomy of the creative exercise.

Enforcement of intellectual property is also affected by the socialist critique of private property. Despite policy changes that have permitted increasingly broad rights to private property,[212] the ideological view that property is an inherently exploitative relationship remains available, if not to reduce popular reliance on private property, certainly to justify official and private intrusions on property rights. Thus, in contrast to the cultural icons that exist in the West about private property, private property in the PRC is a policy creation rather than a basic right.[213] The absence of deeply entrenched notions about the sanctity of private property is of particular relevance to intellectual property relations, where the property in question is abstract rather than tangible. Thus, IPR laws and policies concerning intellectual property protection are seen as products of limited necessity rather than a product of deeply embedded notions about private property and the importance of individual creativity and knowledge as worthy of property protection.

Problems with IPR enforcement also reflect perspectives drawn from a conceptualization of the world in terms of conflicts between the developed North and the developing South. Reflecting United Nations resolutions on the New International Economic Order, Chinese policies express the view that the developed countries of the world have a duty to assist others in development.[214] Implicit in this view are conclusions of dependency theorists that the development of the technology- and capital-rich countries of the "North" was made possible through the exploitation of the less developed countries (LDCs) of the "South." The "right" of the LDCs to receive development assistance carries with it an implied right to acquire technology on the most favorable terms possible. These attitudes are reflected in the compulsory licensing provisions of the PRC Patent Law, which impose on foreign technology owners a duty to make or use the patented product or process in China.[215] In the context of the perceived inadequacies of China's intellectual property protection system, this requirement has been seen as compelling foreign technology owners to make their patents available for unauthorized pirating in China. More specific claims have been raised that the compulsory licensing requirements have been enforced discriminatorily against Western intellectual property owners and have also been used improperly in licensing negotiations.[216]

The thrust of IPR enforcement continues to rely on the dominance of the state.[217] The state's policy interests in economic development have driven the recognition of patent and trademark rights to the extent that the exercise of these rights depends on enforcement being deemed by administrative officials to be consistent with China's development goals. These factors are present in copyright enforcement as well, with the additional factor of copyright approval and enforcement serving as a vehicle for state control over literary, artistic and industrial expression.

Bureaucratic political issues also arise in the rule-making process, which ultimately impedes enforcement. A major component of the enforcement problem concerns the role of administrative enforcement, which devolves significant discretion to local officials. Despite provisions permitting parties claiming infringement to bring actions directly to the courts, enforcement remains largely in the hands of local administrative agencies.[218] Aside from the very real problems that exist where local regulators have parochial interests that discourage the vigorous pursuit of infringement cases, there remains the problem that the local enforcing agencies lack the power to prohibit and punish infringements. The sanctions permitted under the relevant intellectual property laws and regulations emphasize cease-and-desist orders and the role of apology in resolving infringement problems.[219] While the importance of monetary compensation for losses resulting from IPR infringements is gradually being recognized more widely,[220] even where penalties are levied, enforcement requires intervention by the local Public Security Bureau (possibly, but not always with involvement by the local Procuracy or People's Court), whose local parochial interests are not served by vigorous actions against local enterprises. As a result, effective action against infringers is often delayed or prevented altogether. Although there appears to be gradual realization at the central level of the importance of IPR enforcement, the resources and political will necessary to restructure the political and economic interests at the local level in order to make IPR enforcement a reality will be substantial.

The absence of deeply entrenched notions about the sanctity of private property is of particular relevance to intellectual property relations, where the property in question is abstract rather than tangible. Thus, the recognition of intellectual property rights represents a limited exception to the general norms of Chinese socialist ideology, which restrict private property rights, and does not carry with it the requirement of strict and effective enforcement as a condition for that recognition to be meaningful. Despite overwhelming evidence of serious and wide-ranging problems of IPR enforcement, responses to the problem reflect the formalism evident in other aspects of the

Chinese legal regime, as the effectiveness of the intellectual property protection system is asserted on the basis of the enactment of legislation rather than being based on empirical reality. For example, various Chinese "White Papers" on intellectual property rights have made little effort to articulate specific proposals to improve China's intellectual property protection system and instead often criticize calls from the United States and others for improvements in China's IPR protection practices as unfounded.[221]

Corporate property: securities regulation

The role of securities as a form of private property has been affected directly by ideological and policy norms concerning public and private ownership of business enterprises in the Chinese economy.[222] International influences are evident but are subject to limitations born of local bureaucratic and legal culture. After an extended period of debate, China began to erect a system of securities laws and regulations in 1990 that brought reform policies enacted in other sectors of the economy to the finance sector.[223] The effort began in the late 1980s and gathered momentum with the establishment of securities exchanges in Shanghai[224] and Shenzhen.[225] Thereafter, efforts were made to develop a national regulatory framework for securities markets. While the long-term prospects for the development of securities markets in China remain obscure, the regulatory framework provides yet another expression of emerging discourses of property rights.

Local regulatory regimes

With the opening of the Shanghai securities market in December 1990, China began a well-publicized effort to build a legal regime for regulating securities markets. The Shenzhen market was officially opened shortly thereafter, and for a time the regulatory frameworks in these two cities were the major if not the only basis for securities regulation in China. Subject to the limits of national regulations, the local measures applicable in Shanghai and Shenzhen remain effective in these places.

Shanghai

The Shanghai regulations included primarily the Trial Regulations of the Shanghai Securities Exchange on the Activities of the Exchange Market (the Shanghai Exchange Regulations),[226] issued by the SSE's board of directors, and the Methods of Shanghai Municipality for Administration of Securities Transactions (the Shanghai Transaction Regulations),[227] issued by the municipal government. Enacted on November 26, 1990, the Shanghai Exchange Regulations contain detailed provisions on SSE operations and organization, all of which are subject to the authority of the Shanghai Municipal Branch of the People's Bank of China (PBOC/Shanghai).[228] Complementing the

Exchange Regulations, the Shanghai Transaction Regulations govern the issuing and transfer of securities, and related matters,[229] and focus more specifically on the processes for issuing and transferring securities and the parties involved. While reiterating the theme of the Shanghai Exchange Regulations in maintaining PBOC control over securities transactions, the Shanghai Transaction Regulations also depart from the Shanghai Exchange Regulations by opening the possibility of a greater variety of securities being traded[230] and by minimizing the differential treatment between issuing and trading in stocks and bonds.[231] By some accounts, bond regulation is firmly in place in the Shanghai Exchange, although the regulations have not been altogether successful in preventing fraudulent transactions.[232]

The 1990 Shanghai Securities Regulations reiterated principles expressed in the 1984 Provisional Methods Concerning the Issuance of Stock, issued by the PBOC/Shanghai, which limited interest and dividend rates and also restricted the avenues for issuing and transferring securities.[233] The 1990 regulations also underscore the provisions of these earlier measures concerning the authority of the PBOC/Shanghai to approve all securities issues and to control, suspend, or even terminate securities trading.[234]

In November 1991, the PBOC, PBOC/Shanghai, and Shanghai municipal government issued administrative measures and implementing rules for "B shares" – shares denominated in renminbi but allowed to pay dividends in foreign currency.[235] The Shanghai B Share Administrative Measures[236] and Implementing Rules[237] address a wide range of issues, including conversion rates; exchange accounts; securities dealers inside and outside China; issues and trading; clearance procedures; and taxation, fees, and penalties. In addition, the Shanghai Exchange issued a set of Supplementary Operating Rules in February 1992 governing transactions in "B shares", which address issues relating to "B share" accounts, delegated purchase and sale, the mechanics of trade transactions, fees, dispute resolution, and other matters.[238] Taken together, this group of regulations sets the basic framework for the B share market in Shanghai.

Shenzhen

Although transactions in securities were conducted in Shenzhen as early as 1987, when securities were listed by the Shenzhen Development Bank,[239] the formal opening of the Exchange itself remained something of a mystery.[240] As indicated by the 1986 Provisional Methods of Guangdong Province for the Administration of Stocks and Bonds, which empowered enterprises in the province to raise finance by issuing securities,[241] regulatory activity concerning securities markets had been underway in Guangdong for some time.

In July 1990, the Shenzhen municipal government established a "Leading Small Group" (*lingdao xiaozu*), which began drafting regulations for the Shenzhen Exchange.[242] Based on drafting work by the Leading Small

Group, regulations governing the Shenzhen Exchange were formally enacted in May 1991, with subsequent measures issued to address stock trading and other matters.[243] The major regulations governing securities transactions on the Shenzhen Exchange are the Articles of Association for the Shenzhen Securities Exchange (the Shenzhen Exchange Rules) and the Provisional Methods of Shenzhen Municipality for the Issue and Transferring of Shares (the Shenzhen Stock Transaction Regulations), which were submitted for approval to the PBOC Central Branch (with consultation involving the State Commission for Restructuring the Economy and the Bureau for Administration of State Owned Property) after lengthy negotiations between the representatives of the Shenzhen Exchange, the Shenzhen municipal government, the Shenzhen branch of the PBOC (PBOC/Shenzhen).[244]

The Shenzhen Exchange Rules set forth the basic provisions for operation of the Exchange on such issues as the authority of the Shenzhen branch of the PBOC in supervising the Exchange; establishment and operation of the Exchange, as well as sales, purchases, clearing accounts, payment of interest, and other matters; membership; and finance and accounting rules. The focus of these regulations is on the organization and administration of the exchange as an institution, separate and distinct from the transactions associated with it.

By contrast, the Shenzhen Stock Transaction Regulations address transactional matters such as stock issues, stock transactions, and brokers. Unlike the Shanghai enactments, the Shenzhen measures clearly delineate the functional difference between regulation of the exchange itself (through the Shenzhen Exchange Rules) and regulation of stock transactions (through the Shenzhen Stock Transaction Regulations). In December 1991, the PBOC, PBOC/Shenzhen, and Shenzhen municipal government issued Interim Procedures[245] and Implementing Rules[246] for the Shenzhen securities market that are broadly similar to those issued for Shanghai.

China's national securities regulatory regime

While the process of developing a national securities regulatory regime was fraught with policy conflicts over the goals of regulation, nonetheless there was a powerful consensus among proponents of deepening reform, particularly after Deng Xiaoping's momentous Southern Tour (*nanxun*) in 1992, that an expansive legislative initiative should be pursued to establish a national securities regulatory system.[247] Wide recognition of the need to resolve the crisis of functionally insolvent state-owned enterprises combined with increased flexibility in the ideology of public ownership contributed to a growing acceptance of the need for quasi-private financial markets.[248] Rather than focus on the issue of ownership, proponents of expanded securities markets opted for general principles of openness, fairness, and equality, which would then be enshrined in formal legislation.[249] The Company Law, enacted in 1994, primarily addressed the regulation of business enterprises.[250] While it invited opposition by the fact of its imposing formal procedures on government regulation and by its recognition of the possibility of privately owned joint stock and limited liability companies, the Company Law was relatively uncontroversial. The Securities Law was quite another matter and was not enacted until 1999 following years of debate.[251] The Company Law and the Securities Law provide the regulatory foundation upon which local regulations in Shanghai and Shenzhen operate.

The Company Law of the PRC

In December 1993, the NPC promulgated the PRC Company Law, which formalized the rules and procedures for company operations but also added new rules and procedures for company shares.[252] Based on a draft that had been submitted the previous March after undergoing years of refinement and debate,[253] and on various "opinions" on stock companies and limited liability companies,[254] the Company Law came into effect on July 1, 1994, and runs to 230 articles covering the establishment and organization of companies, bond issues, accounting matters, mergers, bankruptcy and liquidation, responsibilities of branches of foreign companies, and other matters. Of particular importance are the provisions concerning companies limited by shares (*gufen youxian gongsi*, also referred to as "joint stock companies"), which were previously authorized to issue B shares,[255] and which under the Company Law may now receive approval for listing their shares on overseas securities exchanges.[256]

Shares of companies limited by shares are to be issued in the form of share certificates carrying equal rights and benefits for each class of stock, and at or above par value.[257] Public offers are to be underwritten by authorized securities institutions.[258] Transactions in shares are subject to approval by the State Council's securities administration department.[259] Additional requirements are aimed at confirming the financial wherewithal of the issuing company.[260] Listing of shares to the public for trading requires additional approval from the State Council or its securities administrative department, as well as from the relevant securities exchange.[261]

In addition to stock issues, companies limited by shares as well as limited liability companies with state investment may issue corporate bonds.[262] Prior to seeking State Council approval, the bond issue must be approved by the shareholders or, in the case of state-owned companies, by the state's authorized investment department.[263] Requirements for approval include:

1   net assets must be not less than RMB30 million for companies limited by shares and not less that RMB60 million for limited liability companies;

2   the aggregate value of bonds may not exceed 40 percent of total net assets;

3   the average distributable profits over the past three years must be suffi-
    cient to defray one year's interest payment on the bonds;
4   the use of funds raised must conform to state industrial policy and must
    be used for approved purposes and to cover losses or for non-production
    expenditure; and
5   the interest rate payable may not exceed State Council limits.[264]

Bonds may not be reissued if (1) the previous issue was not fully subscribed
or (2) the company has defaulted on previously issued bonds or other indebt-
edness, or is late in payment of principal or interest.[265]

Securities regulations

Although many expected a securities law to emerge shortly after the
Company Law was enacted, they were soon disappointed.[266] The debates
over public and private ownership that had characterized the securities
system generally delayed enactment of a securities law. The fundamental
question was whether a socialist society could tolerate capitalist mechanisms
such as securities markets, which fostered private ownership of business
companies' assets.[267] In other words, could China accept privatization of the
means of production, and if so to what extent? The resulting policy compromises saw enactment of an interim series of national regulations in 1992–93
on the issue and trading of securities.[268]

Following the opening of securities exchanges in Shanghai and Shenzhen,
securities regulation in the PRC gradually extended to the national level
through a series of eight separate regulations issued between June and
August 1992.[269] The most important of these measures, and one from
which the others derived, was the "Regulations on Enterprises' Shareholding
System Experiment" (hereafter, the Shareholding System Regulations),
issued jointly by the State Commission on Restructuring the Economy, the
State Planning Commission, the Ministry of Finance, the People's Bank of
China, and the State Council Production Office.[270] The Shareholder System
Regulations set the broad parameters for expanding the use of shares as the
basis for enterprise ownership. A key element of this was protection of shareholder interests. Additional issues included financial management,[271]
taxation,[272] commercial transactions,[273] and the formation and supervision
of joint stock companies.[274]

In April 1993, the State Council issued provisional regulations that
provided formal nationwide standards for the issue and trading of stock.[275]
Emerging from the State Council's January 1993 Circular on Further
Strengthening Macro-Control of Securities Markets,[276] the State Council
rules supplemented regulations already in place at the Shanghai and
Shenzhen exchanges. The January circular was amplified yet again in July
with the State Council Securities Committee's Interim Procedures on the
Management of Stock Exchanges.[277] The 1993 regulations addressed such

matters as stock issues and trading; takeovers; the custody, clearance, and registration of shares; information disclosure; inspection and penalties; and dispute resolution. The regulations also paved the way for the listing of Chinese domestic stocks on foreign markets such as Hong Kong.[278]

Expanding upon the State Council circular of January 1993, the mid-year regulations specified that the State Council Securities Policy Committee (SCSPC) was to have overall charge of administration of the national stock market, while the China Securities Regulatory Commission (CSRC) was to be the SCSPC's executive agency responsible for supervision and regulation.[279] The regulations granted the CSRC broad authority to investigate individuals or companies suspected of violating the regulations, and to examine the business activities of any securities institution without cause. The CSRC subsequently established a special commission to examine and approve share issues.[280]

After a short hiatus following enactment of the Company Law, the Securities Regulatory Commission increased its rule-making activities. By some reports, more than a dozen new regulations were issued in late 1996 and early 1997,[281] among which were formal procedures for the administration of securities exchanges, replacing the interim measures of 1993.[282] In December 1996, regulations were issued on the supervision of companies listed on the Shanghai and Shenzhen exchanges.[283] These rules were aimed primarily at ensuring the accuracy of information released by listed companies and that expenditures and company decisions were lawful and in accordance with company governance documents. New rules on stock issues and trading enacted in January 1997 paid additional attention to ensuring proper and timely payment for securities, so as to avoid the problems of buying on margin and under-capitalized subscriptions.[284]

The rule-making initiative continued into 1998. New regulations on the management of securities and futures consultancies were issued with effect from April 1998, building on circulars issued the previous year.[285] Here again, the emphasis was on procedures for qualification, ongoing supervision, and accuracy of information and consulting services provided. Regulations on capital accretion through additional B share issues were enacted in early 1998, aimed at regularizing the accounting and reporting processes.[286] In April 1998, the People's Bank of China published rules on enterprise bond issues.[287] These included specific rules on debt financing, which previously had been subject to general regulation under the rubric of "securities," which had not been wholly effective because of the regulatory focus on stocks. These rule-making initiatives suggest efforts by various bureaucracies with interests in the securities regulatory process, such as the PBOC and the Securities Regulatory Commission, to articulate principles and assert authority in anticipation of the enactment of the Securities Law. In light of the Securities Law's general absence of specifics on the regulations and regulators that would lose effect upon enactment of the new statute, the rule-making efforts undertaken in advance of the legislation suggest concerted efforts to retain control over regulatory discourses and administrative authority.

The Securities Law of the PRC

The Securities Law (1999) represented a step toward unifying the disparate regulatory regime that had emerged.[288] The statute aimed to standardize the issue and trading of securities, and authorized the State Council to implement centralized and unified regulation of the national securities market, which would include the local exchanges in Shanghai and Shenzhen to the extent that their securities are traded nationally.[289] However, the statute did not repudiate any existing regulations, and it granted that securities approved prior to the law's enactment could continue to be traded (even if by implication these were approved subject to regulatory standards that were superseded by the statute).[290] In many respects, though, the Securities Law reflected the policy priorities of prior regulations, namely to protect the legal rights and interests of investors, safeguard social economic order and public interests, and promote the development of the economy.[291] Thus, the rights and interests of investors were once again subject to the limitations of lawfulness, which in the Chinese context will reflect current Party policy, as well as the needs of social economic order, public interests, and economic development. Securities Regulatory Commission Chairman Zhou Zhengqing indicated that since the commission had "basically completed the work of rectifying illegal stock trading beyond the stock market, the Securities Exchange Center, securities operation organizations, and the futures market, and the work of checking up on and setting standards for original investment funds is proceeding smoothly," the law's chief aim was to provide conditions for sustained development of securities markets under a unified set of rules and procedures.[292]

The concerns of lawmakers with controlling the behavior of unscrupulous issuers of securities were evident in provisions that issues and transactions in securities are subject to principles of openness (*gongkai*), fairness (*gongping*), and justice (*gongzheng*).[293] Concerns over both insider favoritism and oppression were evident in provisions that the parties in such transactions be granted equal legal status and be held to principles of voluntariness (*ziyuan*), compensation (*youchang*), and good faith (*chengshi xinyong*).[294] While the aims were laudable, the patrimonial tenor of the statute was evident, because it will be the state as implementor of Party policy that will ultimately determine issues of fairness, voluntariness, and so on. Criminal penalties were enacted in December 1999 for securities abuses, such as insider trading, underscoring the importance of the public law dimension to securities regulation.[295] Indeed, official commentaries on the law point out that the goals of protecting social and economic order and safeguarding the social and public interest are not "mirages" (*bu shi haishi shenlou*) but rather are the foundation upon which rests the aim to protect investor interests.[296] This

point is made clear by the separation of these principles from the requirement that the issue and trading of securities comply with the law and
administrative regulations and the prohibition of fraudulent and insider
trading and market manipulation.[297]

Specific sections of the Securities Law address issues of securities issuance
and trading; buyouts of listed companies; securities exchanges and companies; institutions for registration, settlement, and other services; associations
of securities companies; administration; and legal liability. The issuing and
trading of securities are subject to familiar requirements of qualification and
reporting, with additional provisions for ongoing disclosure.[298] Issuance of
securities requires the approval of the SSA's Stock Issuance Approval
Commission, subject to evolving substantive and procedural rules.[299]
Complementing the merger and acquisition provisions of the Company Law,
the Securities Law provides for the buyout of listed companies through share
acquisition, again with substantial requirements for reporting to regulators.[300] The statute requires that securities exchanges are subject to State
Council approval and supervision,[301] which on the one hand ensures a
modicum of central control but also frees local exchanges from the parochial
and often conflicting supervision of the PBOC. Securities companies and
institutions for registration, settlement, and other services are also subject to
State Council supervision, as are the associations of securities companies.[302]
The State Council's organ for supervision of securities activities is the
Securities Supervision Administration (*Zengquan jiandu guanli jigou*, SSA),
which has responsibility for the administration and enforcement of securities
laws, along with extensive powers of oversight, inspection, investigation,
and sanction.[303] The rules and regulations governing the SSA's conduct are
required to be kept open (*gongkai*), but the extent of the SSA's duty to
publish these materials remains unclear. And while the SSA will be subject
to the general requirements of Chinese administrative law, the broad scope
of its responsibilities and powers will make challenges to its authority difficult.

Contending influences on China's securities regulatory regime

The proponents of expanding China's securities markets and regulatory
system have been strongly influenced by a variety of foreign jurisdictions,
most notably the United States.[304] The Chinese experts most closely associated with the securities regulatory system received their legal education in
the United States and have continued to look to the NYSE and the SEC
system as models for markets and regulatory regimes.[305] Thus, it is not
surprising to find provisions on information disclosure and insider dealing
in both the Shenzhen and Shanghai exchange regulations that reflect ideals
drawn from the US regulatory regime.[306] Japanese securities regulatory
models have also been consulted by the State Council in the course of its rule
making and legislation on securities regulation.[307] Taiwan company laws

and practice also exerted significant influence.[308] Reflecting these influences, the Securities Law does much to strengthen reporting requirements for the benefit of investors. Thus, the continuing disclosure provisions of the law require that "important events" (ranging from operational and organizational issues to financial questions) be published as well as reported to regulators.[309] Moreover, the Securities Law places stronger limits on the activities of regulators, in part through the requirement that the rules and procedures of the State Council's Securities Supervision Administration must be open. This raises the potential for closer application of administrative law generally to decisions and activities of the SSA.

Despite the influence of liberal norms borrowed from abroad, the state retains a dominant role.[310] Both the Company Law and the Securities Law empower the SSA to approve securities issues but provide scant guidance on the standards to be used throughout the review and approval process. Critics in China have suggested that the law reflects the values of the planned economy and that its provisions requiring state approval for securities issues, for example, unduly restrict the autonomy of market actors.[311] The Company Law privileges the supervisory powers of regulators over the rights of shareholders and other market actors, not least by requiring more information to be disclosed to government regulators than is required to be disclosed to market participants.[312]

As well, the general principles of the Company Law and the Securities Law privilege collective issues of economic order and public interest over the rights of market actors. This allows current policy imperatives to dominate the discretionary decision making by regulatory agencies, protecting in turn Party policies favoring collectivist approaches to property rights. A key issue involves the reform of state-owned enterprises, which remains a fundamental liability hampering economic growth and burdening government resources. Despite efforts at profit sharing, tax incentives, responsibility systems, and other incentives, SOE performance remained problematic throughout the 1990s.[313] Praise for public property ownership through government partnerships reflected a continued commitment to the public ownership of major industrial firms.[314]

Continued emphasis on state control does not mean uniformity of regulatory standards, however, as bureaucratic and policy conflicts result in inconsistency in doctrine and practice. Differences in statutory language between the Company Law and the Securities Law on such issues as information disclosure requirements raise the possibility of conflicting interpretations and approvals of stock issues.[315] Debates continue unresolved among Chinese legal specialists as to whether the Securities Law should simply displace the Company Law on questions of stock issuance.[316] Uncertainty over regulatory standards is likely to increase the already burgeoning number of security-related disputes before the People's Courts as securities investors seize on regulatory weaknesses to pursue their own private interests.[317]

Summary

In contrast to models of Western liberalism, where the norms of liberty and efficiency constrain the state to limit its regulation of private property to the most narrow of possibilities, in China the state continues to occupy a central role in mediating property relations. While international treaties on intellectual property and trade relations will constrain the state's authority to some extent, the contours and the results of the debate over inclusion of a private property protection clause in the 1999 constitutional amendments suggest the extent to which private property rights remain limited. In the areas of land, intellectual property and corporate property, the state retains power to determine the scope of property rights. The challenge for China's management of property relations is to move the state sufficiently away from its position of prominence to dilute the gate-keeping powers of officials, while at the same time ensuring that state regulation of market-based activity is sufficiently effective to prevent economic development undermining the security, health, and well-being of society.

5 Human rights

Social welfare and social control[1]

In contrast to its achievements in the areas of contracts, property, and dispute resolution, China's record on human rights appears to many outside observers to be seriously flawed. On the one hand, China has supported human rights research and scholarship at the highest levels of policy making.[2] International documents on human rights have been translated into Chinese and published with government support.[3] China has approved bilateral scholarly exchange programs aimed at information sharing on human rights doctrine and practice.[4]

On the other hand, even disregarding the 1989 massacre of demonstrators in Beijing and the nationwide campaign of repression that followed,[5] China's policies and practices appear not to have kept pace with its professions to respect human rights. China released its most famous dissident, Wei Jingsheng, from prison in September 1993 in a transparent attempt to placate international opinion at a time when Beijing was bidding to host the 2000 Olympics, only to rearrest him after the bid had been turned down and sentence him to a fourteen-year term for sedition.[6] China signed the International Covenants on Economic, Social and Cultural Rights and Civil and Political Rights but so far has failed to ratify either agreement.[7] Torture and mistreatment of prisoners continue, along with forced confessions, arbitrary arrests, and lengthy incommunicado detention.[8] China has deployed its public security resources and rammed through special legislation to combat its domestic critics and civil organizations such as the Falun Gong sect for allegedly threatening Communist Party rule.[9] Access to information has been restricted through the Law on Protecting State Secrets (1989)[10] and regulations limiting access to the Internet.[11] The Chinese government has banned pro-democracy and human rights activists from returning to China from overseas.[12] Treatment of minority nationalities, especially in sensitive areas like Tibet, has fallen short of international standards.[13] While China has acceded to the Convention on Elimination of All Forms of Discrimination Against Women (CEDAW), implementation has been problematic.[14]

The United States has been particularly critical of China's human rights record,[15] and after initial reluctance, the European Union recently joined the call for reform.[16] A number of international NGOs have also concluded that China's acceptance of international human rights norms is selective, despite efforts at dialog to improve mutual understanding.[17] China has managed to avoid formal criticism at the UN's Commission on Human Rights, largely through a series of successful "no action" motions,[18] while the effects of international monitoring of China's human rights record have been confined to areas of "technical cooperation" such as education and administration, where the Chinese government has already embarked on reforms.[19]

The apparent contradictions between China's increased willingness to engage international norms at the level of abstraction and scholarly discourse and its apparent inability to enforce these norms consistently reflect the extent to which local legal cultures determine the selection and influence of international norms. China's human rights policies can be understood in part by reference to the discourse of the right to development, which China has adopted selectively for its own use. Particularly useful examples of China's human rights practices lie in the areas of labor law and criminal law and procedure, for it is these areas that the Communist Party's ideological commitments to proletarian governance are most sorely tested. In China's labor relations, the authoritarian (patrimonial) state is confronted with conflicting imperatives of economic growth and social welfare for the workers employed in the service of socialist modernization.[20] China's criminal law system poses the contradictory aims of protection of Party and state authority and adherence to generally accepted standards for the rule of law.[21]

The influence of international norms: the right to development

China's human rights laws and practices are influenced significantly by the discourse of the right to development. As a signatory of and advocate for the 1993 Bangkok Declaration on Human Rights,[22] China places strong emphasis on the right to development over the requirements of civil and political rights. Despite criticisms from a wide range of academics of the "Asian values" discourse,[23] alternative views on human rights have emerged that depart from the model often associated with US human rights rhetoric.[24] In its 1991 Human Rights White Paper, the PRC explicitly adopted a position supporting the primacy of economic growth by stressing the right to subsistence as the primary right from which all other rights derive.[25] In explaining the 1991 White Paper, the Director of the State Council Information Office stressed the primacy of the state's management of economic conditions as the basis for development: "We enable our people to have the economic foundation upon which they can enjoy political rights."[26] The stance taken in the Human Rights White Paper is also evident in the yearly reports on economic and social development issued by the PRC government, which consistently give priority to economic achievement over other development needs.[27]

The 1995 Human Rights White Paper reiterated the basic policy position outlined in the 1991 White Paper, thus underscoring the PRC regime's commitment to the primacy of economic development over other human rights issues. Indeed, the 1995 White Paper explicitly stressed the people's right to development on the basis for economic development.[28] While the 1995 document placed considerable emphasis on purported achievements in civil and political rights, these remained confined by law and socialist democratic practices as determined by the Chinese government. In 1997, China issued yet another Human Rights White Paper, which reiterated the theme that subsistence and development were paramount human rights.[29]

The achievement in satisfying human rights to subsistence and development was given prominence yet again in the 2000 Human Rights White Paper.[30] However, civil and political rights continue to be subordinated to the right to development. The 2000 White Paper notes that achievements in the rights to subsistence and development have "initiated a brand-new starting point for further exploration and the progress and development of the cause of human rights" such that China's conditions require "putting the rights to subsistence and development in the first place under conditions of reform, development and stability." The White Paper articulates a sequential timetable for human rights development in which economic development must precede construction of democracy and the legal system, which in turn are aimed to ensure that "the Party and the government control political power and administer the country according to law." Thus, "socialism with Chinese characteristics is ... the only road which can effectively promote human rights in China."

Although many international law scholars challenge the notion that a right to development can take precedence over other human rights,[31] China has used this approach to reject international human rights standards and monitoring. Thus, the 1995 White Paper condemned "unwarranted charges (*heng jia zhi se*) against the internal affairs of some developing countries" purportedly lodged by the United States and other Western countries, and noted China's efforts to support "the struggles of developing countries to safeguard their own rights and interests."[32] In response to the US State Department's 1995 review of China's human rights record, the State Council Information Office rejected out of hand the standards used in the US report while attacking in turn the US domestic record on human rights abuses.[33] The authoritative English-language *China Daily* expressly rejected Western notions of civil and political rights in its December 1996 editorial "Freedom loser when democracy wins."[34] Thereafter, annual reports from the USA criticizing China's human rights record have been met by strident rebuttals from Beijing.

China's views on the right to development have implications for the centrality of the state as the source of rights and as the determinant of the beneficiaries of rights. In contrast to natural rights theories, which view rights as inalienable and intrinsic to the human condition,[35] the PRC

Constitution speaks of rights being granted by the state.[36] Article 33 of the 1982 PRC Constitution goes further and conditions the extension of legal and civil rights on performance of the "duties prescribed by the Constitution and the law." This provision retains its effect despite revisions to the Constitution in 1993 and 1999. Under this approach, rights are not inherent, to be enjoyed by virtue of being human, but rather are specific benefits conferred and enforced at the discretion of the state. Thus, the content and enforcement of rights in such areas as environmental protection, freedom of women from violence and discrimination, religious freedom, and so on depend on the willingness and capacity of state agencies to act, while independent private enforcement measures are discouraged if not suppressed. The state retains a central role in addressing such issues as disparities in income and poverty alleviation,[37] even as it represses popular efforts to remonstrate over declining environmental conditions.[38]

Implications of the right to development: labor rights

The Chinese government's labor policies are caught in a dilemma of conflicting imperatives.[39] The socialist ideology of the CPC would appear to justify granting greater rights to workers in the areas of collective bargaining, work stoppages, and so on, particularly in the context of privatization of production enterprises. Yet the regime also faces the need for continued economic growth, which mandates greater control over worker discipline even as it permits declining conditions of employment. More fundamentally, the state remains committed to protecting its monopoly on authority in labor matters. China's labor law and policy in the reform era reflect many of these tensions as they have played out over the various phases of the reform period.

Ongoing reforms in labor relations

The economic reform programs initiated following the Third Plenum of the 11th Central Committee in 1978 were tentative at first, but they soon moved beyond the confines of either the Maoist or Soviet models that had previously influenced China.[40] Key to this was the political re-emergence of political leaders who emphasized the decline of class struggle and the need to focus on productive forces.[41] For with the end of class struggle, the Party/state no longer needed to concern itself with resolving the problem of exploitation and could recognize greater degrees of autonomy by individuals and groups in the economy. Thus contracts, business firms, and labor relations could be directed not by the Party/state, which was charged with eliminating and avoiding class exploitation, but rather by autonomous actors increasingly freed of state intrusion.

These ideological changes and their policy implications emerged slowly at first. In labor relations, for example, little attention was paid to reforming the state enterprise labor system initially. Instead, the emphasis was placed on reforming enterprise management. Reforms in state planning permitted enterprise managers to contract with a wider variety of business partners, while the two-track pricing system permitted managers greater flexibility in obtaining production inputs.[42] Regulations were enacted to strengthen the autonomy of factory managers from interference by Party secretaries.[43] Thus, the initial policy focus was on increasing the efficiency and productivity of state enterprises, with little attention paid to reforming relations between state enterprises and their workers. In labor relations, the neo-Confucian patrimonial relationship continued.

However, in an effort to address the employment problem for an increasing number of migrant workers – primarily young people seeking work outside their assigned residence (*hukou*) location (these were often Cultural Revolution youths who were returning to the cities after having been sent to rural areas, or peasants seeking an escape from the drudgery of village life) – the government enacted rules on contract labor. The 1986 Regulations on Administration of Labor Contracts by State Enterprises permitted state enterprises to hire occasional workers without actually incorporating them into the enterprise work unit and providing the standard array of accompanying benefits.[44] The labor contracts executed under these rules were generally not available to workers already formally assigned to the enterprise, and in view of the lower level of benefits available under them were not considered desirable.

Even though labor contracts formed pursuant to the 1986 Regulations were essentially "gap fillers" for workers who were not already part of the state enterprise system, the new measures did encourage the gradual emergence of a somewhat free labor market.[45] Even as unskilled workers began to do contract labor in the areas of construction and goods transport – to the extent of reducing the staff needs and costs of state enterprises, skilled workers began to find ways to secure their release from former employers to gain more remunerative employment. This was despite the resistance of state enterprise employers, who were often unwilling to release their skilled workers freely to seek more highly paid employment. Employment agencies began to spring up that would serve as "headhunters" for firms seeking to hire skilled workers and professionals and arrange payment of the fee demanded by state enterprises as the price for releasing their staff members to other units. As well, sidewalk labor markets became an increasingly important source of unskilled workers for short-term projects. In sum, the initial reforms culminated in the emergence of a proto-market for labor.

By the late 1980s, many of the initial reforms had run their course. Enterprise managers were increasingly independent, production inputs and outputs were gradually being freed of state regulatory constraints, and labor was becoming more widely available under the labor contract system. Taking the decision to push reforms one step further, the government embarked on a risky and controversial course of price reform, permitting commodity prices to respond to market forces instead of state planning mandates.[46] This meant that while there was little adjustment in the output quotas demanded of state enterprises, production inputs were subject to ever-increasing prices. The dilemma for enterprises brought on by the problem of prices spiraling upward often resulted in reduced benefits to industrial workers. For those workers formally attached to state enterprises, this meant that bonuses were cut or eliminated, compulsory purchasing of state bonds was enforced, upgrading of worker facilities was postponed or canceled, and general working conditions declined.[47] While much attention focused on the role of unemployed itinerant workers in the political demonstrations of 1989, factory workers formally attached to state enterprises were also extremely active.

For contract workers, the results of price reform were twofold. In many cases, labor contracts were cancelled or not renewed, thus rendering large numbers of workers unemployed. Yet these workers were often unable to return to the rural villages from whence they had come: these areas had adjusted to the migrant laborers' absence, there was no work for them to do, and, moreover, their families remained dependent on their remissions of money from the cities. The result was increasing numbers of unemployed laborers wandering the streets of major cities in search of work. A second consequence was that when short-term labor contracts were available, the terms were even more unfavorable than had been the case previously. In the employer's market that dominated at the time, itinerant laborers had little bargaining power and the inflation resulting from price reform was reducing the ability of employers to offer generous compensation and benefits under these contracts.

The participation of urban workers in the democracy demonstrations of Spring 1989 provided ample testimony to the extent of dissatisfaction. The Chinese government's response was indicative of its concern over worker unrest. A vigorous campaign of discipline and control over urban workers was launched that saw public executions of workers accused of participating in the democracy demonstrations dominate the Chinese public media throughout much of 1989. Indeed, the harshest punishments were reserved for worker demonstrators, particularly in comparison to the relatively lenient treatment of intellectuals and students.

A third stage of reform emerged following Deng Xiaoping's Southern Tour (*nanxun*) in 1992. Responding to Deng's call for accelerated and expanded economic reform, increased attention has been paid to the privatization of Chinese enterprises. While debate continues over the extent of true privatization in the Chinese economy, particularly in light of the evidence that many so-called private enterprises are in fact owned and operated by local government agencies, it is clear that the structure of enterprise control has changed.[48] The transformation of state enterprises through securitization has been accompanied by policies approving expansion of the village and township enterprise sector and the development of private enterprises limited by shares in urban areas.[49] Enterprises now respond to the local interests of corporatist elites, who embody both the economic determinism of business managers and the political power of Party cadres.

Unfortunately, enforcement of these regulations has been problematic. Policy initiatives aimed at the privatization of Chinese enterprises, along with greater attention to efficiency and reduced production costs, have contributed to declining labor conditions for industrial workers.[50] Despite efforts to improve compliance with health and safety regulations, in part through rules on worker accidents and injuries,[51] increased worker unrest has become a major challenge for Chinese labor policy. Between 1986 and 1994, 60,000 labor disputes were recorded (probably matched by a sizeable number of unreported disputes), and 3,000 labor disputes were noted during the first three months of 1994 alone.[52] While Chinese officials have attempted to dismiss such events as an "inevitable" component of economic modernization, the matter is clearly a source of concern, particularly in light of the Tiananmen Square experience.[53] Yet as workers are increasingly forced to take on second and third jobs to earn "gray income" (*huise shouru*), the state's institutions for labor protection and control are increasingly challenged.[54] In 1997, efforts to close or privatize inefficient state enterprises led to further unrest. In March, 20,000 workers in Nanchong, Sichuan province, besieged the city hall for more than thirty hours in one of the worst outbreaks of labor unrest in China since 1949.[55] In December, textile workers in Hefei, Anhui province, staged a sit-in to demand new jobs, following a similar protest in Yibin, Sichuan.[56] Worker unrest has fueled efforts to establish autonomous workers' federations such as the Beijing Workers Autonomous Federation and the China Workers Autonomous Federation, although these have met uniformly with vigorous repression.[57]

Enacting a Labor Law for the PRC

The Chinese government's labor policies are caught in a dilemma of conflicting imperatives. Economic reform and the privatization (or at least corporatization) of production enterprises would appear to justify granting greater rights to workers in the areas of collective bargaining, work stoppages, and so on. On the other hand China's need for continued economic growth requires labor discipline and control. The PRC Labor Law represents the regime's attempt to address these issues. While the law stopped well short of proposals from academics to give workers more voice in state-owned enterprise management,[58] it did formalize a number of benefits for workers, while maintaining the centrality of political control for Party-dominated labor unions.

The Labor Law was enacted at the Eighth Session of the Standing Committee of the Eighth National People's Congress on July 5, 1994, and came into effect on January 1, 1995. The law went through a tortuous drafting process, involving thirty drafts after Deng Xiaoping first proposed the drafting of such a law during a 1978 central work conference.[59] While the delay revealed the extent to which managing labor relations is an essential basis for the distribution of patronage within China's hierarchical and vertically integrated administrative system, the enactment of the legislation revealed the extent of consensus that workers presented a fundamental source of tension in the course of the transition from the planned to the market economy. The final draft was pushed through in response to obvious challenges of declining working conditions in enterprises.[60] While private enterprises and foreign-invested enterprises were the primary source of concern initially,[61] state-owned and cooperative enterprises were also targeted.[62]

Basic principles

The PRC Labor Law extends a number of specific benefits to workers, including "guarantees" of equal opportunity in employment, job selection, compensation, rest, leave, safety and health care, vocational training, social security and welfare, and the right to submit disputes to arbitration. Hiring units are required to fulfill various labor requirements in the areas of hours on employment, rest, leave, worker safety, health care and protection for female and juvenile workers. Juxtaposed against these benefits are a number of obligations that workers must honor, including the duties to fulfill work requirements, improve vocational skills, carry out work safety and health regulations, and observe labor discipline and vocational ethics. The law also contains various enforcement provisions whereby local labor administration departments are charged with the supervision and inspection of labor relations. Subject to these broad principles, the Labor Law contains a multitude of specific provisions on labor contracts, limits to working hours and overtime, wages, social insurance, labor disputes, supervision, legal liability, and labor in foreign-invested enterprises (a provision that is likely to require amendment in the course of China's accession the WTO). A range of implementing regulations are currently being drafted to address these matters in greater detail. Of particular importance are the provisions on labor contracts, trade unions and dispute resolution.

The return to the labor contract system

With the post-Mao economic reform policies beginning in 1978, the labor contract system that had been used during the 1950s was revitalized. After the All China Federation of Trade Unions (ACFTU) approved the use of the labor contract system in state-owned enterprises in April 1979, the labor contract system was increasingly seen as a positive mechanism for improving labor conditions and enterprise efficiency.[63] Initially, the emphasis of regulations was on the foreign business sector. Thus, in July 1980, the "Regulations on Labor Management in Joint Venture Enterprises," promulgated by the State Council, provided for individual and collective labor contracts in joint ventures.[64] These measures were augmented by the "Procedures for Implementation of the Regulations on Labor Management in Joint Venture Enterprises" (1984).[65]

The labor contract system was also gradually being extended to the domestic economy. At the First Session of the 6th NPC in June 1983, Premier Zhao Ziyang alluded to the need for greater flexibility in arrangements for workers in the economy,[66] and the following year's CPC Central Committee "Decision on Reform of the Economic System" asserted the need to expand the labor contract system.[67] The labor contract system was formally extended to state enterprises in July 1986, with the "Interim Provisions on the Implementation of the Labor Contract System for State-Owned Enterprises."[68] Private enterprises were also included, under the "Provisional Regulations on Private Enterprises" (1988)[69] and the "Provisional Regulations on Labor Management in Private Enterprises" (1989),[70] which required private enterprises to sign labor contracts with workers based on the principles of equality, voluntariness, and agreement through consultation, and which authorized the trade unions to represent staff and workers in concluding collective contracts. Following Deng's Southern Tour in 1992, the labor contract system received even greater attention. The 1992 "Regulations for Transferring the Management Mechanism in the State-Owned Industrial Sectors" granted enterprises broader rights to determine the terms of employment through the use of labor contracts with individual workers.[71] Foreign enterprises have seen themselves as particular targets for local government efforts to impose form contracts governing labor relations.[72]

The Labor Law provides rules for contract provisions on term and description of employment, labor protection, remuneration, discipline, termination, liability for breach, and limits to the use of probationary work periods during which benefits may be limited. Article 106 requires that every province, autonomous region, and centrally governed municipality should stipulate the steps for implementation of the labor contract system in accordance with the Labor Law and with the existing conditions. By the end of 1994, a total of thirteen provinces and municipalities had implemented the labor contract system for staff and workers covering 40 million contract workers in all, about 25 percent of the total work force.[73] Provincial and municipal regulations are gradually coming into force, such as the Shanghai municipal government's "Regulations on Labor Contracts of Shanghai Municipality" (1995), which called for popularization of the labor contract system in Shanghai beginning in 1996.

While the contract system is intended to bring greater discipline and control to enterprises in managing labor relations, to a certain extent, the new Labor Law maintains the systems of patronage and co-optation that characterized the Maoist system. Thus, where a Shanghai worker voluntarily sought cancellation of a labor contract in order to take a job at another factory, the original employer was still expected to provide severance pay.[74] Labor contracts remain subject to national and local regulations governing terms of employment, which generally cannot be contracted out of. For example, the Guangdong Provincial Labor Office's 1997 standards for labor and salary will govern the terms of labor contracts in the province.[75]

Continued importance of Party-dominated trade unions

A critical element of the new labor contract system is the continuing role of the CPC-led labor unions under the ACFTL. Article 26 of the 1983 Charter of China's Trade Unions (*Zhongguo gonghui zhangcheng*) passed by the Tenth National Congress of China's Trade Unions authorized basic-level trade union committees to represent staff and workers to sign collective labor contracts. This authorization was repeated in the various regulations on foreign-invested enterprises and on Chinese state and privately owned enterprises. Under the 1992 Trade Union Law of the PRC (*Zhonghua renmin gongheguo gonghui fa*), trade unions were once again given the authority to represent staff and workers in concluding collective contracts with enterprises and institutions.

While labor unions can play a positive role in achieving better working conditions and other benefits, the record of the ACFTU system is somewhat problematic. The ACFTU's primary role as a guarantor of Party power and a "transmission belt" for Party policies undermines its capacity for independent action. And since all local trade unions are subject under law to the overall authority of the ACFTU, there is no legal sanction for the creation of independent labor unions that might challenge the Communist Party's official policies.[76] In addition, recent case reports suggest that the temptation to draw on workers' dues for improper purposes may be overwhelming, again raising concerns that workers' interests are not matters of particularly high concern for union officials.[77]

Dispute resolution

The Labor Law's provisions on dispute resolution may offer workers a basis for appealing against or perhaps avoiding arbitrary decisions by management altogether. In one case, for example, workers were accused of stealing electrical equipment and had their pay docked arbitrarily, while public security officials were only too willing to enforce management orders with little if any investigation.[78] In another case, a worker was summarily suspended for three days without pay after getting into an argument with a supervisor.[79] The supervisor's superiors backed the suspension, and the (reportedly innocent) worker was left without a remedy. Similar incidents have been reported in other enterprises.[80] The hope is that implementation of the

Labor Law will impose more formalized processes for investigation and dispute resolution.

The dispute resolution provisions of the Labor Law build on experiments developed earlier.[81] Of particular importance were the 1987 State Council Regulations on Resolution of Labor Disputes in State Enterprises,[82] which provided for mediation and arbitration of labor disputes. Summarizing previous experiences, the State Council's 1993 Regulations for Handling Labor Disputes provided a framework for the labor disputes that would later be incorporated into the PRC Labor Law. The Ministry of Labor articulated the reasons for the labor dispute system mainly by reference to the increased numbers of labor disputes that accompanied enterprise reforms.[83]

The primary methods for resolving disputes included mediation, which is to be used throughout the entire process of handling labor disputes. According to the Labor Law, mediation should be based on the voluntariness of both parties. Both the process and content of dispute resolution should be in accordance with the law and follow the principle of fairness. The Labor Law requires that equality be accorded to the parties in matters of legal status, rights to apply for mediation, arbitration, or a court judgment, and the various rights to present and explain pertinent facts in labor disputes. The new law requires that mediators, arbitrators, and judges be impartial to the parties involved. In order to protect both parties' rights and interests and especially those of workers, the labor mediation committee, the labor arbitration committee, and the People's Courts are to handle labor disputes in a prompt and timely fashion. These broad principles are taken as the foundation upon which the various procedures for dispute resolution are based.

The first step in dispute resolution is mediation through the mediation committee. If this fails, the dispute will go to arbitration through an arbitration committee, and possibly to the third step of litigation before the People's Court. Under Article 80 of the Labor Law, the labor dispute mediation committee is established inside the employing unit and is composed of representatives of the staff and workers, representatives of the employer, and representatives of the trade union. The committee chair is to be held by a representative of the trade union. Under Article 81, the labor dispute arbitration committee is composed of representatives of the local Labor Administrative Department (who also chairs the committee), representatives from the trade union at the corresponding level, and representatives of the employer. Arbitration is the first level of binding dispute resolution, and the prominent role of the trade union in reviewing its own mediation decision, as well as the absence of direct representation of staff and workers, are particularly noteworthy. Litigation may be undertaken before the People's Courts to appeal an arbitral decision, which has proved helpful in cases where the arbitration organ is overly generous to the employer.[84] However, the institutional and political weaknesses of the court system continue to pose problems, as does the continued inability of the courts to enforce judgments against powerful economic enterprises. Moreover, courts have been seen to lack sufficient expertise to permit them to coordinate dispute resolution proceedings without compromising other aspects of enforcement of the Labor Law.[85] If the case reporting available is any guide, the overwhelming majority of labor disputes that go to some formal resolution are dealt with through arbitration.[86]

Continuing challenges

While the PRC Labor Law represents an important step toward building an effective legal framework for protecting workers' rights in China, a number of issues remain to be resolved. Coinciding with the law's promulgation were official accounts bemoaning the general lack of awareness and basic knowledge of the law[87] and cautioning against lax implementation by the administrative departments concerned.[88] In addition, as with other aspects of China's legal regime, the law represents a formalistic expression of specific rights and obligations but does little to serve as a foundation for meaningful enforcement of fundamental rights for workers. Official reviews of the PRC Labor Law describe it as the complete articulation of the rights of workers.[89] In other words, workers' rights are only those articulated in the law and do not extend beyond the text of the legislation. Of particular interest are statements that the rights of workers in China must be based on China's unique situation and cannot be addressed by reference to foreign labor law criteria.[90] Such an approach to workers' rights leaves little room for articulating and enforcing generalized norms for employer behavior, or for making workers' rights unconditional and independent of various contractual duties.

Although China's labor conditions are unique, two matters discussed by labor specialists in the PRC are of particular importance concerning the Labor Law, namely collective bargaining and dispute resolution. The Labor Law makes reference to collective labor contracts, but it fails to provide meaningful protection for collective bargaining. The obviously unequal bargaining power between individual workers and employers has caused many to view collective bargaining as an essential element of modern labor law. Unfortunately, the Labor Law leaves direct representatives of staff and workers out of the contract bargaining process and omits specific reference to the importance of collective bargaining.

The power disparity between employers and employees is further entrenched through provisions concerning termination of labor contracts. According to Section 25 of the Labor Law, the employing unit may revoke a labor contract if the worker, is "proved not up to the requirements for recruitment during the probation period." Unfortunately, the case record suggests that some staff and workers have been terminated improperly during the probation period.[91] Furthermore, Article 26(3) permits the employer to demand and ultimately to impose revocation of a labor contract with written notification in cases of changed circumstances. This section has been seen as a source of potential abuse, because it lacks provisions concerning the employer's burden of proof and thus leaves room for employers to use changed circumstances improperly as an excuse to summarily dismiss employees. In contrast, while employees have the right to revoke labor contracts "where the employer resorts to violence, intimidation or illegal restriction of the personal freedom" or "fails to provide working conditions as agreed upon in the labor contract," it is difficult for the worker to meet the burden of proof in these cases.

The general inattention to collective bargaining to redress power imbalances in the new Labor Law is puzzling in light of the fact that the concept has been well accepted in the PRC for some time.[92] Shortly after Liberation, collective bargaining rights were reserved for the employees of private enterprises.[93] During the economic reform period of the 1990s, several administrative units noted the importance of collective bargaining in labor relations in foreign-invested enterprises. For example, the "announcement" co-issued by the Labor Department, the Public Security Bureau, and the ACFTU on March 4, 1994, requires that foreign-invested and private enterprises should establish systems for negotiation and collective bargaining.[94] Apparently, despite a willingness to impose collective bargaining on foreign capitalist enterprises, the Chinese government is not yet ready to accept that the socialist market economy entails the potential exploitation of workers by domestic enterprises to the same degree.

A second major issue concerns the independence of trade unions. The new Labor Law entrenches the Party-dominated labor union system as the basic mechanism for enforcing workers' rights.[95] The Chinese Labor Law places significant reliance on the trade unions in:

- representing and safeguarding the legitimate rights and interests of laborers (Article 7);
- requesting reconsideration of termination of a contract by the employer unit and in supporting workers' applications for arbitration or litigation (Article 30);
- representing workers in concluding collective labor contracts (Article 33);
- representing workers on the labor dispute mediation committee (Article 80) and arbitration committee (Article 81); and
- representing workers in supervising the implementation of laws and regulations by the employer (Article 88).

However, the law contains no provisions concerning the formation and structure of a trade union. The PRC Trade Union Law (1992) does include such provisions but contains nothing to suggest that trade unions under the ACFTU will be independent. According to Article 3, all salaried workers are eligible for the membership of a trade union. This would extend to enterprise directors and managers, thus permitting those in charge of the employing unit to join or even to dominate the trade union in their unit. Moreover, the Trade Union Law also grants Party cadres close access to trade union leadership. In fact, CPC cadres have dominated the ACFTU since 1948.[96]

Aside from issues inherent in the text of the Labor Law, a variety of other questions arise concerning effective implementation. Technical issues, for example, arise concerning the standards for workplace safety, environmental conditions, workers' health, and similar matters. These matters are likely to be left to individual ministries and commissions, such as the Ministry of Health, National Environmental Protection Agency, and the Labor Ministry. However, detailed regulations will be needed, and trained implementation staff will be essential. Socio-economic problems will also complicate the problem of enforcement. The development of private firms, which have proliferated in the wake of state-owned enterprise reform, has created new and different conditions for labor, resulting in policy conflicts with the labor system that has developed largely out of the experiences of state-owned enterprises.[97] Also important is the crisis of so-called "migrant workers." The current figures for migrant workers approach fifty million, with official estimates of 120 million "surplus laborers" and the expectation that China will soon have 200 million surplus agricultural workers on the non-agricultural employment market.[98] These conditions have already outstripped the capacity of the government to respond. Many of these migrants are only too happy to take factory jobs, whether in the relatively more secure state sector or the higher-paying village and township enterprise sector, without regard to working conditions and legal rights.

In the context of problems of technical complexity and the swelling numbers of surplus and migrant workers, enforcement of the Labor Law's provisions on workers' rights is hampered further by local corporatist alliances between administrative officials and business enterprises.[99] The economic incentives underlying local corporatist relations have even subverted the financial integrity of the labor unions themselves, as cases have arise where labor union funds are improperly invested, thus putting worker pensions at risk.[100] Furthermore, the local CPC cadre evaluation system places a premium on stability, production, and full employment, while paying little attention to strict enforcement of workers' rights.[101]

While the Labor Law of the PRC represents a major step toward articulating legal norms on the protection of workers rights, it still reflects the imperatives of Chinese government policies of economic growth and the Chinese Communist Party's concerns with political control. Thus provisions on contract labor and the role of trade unions appear to serve the interests of the Party/state to a greater extent than they do the interests of Chinese workers. The new law also faces significant impediments to full implementation. Nonetheless, in the context of the transition to a socialist market economy the Labor Law does represent significant progress in the ongoing challenge of managing labor relations in China.

Social control: the criminal law system

Social control is the trade-off that accompanies state protection of social welfare, as the dictatorship of the proletariat mandates subservience to the Party-led process of social transformation. While the regulation of economic life and social welfare reflects an indirect mechanism for social control, the PRC government's use of law and administrative regulation has perhaps been aimed most directly at ensuring social control and public security. Drawing on a legacy of public and punitive typologies of law from both the Republican and imperial periods of the country's history, the PRC has emphasized law as an instrument of social control to such an extent that many within China and without consider law to be nothing more. The state exercises its monopoly on the legitimate use of force most directly in regulating behavior in society through criminal law and procedure.

During the first three decades of the PRC, social control and public security were achieved primarily through administrative regulation and political campaigns.[102] General political supervision over members of society through such methods as household registration (*hukou*) allowed the Party/state considerable power to control social behavior.[103] The PRC leadership generally shied away from formalizing the standards for conduct upon which might be based the imposition of state sanctions since this would limit the political power of the state. Hence, criminal law and criminal procedure laws were not formally enacted, despite ongoing drafting efforts. The debacle of the Cultural Revolution brought on a reconsideration of this commitment to flexibility and discretion. Driven in part by the need to protect itself, and also by the need to build legitimacy, the post-Mao regime enacted a Criminal Law Code and a Code of Criminal Procedure in 1980, which closely followed the passing of new Regulations on Arrest and Detention in 1979 to replace measures enacted in 1954. With broadly worded provisions of flexible application, these measures had little to do with protecting the rights of criminal defendants but instead were aimed primarily at re-establishing the state's monopoly on the legitimate use of coercive force in the aftermath of the Cultural Revolution.[104] Criminal law reforms were also driven by the need to confront economic crime, which had surged in response to the loosening of state controls under Deng's economic reform program.[105] While the effects of the early criminal law reforms on criminal defendants may well have fallen well short of internationally accepted standards, the newly emerging reliance on legal discourse and institutions represented important departures from the Maoist era.[106] Numerous regulations were issued on the organization, authority, and activities of public security organs to deal with issues such as the transit and registration of persons, identity cards, the registration and operation of vehicles, scalping of train tickets, and so on.[107]

Supplementing these efforts, administrative punishment remained the dominant mechanism for social control.[108] Under the Regulations of the PRC on Security Administration and Punishment (1957, revised 1986,

1994), administrative detention was commonly applied against individuals who committed acts that constituted criminal offenses. The 1980 Criminal Law of the PRC permitted administrative detention to be imposed in lieu of criminal sanctions where the circumstances of a person's crimes were deemed to be minor and not requiring criminal punishment. The more severe administrative systems for reform and re-education through labor, which had been established pursuant to regulations issued by the State Council in 1957, were continued under new rules enacted in 1979.[109] The administrative punishment system denied offenders whatever protection might have been available under the formal criminal justice system, such as relative certainty of sentencing. Under the re-education and reform through labor systems, those whose terms had expired could be detained for longer periods if they were without employment or had served their sentences in sparsely populated areas and were needed in the area.[110] Legislation aimed at reforming the prison system was enacted in 1994, symbolizing an effort to regularize the administration of prisons and labor camps and articulating ideals about the treatment of prisoners.[111]

In addition, the process of "shelter for investigation" (*shourong shencha*) authorized the discretionary arrest and detention of suspicious individuals with little if any legal restrictions imposed.[112] A legacy from the early 1960s, "shelter and investigation" was used to round up unemployed migrants and other perceived ne'er-do-wells, who might be detained for a few months but who also might be sent to re-education through labor facilities. Repeated attempts have been made to formalize the process, most notably in a set of regulations issued in 1985 by the Public Security Ministry, which conferred oversight authority on the People's Procuracy. Although separate notices issued in 1990 by the Procuracy and the Public Security Ministry attempted to curtail abuses of *shourong shencha* procedures, still there was little if any meaningful external scrutiny, and abuses multiplied as a result.[113] With the revisions to the Criminal Procedure Law in 1996, "shelter and investigation" was to be eliminated, although many of the flexible provisions of the process were incorporated into the revised statute.[114] In addition, so-called "custody and repatriation" (*shourong qiansong*) methods have been used widely to detain suspected vagrants arbitrarily and without benefit of legal process.[115]

Revisions to the Criminal Procedure Law[116] and the subsequent amendment of the Criminal Law in 1997[117] were part of a broad effort to reform the criminal justice system in response to domestic socio-economic change[118] and to deflect international human rights criticisms. Efforts to bring international perspectives on criminal law to bear in the Chinese discourse had begun early in the 1990s.[119] Bilateral conferences and exchanges were held with scholars from the United States,[120] Canada,[121] and Japan[122] and added new perspectives to the Chinese debates on criminal law reform.

Revisions to the Criminal Procedure Law purported to improve the provisions of the 1980 law, which were seen as improperly strengthening the power of the prosecution at the expense of a defendant's rights.[123] Driven by principles of fairness (*gongzheng*) and process (*you xu*), the revisions were to achieve a balance between punishing crime and safeguarding human rights by requiring greater attention to evidence of guilt.[124] Criminal defendants gained earlier access to legal counsel as well as greater possibilities for bail, while criminal defense counsel were to be granted expanded access to prosecution evidence and rights to collect evidence.[125] The determination of criminal liability was reserved exclusively for the courts, thus doing away with the Procuracy's previous powers to determine guilt or innocence. The law also imposed on prosecutors the burden to produce reliable and ample (*queshi*, *chongfen*) evidence of the guilt of the accused – not quite the "presumption of innocence" trumpeted by some optimistic observers, but a significant step nonetheless.[126]

The revisions to the Criminal Law also reflected an effort to reduce the potential for arbitrary punishment. The revision provided that an act is not criminal unless specifically stated in the law, thus eliminating the "rule of analogy," which under the 1980 law had permitted criminal conviction for acts not expressly identified as criminal by reference to the most closely analogous provision of the law. The new statute eliminated the provision for counter-revolutionary crimes and addressed the issue of economic crime more directly. The law also purported to reduce the application of the death penalty, in part to conform more closely to international norms and practices.[127]

However, prosecutors retain significant powers to obtain convictions, sometimes justified by reference to policies that remain generally popular, such as anti-corruption efforts.[128] Despite the removal of the "rule of analogy" from the Criminal Law, subsequent interpretations permit criminal convictions for acts for which the defendant is not charged but which are punishable under other provisions of the Criminal Law.[129] While the revised Criminal Law eliminated the crime of counter-revolution, the statute instead uses the crime of "endangering state security," which is not limited by the intent requirement that informed the counter-revolution provisions of the past. Absent the requirement to prove intent, the state may now determine without restriction whether it is endangered by an act with which it disagrees. While the intent requirement may have been of little practical significance, its elimination sends a powerful message that the Party/state will tolerate no threats, intended or not, to its monopoly on political authority.

Revisions to the Criminal Law were intended in large part to ensure continued government authority over economic order in the transition to the market economy, while imposing criminal penalties on economic and market abuses.[130] Accordingly, the revised law extended the reach of the criminal prosecution to a broad array of commercial conduct in areas such as intellectual property, corporate governance and securities, banking and finance, taxation, and general market behavior.[131] Other laws and regulations that operate in conjunction with the criminal law system further entrench the Party/state's power of coercion. The State Secrets Law, for example, permits criminal sanctions to be used to silence or intimidate critics, while the National Security Law allows violations of the State Secrets Law to be included as a crime against national security.[132] In response to public and international inquiries about criminal punishments in China, and particularly allegations about the sale of the internal organs of executed defendants, increased attention has been paid to regulations barring "rumor-mongering" about criminal executions.[133]

Summary

China's human rights doctrines have been heavily influenced by international norms, albeit ones that are not welcomed by proponents of liberal legal discourses. The right to development has been selectively adapted by China to justify human rights approaches that give priority to subsistence and economic development over the protection of political and civil rights. An additional consequence is the continued centrality of the Party/state and its political authority. The examples of labor law and criminal law suggest that China's ability to implement the right to development is problematic in large part because of the unwillingness to restrain the state, and because of the state's inability to control its agents and subordinates. Thus, Labor Law provisions that privilege state employers and Party-led labor unions deprive workers of relief from ever-deteriorating labor conditions. Criminal law and procedural reforms have not addressed fully the power of local police to engage in arbitrary detention. Thus, the privileging of state and Party power impedes the government's ability to protect for its citizens even the limited human rights that the government does recognize. This poses a fundamental challenge to the government – a legacy of lingering and unsettling questions as to whether China's limited approach to human rights, which entrenches the supremacy of the Party/state, can foster sustainable development.

6 Foreign economic relations

The legal regime for foreign business relations in the People's Republic of China reflects a basic tension between policies emphasizing state control and those emphasizing market incentives.[1] These tensions are emblematic of the contradiction between China's troubled legacy of relations with foreign capital during the nineteenth and early twentieth centuries[2] and the post-Mao regime's commitment to attracting foreign business in pursuit of national economic development goals. The relationship between the state and the market has been a key element in the development experiences of Japan and more recently of the East Asian NICs, whose economies seem to have avoided the dependency trap that has befallen developing countries elsewhere in the world.[3] The tensions over development and dependency provide the international context for China's foreign business law regime. This regime is by definition intertwined with international norms and institutions. Thus, the key issue in terms of the influence of foreign norms, is what will be the dominant paradigm informing China's foreign trade and investment policies and laws. China's foreign business law regime reflects efforts to overcome the problems of dependency and to mobilize international economic relations in the service of Chinese development.

Contexts for assessing China's foreign business law regime

While China's development efforts may be viewed as amounting to an independent path toward development,[4] the contrasting perspectives of neo-classical economic theories of development and critical Marxist theories of dependency provide a useful framework within which to view China's own efforts at harnessing foreign trade and investment in pursuit of economic growth.

Critical perspectives: weak states, dependency, and the role of law

Theories of dependency have given rise to a multitude of complementary and sometimes conflicting approaches to understanding the role of foreign investment in developing economies.[5] While they have been shown to be severely flawed in many respects – particularly in tending to overlook local political and policy causes for underdevelopment[6] and to indulge in holistic ideological viewpoints that are not amenable to either falsification or confirmation, even to the point of descending into what one observer has called a fusion of scholarship, politics, and theater[7] – dependency perspectives nonetheless offer useful approaches to viewing the role of the state in managing foreign investment. Thus, rather than engage in what one critical observer terms "an academic industry of criticism that is bandwagoning of the worst sort,"[8] it seems preferable to draw upon those aspects of dependency perspectives concerning the relationships between the state, law, and foreign investment in the dynamic of economic development that are useful in assessing China's foreign investment regime.

Early proponents of dependency portrayed the state rather crudely as a corporatist ally of foreign capital.[9] This alliance is said to be facilitated by the co-optation of local elites, who serve as conduits for investment and also as the primary local beneficiaries.[10] Their commercial and consumption activities are seen to support the objectives of foreign investment by substituting short-term parochial goals for long-term development priorities of building the technological foundations and infrastructure for long-term economic growth.[11] The corporatist state is seen to rely on formalistic and authoritarian legal systems to retain power, where reformist attempts to establish instrumentalist legal regimes aimed at pursuing national goals are met with vigorous repression.[12] Despite its authoritarian power domestically, however, the corporatist state remains fundamentally weak – dependent upon and yet unable to control the foreign capital in whose service it operates.

More sophisticated theories of economic dependency focus criticism not on the state as a wholly compliant ally of foreign capital but on the liberal economic policies and law that ensure minimal state involvement in economic life.[13] As championed initially by the post-World War II US development bureaucracies, often in response to perceived problems with authoritarian rule, liberal economic policies aim to establish market systems supported by private law rules and institutions.[14] Based largely on Max Weber's analysis of the relationship between formal legal rationality and economic growth in Europe, the liberal expectation is that this would permit economic activity to be more predictable and, in turn, induce the entrepreneurship and risk-taking necessary for capital accumulation and long-term economic growth.[15]

However, this approach has been challenged as contributing to underdevelopment.[16] Liberal economic policies undermine the state's regulation of foreign capital, while the transnational character of foreign business inhibits control by local governments through traditional legal mechanisms.[17] Critical studies perspectives draw on many of the same themes articulated by dependency theorists and suggest that the use of liberal private law systems may itself contribute to weakening the state's capacity to control foreign investment and promote development.[18]

These critical approaches to law and development are useful perspectives from which to view China's legal regime for foreign investment. Also useful are perspectives drawn from the East Asian development experience, which operates in part as a response to the problems of dependency.

The Asian development experience

The role of the state was a crucial factor in the development experiences of Japan and the newly industrialized countries of East Asia.[19] These economies have absorbed significant levels of foreign investment while still appearing to avoid many of the economic distortions and pitfalls of so-called "dependent development." While some have argued that this may be ascribed to the influence of informal business networks,[20] others have suggested that the key lies in the culture of neo-Confucianism, which extols education and accomplishment.[21]

While these cultural factors are undoubtedly important, it also appears that the state has played a critical role. In Japan, the state played a central role in managing economic policy,[22] while in South Korea, the state transformed national industrial structures as a precondition for development.[23] In Taiwan, the state facilitated development by mediating relations between foreign capital and local entrepreneurs.[24] In Singapore too, the state has used market-oriented economic policies to channel foreign investment toward the achievement of long-term development goals, including the establishment of export-oriented industries, while also developing indigenous technology and infrastructure.[25] The state has also pursued policies of import substitution, not only in pursuit of restricting imports and preserving the balance of payments[26] but also to limit local access to foreign consumer goods, thus undermining the capacity of international capital to co-opt local elites.[27] This is not to suggest that free markets are ignored but rather that the state has attempted to create market conditions that induce foreign trade and investment to benefit national development goals. The newly developed economies of Asia are not liberal market economies but rather may be seen as bureaucratic market economies, where the development of exports, technology, and infrastructure result from market inducements erected by state bureaucracies charged with managing foreign economic relations. Although there is significant regional variation in the developmental experiences of the East Asian NICs, state management of foreign trade and investment has played a central role in permitting these economies to avoid the pitfalls of dependent development. The success of the state in Japan and the East Asian NICs in harnessing foreign business relations in pursuit of national development stands in contrast to the problems of dependency.

China's developing foreign business regime

Emerging from a legacy of tightly controlled trade relations, mostly with Soviet bloc countries, that had nearly been shut down during the Cultural Revolution, China's "open door policy" took the revolutionary step of permitting foreign direct investment as well as expanded trade relationships.[28] Once the door was opened, however, the trade and investment regime was driven by varying degrees of pressure from foreign businesses and governments seeking improved conditions for business relations. While foreign business law in China has customarily been divided between trade and investment, the realities of business relations and the developing norms of the World Trade Organization and the GATT have driven increased overlap and complementarity between trade and investment relations.[29]

China's foreign trade regime

The legal regime governing China's foreign trade relations is organizationally disparate and is driven substantively by policy concerns. While Chinese foreign trade relations are subject to the general provisions of the Foreign Trade Law (1994),[30] a variety of specific laws and regulations remain in effect to govern different aspects of the system.

The Foreign Trade Law of the PRC

The PRC Foreign Trade Law provides the legislative framework for China's foreign trade system.[31] While intended in part to meet the concerns of China's trading partners over issues of regulatory transparency, and as part of a broader effort to pave the way for China's entry into the GATT and the WTO, the statute also established the authority of the central government to regulate trade and provided general guidance on the role of various government and non-government trade organizations.

BASIC PROVISIONS

The Foreign Trade Law extends to the import and export of goods, technology, and international services (FTL, Article 2). The law addresses the identity and conduct of entities permitted to engage in international trade. The approval and licensing of these "foreign trade operators" (*dui wai maoyi jingying zhe*) requires that they meet certain specified conditions, including having an explicit (*mingque*) scope of foreign business, possession of the site, the capital and staff to engage in foreign trade, a track record (*shixian*) in commissioned import/export trade, or the necessary sources of import/export goods (FTL, Article 9). The law also provides rules governing the import and export of goods, technology, and services (FTL, Chapters 3,

4). Also addressed are the issues of special safeguards to protect local industries from dramatic increases in the number of imported goods (FTL, Article 29), anti-dumping provisions aimed at preventing or remedying the importation of goods priced below "normal value" (*zhengchang jiazhi*) (FTL, Article 30), and anti-subsidy provisions. The Foreign Trade Law authorizes trade promotion efforts through financial institution reform and the creation of foreign trade development funds (FTL, Article 33); import/export credits, tax refunds, and other inducements (FTL, Article 34); support from chambers of commerce for importers and exporters (FTL, Article 35); and other measures. The law also provides for administrative and criminal penalties for violations (Chapter 7) and permits special rules and exceptions to be made for border areas and areas that levy tariffs independently (Chapter 8).

CONFLICTING NORMS IN THE FOREIGN TRADE LAW

The Foreign Trade Law reflects many of the tensions evident in other legislation passed in connection with China's transition to a market economy. On the one hand, with the GATT requirements of national treatment, transparency, and non-discrimination firmly in mind, the Foreign Trade Law gives importance to free and fair operations in international trade (FTL, Article 4); accords most favored nation treatment and national treatment pursuant to treaties to which China is a party (FTL, Article 6); and recognizes autonomy for foreign trade operators (FTL, Articles 4, 11). The law sets forth a basic principle of free import and export of goods and technology, except where provided otherwise by law (FTL Article 15). The Foreign Trade Law recognizes the principle of market access and national treatment in accordance with treaties or agreements to which China is a party (FTL, Article 23).

On the other hand, the Foreign Trade Law also underscores the importance of state control over trade in goods, technology, and services. Indeed, the law was formulated in order to "develop foreign trade, maintain order in foreign trade activities and promote the sound development of the market economy" (FTL, Article 1). Each of these goals, but particularly the last two, empower the state to intervene in trade relations for policy purposes, which are only vaguely defined. Only "foreign trade operators" specifically approved by the government may engage in foreign trade activities – a significant mechanism for maintaining state control (FTL, Article 13).[32] This builds on the tradition of relying on national foreign trade corporations (NFTCs) organized under the Ministry of Foreign Trade and Cooperation (MOFERT) or its provincial or local commissions and bureaux to exercise a near monopoly on foreign trade.[33] While the Foreign Trade Law raises the prospect of the increased independence of foreign trade operators and permits an increasingly wide array of companies to engage in foreign trade, traditional NFTCs continue to occupy a privileged position by virtue of their organizational affiliation with MOFTEC.[34] Foreign trade operators may act as agents commissioned by other enterprises not approved to engage in foreign trade activities (FTL, Article 13). In contrast to the agency trading system under which an NFTC might act as a conduit for a service fee and the Chinese producer or consumer bears the commercial risk of the transaction,[35] the new agency rules require the foreign trade operator to bear contract liability for the trade transactions in which they engage (FTL, Article 12). However, practical problems of contract enforcement remain in light of the higher level of commercial risk in transactions where the trade contract is concluded with a foreign trade operator but the actual producer or customer is a third party.

The import and export of goods and technology may be restricted not only for national security reasons but also to protect local resources, local market capacity, developing local industries, China's international financial position and balance of payments, and other commercial policy concerns (FTL, Article 16). Foreign exchange restrictions remain entrenched in the legislation (FTL, Article 28). The law authorizes not only permanent lists of restricted import/export goods and technology but also interim measures and quotas (FTL, Articles 18–21). Similarly, trade in international services may be restricted not only for national security reasons but also for matters of public interest, environmental protection, protection of nascent industries, foreign exchange balancing or other unspecified reasons provided for in laws or administrative regulations (FTL, Article 24). Trade in goods and technology may be prohibited for reasons of national security or public health, or where required by international treaties (FTL, Article 19), while trade in international services may be prohibited for reasons of national security, public interests, treaty obligations or where otherwise provided for by law or administrative regulation (FTL, Article 25). And while references to the regulation of foreign trade through law and administrative regulation (e.g., FTL Article 32) suggest a commitment to transparency, the practical reality has often been the reverse of this.

Government regulation of foreign trade

The Foreign Trade Law reaffirms the authority of the State Council's department in charge of foreign trade and economic relations to regulate foreign trade. Since the early 1990s, that department has been the Ministry of Foreign Trade and Economic Cooperation (MOFTEC), and it remains the source of virtually all government regulation on trade. MOFTEC exercises powerful control through the system of import and export licenses that govern trade in the areas classified as restricted.

Import licenses are issued pursuant to the Provisional Rules on the Import License System of the PRC (1984, as amended). These rules and their implementing regulations (1984, as amended), along with the

"Various Regulations on Adjusting the Import and Export Licensing Administration" (1988) established a system of state control over imports through the licensing of goods and importers. While China's application to join the GATT/WTO as well as ongoing reforms in foreign trade policy have changed the specifics of applying these rules, the basic system for import licensing remains. Applications for import licenses are subject to the MOFTEC "Note on Applications for Import Licenses" (1996) and the "Standard Rules for Applying for and Issuing Import Licenses" (1999), under which only MOFTEC and its specifically authorized subordinate units may engage in licensing activities. Licensing activities extend to the examination and verification of compliance with quota controls, state plans, foreign exchange control rules, and other governing regulations.

Export licensing is handled by MOFTEC's Bureau for Control of Quotas and Licenses, pursuant to "Regulations on Export License Control" (1996).[36] Under these regulations, all enterprises engaged in importing and exporting must obtain licenses for goods subject to license control, which are identified in various import/export licensing catalogs issued periodically by MOFTEC.[37] The specific forms and procedures for obtaining export licenses are governed by MOFTEC's "Note on Applications for Export Licenses" (1996) and the "Standard Rules for Applying for and Issuing Export Licenses" (1999).

While references to state planning are increasingly rare, the granting of import and export licenses is still subject to the requirements of state policies approved by the State Economic Development and Planning Commission and relayed to MOFTEC.[38] Foreign-invested enterprises are subject to the same requirements, although in 1986 some preferences were made available for them to permit foreign exchange balancing.[39] Import and export licenses are generally valid for one year, although some enterprises may receive multi-year licenses. Among the criteria that determine the issuance of licenses are the terms of state plans, the terms and conditions of import and export quotas, and the scope of authorization of the applicant foreign trade operator. As the Foreign Trade Law suggests, the trade licensing system is aimed at ensuring order in foreign trade activities: ensuring state control for policy purposes, ensuring sound development of the market economy, and encouraging export-led growth and the protection of nascent domestic industries. Specific purposes also include managing foreign exchange balancing (authorized by FTL Articles 16 and 24), and coordinating access to goods for Chinese importers and coordinating market access strategies for Chinese exporters. Finally, the system operates as a powerful political tool of patronage, which dispenses access to foreign goods (for importers) and foreign exchange (for exporters) so as to maximize the political capital of the licensing organs.

Government control over foreign trade is also exercised through the anti-dumping and anti-subsidy provisions of the Foreign Trade Law and regulations on anti-dumping and countervailing duties.[40] Informed by the difficult experience of defending anti-dumping claims filed against its exporters,[41] China formalized anti-dumping and anti-subsidy provisions together with special safeguards in the Foreign Trade Law. These trade protection provisions are consistent with GATT principles, which permit limited retaliatory tariffs to be imposed where dumping or trade subsidies threaten substantial harm to a domestic industry (GATT, Article VI). Reflecting GATT principles, China's regulations require it to be shown that the import price is not a "normal value" (*zhengchang jiazhi*).[42] The "normal value" may be computed by reference to the price of the same or a similar product in the exporting country; the price of the same or a similar product exported to a third country; or the production cost plus reasonable expenses and profit.[43] While China's anti-dumping and anti-subsidy rules reflect an acceptance of GATT norms in the regulation of trade abuses, the fact that China's trading sector remains dominated by state-controlled enterprises raises the likelihood that these measures will be selected and used for political and policy purposes as well as retaliation in response to foreign anti-dumping actions.[44]

While MOFTEC remains the dominant organ of state control over foreign trade, other units also play important roles. The Commodity Inspection Bureau, together with the State Administration of Industry and Commerce, administers the system of inspection of commodity imports and exports pursuant to the Law of the PRC on Import and Export Commodity Inspection (1989) and its Implementing Regulations (1992).[45] While these activities purport to ensure that imports and exports meet various quality requirements and health and safety standards, they are also a potential source of non-tariff barriers. In areas where China has specific industry protection policies in place, commodity inspection procedures tend to compound barriers to market access.[46] Indeed, authoritative commentary on China's accession to the WTO suggests that non-tariff barriers should continue to be used to protect Chinese industries to the extent permitted by the GATT.[47] The PRC Customs Administration also exercises powerful controls over foreign trade activities through its authority to enforce import/export licensing requirements, commodity inspection, and tariff schedules.[48] While tariff rates have been decreasing gradually and are expected to continue a downward trend in conjunction with China's accession to the GATT and the WTO,[49] the Customs Administration is likely to remain a key government actor in the regulation of China's trade relations.

China's foreign investment system[50]

The Chinese legal regime for foreign investment has evolved significantly since its inception following the Third Plenum of the 11th Central Committee of the Chinese Communist Party in 1978.[51] The first foreign investment laws governing joint ventures were little more than broad statements of principle.[52] Gradually, implementing regulations were added that provided additional detail.[53] Efforts were also made to enact basic laws on contracts,[54] taxation,[55] foreign exchange,[56] and other matters. The government gradually came to approve a broader variety of foreign investment enterprises – contractual joint ventures (also known as cooperative enterprises) and wholly foreign-owned enterprises.[57] In ongoing attempts to attract more foreign investment,[58] the government enacted various inducement measures – first emphasizing location as the basis for preferences[59] and later adding substantive criteria as conditions for the receipt of investment incentives.[60] Most recently, efforts have been made to remove disparities in the legal treatment of foreign and Chinese businesses. The tax system is undergoing reform to harmonize the treatment of foreigners and Chinese, both as individual taxpayers[61] and in business operations.[62] China's foreign exchange system has been reformed and the dual currency system eliminated.[63] Efforts are underway to unify the corporate legal status of Chinese and foreign businesses.[64]

Thus, over the past fifteen years, an expansive legal and policy system for foreign investment has emerged in China.[65] Yet China's complex policy-making environment – at once revealing the diverse effects of bureaucratic processes,[66] personalities and clientelism,[67] bargaining dynamics,[68] and other factors – combined with continuing changes in the domestic and world economies, have made doctrinal consistency difficult to achieve. China's foreign investment regime is as much a product of incremental and *ad hoc* responses to challenges as it is an expression of coherent doctrine. Nonetheless, a number of consistent themes have emerged, including the centrality of state control, the importance of developing of export industries, and the acquisition of technology. These themes operate against the background of the forms for doing business in China and suggest the possibility of China mastering the challenge of development.

Conventional forms for foreign investment in China

Initially, foreign investment projects in China were intended to be joint ventures through which foreign capital would be partnered with state-run Chinese enterprises. This was gradually expanded to include wholly foreign-owned enterprises. Foreign companies were also permitted to establish representative offices to engage in sales and market research. Portfolio investment in Chinese securities represents an alternative investment form.

FOREIGN INVESTMENT ENTERPRISES

Foreign investment enterprises take one of three forms: equity joint ventures (EJVs), cooperative joint ventures (CJVs – also referred to as contractual joint ventures), and wholly foreign-owned enterprises (WFOEs).[69] EJVs are limited liability business associations in which the Chinese and foreign parties each take an equity share.[70] EJV participants share profits and losses based on their registered capital contributions, while the liability of each party is also limited based on the extent of its capital contribution. The managerial control of each EJV partner tends to depend on its proportionate capital contribution, although adjustments to the control relationships between the board of directors and the general manager are often made to protect the managerial authority of the foreign investor. EJVs represent the conceptual base upon which alternative investment structures have been built.

CJVs entail a business structure somewhat akin to a strategic partnership. Unlike an EJV, a CJV need not result in the formation of a new limited liability company, although it may be registered as a legal person. Rather, each partner undertakes to perform certain tasks, the management of which is subject to a joint management committee. Despite the fact that originally they were taxed more heavily,[71] CJVs were considered desirable by foreign investors because the absence of state law permitted greater operational flexibility. In particular, CJVs permitted capital contributions to be separated from management rights: management control did not necessarily require majority ownership. By 1988, when the Cooperative Joint Venture Law was enacted, CJVs actually outnumbered EJVs.[72] An important sub-group of CJVs entails the exploration and extraction of natural resources.[73]

WFOEs are limited liability companies established as wholly owned subsidiaries of foreign companies.[74] The foreign investor provides all capital, determines the management structure and procedures, and bears responsibility for all profits and losses. The Chinese government permitted a small number of WFOEs to be established on an experimental basis during the early 1980s, and following the enactment of the Wholly Foreign-Owned Enterprise Law in 1986, the numbers increased steadily.[75]

FOREIGN REPRESENTATIVE OFFICES

Although strictly speaking they are not considered a form of foreign direct investment, foreign representative offices nonetheless entail significant capital commitment by overseas businesses.[76] Representative offices are established through the sponsorship of a host unit – usually a Chinese state enterprise that does frequent business with the representative office's parent company. State approval and registration are governed by the terms of the host unit approval and then serve as the basis for staff residency permits, banking and tax registration, customs matters, and employment of local personnel. Annual business reports are required as a condition for yearly license renewal, and the host unit's sponsorship is subject to periodic renewal. Of particular interest are the rules governing the representative offices of foreign financial institutions. In 1983, the People's Bank of China issued regulations permitting foreign banks to establish representative offices to provide business liaison, consultation, information, and related services, but it expressly prohibited their engagement in "direct profit-making business activities," such as the granting of loans and handling of foreign exchange.[77] These were replaced in 1991 by new measures that granted broader permission for the establishment of branch offices.[78]

New flexibility in business forms

During the 1990s, new legislation and regulations expanded the range of structures permitted for foreign-invested enterprises, particularly in the areas of foreign-invested enterprises limited by shares and holding companies. Central to this effort was the Company Law of the PRC, which codified rules on business forms. This has particular relevance for foreign investment and is a significant step away from the limited framework offered under the original foreign investment enterprise regime. While the limited liability company form was retained, that was the basis for the foreign-invested enterprise regime, the additional possibility of limited liability companies limited by shares has been added. As well, foreign companies are now permitted to open branches in China, which allow greater flexibility and lower capital costs for building market access.

FOREIGN ENTERPRISES LIMITED BY SHARES

Regulations issued in 1995 on foreign-invested enterprises limited by shares permitted foreign investors to break free of the strictures of the joint venture format for FDI.[79] Pursuant to the provisions of the PRC Company Law on companies limited by shares, the new regulations permitted foreign-invested enterprises (FIEs, consisting of joint ventures, cooperative enterprises, and wholly foreign-owned enterprises) to be established as share companies, and it also allowed existing FIEs to convert into this type of company form. Newly established FIEs limited by shares may be created either by promotion or by share offer. In cases of promotion, there must be at least one foreign shareholder among the promoters. In cases of FIEs created by share offer, there must be at least one promoter, who may be either Chinese or foreign but who must have a record of profitability for the previous three years. FIEs limited by shares must have a minimum registered share capital of RMB30 million, not less than 25 percent of which must be purchased and held by foreign shareholders. Existing FIEs seeking to convert to FIEs limited by shares must have a record of profitability for the previous three years. In keeping with the provisions of the Company Law, the regulations focus broadly on the tasks and liabilities of promoters, whether these be investors in a newly formed FIE limited by shares or, in the case of existing FIEs that are being converted, the original investors together with any new investors. The regulations also provided that Chinese state-owned and collective enterprises may convert to FIEs limited by shares, in which case the Chinese and foreign shareholders act as promoters and enter into an agreement and articles of association for establishing the FIE. Applicant companies must have been in operation for at least five years, with a record of profitability during the previous three years prior to application. Shares in the applicant enterprise purchased with freely convertible currency and held by foreign shareholders must represent not less than 25 percent of the registered capital of the resulting FIE. The scope of business of the applicant enterprise must be one that is permitted for foreign enterprises. Lawfully established Chinese companies limited by shares may also convert to FIEs limited by shares, subject to similar requirements.

The regulations provide that approval of applications to form FIEs limited by shares is subject to decision by the Ministry of Foreign Trade and Economic Cooperation. However, other approval organs will almost certainly be involved. Thus, detailed matters of share issue, promotion, and subscription will be subject to additional approvals by the People's Bank of China and the Chinese Securities Regulatory Commission pursuant to the Company Law and various securities regulations, while foreign exchange matters will require approval from the State Administration for Exchange Control.

As with most new regulatory measures, the new rules on FIEs limited by shares contain ambiguities, and the record of performance is still uncertain. Nonetheless, the new regulations provide a range of opportunities for foreign investors to avail themselves of the new corporate forms set forth in the PRC Company Law. Whether by investing in newly established FIEs limited by shares, converting existing FIEs into share companies, or investing in Chinese enterprises that are converting to share companies, foreign investors are now presented with greater access to Chinese securities markets.

HOLDING COMPANIES

In April 1995, MOFTEC issued regulations by which foreign investors could use the holding company format to apply unified corporate management to multiple projects in China.[80] Managerial and accounting efficiencies (including the possibility of consolidated tax returns, currently denied under Chinese tax law) make the holding company structure particularly attractive. A number of large multinationals, such as Philips, had previously begun operations with holding companies in China, but the new measures added a greater degree of certainty to the regulatory framework. The new rules used the terms "investment-oriented company" or "investment company" to designate the holding companies subject to the regulations. Investment companies were defined under the regulations as wholly foreign-owned enterprises and Sino–foreign limited liability joint ventures that are engaged in making direct investments in China. This meant that holding companies would be subject to the general FIE regulatory regime, except where the holding company rules provide otherwise.

The holding company rules require applicants seeking to set up a holding company to have either (1) a total asset value of not less than $400 million one year prior to the date of application, with at least one established FIE with paid-up registered capital of more than $10 million and approval for more than three additional investment projects; *or* (2) have set up more than ten FIEs in China engaging in manufacturing or infrastructure development with total paid-up registered capital in excess of $30 million. Regardless of which of these criteria the foreign applicant meets, the registered capital of the holding company may not be less than $30 million. In the event of a joint-venture holding company, the Chinese partner must have total assets valued at not less than RMB100 million.

The procedure for setting up a holding company requires central MOFTEC approval – provincial FTEC bureaux are not empowered to approve applications for the establishment of holding companies (as they are for certain types of FIE). The scope of business provisions permit holding companies to operate industrial, agricultural, infrastructure, and energy projects, as well as projects in other sectors approved by the state. Holding company projects need not be located in the same place that the holding company is registered, but they are all subject to separate approvals under the standard regulatory regime applicable to FIEs generally. Holding companies are also permitted to provide a number of services to their subsidiary companies, including limited trading services (such as supplying raw materials and equipment, and selling and servicing subsidiary products in the Chinese and international markets); financial services (including foreign exchange balancing and lending activities); personnel services (including recruitment and training); and a broadly defined category of "consultancy services." In the event that the holding company does provide services to subsidiaries, the recipient subsidiary must be either wholly owned by the holding company or be a joint venture between the holding company and other foreign or Chinese investors in which the holding company and foreign investor contribution accounts for more than 25 percent of the registered capital. Under some circumstances, the holding company may also provide services to newly acquired subsidiaries.

The new regulations require that the holding company supply not less than 25 percent of the total registered capital to their subsidiary enterprises in foreign exchange. The holding company investors must also provide requisite letters of guarantee for the financial and technology transfer obligations of the holding company's projects. The regulations also require yearly reporting on investment plans and conditions to MOFTEC, the conduct of arms-length transactions between holding companies and their subsidiaries, full compliance with tax rules (including a commitment not to engage in tax evasion), and adherence to other Chinese laws and regulations.

State control over investment

Consistent with the pattern of Chinese law in the domestic economy and in social welfare and social control issues, the legal regime governing foreign investment underscores the primacy of state power. State control is exercised first and foremost through the processes for approval and supervision of foreign-invested projects, extending to such matters as size, registered capital, scope of business, location, use of resources, and operational feasibility.[81] Recently, the government has published "Guiding Catalogs" on its foreign investment priorities, identifying various sectors as "permitted," "encouraged," "restricted," or "prohibited," at once demonstrating a greater openness and transparency in the regulatory process but also revealing the extent to which state controls remain firmly in place.[82] Once established, investment projects are subject to an additional range of regulatory controls on matters such as pricing, import and export licensing, environmental protection, and labor management. State control over foreign investment activities is also promoted through financial regulation. Foreign exchange controls are imposed on virtually all foreign investment transactions, a process that continued after the liberalization of foreign exchange rules in 1994, albeit in a less expansive manner. Financial supervision is exercised through the tax reporting system. Investment incentives focusing on tax holidays and deferrals require detailed reporting by applicants seeking the benefits of these incentives.

The centrality of state control as an element of China's regulation of foreign investment was aimed initially at achieving rather vaguely conceived goals of popular welfare and to ensure that foreign investment serves China's development goals. Yet the implementation of the regulatory regime has been uneven.[83] Greater certainty that various foreign investment activities will be subject to the jurisdiction of specific laws and regulations has been accompanied by increased uncertainty over the consistency and certainty of enforcement. While corruption has certainly played a role, much of the uncertainty over enforcement stems from decisions and behavior by officials that, while possibly defensible by reference to the formal terms of law and regulation, seem unfamiliar and even improper to foreign businesses.[84]

Legal culture and the behavior of disputants in foreign business cases

Case reporting on disputes involving Chinese and foreign parties provides useful insights into the legal culture aspects of China's foreign business law regime.[85] Cultural aspects of foreign business disputes with Chinese parties often begin early in the commercial relationship, as foreign and Chinese negotiators bring different cultural precepts and expectations to the process.[86] Foreign – and particularly US[87] – pressure for greater transparency in the Chinese regulatory process also reflects cultural differences between the openness required of liberal democratic regimes founded on basic assumptions of equality and the Chinese regime's political culture, which combines Leninism with traditional Chinese patrimonial authoritarianism[88] and does not accept the basic precepts of accountability upon which norms of transparency are based. A stratification of culture is often evident in the differences of interest and perspective at different levels of Chinese and foreign enterprises. Thus, differences between principals and agents arise when the agents, motivated by personal relations and the prospect of personal gain, make representations to potential business partners that are later repudiated.[89] Decisions denying the validity of such contracts suggest significant cultural and political differences over the authority of individual economic actors to conclude business transactions independently.[90]

In a number of these cases, the contractual agreement between the parties operates within a context of continually changing demands. In one case, for example, involving the shipment of galvanized plates, the parties agreed to change the address for delivery after conclusion of the contract but before delivery.[91] Problems arise when requests for change occur later in transactions, such as when changes are sought in the quality and quantity of goods ordered well after the contract has been concluded.[92] In a similar case, the seller of aluminum ingots requested a change in the price and delivery terms well after the letter of credit paying for the goods had been opened.[93] While Chinese requests to modify agreed contract terms have been viewed by foreign businesses as evidence of lack of good faith,[94] in many instances they reflect instead an expectation that the parties to the transaction ought to help one another to respond as volatile (and to the Chinese possibly unknowable) market conditions change.[95] However, requests for changes in contract terms do not always signify expectations of a close relationship; in one case involving a leather production investment project, changed contract terms were the basis for a claim (later accepted by the arbitration tribunal) that the contract had never been formed.[96]

In several cases, fundamental differences of expectation were at the root of conflict. A typical concern, and one that arose in the context of the Beijing Jeep dispute, concerns the nature of the obligation between the parties.[97] For example, a transaction involving a technology and equipment sale and compensation trade agreement gave rise to a dispute over whether the equipment and technology met the contract specifications.[98] The basic issue in dispute seemed to be whether the obligation of the foreign party was limited solely to the contract terms or should be measured by the expectations of the Chinese party. Thus, while the foreign seller/licensor made several attempts to correct perceived inadequacies in the equipment and technology, the Chinese purchaser/licensee remained dissatisfied, not because the terms of the contract were not fulfilled but because the Chinese were unable to reach what they considered to be the ultimate goal of the project. A similar problem arose in the context of a joint venture involving the production of emulsion – the Chinese party claimed that the production line installed by the foreign investor was not sufficiently modern, while the foreign investor argued that it had performed its contract obligations.[99] Chinese importers have not always been concerned strictly with project objectives. In a dispute over the performance of glass-blowing equipment, the Chinese insisted on compensation for non-conforming goods, even when it was established that the equipment, while not meeting contract specifications, would still meet the Chinese project requirements.[100]

Assumptions that the Chinese contracting party's special relationship with its counterpart transcends the contract terms are also evident in responses to discovering that the foreign party does not view the relationship as particularly special. In a case involving the sale of bread preservatives, the Chinese party agreed to revise the contract payment terms then reneged when they concluded that the foreign seller was seeking merely to avoid Customs duties.[101] The Chinese party's response did not seem to be motivated by the desire to enrich the Chinese Customs Service but was due, apparently, to disappointment that the foreign partner would subordinate their relations with the Chinese seller to concerns about avoiding import duties. A Chinese purchaser of packaging materials and equipment revealed a similar level of disappointment in attempting to resist payment of a performance bond insisted upon by the foreign seller.[102]

The conduct of disputes can also be subject to cultural influences, as Chinese norms of collective responsibility for the management of conflict are evident in expectations about mediation and conciliation.[103] Recent Chinese government edicts prodding Chinese companies facing anti-dumping actions to litigate rather than negotiate a settlement suggest both the pervasive influence of the consensual resolution norm and the differences of approach taken by Chinese companies and Chinese administrative agencies. In a dispute between a Chinese and a Thai company, the issue concerned the conformity of documents with the requirements of a letter of credit.[104] The Chinese bank insisted on "strict compliance," while the Thai seller and its negotiating bank claimed that the documentary differences were inconsequential. In this case, both parties engaged in a lengthy process of negotiation, political intercession, and litigation before settling on mediation under the auspices of CIETAC. After negotiations were unavailing, the Thai seller sought a political solution through the local bureau of the State Administration for Industry and Commerce (SAIC) and appealed for a court judgment before pursuing resolution through CIETAC. CIETAC oversaw a mediated solution by which the Thai seller was largely made whole. The Thai company wrote a lengthy missive extolling the virtues of mediation.

In that case, there was no direct dispute between the parties over performance of the terms of the contractual agreement. Rather, the matter was the conformity of documents needed to secure payment on the letter of credit. Normally, this would be a matter separate from the underlying contract.[105] In this case, however, although the contracting parties were unable to negotiate a mutually agreed conclusion to the matter, they revealed a clear willingness to participate in a managed solution. It would appear that their willingness to engage in mediation, ultimately successful, was helped by the fact that between them there was no substantial disagreement on performance of the contract. Thus, the willingness to engage in voluntary dispute settlement in this case depended not on the extent of economic interest but rather, in part at least, on the fact that the relationship was not undermined by either party's contract performance.

In some instances, however, negotiated solutions do not solve the dispute but only serve to sharpen the parties' differences. In a case involving the sale of steel plate for use in a hydroelectric project, for example, a dispute over the alleged failure of timely delivery was settled, and the seller agreed to pay a negotiated measure of compensation.[106] The Chinese importer still filed for arbitration, claiming additional compensation. Communication difficulties during the course of settling a dispute have in some cases served to exacerbate tensions between the parties, contributing to a breakdown in the transaction.[107]

China's accession to the GATT and the WTO: implications for foreign trade and investment

China's application for accession to the General Agreement on Tariffs and Trade (GATT) and the World Trade Organization (WTO) has generated nearly fifteen years of negotiation, diplomatic engagement, and scholarly inquiry.[108] The formal application was submitted in 1986 and initiated the formation of a GATT working party in accordance with GATT procedures on new members. As the process nears conclusion and the final negotiations with the GATT working party proceed, it is appropriate and timely to review the legal implications of China's accession. Membership of the GATT/WTO presents for China a series of institutional and behavioral challenges that are unlikely to be resolved in the near term. These challenges may be understood, first, by reference to the existing foreign economic law regimes of the PRC discussed in the preceding section. Second, Chinese perspectives on membership in the GATT/WTO provide an important context for examining China's accession project. Finally, the terms of the accession protocol will be examined in light of the implications for further legal reform.

Chinese perspectives on accession to the GATT and the WTO

China's efforts to gain accession to the GATT stand against a background of local conditions that suggest significant socio-economic and possibly political costs. While Chinese perspectives on GATT accession include recognition of the potential for GATT/WTO membership to drive reform efforts in China, less supportive perspectives drawing on themes of dependency and nationalism are also important.

Perspectives on Chinese domestic conditions

The social and economic consequences of China's GATT/WTO accession are likely to be severe when viewed in light of China's domestic conditions.[109] On the economic front, the ongoing and apparently intractable issue of reforming state-owned enterprises and the resulting unemployment and underemployment issues have created significant problems. The cost of investing to upgrade these enterprises is high, and the level of foreign investment interest is marginal. The challenge of maintaining high growth rates while avoiding inflation continues to occupy China's best economic planners. Public sector spending on education and health care is lagging behind GDP growth, whereas the demographics of Chinese society suggest that these issues require more investment not less as increased economic competition places a greater premium on education, while an aging population puts greater burdens on the health care system. On the social front, unemployment issues, combined with the problem of a migrant population in excess of 100 million, have created a significant challenge to social order. Moreover, increasing numbers of laborers and migrants in China have become increasingly disaffected with the reform policies, which have thrust them into an uncertain and insecure economic situation. Environmental degradation continues to worsen, with consequences for economic productivity and health. These various policy challenges are compounded by a crisis of governance. Corruption remains a serious problem and is increasingly coupled with popular cynicism about the capacities and interests of government officials and institutions.

Accession to the GATT/WTO is likely to accelerate the processes of liquidation and downsizing of state-owned enterprises that are already underway, with the prospect of increased unemployment, or at best job dislocation and attendant social costs.[110] Increasing imports of equipment, agricultural products, chemicals, pharmaceuticals, and other goods as a result of reduced tariffs will undoubtedly strain China's foreign exchange balance, while the potential for offsets from foreign investment and increased exports remains to be seen. There is significant uncertainty and apprehension in China about the political and social consequences, despite recent statements on movement toward open convertibility of the renminbi. The political consequences of increased foreign investment may also be problematic, either as a result of increased influence over government policy decisions and decision makers to the detriment of local interests, or because of a backlash of resentment against what might be perceived as foreign domination.

Changing perspectives on the foreign

As readers of Chinese literature ranging from Lao She to Wang Shuo can attest, China's relationship with the outside world has long been an ambivalent one.[111] This is particularly true in the area of foreign trade and investment. Characteristic of the conventional system by which China managed its foreign economic relations was the notion of *she wai/dui wai* (foreign-related), a term intended to underscore the differences between matters Chinese and matters foreign. However, developments in China's foreign economic relations during the 1990s have begun to erode the barriers between "domestic" and "foreign" business, if not necessarily removing the competitive and development tensions that the *she wai/dui wai* distinction implies.[112] Ownership and/or control by PRC nationals of businesses registered in Hong Kong or abroad but active in China renders the "foreign" classification problematic. As well, foreign firms are engaged in a wide array of activities within and without China, partly in response to market demands and sometimes in an effort to avoid regulatory intrusion, thus defying easy categorization. Foreign business actors are increasingly engaged in trade relations aimed at securing capital equipment and opening markets, while also conducting local contract transactions for raw materials. The increased penetration of the Chinese market by international financial institutions and the corresponding access by Chinese firms to the international capital and commercial markets have challenged the barriers between "foreign" and "domestic" business yet further.

As the barriers between "domestic" and "foreign" business activities diminish, foreign businesses have come increasingly to compete with Chinese national firms in both domestic and international transactions. As a result, Chinese businesses have come to rely more fully on their connection networks (*guanxi wang*) and, in the case of former trade officials jumping into the sea of commerce (*xia hai*), building competitive advantage based on personal and professional links with regulatory agencies.[113] Competition with foreign firms often takes the form of efforts to gain preferential access to information and in some cases influence over regulators to the disadvantage of foreign firms. Competition can also lead to illegalities, as in cases where Chinese investors seeking the preferential tax treatment and other benefits accorded to foreign investors route domestic investments illegally through offshore accounts to create "false joint ventures," or disregard import licensing and customs requirements in efforts to gain competitive advantage in the market for imports.[114]

Chinese regulators have attempted to address these issues. The enactment of the Unified Contract Law, for example, was driven in large part by the need to remove artificial disparities between contract rules for domestic and international transactions.[115] Elimination of the foreign exchange certificates and unification of the Chinese currency was driven in part by similar considerations.[116] Consideration has been given to the elimination of tax preferences for foreign investment or to grant the same preferences to

Chinese investors.[117] However, these efforts are aimed primarily at ameliorating the perceived injustice of granting preferential treatment to foreign businesses and thus represent efforts to build popular support for governance and regulation that resist foreign dominion. In this sense, efforts to bring uniformity to the Chinese regulation of foreign economic relations reveal a deep-seated ambivalence toward foreign business intrusion in China.

Perspectives on dependency, nationalism, and China's place in the world economy

Inspired in part by a legacy of tensions in North–South relations and the influence of dependency theory, Chinese officials often portray trade regulation efforts by foreign countries in terms of discrimination against China.[118] In this view, trade sanctions permitted under the GATT are seen as thwarting China's competitive advantages in wages and production costs and are an attempt to prevent China's development. Official commentators reject as protectionist and discriminatory suggestions from the United States in particular that China is a non-market economy, citing World Bank reports indicating that most prices in China are set by the market.[119] While questions about direct and indirect subsidies to Chinese producers and the role of mercantilist trade targeting remain unresolved (and often unrecognized in China's submissions to international tribunals), there remains a fundamental ambivalence and suspicion in official Chinese responses to the international trade regime.

The policies of the PRC on WTO accession also reflect a resurgent nationalism in Chinese attitudes about the world trading system.[120] China's official position on accession is that China is resuming the membership in the WTO originally occupied by the Republic of China regime that was a signatory to the original GATT treaties. Thus, issues of Cold War politics and Western imperialism linked to US support for the Republic of China during the Chinese Civil War and subsequently on Taiwan inform official and popular attitudes toward China's GATT accession. China's response to issues concerning the GATT/WTO are viewed as part of a larger picture of relations with the international system dominated by the United States and other industrialized democracies, in which China is denied its deserved status. Nationalism permits China's accession to the WTO to be interpreted as a variant on a unified theme of foreign exploitation and exclusion.

Perspectives questioning the benefits of WTO accession

China's WTO accession effort also reflects debates over the further entrenchment of economic reform policies.[121] Proponents of China's accession to the WTO have highlighted the beneficial effects that greater access to world markets will have on China's economic growth.[122] However, local organizational interests and ideological perspectives have often resisted the conces-sions mandated by GATT members considering China's application. These perspectives and interests have had a significant impact on the positions taken by China during negotiations since 1986. Driven in part by concerns over the impact on domestic conditions in China and by their own organiza-tional imperatives, political and bureaucratic interests have resisted concessions on China's WTO entry.[123] The accession process has challenged the long-held privileges of the state sector.[124] Just as Zhu Rongji has strug-gled to imposed his vision of efficiency and accountability on the economic ministries and departments, so too have Zhu and China's chief GATT nego-tiator Long Yongtu attempted to assure entrenched bureaucratic interests that WTO accession is in China's long-term interest.[125] State enterprises in the telecommunications, electronics, heavy manufacturing (e.g. automo-biles), pharmaceuticals, and forest products have made their concerns over China's pending accession known.[126] China's agriculture and banking sectors have also expressed dismay at the costs expected of them under the plans for China's WTO accession.[127]

The process of accession: from bilateral agreements with China's major trading partners to the protocol of accession

The process of negotiating the protocol of accession required China to conclude bilateral agreements with WTO members. Key among these agree-ments were the accords with the United States, Canada, and the European Union, all of which progressed in fits and starts following Deng Xiaoping's call for deepening reform in 1992. The USA was widely seen to mishandle Zhu Rongji's visit in April 1999, sending him home empty-handed to face a chilly reception and criticism for apparently conceding too much to US demands.[128] The bombing of China's embassy in Belgrade brought a tempo-rary suspension of negotiations in June 1999,[129] although by the Fall discussions had resumed. China's accession effort crossed important hurdles with the conclusion of bilateral agreements with the United States and Canada in Fall 1999 and the European Union in early 2000.[130] The terms of these agreements set specific conditions for market access and regulatory norms that will be incorporated into the protocol of accession.

The bilateral agreements

China's bilateral agreements with the United States, Canada, and the European Union offered a useful glimpse of the "price" of China's accession to the WTO. While the general principles concerning transparency, national treatment, and other matters of broad regulatory significance were retained, the bilateral agreements also indicated the extent to which particular indus-tries were affecting the terms of China's accession to the world trading system.

The US agreement provided for overall tariff reduction from 22.1 to 17 percent.[131] The agreement required China to eliminate import quotas and quantitative restrictions within five years following China's accession. In some cases, these would be phased out more quickly. US tariffs (including those imposed under the Multi-Fibre Agreement) would be phased out by 2005. The bilateral agreement would permit the USA to retain "special safeguards" to protect against import surges for twelve years after China's accession – reflecting US concerns over China's export competitiveness. The USA would also retain a "special anti-dumping methodology" permitting use of non-market economy surrogates for fifteen years after China's accession, with possible earlier sector-by-sector phase-out.

Aside from tariff reduction, the Sino–US bilateral agreement also provided specific market access guarantees for US firms. In agriculture, tariffs would be reduced to 14.5 percent, and export subsidies on agricultural products would be discontinued. A tariff rate quota system would be retained to provide some level of stability on the quantity of agricultural products subject to various tariffs within the agreed limits. The agreement also provided for direct private trade without the intervention of intermediary trading companies. In telecommunications (including mobile services), China agreed to permit foreign ownership up to 49 percent immediately after accession, with an increase to 50 percent in the second year after accession. This would include Internet content and services. Complementing the telecommunications provisions was the extension of the 17 percent tariff limitation to high-technology imports. As well, market access for audio-visual products would be expanded through a mandated increase in the annual imports of foreign films to twenty on a revenue-sharing basis. Foreign firms would have the right to form joint ventures to distribute video and sound recordings. The agreement required significant market opening in the area of financial services. Foreign banks were to be empowered to provide automobile financing in China from the date of accession. Foreign banks will be able to provide local currency services to Chinese enterprises two years after accession and to individuals five years after accession. Foreign banks were to be accorded the same rights as Chinese banks operating in the same geographical area. China agreed to remove geographical and customer restrictions on foreign banks and their branches within five years after accession. In the securities area, China agreed to permit 33 percent foreign ownership of fund management firms immediately upon accession, with this proportion rising to 49 percent in three years. Foreign ownership of securities companies engaged in underwriting would be set at 33 percent. Securities firms with minority foreign ownership would be able to underwrite domestic securities issues and trade in foreign currency-denominated securities.

In the industrial products sector, average tariffs would be reduced to 9.4 percent by 2005 (7.1 percent for priority products). The agreement provided for the elimination of limits on import and distribution rights (wholesale and retail). Foreign firms would also be granted market access for repair and support services, without use of intermediaries. In the automobile sector, import tariffs would be phased out by 2006, with larger incremental reductions in the early years. These provisions complemented the concessions made to the banking sector on automobile financing.

While the Sino–US bilateral agreement was significant in and of itself, its utility as a precedent was diminished by delays over reforms to the US Foreign Trade Act of 1974, which were required to make the agreement effective. After considerable debate, the House of Representatives agreed to grant permanent normal trade relations (PNTR) to China in May 2000, with the Senate following suit in September. But for congressional acquiescence, the reciprocity requirements of the GATT would have permitted China to deny to the USA the concessionary treatment granted under the Sino–US agreement while still granting parallel concessions to other GATT members. Reactions to the bilateral agreement among thoughtful intellectuals in China suggest that many of the tensions in US–China relations will not be removed by the agreement.[132] The impact of US domestic politics notwithstanding, however, the Sino–US agreement provided significant impetus for China's bilateral agreements with Canada and the European Union.

The Sino–Canadian agreement provided for the average import tariffs on priority Canadian industrial and agricultural goods to fall to 5.2 percent.[133] Significant market opening was granted for agricultural products, and the tariff rate quota system was limited to two products, Canola oil and wheat. Tariffs on industrial products would be reduced to 4.5 percent within two years following accession. China's accession to the WTO's Information Technology Agreement would see the elimination of tariffs on imports of information technology. In telecommunications, the Canadian agreement committed China to granting 49 percent foreign ownership, with the additional provision of 50 percent foreign ownership for value-added and paging services. In the areas of service trade, the agreement provided for greater market access for foreign firms and bound China to refraining from imposing new restrictions on service providers currently in the market ("grandfathering") in anticipation of the expansion that will be required upon accession. In the area of financial services, China reiterated the commitments contained in the Sino–US agreement on market access for foreign banking services, insurance, and securities.

While the Sino–Canadian agreement differed from the Sino–US agreement largely in the areas of general tariff reductions in priority agricultural and industrial products, the bilateral agreement between China and the European Union expanded on the provisions on insurance and telecommunications contained in the Sino–US agreement.[134] In the insurance area, the EU secured a commitment to accelerated expansion of market opening for foreign investment. The schedule for market access for foreign investment in telecommunications (including mobile) was also accelerated. The EU agreement also granted expanded authority to the provincial authorities to approve automobile joint-venture plants – a significant effort at removing bureaucratic delays in project approvals.

The accession protocol and implications for reform

The terms of China's accession to the WTO will be set forth in the final protocol of accession. This will reflect the terms and conditions of the various bilateral agreements and will contain such other requirements as are determined by the GATT working party established to oversee China's accession. While China continues to claim developing country status to justify lenient timetables for accession,[135] the process of China's accession has revealed more fundamental differences between China's regulatory approaches and the norms of the GATT.[136] The GATT and the WTO reflect norms of free trade through the principles of tariff reduction, the elimination of non-tariff barriers, and the enforcement of rules on transparency, non-discrimination, national treatment, and most-favored nation treatment.[137] Particular attention has been given to the broad themes of "most-favored nation treatment" (GATT, Article I); "national treatment" (GATT, Article III); and "non-discrimination" (GATT, Article XIII), as well as the requirements on reducing and eliminating tariffs and trade subsidies.[138] These derive from liberal principles accepting the theory of comparative advantage, which essentially relegates the role of government to promoting the efficiency and utility of a state's existing or acquired economic attributes and opposes state actions to inhibit the economic activities of other states through mercantilism and protectionism.[139] Thus, the development of the international free trade system seeks to minimize the capacity for local interests to interfere with transnational economic relations.[140]

The protocol of accession will incorporate industry-specific market access provisions, as well as broad terms and conditions on regulatory norms and processes. The working party's draft protocol of accession on China (1997) set forth many of the general conditions that will be amplified in the final agreement. In Section I.2.A.3, the draft protocol required that China administer all its laws and regulations governing trade and goods services, trade-related aspects of intellectual property rights, and foreign exchange in a uniform, impartial, and reasonable manner. Section I.2.A.5 required China to establish a mechanism by which non-uniform application of the trade regime may be brought to the attention of the national authorities, implying the availability of a system of administrative review. Section I.2.C required China to undertake significant transparency reforms, including publication of laws and regulations, while Section I.2.D required China to establish a system of judicial review. In order to satisfy these requirements, wide-ranging modifications will be required in China's existing laws and regulations, and equally importantly in the decision-making norms of China's economic regulatory bureaucracy.[141]

NATIONAL ADMINISTRATION OF FOREIGN TRADE

The GATT places significant emphasis on state responsibility for compliance as the basis upon which the GATT's substantive free trade principles rely. Compliance with GATT rules by signatory states is in part a matter of internal administration. Accordingly, Article XXIV(12) requires each contracting party to take "necessary measures" to ensure observance of the GATT by regional and local governments and authorities.[142] This provision has been amplified by the "Understanding on the Interpretation of Article XXIV of the General Agreement on Tariffs and Trade" attached to the Uruguay Round.[143] Signatory states are "fully responsible ... for the observance of all provisions of GATT 1994" and are required to "take such reasonable measures as may be available ... to ensure such observance by regional and local governments and authorities." These requirements are linked to the enforcement provisions on dispute resolution coming out of the Uruguay Round.[144] In response to the requirements of Article XXIV(12), federal states adopt various approaches to ensure that their political subdivisions remain in compliance with GATT principles.

Under the Constitution of the PRC, China is a unitary state in which the provincial and local authorities are bound by decisions and edicts from the central government, subject to a modicum of consultation between the central and local authorities.[145] In recent years, however, there has been a significant devolution of power from Beijing to the provinces and counties. The concentration of economic growth in the southern provinces, particularly Guangdong and Fujian, has decreased the capacity of the central government to control local behavior through its traditional mechanisms of political patronage and financial allocations.[146] As well, the gradual dismantling of the state planning apparatus without the establishment of effective replacement institutions to regulate the newly emerging market economy has contributed to a reduced government capacity to control local commercial behavior.[147] Beijing's general inability to control the local authorities is compounded by the crisis of corruption, which not only undermines the regulatory authority and capacity of government institutions[148] but also extends to the state's own information-gathering processes, thus undermining the ability to manage policy effectively.[149] These obstacles to central government control undermine China's capacity to ensure that its political subdivisions reach compliance with GATT requirements, particularly in the foreign trade centers in the southern provinces.

TRANSPARENCY, RULE OF LAW, AND NATIONAL TREATMENT

Enforcement of GATT rules is dependent on the provisions of Article X(1) requiring publication of trade regulations, and uniform, impartial, and reasonable administration of laws and regulations. This has been interpreted to extend to an obligation to afford an opportunity to consult government authorities to learn about laws and practices.[150] Article X(3) requires the contracting parties to establish independent judicial, arbitral, or administrative tribunals or procedures for the prompt review and correction of administrative action regarding customs matters (which include virtually all aspects of trade regulation). Thus the transparency and enforcement provisions of Article X provide the framework for implementing the substantive norms expressed elsewhere in the agreement, for in the absence of transparency about the content and application of trade regulations, trading partners and their businesses cannot know whether or not the central GATT principles of free trade are being granted or denied. The substantive and operational norms complement each other and set the tone for the GATT's regulatory culture. The national treatment requirements of GATT Article III focus on internal taxes and regulation and prohibit the use of these measures to afford protection to domestic production. National treatment disciplines attempt to prevent non-tariff regulatory efforts that discriminate against imported goods – imports are to receive treatment no less favorable than treatment accorded to comparable local products.[151] As the reach of GATT disciplines extends beyond trade to include services, investment, and intellectual property, national treatment principles also expanded. Under the WTO, national treatment requirements are seen to extend beyond goods to include market actors and their assets – financial, intellectual, and material.[152]

In order to comply with the requirements of the GATT and the WTO, China has begun a wide-ranging campaign of revising existing legislation and administrative regulations. Substantive law in most economic sectors, including customs, foreign exchange, taxation, intellectual property, enterprise law, bankruptcy, and pricing will need to be revised to accord with WTO requirements.[153] Much of this effort is led by MOFTEC's Department of Treaties and Law, although cooperation with other State Council ministries, the State Council's Legal Affairs Bureau (*Fa zhi ju*), and the National People's Congress Legal Affairs Work Committee (*Fa gong wei*) will be needed to bring these efforts to fruition. While significant regulatory reform will undoubtedly be required in order to ensure that the various sectoral market opening commitments made by China will be met, of equal or greater importance are the systemic reforms required to bring the legal and regulatory system as a whole into compliance.

Conclusion

The law governing China's foreign economic relations reflects the dynamics of selective adaptation seen elsewhere in the Chinese legal system. However, unlike other areas of legal institutions, contracts, property, and human rights, the foreign economic law system is subject to direct pressures for reform by foreign interests. Thus, the system that has emerged is perhaps more reflective of foreign norms and practices than are the legal regimes of primarily domestic concern. Nonetheless, local legal cultural norms supporting Party and state control remain dominant. With the application for accession to the WTO and the negotiations that have ensued, however, China's foreign business law system faces significant pressures to conform to the liberal norms of governance associated with the world market system. Undoubtedly, China will resist uncritical assimilation of these norms, and local legal culture will remain an important mediating force in this regard.

Conclusion

Prospects for China's legal reform project

The Chinese legal system has changed considerably over the past two decades, but particularly since 1992. Increased interaction with the world economy and the dynamic of globalization has brought a range of powerful foreign influences to bear. China's response to the opportunities and challenges offered by norms of globalized liberalism has been one of selective adaptation, by which foreign legal norms are mediated by local legal culture. But it is not always popular legal culture that diminishes the influence of globalization. More often, the record of Chinese legal reform in the areas of legal institutions, contract, property, human rights, and foreign economic relations reveals a relatively consistent pattern by which foreign legal norms and institutional arrangements are adjusted to meet local political and ideological imperatives, as identified and approved by the Party/state. However, China's accession to the GATT and WTO imposes limits on this process. The GATT/WTO disciplines of transparency, rule of law, and national treatment in particular will require wide-ranging changes in the areas of legal institutions, contracts, property, human rights (labor and criminal law), and foreign economic relations, which have been the subject of this book.

Reform of basic legal institutions

Perhaps the most fundamental legislative changes that will be needed for China to conform to the GATT/WTO will be revision of the PRC Constitution, which permits control by the Chinese Communist Party in the operation of the legal system. References to the principle of Party leadership contained in Article 12 and set forth in many interpretative documents and official speeches may require amendment, to the extent that these authorize Party control over the regulation of trade and investment activities. The rule-of-law requirements of GATT Article X(3)(b) on independent adjudication and review of trade regulation matters will dictate that the Party's internal (*neibu*) non-public decision-making processes not be permitted to govern the regulation of economic and commercial affairs.[1]

As well, the provisions of PRC Constitution Article 16 subordinating the role of private property may require revision in order to ensure that it does not impose local content requirements or other discriminatory treatment on foreign market actors in violation of the GATT's national treatment principles.[2] Also, to the extent that the preference given by the PRC Constitution to the public sector privileges the competitive position of state-owned Chinese firms, issues arise concerning compliance with the non-discrimination provisions of GATT Article XVII.[3]

In the area of legislative procedure, the Legislation Law of the PRC may require further reinterpretation and possible revision in order to comply with the transparency requirements of GATT Article X on the question of public consultation in the process of trade regulation. While the experience of the Unified Contract Law during 1997–98 suggested an increased commitment to a public legislative process, this will need to be extended to other areas of trade-related legislation and regulatory rule making. As well, the rules and processes for technical amendments to legislation and regulation will need to be formalized to ensure that legislative changes made through the transparent public consultative processes required by the GATT are reflected in revisions to ancillary laws and regulations.

In the area of administrative law reform, GATT Article X(3)(b)'s requirements regarding prompt review and correction of administrative action may require amendments to the current regimes for administrative reconsideration and judicial review. The Administrative Litigation Law is likely to need amendment to broaden the scope of judicial review and to ensure uniform and fair application of the criteria for determining when an administrative decision is "unlawful," the standard of review now set forth in ALL Article 5. Amendments to the Administrative Reconsideration Law will be needed to articulate clear standards for the exhaustion of administrative remedies as a prelude to judicial review. In addition, an administrative procedure law may be needed to ensure compliance with GATT transparency principles in rule making and in the uniform, impartial, and reasonable administration of laws and regulations on foreign trade.[4]

The PRC court system, and particularly laws governing court organization, civil procedure, judges, and lawyers, may require revision in order to bring the judicial dispute settlement system into compliance with GATT/WTO rule-of-law requirements. Restrictions against foreign lawyers may well be deemed a violation of the WTO's General Agreement on Trade in Services (GATS).[5] While China's Supreme People's Court is already engaged in reforming the civil trial system to accord with WTO rule-of-law requirements,[6] GATT transparency requirements are likely to mandate more expansive reforms, possibly including the removal of Party committees and Party-led adjudication committees from judicial decision making – in practice as well as in formality. The provisions of Article 14 of the PRC Civil Procedural Law on supervision by the People's Procuracy of civil trials (interpreted generally to include trials involving judicial review of administrative action and proceedings in the Foreign Economic Law Chambers) may require amendment in order to ensure that such supervision complies with GATT rules on transparency and independent adjudication. The jurisdictional provisions of the Civil Procedure Law, Articles 36–9, on the transfer of complex and difficult cases, as well as the provisions of Article 138 on reasons for judgments, will require amendment in order to comply with transparency requirements. GATT requirements will also mean strengthening the procedures and practices for enforcing foreign arbitral awards in Chinese courts.[7]

Reform of contract and property law

In the area of contracts, the transparency requirements of the GATT will require greater clarity of the norms and standards set forth in the Unified Contract Law providing that contracts may be avoided on grounds of violating norms of morality, good faith, state and public interest, social and economic order, and so on, to the extent that these may serve as an exercise in trade regulation. The publication of these norms will be required in order for the UCL provisions on contract effectiveness to comply with the transparency principles set forth in GATT Article X. Transparency rules will also require greater clarity in the provisions of UCL Article 44 that contract approvals should be sought where necessary, as well as in the ancillary regulatory systems upon which this provision is based.

In the area of property law, transparency requirements will mandate greater clarity in the management of land-use rights, particularly in the area of registration rules and the rights to transfer and dispose of land-use rights. In the intellectual property area, transparency and national treatment principles will require broader access by IPR holders to enforcement processes and institutions.[8] National treatment requirements will mandate equal access by foreign companies to the People's Courts, as well as enforcement in practice of national treatment and non-discrimination requirements in the enforcement of foreign and domestic intellectual property rights.[9] Transparency principles may require broader access by market actors to the rule-making processes that attend the identification and enforcement of intellectual property rights.

In the area of corporate property, WTO accession will require reforms in China's financial markets. Privatization of industry, a key element of the reforms that will be required following China's accession to the GATT/WTO, will gradually draw the SOEs out of the state bureaucratic economy and into a more market-oriented environment.[10] Experience to date suggests that the investors in privatization will be drawn largely from former SOE managers and senior executives armed with concessionary financing from state banks.[11] While policy lending has long been a mainstay of the Chinese banking system, the problem is likely to be exacerbated by increased demands for capital needed to fund the privatization process.[12]

Banking reforms already underway in China will face significant new pressures, born of the calls for fair access by foreign investors seeking opportunities to acquire potentially profitable SOEs. While competition with foreign banks will increase, China's Central Bank governor Dai Xianglong recently indicated a commitment to continued government support: "The government will still take measures necessary to back up and protect banks in the mainland for a certain period of time."[13] However, China's market access commitments in the banking sector will require the removal of current restrictions against foreign bank activities in China,[14] leaving foreign banking activity under the jurisdiction of the Commercial Bank Law (1995).[15] Revisions to that law's provisions governing approval for the establishment of commercial banks and supervision will be required to comply with GATT transparency and national treatment rules.[16] Banking reforms will also be needed to ensure that enforcement of letters of credit conforms to international standards.[17]

Financing for privatization will also be possible through the securities markets, although reforms in the securities regulatory system and associated service sectors in accounting will be needed.[18] Despite some hesitation over the prospects of opening China's financial markets,[19] gradual expansion of market access for foreign investors – either directly or through listing by foreign-invested enterprises in China – appears to be inevitable.[20] Regulatory efforts to restrict foreign participation in securities businesses made in advance of China's accession[21] will require revision to conform with the requirements of the bilateral market access agreements and the protocol of accession. Revisions to the Securities Law and the Company Law provisions governing supervision of securities markets and approval of securities issues and trades will be necessary to ensure compliance with GATT transparency requirements, where such administrative activities are linked to foreign trade matters such as in the case of FIEs limited by shares. GATT national treatment requirements will mandate greater uniformity in the administration of securities regulations in such areas as information disclosure, approvals, and supervision between foreign and domestic companies.

Reforms in human rights (labor and criminal law)

China's accession to the WTO will require revisions to human rights legislation in the areas of labor and criminal law. For example, transparency requirements will mandate clarity in the norms and procedures for application of labor law standards to trade-related enterprises and may also require broader access and opportunities for consultation by foreign firms during the processes of rule making and enforcement of labor relations matters. National treatment principles will require that the rules governing labor in foreign businesses conform to those governing labor standards in domestic and especially state-owned enterprises. Currently, labor relations in FIEs are governed by administrative regulations such as the "Regulations on Labor

Management in Foreign-Funded Enterprises" (1994) and "Various Opinions of the Ministry of Labor on Collective Bargaining in Foreign Funded Enterprises" (1997).[22] While ostensibly subject to the Labor Law of the PRC, these regulations impose special rules on foreign businesses that may not withstand scrutiny under the GATT's national treatment principles.

The application of PRC criminal law to many aspects of commercial activity raises the prospect of the application of WTO standards. For example, transparency norms will require greater clarity and consistency in the standards for applying criminal law to commercial activity in such areas as intellectual property rights, securities law, and price and competition law. National treatment principles will require that regulatory standards are applied uniformly between foreign and domestic market actors.

Reforms in foreign economic relations

The market access commitments made by China in the course of negotiating accession to the WTO will obviously require substantial revision to the laws and regulations governing foreign trade and investment in such sectors as agricultural production, telecommunications (including the Internet), financial services (including banking, insurance, and securities); and manufacturing (especially automobiles). More fundamentally, however, the transparency and national treatment principles of the GATT/WTO will require substantial reform to the legal and regulatory systems governing the administration of trade and investment. In the trade area, transparency norms will require greater openness in the processes for approving the status of foreign trade operators under Article 9 of the Foreign Trade Law, while national treatment requirements will mandate equal treatment for local and foreign firms. Transparency requirements will also mandate more open decision making in areas such as import and export licensing, Customs regulations, commodity inspection, and the interpretation and enforcement of health and safety standards on imports and exports under the Foreign Trade Law and the various regulations on import/export licensing and commodity inspection. WTO rules on technical barriers to trade will mandate removal – in practice as well as in law – of non-tariff barriers in the areas of import and export licensing, import quotas, commodity inspection, and so on.[23] Transparency requirements will also mandate that the processes for tariff reduction and elimination be made more accessible to foreign importers and exporters.

In the area of investment, national treatment principles of the GATT and the WTO Agreement on Trade-Related Investment Measures (TRIMs) will require elimination of import substitution rules as well as reform of disparate regulatory treatment of foreign and domestic companies in the areas of tax law, environmental protection, labor standards, investment ratios and minimum investment requirements, foreign exchange, and other areas.[24] China's accession to the WTO will bring into play the national treatment and transparency requirements of the General Agreement on Trade in Services (GATS), requiring significant openings in the areas of financial and accounting services, as well as other sectors such as engineering and legal services.[25] In a very important sense, the fundamental *she wai/dui wai* principles that inform China's administration of its foreign business regime must be reformed in order to comply with GATT/WTO requirements. Transparency and national treatment principles will also require greater openness and uniformity in the enactment and application of administrative regulation in such areas as project approval, tax and foreign exchange administration, company registration, price administration, and labor relations. Transparency principles may also require that the Chinese Communist Party's internal decision-making processes not intrude on the conduct of labor unions established in foreign-invested companies.

Thus, virtually all aspects of the PRC legal system will require further reform as a result of China's accession to the WTO. While China can be expected to continue to interpret and apply the norms, institutions, and processes of the GATT/WTO in ways that are heavily influenced by local legal culture, the process of selective adaptation that has governed China's borrowing of globalized legal norms will be increasingly restricted.

While long-term compliance remains a reasonable expectation, what is needed more immediately is a higher degree of certainty about the reality of China's WTO behavior. Rather than focus on full compliance, attention should be paid to the issue of "appropriate compliance," which may in fact mean "acceptable non-compliance" as the likely reality in the near term. Preparing for non-compliance is likely to be preferable to hinging government policies and private sector strategies on inflated expectations about China's ability to adhere strictly to GATT/WTO rules within the mandated schedules.

In determining what constitutes appropriate compliance, existing WTO members can play a constructive role in identifying clear parameters for acceptable behavior and encouraging China to accelerate its transition to full compliance. The WTO dispute settlement procedures under the dispute settlement understanding are likely to provide useful avenues for redress in cases of serious breach of duty by China.[26] However, resort to WTO dispute settlement procedures necessarily intrudes on diplomatic relations and is not necessarily an optimal solution in all cases of non-compliance.[27] WTO members should recognize the extent of legal and political transformation that will be required of China to achieve full compliance with the requirements of the GATT/WTO.[28] Reliance on the WTO trade policy review mechanism as a monitoring process on Chinese compliance may facilitate accommodation between the WTO system and Chinese traditions of governance in the areas of market access, transparency, rule of law, and national treatment.[29] A key additional element will be confidence building by WTO members to strengthen appreciation among

Chinese leaders and institutions about the benefits of WTO compliance and participation.

As suggested in the Introduction, this book is largely an attempt to build realistic expectations about the performance of China's legal regimes. China's accession to the WTO will not diminish this task but rather is likely to raise further challenges.[30] The challenge for China is to achieve compliance with GATT/WTO requirements while remaining true to its local cultural and developmental imperatives. The challenge for foreign participants and observers in China's legal reform project is to adopt realistic expectations about the dynamics and likely outcomes of this process.

Appendix A: Table of laws, regulations, and treaties

Administrative Litigation Law of the PRC (1989), CCH Australia Ltd, *Laws for Foreign Business*, (hereafter, "CCH"), paras 19–558.

Administrative Measures of the People's Bank of China on Establishment in China of Resident Representative Offices by Foreign Financial Institutions (1991), CCH paras 7–542.

Administrative Measures on Foreign Investment Financial Institutions (1994), CCH paras 8–692.

Administrative Protection of Pharmaceutical Regulations (1993), *China Law & Practice*, March 25, 1993, p. 37.

Administrative Reconsideration Law (1989), Beijing Xinhua Domestic Service (April 29, 1999), *FBIS Daily Report: China* (FBIS-CHI-1999–0512).

Administrative Supervision Law of the PRC (1997), Chinalaw.net (electronic service).

Agreement on Market Access Between the PRC and the United States of America (1989), USTR, November 15, 1999.

Agreement on Trade-Related Investment Measures (1994), World Trade Organization (ed.), *The Legal Texts: The Results of the Uruguay Round of Multilateral Trade Negotiations*, Cambridge: Cambridge University Press, 1999, p. 143.

Agreement on Trade-Related Aspects of Intellectual Property Rights (1994) *International Legal Materials*, 1994, vol. 33, p. 1197.

Announcement of the People's Bank of China on Further Reforming the Foreign Exchange Management System (December 28, 1993), *China Economic News* January 10, 1994, p. 9.

Anti-dumping and Anti-subsidy Rules of the PRC (1997), CCH paras 19–620.

Arbitration Law of the PRC (1994), CCH paras 10–470.

Beijing Municipality Patent Dispute Mediation Procedures (1988), *China Law & Practice*, August 21, 1989, p. 54.

Berne Convention for the Protection of Literary and Artistic Works, TIAS, WIPO Doc. 287(E). As revised at Stockholm 1967, UNTS 828/221.

Circular on Study of Administrative Procedure (1990), Beijing Xinhua English Service (January 15, 1990), *FBIS Daily Report: China*, January 19, 1990 at 20.

Civil Procedure Law of the PRC (1991), CCH paras 19–200.

Commercial Bank Law of the PRC (1995), CCH paras 8–350.

Company Law of the PRC (1994), *China Economic News*, Supplement No. 2, March 7, 1994.

Computer Software Protection Regulations of the PRC (1991), CCH paras 11–704.

Constitution of the PRC (1978, revised 1982, 1992, 1999), Beijing: Law Publishing, n.d.

Contract Law of the PRC (1999), *China Law & Practice*, May 1999, pp. 19–82.

Convention on Contracts for the International Sales of Goods, UN Doc. A/Conf.97/18, Annex I (1980), 19 *International Legal Materials*.

Convention on the Settlement of Disputes between States and the Nationals of Other States (1965), 575 UNTS 159.

Copyright Law of the PRC (1990, revised 2001), CCH paras 11–700.

CPC General Political Committee, "Suggestions Concerning Strengthening Resettlement and Training Work for Released Labor Reform and Labor Re-education Prisoners" (1995).

Criminal Law of the PRC (1997), Chinalaw website: www.qis.net/chinalaw.

Customs Law of the PRC (1987), CCH paras 50–300.

Decision of the State Council on Questions of Re-education and Rehabilitation Through Labor (1957).

Decision on the Use of Interim Regulations Concerning Value-Added Taxes, Consumption Taxes and Business Taxes on FFEs and Foreign Enterprises (1993), *China Economic News*, January 31, 1994, p. 7.

Detailed Implementing Rules for the Measures of Shanghai Municipality for the Administration of Special Renminbi-Denominated Shares (November 25, 1991), enacted by Shanghai Branch of the People's Bank of China, translation by Baker and McKenzie.

Detailed Implementing Rules of the Copyright Law of the PRC (1991), CCH paras 11–702.

Detailed Implementing Rules of the Trademark Law of the PRC (1983, revised 1988, 1993, 1995), CCH paras 11–510.

Detailed Rules for the Implementation of the Foreign Enterprise Income Tax Law of the PRC (Foreign Enterprise Income Tax Implementing Regulations) (1982), *China's Foreign Economic Legislation Vol. II*, Beijing: Foreign Languages Press, 1982, pp. 64–74.

Detailed Rules for the Implementation of the Individual Income Tax Law of the PRC (1980), CCH paras 300–520(4).

Detailed Rules for the Implementation of the Income Tax Law of the PRC for Joint Ventures with Chinese and Foreign Investment (1980), *China's Foreign Economic Legislation Vol. I*, Beijing: Foreign Languages Press, 1982, pp. 45–55.

Directive Concerning the Strict Prohibition on Parading on the Streets in front of the Masses Criminals who are about to be Executed (1986).

Economic Contract Law of the PRC (1981), Jerome A. Cohen, *Contract Laws of the PRC*, Hong Kong: Longman, 1988, pp. 49–61.

Enterprise Bankruptcy Law of the PRC [for trial implementation] (1986), CCH paras 13–522(4).

Establishment of Companies with an Investment Nature by Foreign Investors Tentative Provisions – Supplementary Provisions (August 24, 1999), *China Law & Practice,* October 1999, p. 23.

Explanation of Questions Related to Interim Provisions on Investment Companies Established with Foreign Investment (February 16, 1996).

Final Declaration of the Regional Meeting for Asia of the World Conference on Human Rights (Bangkok Declaration, April 2, 1993), *Human Rights Law Journal*, 1993, vol. 14, p. 370.

Foreign Economic Contract Law of the PRC (1985), CCH paras 5–550.

Foreign Enterprise Income Tax Law of the PRC (1981), *China's Foreign Economic Legislation Vol. I*, Beijing: Foreign Languages Press, 1982, pp. 55–63.

Foreign Trade Law of the PRC (1994), *China Economic News*, May 23, 1994, p. 8; May 30, 1994, p. 7.

GATT Working Party, Draft Protocol on China (1997).

General Agreement on Tariffs and Trade, *Basic Instruments and Selected Documents* (BISD).

General Agreement on Trade in Services (1994), World Trade Organization (ed.), *The Legal Texts: The Results of the Uruguay Round of Multilateral Trade Negotiations*, Cambridge: Cambridge University Press, 1999, p. 284.

General Office of the State Council Working Conference on Intellectual Property (ed.), Report of Chinese Enforcement Actions Under the 1995 IPR Agreement (June 17, 1996).

General Office of the State Council Working Conference on Intellectual Property (ed.), Status Report of the Enforcement of IPR Laws in China 1996 (May 1997).

General Office of the State Council Working Conference on Intellectual Property (ed.), 1999 White Paper on Intellectual Property Rights Enforcement (2000).

General Principles of Civil Law (1986), CCH paras 19–150.

Guangdong sheng gupiao zhaiquan guanli zanxing banfa (Provisional Methods of Guangdong Province for the Administration of Stocks and Bonds) September 30, 1986; *Zhonghua renmin gongheguo sifabu falu zhengce yanjiu shi* (Laws and Policy Research Office of the PRC Ministry of Justice); *Hengxiang jingji lianhe falu fa gui zhengce huibian* (Compilation of Laws and Statutes and Regulations on Horizontal Economic Linkages), Beijing, 1987, pp. 353–7.

Guangdong sheng jingji tequ tiaoli (Regulations of Guangdong Province for special economic zones) 1985; *Zhongguo jingji tequ kaifa qu falu fagui xuanbian* (Selection of Laws and Regulations for China's Special Economic Zones and Development Zones), Beijing: Zhanlan Publishing, 1987, p. 2.

Guanyu difang renmin zhengfu guiding ke xiang renmin fayuan qisu de xingzheng anjian fayuan ying fou shouli wenti de pi fu (Response to a Question as to Whether Courts Should Accept Administrative Cases of Local Government Regulations Submitted to the People's Courts for Litigation) 1987; *Zhonghua renmin gongheguo zui gao renmin fayuan gongbao* (PRC Supreme Court Bulletin), 1987, no. 4, p. ~22.

Guanyu faxing gupiao de zanxing guanli banfa (Provisional Methods for Issuing Stock) August 10, 1984; Shanghai Shi Renmin Zhengfu Bangongting (General Office of the Shanghai Municipal Government) and Shanghai Renmin Zhengfu Jingji Fagui Yanjiu Zhongxin (Economic Laws and Regulations Research Center of the Shanghai Municipal Government) (eds) *Shanghai shi fagui guizhang huibian – 1949–1985* (Compilation of Statutes and Regulations and Rules of Shanghai Municipality), Shanghai: Shanghai People's Press, 1986.

Guanyu moshou, chuli weifan zhi an guanli suode caiwu he shiyong gongju de zanxing guiding (Provisional Regulations on Confiscation and Handling of Property Obtained and Instrumentalities Used in Violation of Security Administration) December 20, 1986; *Xingzheng shenpan shouce* (Handbook on Administrative Adjudication), Beijing: People's Court Press, 1988, p. 789.

Guanyu [Shenzhen shi gupiao faxing yu jiaoyi guanli zanxing banfa] he [Shenzhen zhengquan jiaoyi suo zhangcheng} de pifu (Official Reply Concerning the Provisional

Methods of Shenzhen Municipality for the Issue and Transferring of Shares and the Articles of Association for the Shenzhen Securities Exchange, 1991), Document Yin Fu [1991] No. 154, April 11, 1991.

Guanyu zhi an guanli chufa zhong danbao ren he baozheng jin de zanxing guiding (Provisional Regulations on Guarantors and Guarantee Payments in Security Administration Punishments) December 20, 1986; *Xingzheng shenpan shouce* (Handbook on Administrative Adjudication), Beijing: People's Court Press, 1988, p. 787.

Gufen you xian gongsi guifan yijian (Opinion on Standards for Limited Liability Stock Companies), *Renmin ribao (People's Daily)*, June 19, 1992.

Guojia xingzheng jiguan gongzuo renyuan tanwu huilu xingzheng chufen zanxing guiding (Provisional Regulations on Handling Corruption by State Administrative Institution Officials), *Fazhi ribao* (Legal System Daily), September 14, 1989, p. 2.

Guojia xingzheng jiguan gongzuo renyuan tanwu huilu xingzheng chufen zanxing guiding shishi xize (Implementing Regulations for the Provisional Regulations on Handling Corruption by State Administrative Institution Officials) (1989), *Fazhi ribao* (Legal System Daily), September 14, 1989, p. 2.

Guowuyuan banggongting guanyu guanche shishi «Zhonghua renmin gongheguo zhongcai fa» xuyao mingque de jige wenti de tongzhi (Circular of the General Office of the State Council on Certain Issues to be Clarified on Implementing the Arbitration Law of the PRC), *Guowuyuan gongbao (State Council Bulletin)*, no. 18, July 9, 1996.

Guowuyuan xingzheng fagui zhiding chengxu zanxing tiaoli (Provisional Measures of the State Council on the Procedure for Enacting Administrative Regulations), 1987.

Guoying qiye laodong zhengyi chuli zanxing guiding (Regulations on Resolution of Labor Disputes in State Enterprises) 1987; *Siying qiye changyong falu shouce* (Handbook of Commonly Used Laws for Private Enterprises), Beijing: Law Publishing, 1988, p. 10.

Guoying qiye shixing laodong hetong zhi zanxing guiding (Provisional Regulations for Implementation of the Labor Contract System by State Enterprises) 1986; Song X. (ed.), *Shiyong laodong fa daquan* (Encyclopedia on the Use of Labor Law), Changchun: Jilin Documentary History Press, 1989, p. 58.

Implementation Rules of the Patent Law of the PRC (1992), CCH paras 11–603.

Implementing International Copyright Treaties Provisions (1992), *China Law & Practice*, January 14, 1993, p. 36.

Implementing Measures of the Ministry of Foreign Economic Relations and Trade Concerning Application for Import and Export Licenses by Foreign Investment Enterprises (1987), CCH paras 51–617.

Implementing Regulations Administrative Measures on Foreign Investment Financial Institutions (1996), CCH paras 8–693.

Implementing Regulations for the Law of the PRC on Import and Export Commodity Inspection (1992), CCH paras 52–525.

Implementing Regulations for the Law of the PRC on Joint Ventures Using Chinese and Foreign Investment (1983, revised 1986), CCH paras 6–550.

Implementing Rules for China's Law on Wholly Foreign Owned Enterprises (1990), *East Asian Executive Reports*, February 1991, p. 25.

Income Tax Law of the PRC Concerning Joint Ventures with Chinese and Foreign Investment (1980), *China's Foreign Economic Legislation Vol. I*, Beijing: Foreign Languages Press, 1982, pp. 36–44.

Income Tax Law of the PRC for Foreign Investment Enterprises and Foreign Enterprises (1991), CCH paras 32–505.

Individual Income Tax Law of the PRC (1980, revised 1993), CCH paras 30–500(4).

Interim Procedures Concerning Capital Accretion Through Additional Issues of B-Shares by Domestically Listed Companies, *China Economic News* 198, no. 22, June 15, 1998, pp. 8–10.

Interim Procedures Governing the Supply and Marketing of Goods and Materials by Experimental Shareholding Enterprises (1992), *FBIS Daily Report: China*, July 6, 1992, p. 58.

Interim Procedures on Administration of Securities and Futures Investment Consultancy (1998), *China Economic News* 16(4) (May 1998), pp. 7–12.

Interim Procedures on Control of Shenzhen Special (B-Type) RMB Stocks, *China Economic News*, January 27, 1992, p. 7.

Interim Procedures on Management of Stock Exchanges, (July 7, 1993), *China Economic News* 30 (August 9, 1993), pp. 6–9, and 31 (August 16, 1993), pp. 6–8.

Interim Provisions on Administering Land Assets of Experimental Shareholding Enterprises (July 9, 1992).

Interim Provisions on Management of the Issuing and Trading of Stocks, *China Economic News*, June 7, 1993, p. 7 and June 14, 1993, p. 7.

Interim Regulations Concerning the Control of Resident Offices of Foreign Enterprises (1980), CCH paras 7–500(4).

Interim Regulations Governing Labor and Wages in Enterprises Experimenting with Share-Holding Systems (June 1, 1992).

International Covenant on Civil and Political Rights (1966), 999 UNTS 171.

International Covenant on Economic, Social and Cultural Rights (1966), 993 UNTS 3.

Labor Law of the PRC (1994), *China Law & Practice*, August 29, 1994, pp. 21–36.

Land Administration Law of the PRC (1986, revised 1988, 1998), CCH paras 14–701.

Law of the PRC on Import and Export Commodity Inspection (1989), CCH paras 52–520.

Law of the PRC on Joint Ventures Using Chinese and Foreign Investment (1979, revised 1990, 2001), CCH paras 6–500.

Law of the PRC on Sino–Foreign Cooperative Enterprises (1988), CCH paras 6–100.

Law of the PRC on Wholly Foreign-Owned Enterprises (1986), CCH paras 13–506.

Legislation Law of the PRC (2000), *China Economic News* May 29, 2000, pp. 2–8.

Maritime Law of the PRC (1992), CCH paras 15–642.

Marrakech Agreement Establishing the World Trade Organization (1994), *International Legal Materials*, 1994, vol. 33, p. 1226.

Measures for the Administration of Foreign Securities-Based Organizations Representative Offices in China (1999), *FBIS Daily Report: China* (FBIS-CHI-1999–0614), June 15, 1999.

Measures of Shanghai Municipality for Administration of Special Renminbi-Denominated Shares (November 22, 1991), enacted by the People's Bank of China and the Shanghai Municipal Government, translation by Baker and McKenzie.

Memorandum of Understanding Between the Government of the PRC and the Government of the United States of America on the Protection of Intellectual Property (1992).

Ministry of Foreign Economic Cooperation and Trade (hereafter, "MOFTEC"), Note on Applications for Export Licenses (1996), CCH paras 51–640.

MOFTEC and SAIC, Administration of Trademarks in Foreign Trade Provisions, *China Law & Practice*, February 1996, p. 34.

MOFTEC Guiding Catalog on Foreign Investment (1998), *China Economic News*, Supplement No. 1, March 2, 1998.

MOFTEC Interim Provisions on Investment Companies Established with Foreign Investment (April 4, 1995), CCH paras 13–400.

MOFTEC Note on Applications for Export Licenses (1996), CCH paras 51–640.

MOFTEC Note on Applications for Import Licenses (1996), CCH paras 51–636.

MOFTEC Standard Rules for Applying for and Issuing Export Licenses (1999).

MOFTEC Supplementary Regulations on the Interim Provisions on Investment Companies Established with Foreign Investment (1999), CCH paras 13–402.

National People's Congress Standing Committee, Decision Regarding the Handling of Offenders Undergoing Reform through Labor and Persons Undergoing Rehabilitation through Labor who Escape or Commit New Crimes (1981).

New York Convention on Recognition and Enforcement of Foreign Arbitral Awards, 21 UST 2517; TIAS 6997; 330 UNTS 3.

Notice Concerning the Enforcement of United Nations Convention on the Recognition and Enforcement of Foreign Arbitral Awards Acceded to by Our Country, PRC Supreme People's Court, Circular No. 5, April 10, 1987.

Notice on Strictly Preventing Reactionary Publications from Using Our Execution of Criminals to Engage in Rumor-Mongering and Slander (1984).

Paris Convention for the Protection of Industrial Property (1984) (as updated by the Stockholm Act of 1967), 21 UST 1583; 24 UST 2140; TIAS 6923, 7727; 828 UNTS 107.

Patent Administrative Authority Adjudicating Patent Disputes Procedures (1989), *China Law & Practice*, May 7, 1990, p. 40.

Patent Law of the PRC (1985, revised 1993, 2000), CCH paras 11–600.

PRC Criminal Law (Amended) [excerpts], *China Law & Practice* June 1997, p. 39.

PRC Lawyers Law, *China Law & Practice*, July/August 1996, p. 31.

PRC Pricing Law, *China Law & Practice*, March 1998, p. 51.

PRC State Council Circular on Enacting Legislation Law, Beijing Xinhua Domestic Service (June 15, 2000), *FBIS Daily Report: China* (FBIS-CHI-2000–0615).

PRC, Administration of Urban Real Property Law, *China Law & Practice*, October 3, 1994, p. 23.

Prison Law of the PRC (1994), *National People's Congress Reports*, December 31, 1994, no. 8.

Procedures for Checking of Listed Companies, *China Economic News*, no. 6, February 17, 1997, pp. 7–8.

Procedures for Implementation of the Regulations on Labor Management in Joint Venture Enterprises (1984), Ministry of Labor *et al.*, *Laodong fa shouce* (Labor Law Handbook), Beijing: Economic Management Press, 1988, p. 290.

Procedures Governing Inspections over Imported Automobiles (2000), *China Economic News* no. 9, March 6, 2000, pp. 10–11.

Procedures of the People's Bank of China for the Establishment of Representative Offices in China by Overseas and Foreign Financial Institutions (1983), CCH paras 7–540(4).

Procedures on the Administration of Issuance and Transfer of Enterprise Bonds, *China Economic News* Supplement no. 6, June 22, 1998, pp. 1–10.

Provisional Measures for Dealing with the Release of Reform Through Labor Criminals at the Expiration of their Term of Imprisonment and for Placing Them and Getting Them Employed (n.d.).

Provisional Measures on Re-education and Rehabilitation through Labor (1982).

Provisional Regulations of the PRC Governing Foreign Exchange Control (1980), CCH paras 8–550.

Provisional Regulations on Auditing at Experimental Shareholding Enterprises, *FBIS Daily Report: China*, July 22, 1992, p. 37.

Provisional Regulations on License Control of Securities and Futures-Related Business Carried out by Certified Public Accountants, *China Economic News* no. 11, 23 March 1998, pp. 6–8; and no. 12, March 30, 1998, pp. 8–10.

Provisional Regulations on Several Issues Concerning the Establishment of Foreign Investment Enterprises Limited by Shares (1995), CCH paras 13–405.

Provisional Regulations on the Macroeconomic Control of Experimental Joint-Stock Enterprises in Regulations on Forming Joint-Stock Enterprises, *FBIS Daily Report: China*, July 14, 1992, p. 37.

Provisional Regulations on the Process of New Stock Issuances and Subscriptions, *China Economic News* no. 10, March 17, 1997, pp. 6–10.

Provisional Rules on the Import License System of the PRC (1984).

Provisions of the State Council of the PRC for the Encouragement of Foreign Investment (1986), *The China Business Review*, January–February 1987, pp. 14–15.

Qiye zhi gong shangwang shigu baogao he chuli guiding (Regulations on the Reporting and Resolution of Injuries and Accidents Involving Enterprise Workers and Staff) 1991; Xin S. and Ye X. (eds) *Xinbian changzhang jingli shiyong jingji falu quanshu* (Newly Compiled Compendium of Practical Economic Laws for Factory Directors and Managers), Beijing: Procuracy Press, 1993, p. 1787.

Quanguo renmin daibiao dahui changwu weiyuanhui guanyu chengzhi qinfan zhuzuoquan de fanzui de jueding (caoan) (Decision (draft) of the NPC Standing Committee on Punishing Crimes of Violating Copyright) February 4, 1994.

Quanguo renmin daibiao dahui changwu weiyuanhui guanyu shouquan Guangdong sheng, Fujian sheng renmin daibiao hui ji qita changwu weiyuanhui zhiding suo shu jingji tequ de ge xiang danxing jingji fagui de jueyi (Decision of the Standing Committee of the National People's Congress Authorizing the People's Congresses of Guangdong and Fujian Provinces and Their Standing Committees to Enact Various Specific Laws and Regulations for the Special Economic Zones under their Jurisdiction) 1981, in *Zhongguo jingji tequ kaifa qu falu fagui xuanbian* (Selection of Laws and Regulations for China's Special Economic Zones and Development Zones), Beijing: Zhanlan publishing, 1987, p. 1.

Quanmin suoyouzhi gongye qiye zhuanhuan jingying ji zhi tiaoli (Regulations for Transferring the Management Mechanism in the State-Owned Industrial Sectors) (1992); Xin S. and Ye X. (eds) *Xinbian changzhang jingli shiyong jingji falu quanshu* (Newly Compiled Compendium of Practical Economic Laws for Factory Directors and Managers), Beijing: Procuracy Press, 1993, p. 122.

Regulations Concerning Reconsideration of Administrative Measures, *FBIS Daily Report: China*, January 3, 1991, p. 20.

Regulations for Handling Labor Disputes (1993), *FBIS Daily Report: China*, August 2, 1993, p. 27.

Regulations on Administrative Reconsideration, Beijing Xinhua Domestic Service (October 13, 1994), *FBIS Daily Report: China* (FBIS-CHI-94–207), October 26, 1994, p. 28.

Regulations on Enterprises' Shareholding System Experiment (May 15, 1992).

Regulations on Export License Control (1996), *China Economic News* no. 23, June 24, 1996, pp. 5–8; and no. 24, July 1, 1996, pp. 6–8.

Regulations on Labor Management in Foreign Funded Enterprises (1994), *China Economic News*, March 13, 1995, p. 7.

Regulations on Labor Management in Joint Venture Enterprises (1990), Ministry of Labor *et al.*, *Laodong fa shouce* (Labor Law Handbook), Beijing: Economic Management Press, 1988, p. 288.

Regulations on Social Organizations, Beijing Xinhua Domestic Service (November 3, 1998), *FBIS Daily Report: China* (FBIS-CHI-98–309), November 5, 1998.

Regulations on Stock Issuance Approval Commission, Beijing Xinhua Domestic Service (October 13, 1999), *FBIS Daily Report: China* (FBIS-CHI-1999–1206), December 8, 1999.

Report on Just Implementation of Law by PRC's People's Courts (1999), Beijing Xinhua Domestic Service (March 11, 2000), *FBIS Daily Report: China* (FBIS-CHI-2000–0311) March 30, 2000.

Rules for the Implementation of Foreign Exchange Controls Relating to Enterprises with Overseas Chinese Capital, Enterprises with Foreign Capital, and Chinese/Foreign Equity Joint Ventures (1983), CCH paras 8–670.

Rules for the Implementation of the Interim Procedures on Control of Shenzhen Special (B-Type) RMB Stocks, *China Economic News*, 3 February 1992, p. 7.

Secured Interests Law of the PRC (1995), CCH paras 5–605.

Securities Law of the PRC (1998), *China Economic News* 1999, Supplement No. 3, March 15, 1999, pp. 1–18.

Several Questions Concerning the Establishment of Foreign Investment Companies Limited by Shares Tentative Provisions (January 10, 1995), *China Law & Practice*, August 11, 1995, p. 52.

Shangbiao guanli tiaoli (Administrative Regulations for Trademarks), Trademark Office of the State Administration for Industry and Commerce, *Shangbiao fagui ziliao xuanbian* (Selected Laws and Regulations and Materials on Trademarks), Beijing: Law Publishing, 1985, p. 52.

Shanghai Municipality, PRC Land Administration Law Implementing Measures, *China Law & Practice*, December 15, 1994, pp. 32–49.

Shanghai Patent Dispute Mediation Tentative Procedures (1988), *China Law & Practice*, August 21, 1989, p. 59.

Shanghai Securities Transaction Regulations, *FBIS Daily Report: China*, December 20, 1990, p. 46.

Shanghai shi zhengquan jiaoyi guanli banfa (Methods of Shanghai Municipality for Administration of Securities Transactions), *Jiefang ribao* (*Liberation Daily*), December 12, 1990, p. 3.

Shanghai zhengquan jiaoyi suo jiaoyi shichang yewu shixing guize (Trial Regulations of the Shanghai Securities Exchange on the Activities of the Exchange Market)

November 26, 1990, Shanghai: Shanghai Securities Exchange Board of Directors, 1990.

Shenzhen shi gupiao faxing yu jiaoyi guanli zanxing banfa (Provisional Methods of Shenzhen Municipality for the Issue and Transferring of Shares) May 15, 1991.

Shenzhen shi renmin zhengfu «Guanyu chengli Shenzhen shi zhengquan shichang Lingdao Xiaozu» de tongzhi (Notice of the Shenzhen Municipal People's Government Concerning the Establishment of the Leading Small Group for the Shenzhen Securities Market), *Shenzhen Zhengquan Shichang Nianbao, 1990* (Annual Report on Shenzhen Securities Market, 1990), p. 229.

Shenzhen zhengquan jiaoyi suo zhangcheng (Articles of Association for the Shenzhen Securities Exchange) (1991).

Siying qiye laodong guanli zanxing guiding (Provisional Regulations on Labor Management in Private Enterprises) (1989), *Laodong fa yu laodong zhengyi shiyong shouce* (Practical Handbook on Labor Law and Labor Disputes), Beijing: China Economy Press, 1994, p. 672.

Standing Committee of the National People's Congress, Amendment of the Trademark Law Decision (1993), *China Law & Practice*, April 29, 1993, p. 42.

State Compensation Law of the PRC, Beijing Xinhua Domestic Service May 12, 1994, *FBIS Daily Report: China* (FBIS CHI-94–096), May 18, 1994, pp. 33–7.

State Council Circular on Further Strengthening Macro-Control of Securities Markets, *FBIS Daily Report: China*, January 25, 1993, p. 24.

State Council Information Office, "Text of Human Rights White Paper," *FBIS Daily Report: China* (Supplement), November 21, 1991.

State Council Information Office, "The Progress of Human Rights in China," Xinhua Domestic Service, December 27, 1995, *FBIS Daily Report: China*, December 28, 1996, pp. 8–26.

State Council Information Office, "White Paper: Fifty Years of Progress in China's Human Rights," February 2000.

State Council Regulations for Handling Labor Disputes, *FBIS Daily Report: China*, August 2, 1993, p. 27.

State Regulations on Shareholding Experiment, *FBIS Daily Report: China*, June 22, 1992, p. 31.

State Secrecy Protection Regulations for Computer Information Systems on the Internet (2000), China Online.

Stipulations on Labor Contracts for Shanghai Municipality, *Shanghai Legal System*, December 18, 1995.

Stock Exchange Administration Procedures, *China Law & Practice*, July 1996, p. 9.

Supplementary Operating Rules for the Trading Market (Special Renminbi-Denominated Shares) of the Shanghai Securities Exchange (February 18, 1992), enacted by the Shanghai Securities Exchange, translation by Baker and McKenzie.

Supplementary Provisions on Re-education and Rehabilitation through Labor (1979).

Supreme People's Court, Disposal by Different Levels of People's Courts of Applications for Review in Civil and Economic Cases Tentative Provisions (1989), *China Law & Practice*, December 11, 1989, p. 38.

Supreme People's Court, Explanation of Several Questions Concerning the Application of the Foreign Economic Contract Law (October 19, 1987), *China Law & Practice*, May 2, 1988, pp. 52–64.

Supreme People's Court, *Guanyu guanche zhixing «Minshi susong fa (caoan)» ruogan wenti de yijian* (Opinion on Several Issues of Fully Implementing the "Civil Procedure Law (Draft)", August 30, 1984, *Minshi falu shiyong daquan* (Practical Compendium on Civil Law), Beijing: People's University Press, 1990, pp. 644–58.

Supreme People's Court, *Guanyu guanche zhixing «Minshi susong fa» ruogan wenti de yijian* (Opinion on Several Issues of Fully Implementing the "Civil Procedure Law"), July 14, 1992, *Zhonghua renmin gongheguo zui gao renmin fayuan gongbao* (PRC Supreme Court Bulletin), 1992, no. 3, p. 70.

Supreme People's Court, *Guanyu guanche zhixing «Zhonghua renmin gongheguo min fa tongze» ruogan wenti de yijian (shixing)* (Trial Opinion on Certain Questions Concerning the Full Implementation of the General Principles of Civil Law of the PRC), January 26, 1988, *Zhonghua renmin gongheguo zui gao renmin fayuan gongbao* (PRC Supreme Court Bulletin) (1988), No. 2, at 17.

Supreme People's Court, *Guanyu guanche zhixing minshi zhengce falu ruogan wenti de yijian* (Opinion on Various Issues of Fully Implementing Civil Policy and Law), August 30, 1984, *Minshi falu shiyong daquan* (Practical Compendium on Civil Law), Beijing: People's University Press 1990, pp. 66–80.

Supreme People's Court, *Guanyu quanguo jingji shenpan gongzuo zuotanhui jiyao (jielu)* (Outline of Work Conference on Economic Adjudication – excerpts), n.d., Economic Adjudication Chamber of the Supreme People's Court (ed.), *Hetong fa shijie yu shiyong* (Interpretation and Application of Contract Law), Beijing: Xinhua Press, 1999, p. 1693.

Supreme People's Court, *Guanyu renmin fayuan shenli jingji xingzheng anjian bu ying jinxing tiaojie de tongzhi* (Notice Concerning People's Courts Not Conducting Mediation in Handling Economic Administrative Cases), Zui gao renmin fayuan yanjiu shi (Research Office of the Supreme People's Court), November 6, 1985, *Xingzheng shenpan shouce* (Handbook on Administrative Adjudication), Beijing: People's Court Press, 1988, p. 784.

Supreme People's Court, *Guanyu renzhen xuexi xuanchuan guanche xiuding de «Zhonghua renmin gongheguo xingfa» de tongzhi* (Notice on Serious Studying, Propagandizing and Fully Implementing the Revised Criminal Law of the PRC), March 25, 1997.

Supreme People's Court, *Guanyu shiyong «Shewai jingji hetong fa» ruogan wenti de jieda* (Interpretation and Answer on Several Issues in Application of the Foreign Economic Contract Law) October 19, 1987, *Minshi falu shiyong daquan* (Practical Compendium on Civil Law), Beijing: People's University Press, 1990, pp. 368–73.

Supreme People's Court, *Guanyu shiyong «Zhonghua renmin gongheguo minshi susong fa» ruogan wenti de yijian* (Opinion on Several Issues of Using the Civil Procedure Law of the PRC), n.d., Civil Adjudication Chamber of the Supreme People's Court (ed.), *Minshi shouce* (Handbook on Civil Affairs), Beijing: People's Court Press, 1994, p. 74.

Supreme People's Court, *Guanyu zai jingji shenpan gongzuo zhong guanche zhixing «Minshi susong fa {shi xing}» ruogan wenti de yijian* (Opinion on Several Questions of Fully Implementing the Civil Procedure Law [For Trial Implementation] During the Course of Economic Adjudication Work), September 17, 1984, *Minshi falu shiyong daquan* (Practical Compendium on Civil Law), Beijing: People's University Press, 1990, pp. 658–63.

Supreme People's Court, *Guanyu zhixing «Zhonghua renmin gongheguo xingshi susong fa» ruogan wenti de jieshi* (Interpretation on Certain Issues Related to the Implementation of the Criminal Procedure Law of the PRC), *Zhongguo fazhi bao (China Legal System Gazette)*, September 9, 1998, p. 1.

Supreme People's Court, Implementing International Treaties Provisions, *China Law & Practice* January 14, 1993, p. 36.

Supreme People's Court, Several Issues Concerning Application of the PRC Contract Law Interpretation (1), *China Law & Practice*, March 2000.

Supreme People's Court, People's Bank of China, *Guanyu fayuan dui xingzheng jiguan yi fa shenqing qiangzhi zhixing xuyao yinhang xiezhu zhixing de anjian ying ruhe banli wenti de lianhe tongzhi* (Joint Notice Concerning Questions as to how to Handle Cases where Administrative Organs Apply According to Law for Compulsory Enforcement and Request the Banks to Assist in Enforcement), January 11, 1989, *Zhonghua renmin gongheguo zui gao renmin fayuan gongbao* (PRC Supreme Court Bulletin), 1989, no. 1, p. 17.

Supreme People's Court, Supreme People's Procuracy, and Ministry of Public Security, Notice on Resolutely Putting a Stop to [the Practice of] Parading Through the Street and Exhibiting to the Public Convicted and Not-Yet-Convicted Criminals (1988).

Temporary Provisions on Issues Concerning Tax Revenue of Experimental Shareholding Enterprises (June 12, 1992), *FBIS Daily Report: China*, July 6, 1992, p. 57.

Temporary Provisions on Several Issues Concerning Financial Management in Experimental Shareholding Enterprises (June 27, 1992) *FBIS Daily Report: China*, July 6, 1992, p. 52.

Text of PRC Constitutional Amendment, Beijing Xinhua Domestic Service, March 16, 1999, *FBIS Daily Report – China* (FBIS-CHI-1999–0316).

Trademark Law of the PRC (1982, revised 1993), CCH paras 11–500.

UN Convention on Collection of Evidence Abroad, TIAS 7444; 847 UNTS 231.

UN Convention on Service Abroad of Judicial and Extrajudicial Documents in Civil or Commercial Matters, TIAS 6638; 658 UNTS 163.

Understanding on Rules and Procedures Governing the Settlement of Disputes (1994), *International Legal Materials*, 1994, vol. 33, p. 1226.

Understanding on the Interpretation of Article XXIV of the General Agreement on Tariffs and Trade (1994), *International Legal Materials*, 1994, vol. 33, p. 1161.

Universal Copyright Convention (1992), 6 UST 2731; TIAS 3324; 216 UNTS 132. As revised 1971, 25 UST 1341; TIAS 7868.

Universal Declaration of Human Rights (1948), UNGA Res. 217 (III), UN GAOR, Third Session, Supplement No. 13 at 71, UN Doc a/810.

Various Opinions of the Ministry of Labor on Collective Bargaining in Foreign-Funded Enterprises (1997), *China Law & Practice*, November 1997, p. 25.

Various Regulations on Adjusting the Import and Export Licensing Administration (1988).

World Intellectual Property Organization Convention, 21 UST 1749; TIAS 6932; 828 UNTS 3.

Xingzheng fagui zhiding chengxu zanxing tiaoli (Provisional Regulations on the Procedures for Enacting Administrative Laws and Regulations), State Council, April 21, 1987.

Xingzheng fuyi tiaoli (Regulations on Administrative Reconsideration), *Fazhi ribao* (Legal System Daily) December 28, 1990.

Zhengquan shichang lingdao xiaozu huiyi jiyao (xuandeng san) (Summary of Minutes of the Leading Small Group of the Shenzhen Securities Market – Selection Three), *Shenzhen Zhengquan Shichang Nianbao 1990* (Annual Report on the Shenzhen Securities Market 1990), p. 113.

Zhongguo gonghui zhangcheng (Charter of China's Trade Unions), *Gonghui fa shouce* (Handbook of Trade Union Law), Beijing: Democracy and Legal System Press, 1994, p. 380.

Zhongguo Renmin Yinhang Shanghai Shi Fenhang guanyu faxing gupiao de zanxing guanli fangfa (Provisional Methods of the Shanghai Municipal Branch of the People's Bank of China Concerning the Issuance of Stock), Guo Zhenying (ed.), *Zhongguo shehui zhuyi gufen jingji wen da* (Questions and Answers on China's Socialist Share Economy), Beijing: Aeronautics Academy Press, 1986, p. 361.

Zhongguo wuquan fa (caoan) (Chinese Property Law (draft)), Liang Huixing (ed.), *Zhongguo wuquanfa caoan jianyi gao* (Outline of Opinion on a Draft Chinese Property Law), Beijing: Social Science Manuscripts Press, 2000, p. 5.

Zhonghua renmin gongheguo baoshou guojia mimi fa (Law of the PRC on Protecting State Secrets), 1989, State Council Legal Affairs Bureau (ed.), *Zhonghua renmin gongheguo xin fagui huibian* (New Compilation of Laws and Regulations of the PRC), Beijing: Xinhua Press, 1988, no. 2, pp. 16–22.

Zhonghua renmin gongheguo baoshou guojia mimi fa shishi banfa (Implementing Methods for Law of the PRC on Protecting State Secrets) (1990), State Council Legal Affairs Bureau (ed.), *Zhonghua renmin gongheguo xingzheng fagui quanshu* (Compendium of Administrative Laws and Regulations of the PRC), Beijing: Xinhua Press, 1993, p. 1401.

Zhonghua renmin gongheguo cujin keji chengguo zhuanhua fa (jielu) (Law of the PRC on Promoting Dissemination of the Technical Results – Excerpts), Economic Adjudication Chamber of the Supreme People's Court (ed.), *Hetong fa shijie yu shiyong* (Interpretation and Application of Contract Law), Beijing: Xinhua Press, 1999, p. 1690.

Zhonghua renmin gongheguo faguan fa (Judges Law of the PRC) (1995), State Council Legal Affairs Bureau (ed.), *Zhonghua renmin gongheguo fagui huibian* (hereafter "State Council *Fagui huibian*") (Compilation of Laws and Regulations of the PRC 1993), 1–12, Beijing: Xinhua Press, 1996, p. 58.

Zhonghua renmin gongheguo gonghui fa (Trade Union Law of the PRC), 1992, *Gonghui fa shouce* (Handbook of Trade Union Law), Beijing: Democracy and Legal System Press, 1994, p. 63.

Zhonghua renmin gongheguo guojia anquan fa (National Security Law of the PRC) (1993), State Council *Fagui huibian* (Compilation of Laws and Regulations of the PRC 1993), 1–12, Beijing: Law Publishing, 1994, p. 5.

Zhonghua renmin gongheguo hetong fa lifa fangan (Legislative Proposal for PRC Contract Law), *Zhengda faxue pinglun* (Chengchi University Jurisprudence and Discussion), 1995, no. 53, pp. 433–43.

Zhonghua renmin gongheguo hetong fa shiyi gao (Tentative Draft Contract Law of the PRC), Civil Law Office of the NPC Standing Committee Legal Affairs Committee (ed.), *«Zhonghua renmin gongheguo hetong fa» ji qi zhongyao caogao jieshao* (Introduction to the Contract Law of the PRC and its Important Drafts), Beijing: Law Publishing, 1999, pp. 15–100.

Zhonghua renmin gongheguo jingji hetong fa tongze (General Principles of PRC Economic Contract Law), September 22, 1992.

Zhonghua renmin gongheguo jingji hetong zhongcai tiaoli (Regulations of the PRC on Arbitration of Economic Contracts), August 22, 1983, *Guowuyuan gongbao* (State Council Gazette), 1983, p. 803.

Zhonghua renmin gongheguo jishu hetong fa (Technology Contracts Law of the PRC), State Council *Fagui huibian* (Compilation of Laws and Regulations of the PRC) 1987, 1–12, Beijing: Law Publishing, 1988, p. 873.

Zhonghua renmin gongheguo jixuanji xinxi wangluo guoji lianwang guanli zanxing guiding (Provisional Regulations of the PRC on Administration of Computer Information Systems and the International Internet) (1996).

Zhonghua renmin gongheguo min fa tongze (General Principles of Civil Law of the PRC), *Renmin ribao – hai wai ban* (*People's Daily* – overseas edition), April 17, 1986, p. 2.

Zhonghua renmin gongheguo minshi susong fa (shi xing) (Civil Procedure Law of the PRC [for Trial Implementation]), *Renmin ribao* (*People's Daily*), March 11, 1982.

Zhonghua renmin gongheguo quanmin suo you zhi gongye qiye fa (Law of the PRC on Enterprises Owned by the Whole People), State Council Legal Affairs Bureau (ed.), *Zhonghua renmin gongheguo xin fagui huibian* (Compilation of New PRC Laws and Regulations), Beijing: Xinhua Press, 1988, no. 1, p. 27.

Zhonghua renmin gongheguo renmin fayuan zuzhi fa (Organization Law of the PRC for the People's Courts), Legal System Work Committee of the NPC Standing Committee (ed.), *Zhonghua renmin gongheguo falu ji youguan fagui huibian – 1979–1984* (Compilation of Law and Related Regulations of the PRC – 1979–1984), Beijing: Law Publishing, 1984, pp. 77–86.

Zhonghua renmin gongheguo siying qiye zanxing guiding (Provisional Regulations of the PRC on Privately Managed Enterprises), 1988, Law and Regulation Editorial Office of Law Publishing House (ed.), *Siying qiye changyong falu shouce* (Handbook of Commonly Used Laws on Private Enterprises), Beijing: Law Publishing, 1988, pp. 1–9.

Zhonghua renmin gongheguo xingshi susong fa (Criminal Procedure Law of the PRC), 1996, *Renmin ribao* (*People's Daily*), March 25, 1996, p. 2.

Zhonghua renmin gongheguo zhengquan fa (Securities Law of the PRC), 1998, *Fazhi ribao* (*Legal System Daily*), December 30, 1998, pp. 2–3.

Notes

Introduction

1 See "Zhongguo gongchandang di shi yi jie zhongyang weiyuanhui di san ci quanti huiyi gongbao" (Communiqué of the Third Plenum of the Eleventh CCP Central Committee), *Hongqi* (Red Flag), 1979, no. 1, pp. 14–21.

Chapter 1

1 See Peng Zhen, "Guanyu shehui zhuyi fazhi de jige wenti" (Several Issues Concerning the Socialist Legal System), speech to Central Party School, September 1, 1979, in *Hongqi* (Red Flag), no. 11, p. 3. In his speech to the founding meeting of the China Law Society, Peng Zhen specifically urged that the foreign serve China and the past serve the present (*yang wei zhong yong, gu wei jin yong*). See "Zhongguo faxuehui zai jing zhengshi chengli" (The China Law Society Is Formally Established in Beijing), *Faxue yanjiu* (Studies in Law), 1982, no. 5, p. 8.

2 See generally, S. Leng and H. Chiu, *Criminal Justice in Post-Mao China*, Albany: State University of New York Press, 1985.

3 See J.V. Feinerman, "Legal Institution, Administrative Device, or Foreign Import: The Roles of Contract in the People's Republic of China," in P.B. Potter (ed.), *Domestic Law Reforms in Post-Mao China*, Armonk, NY, and London: M.E. Sharpe, 1994; P.B. Potter, *The Economic Contract Law of the PRC: Legitimacy and Contract Autonomy in China*, Seattle and London: University of Washington Press, 1992.

4 See Wang Liming (ed.), *Minshang fa yanjiu* (Studies in Civil and Commercial Law), Beijing: Law Publishing, 1998; A.H.Y. Chen, "The Developing Chinese Law and the Civil Law Tradition," in M. Brosseau, S. Pepper, and S.K. Tsang (eds) *China Review 1996*, Hong Kong: Chinese University Press, 1996, pp. 29–59; E.J. Epstein, "Codification of Civil Law in the People's Republic of China: Form and Substance in the Reception of Concepts and Elements of Western Private Law," *University of British Columbia Law Review*, 1998, vol. 32, no. 1, pp. 153–98; W.C. Jones, "The Significance of the Opinion of the Supreme People's Court for Civil Law in China," in P.B. Potter (ed.), *op. cit.*; *ibid.*, "Some Questions Regarding the Significance of the General Provisions of Civil Law of the People's Republic of China," *Harvard Journal of International Law*, 1987, vol. 28, p. 311.

5 See "Renmin Ribao Discusses Civil Procedure Law," *Beijing Renmin Ribao*, March 11, 1982, in *FBIS Daily Report: China*, March 16, 1982, p. K1; "Jurist Answers Questions on Civil Procedure Law," Beijing Xinhua Domestic Service,

March 14, 1982, in *FBIS Daily Report: China*, March 16, 1982, p. K3. Also see Jiang Liu, "Min su fa de lifa yuanze yu guoqing" (Legislative Principles and National Conditions in the Civil Procedure Law), *Faxue* (Jurisprudence), 1982, no. 5, pp. 30–2; "Trial Implementation of Civil Procedure Law Initiated," *Beijing Renmin Ribao*, March 29, 1982, in *China Report: Political, Social, Military*, May 12, 1982, p. 90; Jiang Wei, "Minshi susong fa gai shuo" (Speaking Conceptually of the Civil Procedure Law), *Bai ke zhishi* (Encyclopedia of Knowledge), 1982, no. 1, pp. 6–9.

6 See generally, *The China Quarterly Special Issue: China's Legal Reforms*, no. 141, 1995. On environmental law, see L. Ross and M.A. Silk, "Environmental Law and Policy in China," *Chinese Law and Government*, Spring 1986; V. Smil, "China's Environmental Morass," *Current History*, September 1989. On business regulation, see J.V. Feinerman, "Economic and Legal Reform in China, 1978–91," *Problems of Communism*, September–October 1991, pp. 62–75; P.B. Potter, *Foreign Business Law in China: Past Progress, Future Challenges*, San Francisco: 1990 Institute, 1995. On intellectual property, see Zheng C. (with M. Pendleton), *Chinese Intellectual Property and Technology Transfer Law*, London, Sweet & Maxwell, 1987. On dispute resolution, see Asia Law and Practice (ed.), *Dispute Resolution in the PRC*, Hong Kong, Asia Law and Practice, 1995; A. Crawford and C. Salbaing, "Resolving International Commercial Disputes in China," in Streng and Wilcox (eds), *Doing Business in China*, looseleaf, interjura.

7 There are many examples of participants in these programs going on to exert significant influence on legal norms. See, e.g., Jiang Bixin (participant in the Canadian Development Agency's Senior Judges Training Program Supreme People's Court Administrative Tribunal) (ed.), *Xingzheng susong yu tudi guanlifa: xin jie* (Administrative Litigation of Land Administration Law: New Interpretations), Beijing: Current Events Press, 1999; Wang Liming (participant in the Ford Foundation's Committee on Legal Educational Exchanges with China) (ed.), *Minshang fa yanjiu* (Studies in Civil and Commercial Law), *op. cit.*; Wang Weiguo (participant in education exchanges with Sweden and Canada), "Lun hetong wuxiao zhidu" (On the System for Invalidating Contracts), *Faxue yanjiu* (Studies in Law), 1994, no. 3, pp. 11–24; and Shen Zongling (participant in exchanges with the United States and Canada) (ed.), *Lifaxue yu bijiaofa lunji* (Theoretical Compilation on Jurisprudence and Comparative Law), Beijing: Peking University Press, 1999. Numerous Chinese judges have had training or experience on exchange programs abroad, including Luo Haocai, Cao Jianming, and Ma Huaide (Supreme People's Court), and Lu Guoqiang (Shanghai High Court). Many deans and senior law professors have similar training, including Yu Jinsong (Wuhan University), Xin Chunying (CASS Law Institute), Wu Zhipan (Peking University), Wang Chenguang (Tsinghua University), Li Changdao (Fudan University), Li Buyun (CASS Law Institute), and Fang Liufang (Chinese University of Politics and Law). Thanks to Jim Feinerman for assistance in compiling these last references.

8 See Geng Cheng, "Shichang jingji yu fazhi de guojihua" (Internationalization of the Market Economy and Legal System), *Jingji fazhi* (Economic Legal System), 1994, no. 11, pp. 2–4; Chen An, "Lun shiyong guoji guan lie yu you fa bi yi de tongyi" (On the Unity of Using International Custom and Usage and Having Law to Follow), *Zhongguo shehui kexue* (Chinese Social Science), 1994, no. 4, pp. 77–90; Guo Daohui, "Shichang jingji yu faxue lilun fazhi guannian de bianhua" (Market Economy and the Change in Legal Theory and Concepts of the Legal System), *Faxue* (Jurisprudence), 1994, no. 2, pp. 2–6; and Shen Zongling, "Dangdai zhongguo jiejian waiguo falu de shili" (Examples of Borrowing Foreign Law in Contemporary China), *Zhongguo faxue* (Chinese Jurisprudence),

1997, no. 5, pp. 22–40. Also see Committee on Scholarly Communication with China (ed.), *China Exchange News Special Issue: Law and Legal Studies in the People's Republic of China*, 1994.

9 See, e.g., Wang Liming, "Lun wanshan qinquan fa yu zhuangjian fazhi shehui de guanxi" (On the Relationship between Perfecting Tort Law and Building a Society Ruled by Law), *Faxue pinglun* (Legal Studies Commentary), 1992, no. 1, pp. 4–19; Kong Yangjun and Yang Yu, "Qinquan zeren yaojian yanjiu" (Research on the Requirements for Tortious Liability) (parts 1 and 2), *Zhengfa luntan* (Politics and Law Forum), 1993, no. 1, pp. 42–7, and no. 2, pp. 50–5 and 71.

10 See generally, Wang Zejian, "Taiwan de minfa yu shichang jingji" (Taiwan's Civil Law and Market Economy), *Faxue yanjiu* (Studies in Law), 1993, no. 2, pp. 62–78; Zhuang Jingfeng, "Taiwan touze lifa jidian zhide jiajian de jingyan" (Experience of Various Direct Borrowings from Taiwan Investment Legislation), *Zhongguo faxue* (Chinese Jurisprudence), 1989, no. 4, pp. 74–9.

11 See generally, K. Jayasuriya (ed.), *Law, Capitalism and Power in Asia*, London: Routledge, 1999; A. Woodiwiss, *Globalization, Human Rights and Labour Law in Pacific Asia*, Cambridge: Cambridge University Press, 1998; T. Ginsburg, "Does Law Matter for Economic Development?" *Law & Society Review*, 2000, vol. 34, no. 3, pp. 829–56; D. Trubek *et al.*, "Global Restructuring and the Law: The Internationalization of Legal Fields and the Creation of Transnational Arenas," working paper, University of Wisconsin-Madison, 1993; James A. Gardner, *Legal Imperialism: American Lawyers and Foreign Aid in Latin America*, Madison: University of Wisconsin Press, 1980.

12 See generally, "Property: Questioning Efficiency, Liberty and Imperialism," in N. Mercuro and W.J. Samuels (eds), *The Fundamental Interrelationships Between Government and Property*, Stamford, Conn.: JAI Press, 1999, pp. 177–90; D. Barry and R.C. Keith, *Regionalism, Multilateralism and the Politics of Global Trade*, Vancouver: University of British Columbia Press, 1999; F. Jameson and M. Miyoshi (eds) *The Cultures of Globalization*, Durham, NC: Duke University Press, 1998; F.J. Lechner and J. Boli (eds) *The Globalization Reader*, Malden, Mass.: Blackwell, 2000; F. Rajaee, *Globalization on Trial: The Human Condition and the Information Civilization*, Ottawa: International Development Research Centre, 2000; and J. Tomlinson, *Globalization and Culture*, Chicago: University of Chicago Press, 1999.

13 D. Kennedy, "Receiving the International," *Connecticut Journal of International Law*, 1994, vol. 10(1), p. 1.

14 See generally, G.W. Noble and J. Ravenhill (eds), *The Asian Financial Crisis and the Architecture of Global Finance*, Cambridge: Cambridge University Press, 2000; and G. Segal and D.S.G. Goodman (eds), *Towards Recovery in Pacific Asia*, London: Routledge, 2000. For discussion of the applicability of liberal models of financial regulation to developing economies, see S. Haggard and C.H. Lee, *Financial Systems and Economic Policy in Developing Countries*, Ithaca, NY: Cornell University Press, 1995; and S. Haggard, C.H. Lee, and S. Maxfield (eds), *The Politics of Finance in Developing Countries*, Ithaca, NY: Cornell University Press, 1993.

15 R.H. Wagner, "Economic Interdependence, Bargaining Power and Political Influence," *International Organization*, 1988, vol. 42(3), p. 461.

16 Citations for all laws, regulations, and treaties are provided in Appendix A: Table of Laws, Regulations, and Treaties.

17 See L.M. Friedman, *The Legal System: A Social Science Perspective*, Englewood Cliffs, NJ: Prentice Hall, 1975, p. 15.

18 See H.W. Ehrmann, *Comparative Legal Cultures*, Englewood Cliffs, NJ: Prentice Hall, 1976, pp. 6 *et seq.*

19 See S.B. Lubman, "Studying Contemporary Chinese Law: Limits, Possibilities and Strategy," *American Journal of Comparative Law*, 1991, vol. 36, p. 333.

20 See M.A. Glendon, *Comparative Legal Systems*, St Paul, Minn.: West, 1985.

21 See C. Varga (ed.), *Comparative Legal Cultures*, Aldershot: Dartmouth, 1992. Interestingly, Paul Bohannon's seminal work on "double institutionalization" in the anthropology of law is included in Varga's collection only as the focus of Diamond's critique.

22 For a discussion of "reception" as a process by which adherence to proposed norms proceeds based on an underlying affinity with existing social values, see R.M. Unger, *Knowledge and Politics*, New York: Free Press, 1975.

23 See M. McAuley, "Political Culture and Communist Politics: One Step Forward Two Steps Back," in A. Brown (ed.), *Political Culture and Communist Studies*, Hampshire and London: Macmillan, 1984, p. 31.

24 See P. Bohannon, "The Differing Realms of Law," *American Anthropologist*, December 1965, vol. 67, no. 6, p. 33. Also see A.S. Diamond, "The Rule of Law Versus the Order of Custom," in D. Black and M. Mileski (eds), *The Social Organization of Law*, New York and London: Seminar Press, 1973, p. 318; and H.J. Berman, *Law and Revolution: The Formation of the Western Legal Tradition*, Cambridge, Mass., and London: Harvard University Press, 1983, p. 79.

25 See C. Geertz, "Ideology as a Cultural System," in D.E. Apter (ed.), *Ideology and Discontent*, New York: Free Press; London: Collier-Macmillan, 1964, p. 64.

26 See O. Seliktar, "Identifying a Society's Belief Systems," in M. Herman (ed.), *Political Psychology*, San Francisco and London: Jossey-Bass, 1986, pp. 321–2.

27 See generally, S.N. Eisenstadt and L. Roniger, *Patrons, Clients and Friends: Interpersonal Relations and the Structure of Trust in Society*, Cambridge: Cambridge University Press, 1984; and R.K. Merton, *Social Theory and Social Structure* (revised and enlarged edition), New York: Free Press, 1965, reprinted in R.M. Cover and O.M. Fiss, *The Structure of Procedure*, Mineola, NY: Foundation Press, 1979, p. 377.

28 See generally, K. Lieberthal, *Governing China: From Revolution through Reform*, New York and London: W.W. Norton, 1995. For a discussion of earlier views, see S.N. Eisenstadt, "Tradition, Change and Modernity: Reflections on the Chinese Experience," in P. Ho and T. Tsou (eds), *China in Crisis*, Chicago: University of Chicago Press, 1968, pp. 753–74.

29 See, e.g., Gong Piyang, "Zhongguo fa zhi xiandaihua mianju de si da maodun" (Four Major Contradictions in the Modernization of Chinese Law), *Tansuo yu zhengming* (Inquiry and Debate), 1995, no. 3, pp. 3–6.

30 See generally, A. Kent, *Between Freedom and Subsistence: Human Rights in China*, Hong Kong: Oxford University Press, 1993; and D.E. Christensen, "Breaking the Deadlock: Toward a Socialist Confucianist Concept of Human Rights in China," *Michigan Journal of International Law*, 1992, vol. 13, p. 469. The importance of Confucianism as a basis for a collectivist legal order is the focus of many officially sanctioned studies of Chinese legal culture. See, e.g., Chinese Society for the Study of Confucianism and Legal Culture (ed.), *Confucianism and Legal Culture*, Shanghai: Fudan University Press, 1992.

31 See, e.g., B. Yang, *The Ugly Chinaman and the Crisis of Chinese Culture*, D.J. Cohn and J. Qing (trans.), St Leonards, New South Wales: Allen & Unwin, 1992; and Wang Ruoshui, "Wei rendao zhuyi bianhu" (In Defense of Humanism), in Wang Ruoshui (ed.), *Wei rendao zhuyi bianhu*, Beijing: United Press, 1986, pp. 217–33. Also see A. Kent, *op. cit.*, pp. 136–53.

32 See generally, W. Tang and W.L. Parish, *Chinese Urban Life Under Reform*, Cambridge: Cambridge University Press, 2000, chap. 2; E.J. Perry and M. Selden (eds), *Chinese Society: Change, Conflict and Resistance*, London and New York: Routledge, 2000.

33 See Dao Xuezheng, "Fazhi jianshi she zhengzhi tizhi gaige de zhongyao neirong" (Legal System Construction Is an Important Component of Political System Reform), *Lilun yuetan* (Theory Monthly), 1987, no. 9, pp. 33–7.

34 See Li Fuqi, "Shehui zhuyi chuji jieduan minzhu yu fazhi jianshe de jiangcheng" (Progress in Democracy and Legal System Construction in the Preliminary Stage of Socialism), *Zhongguo faxue* (Chinese Legal Studies), 1988, no. 2, pp. 3–9.

35 See Zhao Ziyang, "Advance Along the Road to Socialism With Chinese Characteristics," October 25, 1987, in *Documents of the Thirteenth National Congress of the Communist Party of China*, Beijing: Foreign Languages Press, 1987, pp. 3–77.

36 See Yu Qingwu, "Lun Zhongguo minfa wenhua de zhuangjian" (The Creation of China's Civil Law Culture), *Tianjin shehui kexue* (Tianjin Social Sciences), 1994, no. 3, pp. 96–100.

37 See, e.g., Zheng Yuanmin and Zhou Zhong, "Zhuanxing shiqi shehui jiazhiguan de biange yi tiaokong" (Change, Control and Adjustment of Social Values in the Period of Transformation), *Zhengzhi yu falu* (Politics and Law), 1996, no. 1, pp. 26–9.

38 See Qiao Wei, "Ping 'Quanli benwei shuo'" (Critiquing "Speaking of Rights Standards"), *Qiushi* (Facts), 1990, no. 13, pp. 10–15.

39 See "Zhongguo shehui fazhan yu quanli baohu bitan" (Notes and Discussion on China's Social Development and the Enforcement of Rights), *Faxue yanjiu* (Legal Studies Research), 1994, vol. 3, pp. 3–14.

40 See, e.g., Wang Chenguang and Liu Wen, "Shichang jingji he gong fa yu sifa de huafen" (The Market Economy and the Divide between Public and Private Law), *Zhongguo faxue* (Chinese Jurisprudence), 1993, no. 5, pp. 28–36.

41 See, e.g., P.B. Potter, "Riding the Tiger – Legitimacy and Legal Culture in Post-Mao China," *The China Quarterly*, 1994, no. 38, pp. 325–58; *ibid.*, "Socialist Legality and Legal Culture in Shanghai: A Survey of the Getihu," *Canadian Journal of Law and Society*, 1994, vol. 9, pp. 41–72.

42 See generally, D. Bodde and C. Morris, *Law in Imperial China*, Philadelphia: University of Pennsylvania Press, 1967; Ch'u T., "Chinese Class Structure and Its Ideology" in J.K. Fairbank (ed.), *Chinese Thought and Institutions*, Chicago and London: University of Chicago Press, 1957.

43 See, e.g., Ch'u T., *Law and Society in Traditional China*, Paris: Mouton Press, 1961; H. Gates, *Chinese Working Class Lives: Getting By in Taiwan*, Ithaca, NY, and London: Cornell University Press, 1987, pp. 72 and 145 *et seq.*

44 Ch'u T., "Chinese Class Structure and Its Ideology," *op. cit.*, p. 239.

45 See generally, D.J. Munro, *The Concept of Man in Contemporary China*, Ann Arbor: University of Michigan Press, 1977, pp. 1–22, 178–82.

46 See generally, H.J. Berman, *op. cit.*; and M. Tigar and M. Levy, *Law and the Rise of Capitalism*, New York: Free Press, 1977.

47 See A.J. Nathan, *Chinese Democracy*, Berkeley and Los Angeles: University of California Press, 1985, pp. 104 *et seq.*

48 See generally, D. Bodde and C. Morris, *op. cit.*; S. Van Der Sprenkel, *Legal Institutions in Manchu China*, New York: Athlone Press, 1962; Ch'u T., "Chinese Class Structure and Its Ideology," *op. cit.*

49 See generally, Ch'u T., *Law and Society in Traditional China*, *op. cit.*

50 See, e.g., R. Brockman, "Commercial Contract Law in Late Nineteenth-Century Taiwan," in J.A. Cohen, R.R. Edwards, and F. Chen (eds), *Essays on China's Legal Tradition*, Princeton, NJ: Princeton University Press, 1980, p. 76.

51 M.H. Fried, *The Fabric of Chinese Society*, New York: Praeger, 1953, p. 193.

52 M.H. Fried, *op. cit.*, pp. 195 *et seq.*

53 See generally, V. Shue, *The Reach of the State: Sketches of the Chinese Body Politic*, Stanford, Calif.: Stanford University Press, 1988, chap. 3.

54 P. Li, "In Search of Justice: Law and Morality in Three Chinese Dramas," *ibid.*, p. 104. Also see C. Shih, *Injustice to Tou O (Tou O Yuan): A Study and Translation*, Cambridge: Cambridge University Press, 1972.

55 See *Chin Pingmei: The Adventurous History of His Men and His Six Wives*, New York: Capricorn Books, 1960; *The Dream of the Red Chamber: A Chinese Novel of the Early Ch'ing Period*, New York: Grosset and Dunlap, 1968. Also see generally, C.T. Hsia, *The Classic Chinese Novel: A Critical Introduction*, New York and London: Columbia University Press, 1968.

56 *Cf.* L. Nader, *Law in Culture and Society*, Chicago: Aldine Press, 1969, p. 8.

57 See, e.g., Yu X., "Legal Pragmatism in the People's Republic of China," *Journal of Chinese Law*, 1989, vol. 3, p. 29. Also see generally, R.C. Keith, *China's Struggle for the Rule of Law*, New York: St Martin's Press, 1994, pp. 218–21.

58 See, e.g., Supreme People's Court, "Guanyu guanche zhixing minshi zhengce falu ruogan wenti de yijian" (Opinion on Various Issues of Fully Implementing Civil Policy and Law), 1990.

59 See Zhang Youyu, "Yi bu juyou xian jieduan zhongguo tese de xianfa" (A Constitution that Reflects the Special Characteristics of China in the Present Stage), *Zhongguo faxue* (Chinese Jurisprudence), 1988, no. 2, pp. 36–40.

60 See D. Bodde and C. Morris, *op. cit.*; and M. Dutton, *Policing and Punishment in China: From Patriarchy to "The People,"* Hong Kong: Oxford University Press, 1992.

61 See generally, S.B. Lubman, "Methodological Problems in Studying Chinese Communist 'Civil' Law," in J.A. Cohen (ed.), *Contemporary Chinese Law: Research Problems and Perspectives*, Cambridge, Mass.: Harvard University Press, 1970.

62 See, e.g., V.H. Li, "The Evolution and Development of the Chinese Legal System," in J. Lindbeck, *China: Management of a Revolutionary Society*, Seattle and London: University of Washington Press, 1970, esp. pp. 240–1. Also see L. Ladany, *Law and Legality in China: The Testament of a China-watcher*, M. Nath (ed.), London, Hurst & Co., 1992, chap. 3.

63 See, e.g., Peng Zhen, "Guanyu qi ge falu caoan de shuoming" (Explanation of Seven Draft Laws), in Peng Zhen, *Lun xin shiqi de shehuizhu minzhu yu fazhi jianshe* (On the Establishment of Socialist Democracy and Legal System in the New Period), Beijing: Central Digest Publishers, 1989, p. 1.

64 See Liu Peixue, "Tan tan «yao fazhi bu yao renzhi» de kouhao," (Discussing the Slogan "Rule of Law Not Rule of Man") *Neibu wengao* (Internal Manuscripts), 1991, no. 7, pp. 7–8; and Zheng Jingru, "Ye tan 'yao fazhi bu yao renzhi' de kouhao," (Discussing Again the Slogan "Rule of Law Not Rule of Man") *Neibu wengao*, 1991, no. 14, pp. 21–2.

65 See "Xiao Yang on Constitutional Amendments," Beijing Xinhua Domestic Service, March 9, 1999, in *FBIS Daily Report: China* (FNIS-CHI-1999–0312), March 16, 1999.

66 See, e.g., Shi Tong, "Zhengfa jiguan sixiang zhengzhi gongzuo de jidian sikao," (Various Considerations in the Ideological and Political Work of Political–Legal Organs), *Neibu wengao* (Internal Manuscripts), 1992, no. 3, pp. 26–7. Also see Gao Xinting, "Provide Better Legal Guarantee for Cross-Century Development," *Liaowang* (Outlook), January 11, 1999, in *FBIS Daily Report: China* (FBIS-CHI-99–029), January 29, 1999.

67 See Qiu Dunhong, "Gaige dangnei jiandu zhi de jige jianyi" (Several Suggestions on Reforming the Party's Internal Supervision System), *Neibu wengao* (Internal Manuscripts), 1991, no. 4, pp. 22–4 and 30.

68 See, e.g., "Zou yifa zhiguo zhi lu: Jiang Zemin yu Zhongguo shehui zhuyi fazhi jiangcheng" (Advance Along the Road of Ruling the Country According to Law: Jiang Zemin Speaking on Jiang Zemin and China's Rule of Socialist Law), *Fazhi ribao* (Legal System Daily), April 22, 2000, pp. 1–2.

69 See, e.g., Song Haobo, "Luelun woguo jingji tizhi gaige zhong de falu yaoqiu" (Tentative Theory on the Legal Requirements of Economic Structural Reform), *Faxue yanjiu* (Studies in Law), 1985, no. 3, pp. 1–6; and Jun Guomin, "Lun gongmin de jingji jibenquan yu jingji susong" (On Citizens' Basic Economic Rights and Economic Litigation), *Xiandai faxue* (Modern Law), 1996, no. 5, pp. 75–7.

70 See generally, D.C. Clarke, "Regulation and Its Discontents: Understanding Economic Law in China," *Stanford Journal of International Law*, 1992, vol. 28, no. 2, pp. 283–322; and E.J. Epstein, *op. cit.*

71 See, e.g., Li Jingbing, "Minfa zhong bixu zhongshen de liang ge guannian" (Two Concepts that Should Be Reaffirmed in Civil Law), *Zhongguo faxue* (Chinese Jurisprudence), 1993, no. 4, pp. 10–17.

72 In theory, the flexibility and discretion conferred on Chinese decision makers is controlled through ideological training in much the same way that the discretion of Imperial Chinese officials was controlled through Confucian training. See generally, J. Levenson, *Confucian China and Its Modern Fate*, Berkeley: University of California Press, 1958.

73 See generally, J.V. Feinerman, "Economic and Legal Reform in China, 1978–91," *op. cit.*; and S.B. Lubman, "Emerging Functions of Formal Legal Institutions in China's Modernization," in Joint Economic Committee of US Congress (ed.), *China Under the Four Modernizations*, Washington: US Government Printing Office, 1982, p. 235. *Cf.* P.B. Potter, "Riding the Tiger: Legitimacy and Legal Reform in Post-Mao China," *op. cit.* Also see T.C. Grey, "Langdell's Orthodoxy," *University of Pittsburgh Law Review*, 1983, vol. 45, p. 1.

74 For a discussion of the problem of policy making and trade-offs, see S.L. Shirk, *The Political Logic of Economic Reform in China*, Berkeley: University of California Press, 1993.

75 See P.B. Potter, "Civil Obligations and Legal Culture in Shanghai: A Survey of the Getihu," *op. cit.*

76 See P.B. Potter, "*Guanxi* and the PRC Legal System: From Contradiction to Complementarity," Woodrow Wilson Center for Scholars occasional papers, 2000.

77 See J.T.G. Arias, "A Relationship Marketing Approach to *Guanxi*," *European Journal of Marketing*, 1998, vol. 32, no. 1/2, p. 145; H. Chin and G. Graen, "*Guanxi* and Professional Leadership in Contemporary Sino–American Joint Ventures in Mainland China," *Leadership Quarterly*, Winter 1997, vol. 8, no. 4, pp. 451–65.

78 See C.R. Xin and J.L. Pearce, "*Guanxi*: Connections as Substitutes for Formal Institutional Support," *Academy of Management Journal*, December 1996, vol. 39, no. 6, pp. 1641–58.

79 See A. Walder, "Local Governments as Industrial Firms: An Organizational Analysis of China's Transitional Economy," *American Journal of Sociology*, September 1995, vol. 101, no. 2, pp. 263–301.

80 See D.C. Wank, "The Institutional Process of Market Clientelism: *Guanxi* and Private Business in a South China City," *The China Quarterly*, September 1997, no. 147, pp. 820–38.

81 See J. Unger, "'Bridges': Private Business, The Chinese Government and the Rise of New Associations," *The China Quarterly*, September 1996, no. 147, pp. 795–819.

82 See D.C. Wank, *op. cit.*

83 See A. Smart, "Gifts, Bribes and *Guanxi*: A Reconsideration of Bourdieu's Social Capital," *Cultural Anthropology*, August 1993, vol. 8, no. 3, pp. 388–408.

84 For a useful example of the way in which the fairness/efficiency debates of Western jurisprudence have been adapted to Chinese law contexts, see Xie

Pengcheng, *Jieben falu jiazhi* (Basic Legal Values), Jinan: Shandong People's Press, 2000.

85 For discussion of formation of political groups based on organizational experience, see J. Domes, "Intra-Elite Group Formation and Conflict in the PRC," in D.S.G. Goodman (ed.), *Groups and Politics in the People's Republic of China*, Cardiff, UK, University College Cardiff Press, 1984, pp. 26–39. For discussion recognizing that organizational priorities influence political decision making, see K. Lieberthal and M. Oksenberg, *Policy Making in China*, Princeton: Princeton University Press, 1988, pp. 404 *et seq.*, and sources cited; and S.L. Shirk, "The Politics of Industrial Reform," in E.J. Perry and C. Wong, *The Political Economy of Reform in Post-Mao China*, Cambridge, Mass.: Harvard University Press, 1985, p. 195. For a contrary view, see L. Pye, *The Dynamics of Chinese Politics*, Cambridge: Oelgeschlager, Gunn & Hain, 1981.

86 See generally, W.P. Alford and Fang L., "Legal Training and Education in the 1990s: An Overview and Assessment of China's Needs," 1994. Also see Zhu Lanye, "Powerful Attorneys: Chinese Educators on Legal Training and Law in China" and P.B. Potter, "Class Action: Educating Lawyers in China," both in Committee on Scholarly Communication With China (ed.), *op. cit.*

87 See, e.g., Li Buyun, *Zouxiang fazhi* (Proceeding Toward Rule of Law), Changsha: Hunan People's Press, 1998; and articles contained in Xia Yong (ed.), *Zuoxiang quanli de shidai: Zhongguo gongmin quanli fazhan yanjiu* (Proceeding Toward an Era of Rights: A Study of the Development of Citizens' Rights in China), Beijing: University of Politics and Law Press, 1995. For a discussion, see A.H.Y. Chen, "Toward a Legal Enlightenment: Discussions in Contemporary China on the Rule of Law," *UCLA Pacific Basin Law Journal*, 1999/2000, vol. 17, nos 2 and 3, pp. 125–65.

Chapter 2

1 *Constitution of the PRC*, Article 62. Citations for all laws, regulations, and treaties are provided in Appendix A: Table of Laws, Regulations, and Treaties. The NPC also has nominal authority to make personnel decisions for national offices, although in reality these are driven by CPC Politburo preferences. Among the many excellent studies of the Chinese legislative process are K.J. O'Brien, "China's National People's Congress: Reform and Its Limits," *Legislative Studies Quarterly*, 1988, vol. XIII, no. 3, pp. 343–74; K.J. O'Brien, *Reform Without Liberalization: The National People's Congress and the Politics of Institutional Change*, New York: Cambridge University Press, 1990; M.S. Tanner, "Organizations and Politics in China's Post-Mao Law-Making System," in P.B. Potter (ed.), *Domestic Law Reforms in Post-Mao China*, Armonk, NY: M.E. Sharpe, 1994, pp. 56–93; and M.S. Tanner, "How a Bill Becomes Law in China: Stages and Processes in Lawmaking," *The China Quarterly Special Issue: China's Legal Reforms*, 1995, no. 141, pp. 39–64.

2 Peng Zhen, "Guanyu qige falu caoan de shuoming" (Explanation of the Seven Draft Laws) in *Peng Zhen wenxuan* (Collected works of Peng Zhen), Beijing: People's Press, 1991, p. 371.

3 See K.J. O'Brien, "Agents and Remonstrators: Role Accumulation by Chinese People's Congress Deputies," *The China Quarterly*, June 1994, no. 138.

4 "PRC: Legislative Process at NPC Examined," Beijing Xinhua English Service, 17 March 1996, in *FBIS Daily Report: China*, 19 March 1996, p. 36. Also see M.S. Tanner, "How a Bill Becomes Law in China," *op. cit.*, pp. 46–49; M.S. Tanner, "Organizations and Politics in China's Post-Mao Law-Making System," *op. cit.*, p. 64.

5 See L. Ladany, "China's New Power Centre?" *Far Eastern Economic Review*, June 26, 1984, p. 38. Also see M.S. Tanner, "Organizations and Politics in China's Post-Mao Law-Making System," *op. cit.*, p. 56; K.J. O'Brien, *Reform Without Liberalization*, *op. cit.*, *passim*; and K.J. O'Brien, "China's National People's Congress," *op. cit.*, p. 343.

6 Compare *Constitution of the PRC, 1978*, Article 25 with *Constitution of the PRC, 1982*, Article 67.

7 Peng Zhen, "Tan tan ren da changweihui de gongzuo" (Discussing the Work of the NPC Standing Committee), January 24, 1984, in Peng Zhen, *Lun xin shiqi de shehui zhuyi minzhu yu fazhi jianshe* (On the Construction of Socialist Democracy and the Legal System during the New Period) (hereafter, "*XSMF*"), Beijing: Party Documents, 1989, p. 214. Also see Peng Zhen, "Guanyu lifa gongzuo" (On Legislative Work), January 23, 1985, in *Peng Zhen wenxuan* (Collected Works of Peng Zhen), *op. cit.*, p. 503; and in *XSMF*, *op. cit.*, p. 244; "Jiaqiang minzhu yu fazhi jianshe, jiaqiang ren da changweihui gongzuo" (Strengthen the Building of Democracy and the Legal System, Strengthen the Work of the NPC Standing Committee), June 27, 1986, in *XSMF*, *op. cit.*, p. 324.

8 Peng Zhen, "Zuo hao sheng ji ren da changweihui de gongzuo" (Do a Good Job with the Provincial Level People's Congresses), June 24, 1983, in *XSMF*, *op. cit.*, p. 196.

9 Peng Zhen, "Yi bu yao shizhi, yi bu yao yuequan" (First, We Cannot Forget our Duties; Second, We Cannot Exceed our Authority), June 22, 1987, in *XSMF*, *op. cit.*, p. 360.

10 See "Chairman Qiao Shi Speaks at Closing," Beijing Xinhua English Service, March 31, 1993, in *FBIS Daily Report: China*, March 31, 1993, p. 34.

11 See Shao K., "A Challenge to the Dictatorship of the Chinese Communist Party," *China Focus*, November 1, 1994, vol. 2, no. 11, pp. 1, 8.

12 See "Qiao Shi Speech at NPC Closing Session Published," Beijing Xinhua Domestic Service, March 17, 1996, in *FBIS Daily Report: China*, March 18, 1996, pp. 24–6.

13 See "Qiao Shi Interviewed on NPC Legislative Work," *Renmin ribao*, March 1, 1996, p. 1, in *FBIS Daily Report: China*, March 5, 1996, p. 27.

14 See "Qiao Shi's Words on Democracy in China," *China News Digest* (electronic media), June 2, 1997; "The 15th CCP National Congress Closed, Qiao Shi Is Out," *China News Digest* (electronic media), September 19, 1997. In light of Qiao Shi's dismissal, the inclusion of a reference to Peng Zhen in the Congress's minute of silence for deceased leading comrades was particularly ironic, because Qiao Shi was to a large extent building on Peng's legacy and was getting into political trouble for it.

15 See "Li Peng on Rule by Law at NPC Session," Beijing Xinhua Domestic Service, March 21, 1998, in *FBIS Daily Report: China* (FBIS-CHI-98–082), March 23, 1998.

16 See "Li Peng Addresses the NPC Legal System Lecture," Beijing Xinhua Domestic Service, October 20, 1998, in *FBIS Daily Report: China* (FBIS-CHI-98–300), October 27, 1998.

17 See Wu D. *et al.*, *Lifa zhidu bijiao yanjiu* (Comparative Study of the Legislative System), Beijing: Law Publishing, 1981, pp. 18–19.

18 See Zhou Wangsheng, *Lifa xue* (Legislation), Beijing: Peking University Press, 1988, pp. 224–38.

19 See Li Peizhuan, *Zhongguo shehui zhuyi lifa de lilun yu shixian* (Theory and Practice of Socialist Legislation in China), Beijing: China Legal System Press, 1991, pp. 6, 26–31.

20 See, e.g., Zhou Wangsheng, *Lifa lun* (Theory of Legislation), Beijing: Peking University Press, 1994.

21 See "Zhonghua renmin gongheguo lifa fa (zhuanjia jianyi gao)" (Legislation Law of the PRC (Specialists' Draft)), in Li Buyun (ed.), *Lifa fa yanjiu* (Study of Legislation Law), Changsha, Hunan People's Press, 1999, pp. 3–36.

22 See Legislation Law of the People's Republic of China (2000).

23 See PRC State Council Circular on Enacting Legislation Law (June 15, 2000); "At PRC's NPC Meeting Draft Legislative Law Explained," Beijing Xinhua Domestic Service, March 9, 2000, in *FBIS Daily Report: China* (FBIS-CHI-2000–0309), March 16, 2000.

24 See "NPC Leaders Discuss Lawmaking," Beijing Xinhua Domestic Service, March 9, 2000, in *FBIS Daily Report: China* (FBIS-CHI-2000–0310), March 9, 2000.

25 *Ibid.*

26 For an authoritative discussion of Party management of so-called non-government organizations, see "Wei Jianxing on NGO Management," Beijing Xinhua Domestic Service, December 1, 1998, in *FBIS Daily Report: China* (FBIS-CHI-98–335), December 1, 1998. Regulations on registration and management of social organizations prohibited their "oppos[ing] the basic principles defined by the Constitution" – a clear reference to the Four Basic Principles that entrench Party leadership. See "Regulations on Social Organizations" (1998).

27 See, e.g., Zhang Zisheng, "Luelun lifa guihua: Cong «chengshu yi ge, zhiding yi ge» de lifa zhuangtai tanqi" (Considering Legislative Plans: Speaking from the View on Legislation of "When Ripe, then Enact"), *Faxue* (Legal Studies), 1995, no. 7, pp. 44–7.

28 See Meng Qinguo, "Jingji tizhi gaige shiqi de minshi lifa" (Civil Legislation in Period of Economic Structure Reform), *Zhongguo shehui kexue* (Chinese Social Science), 1988, no. 6, pp. 77–90.

29 See Tong Rou, "Shiyi jie san zhong quan hui yu minfa de diwei" (The Third Plenum of the 11th Central Committee and the Position of Civil Law), *Zhongguo renmin daxue xuebao* (Journal of Chinese People's University), 1988, no. 6, pp. 3–4.

30 See generally, E.L. Rubin, "Administrative Law and the Complexity of Culture," in A. Seidman, R. Seidman, and J. Payne (eds), *Legislative Drafting for Market Reform: Some Lessons From China*, New York: St Martin's Press, 1997.

31 See P.B. Potter, "The *Administrative Litigation Law of the PRC*," *Chinese Law and Government*, Fall 1991 and "Judicial Review and Bureaucratic Reform: The Administrative Litigation Law of the PRC," in P.B. Potter (ed.), *Domestic Law Reforms in Post-Mao China*, *op. cit.*, p. 270.

Also see J. Fa and S. Leng, "Judicial Review of Administration in the People's Republic of China," *Occasional Papers/Reprints Series in Contemporary Asian Studies*, 1992, no. 1.

32 See "Guanyu zhi an guanli chufa zhong danbao ren he baozheng jin de zanxing guiding" (Provisional Regulations on Guarantors and Guarantee Payments in Security Administration Punishments); "Guanyu moshou, chuli weifan zhi an guanli suode caiwu he shiyong gongju de zanxing guiding" (Provisional Regulations on Confiscation and Handling of Property Obtained and Instrumentalities Used in Violation of Security Administration). Each of these regulations provides for recompense to individuals fined or whose property is seized for violations of the Security Administration Punishment Act but who are later vindicated on appeal.

33 Liu Yanshou, "Jiaqiang xingzheng lifa he xingzheng sifa gongzuo" (Strengthen Administrative Legislation and Administrative Adjudicatory Work), *Guangming ribao* (Bright Daily), April 11, 1982, p. 3.

34   Yin Liangpei, "Yingdang dali jiaqiang xingzheng fa de yanjiu he jianshe" (We Should Exert Every Effort to Strengthen Research and Establishment of Economic Law), *Liaoning daxue xuebao* (Liaoning University Journal), 1982, no. 5, p. 57.

35   "Wang Hanbin zuo xingzheng susong fa caoan shuoming" (Wang Hanbin Delivers Explanation of the Draft Administrative Litigation Law), *Renmin ribao* (People's Daily), March 29, 1989, p. 2.

36   For discussion of reasons for delaying the effective date of the ALL, see "Yang Shangkun qianshu zhuxi ling gongbu xingzheng susong fa" (Yang Shangkun Signs as President the Order for Promulgation of the Administrative Litigation Law), *Fazhi ribao* (Legal System Daily), April 10, 1989, p. 1. For reports on meetings held to build support for the ALL, see "Forum Discusses Administrative Procedural Law," Beijing Xinhua Domestic Service, June 23, 1990, in *FBIS Daily Report: China*, June 26, 1990, p. 32; and "Yao Yilin on Administrative Procedures Law," Beijing Xinhua Domestic Service, September 1, 1990, in *FBIS Daily Report: China*, September 4, 1990, p. 32.

37   "Zui gao renmin fayuan xingzheng shenpan ting zhengshi jianli bing kaizhan gongzuo" (Administrative Adjudication Chamber of the Supreme People's Court is Formally Established and Begins Work), *Zhonghua renmin gongheguo zui gao renmin fayuan gongbao* (PRC Supreme Court Bulletin), 1988, no. 4, p. 10.

38   Chang Hong, "1 Oct Law Will Permit Citizens to Sue Officials," *China Daily*, September 28, 1990, p. 1, in *FBIS Daily Report: China*, September 8, 1990, p. 11.

39   Juridical persons may include economic enterprises and business units, state organs, social groups or other legal organizations. See "Zhonghua renmin gongheguo min fa tongze" (*General Principles of Civil Law of the PRC*), Chap. III.

40   See generally, P.H. Corne, *Foreign Investment in China: The Administrative Legal System*, Hong Kong: Hong Kong University Press, 1997.

41   See, e.g., Wang Yuming, "«Xingzheng susong fa» shixing de jiji zhengzhi xiaoyong" (The Positive Political Utility of Implementing the "Administrative Litigation Act"), *Fa zhi jianshe* (Building the Legal System), 1990, no. 4, p. 2.

42   See generally, Chen Weixin, "Tan xingzheng susong zhengju wenti" (A Discussion of Evidence Issues in Administrative Litigation), *Fa zhi ribao* (Legal System Daily), July 19, 1989, p. 3; Ye Bifeng, "Xingzheng chengxu zhong de tingzheng zhidu" (The Hearing System in Administrative Procedure), *Faxue yanjiu* (Studies in Law), 1989, no. 4, p. 60.

43   Chen Weixin, *op. cit.* and Ye Bifeng, *op. cit.*. Also see Zhang Lingyuan and Du Xichuan, *«Zhonghua renmin gongheguo xingzheng susong fa» shiyi* (Explanation of the "Administrative Litigation Act of the PRC"), Beijing, 1989, p. 103 *et seq.*; and Zhang Ling, "Xingzheng jiguan zai xingzheng susong zhong de quanli he yiwu" (The Rights and Obligations of Administrative Organs in the Course of Administrative Litigation), *Fa zhi ribao* (Legal System Daily), September 29, 1989, p. 3.

44   The Supreme People's Court indicated that in cases involving challenges to administrative fines, for example, the court should decide whether or not the fine was valid and that no compromise or incremental decision should be allowed. See "Zui gao renmin fayuan guanyu renmin fayuan shenli jingji xingzheng anjian bu ying jinxing tiaojie de tongzhi" (Notice of the Supreme People's Court Concerning People's Courts Not Conducting Mediation in Handling Economic Administrative Cases). Also Ying Songnian, *Xingzheng susong zhishi shouce* (Handbook of Knowledge on Administrative Litigation), Beijing, 1988, pp. 42–3.

45   E.g., Wang Yuanming, "Xingzheng peichang zeren yuanze zhi wo jian" (The Principle of Liability for Administrative Compensation From My View), *Fa zhi*

ribao (Legal System Daily), August 23, 1989, p. 3. Huang S., *Xingzheng susong fa 100 wen* (100 Questions on the Administrative Litigation Law), Beijing, 1989, pp. 224–32. Also see «Xingzheng susong fa» tong shi bian xie zu (Group for Compiling and Writing the General Explanation of the "Administrative Litigation Law"), «*Xingzheng susong fa*» *tong shi* (General Interpretation of the "Administrative Litigation Law"), Beijing, 1989, pp. 150–7. This provision is derived from Article 41 of the 1982 Constitution.

46 See, e.g., Luan Yanmin and Chen Donghao, "Guanyu wo guo xingzheng peichang lifa de ji ge shexiang" (Concerning Various Tentative Plans For Our Administrative Compensation Legislation), *Faxue zazhi* (Legal Studies Magazine), 1990, no. 4, p. 6.

47 See generally, Wang Liming, Zhang Huanguang, and Hu Jianmiao, *Xingzheng guan si mantan* (Informal Discussion of Administrative Suits), *People's Daily Press*, Beijing, 1988, pp. 14–79.

48 For discussion of the problems of bureaucratic organs delaying or refusing to complete administrative reconsideration procedures, thus effectively barring judicial review under prior regulations, see, e.g., Zhang Lingyuan and Du Xichuan, op. cit., pp. 120–1.

49 See, e.g., Zhu Feng, "Xingzheng susong fa ying queli xingzheng fuyi qianzheng yuanze" (The Administrative Litigation Law Should Establish the Principle of Primacy of Administrative Reconsideration), *Fa zhi ribao* (Legal System Daily), December 28, 1988, p. 3. Also see "Xing su fa caoan yinqi ge fang guanzhu yi yue lai qunzhong tichu xuduo jianyi" (The Administrative Litigation Law Elicits Interest From All Sides, In the Past Month the Masses Have Submitted Numerous Opinions), *Fa zhi ribao* (Legal System Daily), December 14, 1988, p. 1.

50 The need for regulations on the *fu yi* process was recognized in the State Council's January 1990 circular on implementation of the law (see "Circular on Study of Administrative Procedure," *op. cit.*), but calls for the regulations accelerated after the ALL came into effect. See, e.g., Tan Zongze and Wang Lianchange, "Shi lun wo guo xingzheng fuyi zhidu de jianshe" (Preliminary Discussion of Our System of Administrative Reconsideration), *Faxue zazhi* (Legal Studies Magazine), 1990, no. 3, p. 10; Ying Songnian and Dong Hao, "Xingzheng fuyi jigou yu guansha wenti zhi yanjiu" (Study of the Organs and Jurisdiction of Administrative Reconsideration), *Faxue zazhi* (Legal Studies Magazine), 1990, no. 4, p. 4; and Su Jian, "Jishi zhiding he banbu «Xingzheng fuyi tiaoli»" (Immediately Enact and Promulgate "Regulations for Administrative Reconsideration"), *Faxue* (Jurisprudence), 1990, no. 8, p. 19.

51 See "Xingzheng fuyi tiaoli" (Regulations on Administrative Reconsideration) (1990). For English text, see "Regulations Concerning Reconsideration of Administrative Measures," in *FBIS Daily Report: China*, January 3, 1991, p. 20.

52 See *ibid.*, Chap. VI (concerning requirements to be met by applicants for reconsideration) and Chap. VII (concerning requirements for agency conducting reconsideration).

53 See Ying Songnian and Dong Hao, "Xingzheng fuyi shiyong falu wenti zhi yanjiu" (A Study of the Issue of the Utilization of Law in Administrative Reconsideration), *Zhengfa luntan (Zhongguo zheng fa daxue xuebao)* (Politics and Law Forum: Journal of the Chinese University of Politics and Law), 1990, no. 1, p. 46.

54 "Regulations on Administrative Reconsideration" (1984). Also see Zhang Chunseng and Tong Weidong, "Wo guo xingzheng fuyi de fazhan he wanshan" (Development and Perfecting of our Administrative Reconsideration System) *Zhongguo faxue* (Chinese Jurisprudence), 1999, no. 4, pp. 47–51.

55 See Administrative Reconsideration Law (1999). Also see "NPC Supports Law on Administrative Appeal," Beijing Xinhua English Service, October 30, 1998, in *FBIS Daily Report: China* (FBIS-CHI-98–303), November 2, 1998.

56 See, e.g., "Yi jian nongye chengbao hetong jiufen an" (A Case of an Agricultural Responsibility Contract Dispute), *Zhongguo fazhi bao* (Chinese Legal System Gazette), April 18, 1984, p. 3; "Taiyuan shi huayi shangdian shou jingji zhicai" (The Huayi Store of Taiyuan City Bears Economic Sanctions), *Zhongguo fazhi bao* (Chinese Legal System Gazette), April 4, 1984, p. 1.

57 See "Zuigao renmin fayuan guanyu zai jingji shenpan gongzuo zhong guanche zhixing «Minshi susong fa [shi xing]» ruogan wenti de yijian" (Opinion of the Supreme People's Court on Several Questions of Fully Implementing the "Civil Procedure Law [For Trial Implementation]" During the Course of Economic Adjudication Work). Also see "Zui gao renmin fayuan, zhongguo renmin yinhang guanyu fayuan dui xingzheng jiguan yi fa shenqing qiangzhi zhixing xuyao yinhang xiezhu zhixing de anjian ying ruhe banli wenti de lianhe tongzhi" (Joint Notice by the Supreme People's Court and the People's Bank of China Concerning Questions as to how to Handle Cases where Administrative Organs Apply According to Law for Compulsory Enforcement and Request the Banks to Assist in Enforcement), 1989.

58 See "Guowuyuan jingji fa gui yanjiu zhongxin bangongshi" (Administrative Office of the Economic Laws and Regulations Research Center of the State Council), *Zhonghua renmin gongheguo jingji hetong fa tiaowen shiyi* (The Economic Contract Law of the PRC: Explanation of the Articles), Beijing, 1982, pp. 122–4.

59 See, e.g., Zhang Yong, "Shi lun xingzheng susong zhong de zhixing quan" (Tentative Discussion of Enforcement Powers in Administrative Litigation), *Faxue jianshe* (Building the Legal System), 1990, no. 4, p. 9.

60 The courts are to defer review of the propriety of administrative decisions pending future refinements of China's administrative law system. See, e.g., Wang Hanbin, "Zhonghua renmin gongheguo xingzheng susong fa (caoan) de shuoming" (Explanation of the (Draft) Administrative Litigation Law of the PRC), *Renmin ribao* (People's Daily), April 10, 1989, p. 2.

61 Wang Mincan, *Xingzheng fa gaiyao* (Introductory Outline to Administrative Law), Beijing, 1983, p. 221.

62 Zhang Shuyi, "Xingzheng susong fa (caoan) ruogan zhenglun wenti sikao" (Inquiry Into Various Controversial Issues of the (Draft) Administrative Litigation Law), *Faxue* (Jurisprudence), 1989, no. 3, p. 8.

63 Zhang Shuyi, "Xingzheng fagui jieshou si fa shencha xi" (Analysis of Administrative Laws and Regulations Accepting Judicial Scrutiny), *Fa zhi ribao* (Legal System Daily), March 24, 1989, p. 3. Also see "Guanyu difang renmin zhengfu guiding ke xiang renmin fayuan qisu de xingzheng anjian fayuan ying fou shouli wenti de pi fu" (Response to a Question as to Whether Courts Should Accept Administrative Cases of Local Government Regulations Submitted to the People's Courts for Litigation) (1987).

64 See Wang Xuezheng, "Zai xingzheng susong zhong de keneng yudao de wenti" (Questions That May Be Encountered in Administrative Litigation), *Faxue zazhi* (Legal Studies Magazine), 1990, no. 3, p. 24.

65 See, e.g., "Xingzheng susong fa caoan zuotan hui jieshu" (Conference on the Administrative Litigation Law Closes), *op. cit.*; "Dui xingzheng susong fa caoan ji ge wenti de jianjie" (Opinions on Several Questions of the Draft Administrative Litigation Law), *op. cit.*

66 See, e.g., Jiang Bixin, "Lun xingzheng susong zhong de sifa bian geng quan" (Discussion of the Authority of Judicial Revision in the Course of Administrative Litigation), *Faxue yanjiu* (Legal Studies), 1988, no. 6, p. 31.

Jiang's position with the Supreme People's Court at the time that this article was published suggests the article was an effort to win support for the authority of the courts generally to amend administrative decisions.

67 See, e.g., Wang Hanbin, *op. cit.*

68 See *ibid.*

69 For compendia of case decisions involving the Administrative Litigation Law, see, e.g.,Wang Guichen *et al.* (eds), *Renmin fayuan yinan panli pingxi: xingzheng juan* (Analysis of Difficult Judgments of the People's Courts: Administrative Volume), Changchun: Jilin Publishers, 1999; Administrative Adjudication Chamber of the Supreme People's Court (ed.), *Xingzheng susong yu tudi guanli fa* (Administrative Litigation and the Land Administration Law), Beijing: Times Press, 1999; Liang Huaren and Zhang Jiyang (eds), *Changjian anjian guifanhua shenli zhinan* (Guide to the Standardization of Commonly Seen Cases) (3 vols), Beijing: University of Law and Politics Press, 1992. Administrative law cases also appear in the series, Zuiguo renmin fayuan Zhonyguo xingyoung faxve yanjiu suo (China Legalization Research Institute of the Supreme People's Court) (ed.), *Renmin fayuan anli xuan* (Compilation of Cases from the People's Courts), quarterly.

70 See R. Heufers *et al.*, "The Impact of the Administrative Procedure [*sic*] Law on Legal Security in the People's Republic of China," occasional paper, Friedrich Naumann Foundation, Beijing, 1996. Also see generally, P.B. Potter, "Administrative Litigation and Political Rights in China," *Human Rights Tribune*, 1992, vol. 3, no. 2, pp. 4–7.

71 See Jiang Mingan, "Zhongguo xingzheng fazhi fazhan jingcheng diaocha baogao" (Report on Investigation of the Development and Progress of China's Administrative Rule of Law), Beijing: Law Publishing, 1998, p. 324.

72 See State Compensation Law of the PRC (1994).

73 See Jiang Mingan, "Zhongguo xingzheng fazhi fazhan jingcheng diaocha baogao" (Report on Investigation of the Development and Progress of China's Administrative Rule of Law), Beijing: Law Publishing, 1998, p. 324.

74 See "Report on Just Implementation of Law by PRC's People's Courts in 1999," Beijing Xinhua Domestic Service, March 11, 2000, in *FBIS Daily Report: China* (FBIS-CHI-2000–0311), March 30, 2000.

75 See "Xingzheng fagui zhiding chengxu zanxing tiaoli" (Provisional Regulations on the Procedures for Enacting Administrative Laws and Regulations) (1987).

76 See Administrative Supervision Law of the PRC, 1997.

77 See Ma Huaide, "Xingzheng jiandu yu jiuji zhidu de xin tupo" (A New Breakthrough in the Administrative Supervision and Remedy System), in *Zhengfa luntan* (Politics and Law Forum), 1999, no. 4, pp. 66–72. Also see Lin Zhe, *Quanli fubai yu quanli zhiyue* (Corruption of Authority and Limitations on Authority), Beijing: Law Publishing, 1997.

78 See Yang Haikun and Huang Xuexian, *Zhongguo xingzheng chengxu fadianhua: Cong bijiao jiaodu yanjiu* (Codification of Chinese Administrative Procedure: Studied from a Comparative Perspective), Beijing: Law Publishing, 1999.

79 See generally, General Office of the Supreme People's Court of the PRC, "A Brief Introduction to the People's Courts of the People's Republic of China," 1988. For a retrospective assessment, see S. Finder, "Inside the People's Courts: China's Litigation System and the Resolution of Commercial Disputes," *China Law & Practice*, February 1996, pp. 16–21.

80 Zhonghua renmin gongheguo renmin fayuan zuzhi fa (Organization Law of the PRC for the People's Courts) (1980). For an overview of the court system in China, see R. Brown, *Understanding Chinese Courts and Legal Process: Law with Chinese Characteristics*, The Hague: Kluwer, 1997.

81 For regulations on review of cases, see Supreme People's Court, "Disposal by Different Levels of People's Courts of Applications for Review in Civil and Economic Cases Tentative Provisions" (1989).

82 See PRC Supreme People's Court Economic Adjudication Chamber (ed.), *Zuigao renmin fayuan sheli de er shen zai shen jingji jiufen anli xuanbian* (Compilation of Second and Revisited Economic Case Decisions by the Supreme People's Court), Beijing: People's Court Press, 1994.

83 See J.V. Feinerman, "The History and Development of China's Dispute Resolution System," in Asia Law & Practice (ed.), *Dispute Resolution in the PRC*, Hong Kong, Asia Law & Practice, 1995, pp. 5–21.

84 See "Civil Cases Involving Foreigners," Beijing Xinhua English Service, December 5, 1990, in *FBIS Daily Report: China* (FBIS-CHI-90–235), December 6, 1990, p. 24.

85 See generally, E.J. Epstein, "Evolution of China's General Principles of Civil Law," *The American Journal of Comparative Law*, 1986, vol. 34, no. 4, p. 705.

86 See C. Salbaing, "Dispute Settlement in China," in Streng and Wilcox (eds), *Doing Business in China*, Irvington-on-Hudson, NY: Transnational Juris, looseleaf, chap. 21.

87 See generally, N. Kaplan, J. Spruce, and M.J. Moser, *Hong Kong and China Arbitration Cases and Materials*, Singapore: Butterworth, 1994; S.A. Harpole, "Procedures and Practices Under the China International Economic and Trade Arbitration Commission," in Asia Law & Practice (ed.), *op. cit.*, pp. 51–62.

88 "Zhonghua renmin gongheguo jingji hetong zhongcai tiaoli" (Regulations of the PRC on Arbitration of Economic Contracts) (1983). Also see "Arbitration Committees to Handle Contract Disputes," Beijing Xinhua Domestic Service, September 1, 1983, in *FBIS Daily Report: China*, September 2, 1983, pp. K3–K4; Wu Tong, "Wo guo guonei jingji hetong zhongcai xianghe chuzou" (Where is Our Arbitration of Domestic Economic Contracts Going), *Zhongguo faxue* (Chinese Jurisprudence), 1991, no. 2, pp. 82–4.

89 For discussion, see generally, Zhang Y., "Towards the UNCITRAL Model Law: A Chinese Perspective," *Journal of International Arbitration*, 1994, vol. 11(1), p. 87; Chen M., "The Arbitration Act of the People's Republic of China," *Journal of International Arbitration*, 1995, vol. 12, no. 4, pp. 29–49; S.A. Harpole, "Procedures and Practices Under the China International Economic and Trade Arbitration Commission," *op. cit.*

90 See *Guowuyuan banggongting guanyu guanche shishi 'Zhonghua renmin gongheguo zhongcai fa' xuyao mingque de jige wenti de tongzhi* (Circular of the General Office of the State Council on Certain Issues to be Clarified on Implementing the Arbitration Law of the PRC, 1996). Also see Zhang Y., "Domestic Commissions' Foreign Powers Leave CIETAC Defending Its Turf," *China Joint Venturer*, September 1997, pp. 11–17.

91 See S.B. Lubman, "Setback for China-Wide Rule of Law," *Far Eastern Economic Review*, November 17, 1996, p. 38.

92 See Zhang Youyu, "Lun woguo minshi susong fa de jiben yuanze he tedian" (On the Basic Principles and Special Characteristics of our Civil Procedure Law), *Faxue yanjiu* (Studies in Law), 1982, no. 3, pp. 55–60.

93 See Zuigao renmin fayuan, "Guanyu guanche zhixing «Minshi susong fa (caoan)» ruogan wenti de yijian" (Opinion on Several Issues of Fully Implementing the "Civil Procedure Law (Draft)", *Minshi falu shiyong daquan* (Practical Compendium on Civil Law), Beijing: People's University Press, 1990, pp. 644–58.

94 See *Minshi falu shiyong daquan* (Practical Compendium on Civil Law), Beijing: People's University Press, 1990, pp. 658–788.

95 See Wang Hanbin, "Guanyu «Zhonghua renmin gongheguo minshi susong fa (shixing)» xiuding caoan de shouming," (Explanation of Revised Draft of the Civil Procedure Law of the PRC – for Trial Implementation), in *Minshi falu shiyong daquan* (Practical Compendium on Civil Law), Beijing: People's University Press, 1990, pp. 657–67; See "Wang Hanbin Explanation of Civil Procedure Law," *Beijing Renmin ribao* (People's Daily), April 14, 1991, in *FBIS Daily Report: China* (FBIS-CHI-91–115), June 14, 1991, p. 88; "Civil Law Revision Considered," Beijing Xinhua Domestic Service, December 20, 1990, in *FBIS Daily Report: China* (FBIS-CHI-90–246), December 21, 1990, p. 17; "Civil Procedure Law Explained," Beijing Xinhua Domestic Service, December 20, 1990, in *FBIS Daily Report: China* (FBIS-CHI-90–250), p. 15; "Civil Procedure Law Examined," Beijing Xinhua Domestic Service, December 22, 1990, in *FBIS Daily Report: China* (FBIS-CHI-90–247), p. 24.

96 See Wang Cunxue (ed.), *Zhongguo jingji zhongcai he susong shiyong shouce* (Practical Handbook on China's Economic Arbitration and Litigation), Beijing: China Development Press, 1993, pp. 12–13.

97 General Principles of Civil Law, 1986, Article 7.

98 See Wang Farong *et al.*, *Zhongguo minshi shenpan xue* (The Study of China's Civil Litigation), Beijing: Law Publishing, 1992, pp. 4–5.

99 See Wang Cunxue (ed.), *op. cit.*, p. 355. Also see Pan Jianfeng, "Minshi susong fazhi jianshe sishi nian" (Forty Years of Development of the Civil Procedure Law System), *Zhongwai faxue* (Chinese and Foreign Legal Studies), 1989, no. 5, pp. 9–16; "Renzhen shishi minfa tongze he minshi susong fa: «minfa tongze banbu wu zhou nian, minshi susong fa shishi» zuotanhui bufen fayan gaoyao" (Earnestly Carry Out the General Principles of Civil Law and the Civil Procedure Law: Excerpts of Speeches to the Conference on the Fifth Anniversary of the GPCL and on Implementing the Civil Procedure Law), *Zhongguo faxue* (Chinese Jurisprudence), 1991, no. 4, pp. 22–31.

100 See Ma Yuan (ed.), *Minshi shenpan de lilun yu shiwu* (Theory and Application of Civil Adjudication), Beijing: People's Court Publishers 1992, pp. 53–4.

101 See Zuigao renmin fayuan, "Guanyu guanche «Minshi susong fa» ruogan wenti de yijian" (Opinion on Several Issues of Fully Implementing the "Civil Procedure Law") (1992).

102 See "Supreme Court Issues Open Trial Regulations," *Beijing Xinhua Daily Report: China* (FBIS-CHI-1999–0316), March 17, 1999.

103 See, e.g., China Senior Judges Training Centre and Chinese People's University Law Faculty (ed.), *Zhongguo shenpan anli yaolan* (Compendium of Chinese Case Decisions), Beijing: Public Security University Press, periodical; Legal Research Institute of the PRC Supreme People's Court (ed.) *Renmin fayuan anli xuan* (Compilation of Court Cases), Beijing: Public Security University Press, periodical; Shanghai High People's Court (ed.), *Shanghai fayuan zuixin anli qingxuan* (Selected Most Recent Decisions by the Shanghai Courts), Shanghai: Shanghai People's Press, periodical; Wang Zhaoying (ed.), *Guoji jingji fa jiaoxue anli* (Teaching Cases on International Economic Law), Beijing: China University of Politics and Law Press, 1999; Li Ziping (ed.), *Shewai jingji fa anli* (Cases in Foreign Economic Law), Nanchang: Jiangxi Higher Education Press, 1997; Liu Ruifu (ed.), *Zhonghua renmin gongheguo falu panli fenxi quanshu* (Compendium of Analysis of Legal Decisions), Beijing: International Culture Press, 1995; Wang Cunxue, *op. cit.*, *New Selections of the Foreign-Related Economic Cases in China*, Shanghai: Economic Information Agency, 1992; Qi Tianchang (ed.), *Hetong an li pingxi* (Discussion of Contract Cases), Beijing: Chinese University of Politics and Law Press, 1991; Zhang Huilong, *She wai jingji fa anli jiexi* (Analysis of Sino-Foreign Economic Law Cases), Beijing: Youth Publishers, 1990.

104 See the casebook series *Renmin fayuan yinan panli pingxi* (Critical Analysis of Difficult Decisions by the People's Courts), Changchun: Jilin People's Press, 1999.

105 See "PRC Judiciary's Xiao Yang Supports Reform," Beijing Xinhua Domestic Service, December 14, 1999, in *FBIS Daily Report: China* (FBIS-CHI-2000–0116), January 19, 2000.

106 See "NPC, CPPCC on Court Supervision," Beijing Xinhua Domestic Service, March 10, 2000, in *FBIS Daily Report: China* (FBIS-CHI-2000–0310), March 16, 2000.

107 See generally, J.A. Cohen, "Reforming China's Civil Procedure: Judging the Courts," *American Journal of Comparative Law*, 1997, vol. 45, no. 4, pp. 793–804.

108 See "Supreme People's Court on Providing Services for Economic Development," Beijing Xinhua Domestic Service, March 2, 2000, in *FBIS Daily Report: China* (FBIS-CHI-2000–0302), March 2, 2000.

109 See "Luo Gan on Measures to Tighten Judicial Discipline," Beijing Xinhua Domestic Service, December 21, 1998, in *FBIS Daily Report: China* (FBIS-CHI-98–357), December 28, 1998.

110 See generally, D.C. Clarke, "Dispute Resolution in China," *Journal of Chinese Law*, 1991, vol. 5, p. 245; S.B. Lubman, "Studying Contemporary Chinese Law: Limits, Possibilities and Strategy," *American Journal of Comparative Law*, 1991, vol. 39, p. 333; and P.B. Potter, "Riding the Tiger: Legitimacy and Legal Culture in Post-Mao China," *The China Quarterly*, June 1994, vol. 138, pp. 325–58.

111 See D.C. Clarke, "Dispute Resolution in the PRC: Power, the Courts and Enforcement of Judgments," *Columbia Journal of Chinese Law*, 1996.

112 See "Continuing Reform in PRC Courts," Beijing Xinhua Hong Kong Service, March 19, 2000, in *FBIS Daily Report: China* (FBIS-CHI-2000–0413), April 14, 2000; "China: Supreme Court, Procuratorate Report Work," Beijing Xinhua Domestic Service, September 14, 1998, in *FBIS Daily Report: China* (FBIS-CHI-98–260), September 17, 1998; and Han Zhubin, "Stresses Need to Better Handle Appeals, Tips," Beijing Xinhua Domestic Service, September 25, 1998, in *FBIS Daily Report: China* (FBIS-CHI-98–271), September 28, 1998. Also see Shao Chongzhu (ed.), *Zhong gong fan tan da an zhong an* (Big Cases and Serious Cases on the Chinese Communists' Fight Against Corruption), Hong Kong: So Far (*Xiafeier*) Publishers, 1998, pp. 337 (Hebei High Level People's Court), 339 (Wuxi Procuracy), and 346 (Nanjing Middle Level People's Court).

113 See "Supreme Procuratorate President on Educating Judicial Workers in Work Report to NPC," Beijing Xinhua Domestic Service, March 10, 1999, in *FBIS Daily Report: China* (FBIS-CHI-1999–0316), March 17, 1999. The reference to the Supreme People's Procuratorate is the result of inaccurate translation – the reported speech was given by Xiao Yang, President of the Supreme People's Court.

114 See generally, S. Finder, "Litigation in the Chinese Courts: A New Frontier for Foreign Business," *China Law & Practice*, February 1996, pp. 18–19.

115 For a preliminary discussion, see S.B. Lubman, "Setback for the China-Wide Rule of Law," *op. cit.*

116 See A. Smart, "Gifts, Bribes and *Guanxi*: A Reconsideration of Bourdieu's Social Capital," *Cultural Anthropology*, August 1993, vol. 8, no. 3, pp. 388–408; and M. Yang, *Gifts, Favors, and Banquets: The Art of Social Relationships in China*, Ithaca, NY: Cornell University Press, 1994. I have personally observed the practice of judges meeting with one of the disputants and/or their counsel over dinner to investigate the circumstances of the case

and to hear one side's arguments informally. In most jurisdictions of Europe and North America, these *ex parte* meetings would be considered a violation of a judge's duty of disinterestedness, but in China they are often not considered improper.

117 See P.B. Potter, "Riding the Tiger: Legitimacy and Legal Culture in Post-Mao China," *op. cit.* Chinese and foreign lawyers practicing in China interviewed during 1997–98 underscored that judicial decision making continues to exhibit the characteristics of formalism described here.

118 See "Court President on Ranks of Judges, Police," *Liaowang* (Outlook), August 31, 1998, in *FBIS Daily Report: China* (FBIS-CHI-98–264), September 25, 1998.

119 See Guo Yuyuan (ed.), *Renmin fayuan anli leibian pingxi (jingji shenpan zhuan)* (Analysis of Categories of People's Court Cases: Economic Judgments), Changchun: Jilin Renmin Chubanshe, 1998.

120 See case no. 33, in Zuigao renmin fayuan Zhongguo yingyong faxue yanjiusuo (China Legalization Research Institute of the PRC Supreme People's Court) (ed.), vol. 13, pp. 129–36.

121 These problems were noted formally during the process of revising the Civil Procedure Law in 1990–91, but they appear to continue nonetheless. See "NPC Group Sponsors Civil Procedure Law Forum," Beijing Xinhua Domestic Service, January 23, 1991, in *FBIS Daily Report: China* (FBIS-CHI-91–016), January 23, 1991, p. 21. Also see "NPC, CPPCC on Court Supervision," Beijing Xinhua Domestic Service, March 10, 2000, in *FBIS Daily Report: China* (FBIS-CHI-2000–0310), March 16, 2000.

122 For an example of rhetoric linking ideological purity with impartial and effective judicial institutions, see "Li Peng Addresses NPC Legal System Seminar," Beijing Xinhua Hong Kong Service, August 30, 1998, in *FBIS Daily Report: China* (FBIS-CHI-98–251), September 8, 1998.

123 On judges, see *Zhonghua renmin gongheguo faguan fa* (Judges' Law of the PRC), 1995; "Efforts Urged to Eradicate Judicial Corruption," *Beijing Zhongwen xinwenshe*, September 25, 1998, in *FBIS Daily Report: China* (FBIS-CHI-98–270), September 29, 1998; "NPC to Strengthen Judicial Supervision," Beijing Xinhua Domestic Service, September 15, 1998, in *FBIS Daily Report: China* (FBIS-CHI-98–260), September 21, 1998; and "Supreme Court Promulgates Two Documents," Beijing Xinhua Domestic Service, September 17, 1998, in *FBIS Daily Report: China* (FBIS-CHI-98–262), September 19, 1998. On lawyers, see "PRC Lawyers Law" (1996); Li Y., "Lawyers in China: A 'Flourishing' Profession in a Rapidly Changing Society?" *China Perspectives*, May 11, 2000; P. Sherrington and V. Chan, "New Lawyers Law Needs Further Legislative Clarification," *China Law & Practice*, July/August 1996, pp. 28–30; and K. Song, "China's New Law on Lawyers Will Move System Closer to International Standards," *East Asian Executive Reports*, August 15, 1996, pp. 9–14.

124 See A. Connerty, "Trade with China," *JCI Arbitration*, 1998, vol. 64, pp. 129–36; S.A. Harpole, "Arbitration in China," *Dispute Resolution Journal*, 1997, vol. 51, no. 2, pp. 72–7; and P.B. Potter and M. Donnelly, "Cultural Aspects of Trade Dispute Resolution in Japan and China," Asia Pacific Foundation, 1996.

125 For examples, see Huang Y., "The Stylization and Regularization of the Management and Operation of the Chinese Arbitration Institute," *Journal of International Arbitration*, 1994, vol. 11(2), p. 77; and "Mediation in the Settlement of Business Disputes," *Journal of International Arbitration*, 1991, vol. 8(4), p. 23.

126 See generally, D. Bodde and C. Morris, *Law in Imperial China*, Philadelphia: University of Pennsylvania Press, 1967, pp. 5–6; A. Coates, *Myself a Mandarin,*

London: Frederick Muller, 1968; and R. Van Gulik, *Celebrated Cases of Judge Dee*, New York: Dover Publications, 1976.

127 See generally, Huang Y., "The Ethics of Arbitrators in CIETAC Arbitration," *Journal of International Arbitration*, 1995, vol. 12(2), p. 5.

128 See, e.g., Si X., "CIETAC Arbitration: Joint Venture Case Studies No. 1," in China Law & Practice (ed.), *Dispute Resolution in the PRC: A Practical Guide to Litigation and Arbitration in China*, Hong Kong, China Law & Practice, 1995, case no. 1 (joint venture contract amendments not formally approved were deemed invalid, but the applicant also denied benefit of the bargain under the original contract); case no. 2 (rigid and unsupported conclusion that continued cooperation was impossible resulted in liquidation of joint venture to the benefit of the Chinese party); and case no. 3 (conclusion that bureaucratic department lacked authority to issue loan guarantee resulted in foreign party losing benefit of joint-venture contract); Guo X., *Case Studies of China International Economic and Trade Arbitration*, Hong Kong: Sweet & Maxwell, 1996; case no. 28 (contract outside buyer's approved scope of business deemed invalid and damages shared by buyer and seller); and case no. 31 (conclusion that contract price had been understated to avoid customs duty resulted in denying parties benefit of any contract relation despite partial performance by both).

129 See Guo X., *Case Studies of China International Economic and Trade Arbitration, op. cit.*, cases no. 23 and 24.

130 See, e.g., Li Ziping (ed.), *Shewai jingji fa anli* (Cases in Foreign Economic Law), Nanchang: Jiangxi Higher Education Press, 1997, case no. 4 (dispute over revocation of offer resolved by reference to Vienna Convention on Contracts for the International Sales of Goods – CISG Convention); cases no. 7, 10, and 14 (disputes over non-conforming goods resolved by reference to CISG convention); cases no. 11 and 46 (disputes over delivery terms resolved by reference to ICC definitions of FOB); cases no. 13 and 26 (disputes over non-conforming delivery resolved by reference to CISG Convention and international practice); case no. 24 (dispute over bill of lading resolved by reference to international practice); cases no. 28 and 29 (shipping disputes resolved by reference to Hague–Visby rules); case no. 33 (dispute over collection resolved by reference to Uniform Rules on Collection); Guo X., *Case Studies of China International Economic and Trade Arbitration, op. cit.*; case no. 3 (dispute over pricing provision resolved by reference to the CISG Convention); case no. 8 (dispute over quality of goods resolved by reference to the CISG Convention); case no. 10 (dispute over return of non-conforming goods resolved by reference to the CISG Convention); *Selected Works of China International Economic and Trade Arbitration Commission*, Hong Kong, Sweet & Maxwell (1995); cases no. 2 and 10 (disputes over non-conforming goods resolved by reference to interpretation of the term "FOB" in international practice); case no. 75 (dispute over contract modification resolved by reference to CISG Convention).

131 See Liu Wenhua (ed.), *Shewai jingji jiufen jingjie* (Introduction to Foreign Economic Disputes), Beijing: China Economy Press, 1997. In this book, the Chinese party is almost invariably referred to as a "*woguo gongsi*" (our country's company) and "*wofang*" (our side).

132 See S. Huang, "Several Problems in Need of Resolution in China by Legislation on Foreign Affairs Arbitration," *Journal of International Arbitration*, 1993, vol. 10(3), p. 95.

133 See Zhu Kepeng "Lun guoji shangye zhongcai zhong de fayuan ganyu" (Judicial Intervention in International Commercial Arbitration), *Faxue pinglun* (Theory and Discussion on Law), 1995, no. 4, p. 46.

134 See, e.g., R.A. Aronson, "Testimony before the House Ways and Means Trade Subcommittee, May 23, 1995," *Federal Information Systems*, 1995; M. Bersani, "Enforcement of Arbitration Awards in China," *China Business Review*, May–June, 1992, p. 6 and "Enforcement of Arbitration Awards in China," *Journal of International Arbitration*, 1993, vol. 10, no. 2, p. 47; and A. Mora, "The Revpower Dispute: China's Breach of the New York Convention?" China Law & Practice (ed.), *op. cit.*, p. 151.

135 See "Joint Venture Dispute Triggers Jurisdictional Concerns," *Chinese Law & Practice*, February 1996, pp. 24–8.

136 See Wang S., *Resolving Disputes in the PRC: A Practical Guide to Arbitration and Conciliation in China*, Hong Kong: Sweet & Maxwell Asia, 1996, p. 165 and cases cited on pp. 178–80.

137 See "US Court recognizes Chinese arbitral award," *Chinese Law & Practice*, September 1996, pp. 48–51.

138 See Li Buyun (ed.), *Lifa fa yanjiu* (Study of Legislation Law), Changsha: Hunan People's Press, 1999.

139 See Hu Jianlin, "Guo wai xingzheng sifa tizhi" (Foreign Systems for Administrative Adjudication), *Faxue yanjiu* (Studies in Law), 1989, no. 2, pp. 88–9; and Jiang Bixin, "Guo wai xingzheng susong zhong de sifa biangengquan" (The Juridical Authority of Revision in Foreign Administrative Litigation), *Faxue ribao* (Legal System Daily), June 24, 1989, p. 4.

140 See, e.g., B. Schwartz, "Fashioning an Administrative Law System," *Administrative Law Review*, 1988, vol. 40, no. 3, pp. 415–32.

141 See, e.g., Liu Zhaoxing, "Lianbang deguo de xingzheng susong fa ji xingzheng susong zhidu" (The Administrative Litigation Law and Administrative Litigation System of the Federal Republic of Germany), *Faxue yanjiu* (Studies in Law), 1988, no. 1, pp. 87–90; Liu Hai, "Riben guojia xingzheng jiguan de jiben tedian" (The Basic Features of National Administrative Organs in Japan), *Fazhi ribao* (Legal System Daily), June 24, 1989, p. 4; and Zhang Ling, "Riben xingzheng susong fa zhong de kanggao susong" (Litigation over Refusal of Complaint in Japan's Administrative Litigation Law), *Fazhi ribao* (Legal System Daily), June 24, 1989, p. 4.

142 See, e.g., "Guojia xingzheng jiguan gongzuo renyuan tanwu huilu xingzheng chufen zanxing guiding" (Provisional Regulations on Handling Corruption by State Administrative Institution Officials) and "Guojia xingzheng jiguan gongzuo renyuan tanwu huilu xingzheng chufen zanxing guiding shishi xize" (Implementing Regulations for the Provisional Regulations on Handling Corruption by State Administrative Institution Officials), 1989.

143 See "Guo Luoji kangsu Li Tieying" (Guo Luoji rebuts Li Tieying), *Zhongguo zhi chun* (China Spring), March 1992, pp. 9–13; and "Guo Luoji de shangsu zhuang" (Guo Luoji's Appeal), *Zhongguo zhi chun* (China Spring), May 1992, pp. 44–8.

144 See, e.g., Supreme People's Court Administrative Tribunal (ed.), *Xingzheng susong yu tudi guanlifa: Xin jie* (Administrative Litigation of Land Administration Law: New Interpretations), Beijing: Current Events Press, 1999.

145 See "*Renmin ribao* Discusses Civil Procedure Law," *Beijing Renmin ribao*, March 11, 1982, in *FBIS Daily Report: China*, March 16, 1982, p. K1; "Jurist Answers Questions on Civil Procedure Law," Beijing Xinhua Domestic Service, March 14, 1982, in *FBIS Daily Report: China*, March 16, 1982, p. K3.

146 See, e.g., Jiang Liu, "Min su fa de lifa yuanze yu guoqing" (Legislative Principles and National Conditions in the Civil Procedure Law), *Faxue* (Jurisprudence), 1982, no. 5, pp. 30–2; "Trial Implementation of Civil

Procedure Law Initiated," *Beijing Renmin ribao*, March 29, 1982, in *China Report: Political, Social, Military*, May 12, 1982, p. 90.

147 See Jiang Wei, "Minshi susong fa gai shuo" (Speaking Conceptually of the Civil Procedure Law), *Bai ke zhishi* (Encyclopedia of Knowledge), 1982, no. 1, pp. 6–9.

148 See, e.g., Bi Yuquian, *Minshi zhengju fa panli shiwu yanjiu* (Practical Study of Adjudication in Civil Evidence Law), Beijing: Law Publishing, 1999.

149 See Zhang Yulin, "Towards the UNCITRAL Model Law: A Chinese Perspective," *op. cit.*

150 See generally, M.J. Moser, "China's New International Arbitration Rules," *Journal of International Arbitration*, 1994, vol. 11(3), p. 5; Shen M., "Lun wo guo zhongcai zhidu de xin fazhan" (New Developments in Our Country's Arbitration System), *Faxue pinglun* (Theory and Discussion on Law), 1995, no. 4, p. 40; Guo X., "The Validity and Performance of Arbitration Agreements in China," *Journal of International Arbitration*, 1994, vol. 11(1), p. 47; and G. Liu and A. Lourie, "International Commercial Arbitration in China: History, New Developments and Current Practice," *John Marshall Law Review*, 1995, vol. 28, p. 539.

151 See, e.g., Yuan Quan and Guo Yujun, "ADR – Xifang shengxing de jiejue minshangshi zhengyi de remen zhidu" (ADR – A Popular System Currently in the West for Resolving Civil and Commercial Disputes), *Faxue pinglun* (Legal Studies Commentary), 1999, no. 1, pp. 89–94.

152 See "Notice Concerning the Enforcement of United Nations Convention on the Recognition and Enforcement of Foreign Arbitral Awards Acceded to by Our Country," 1987.

153 See generally, Soley, "ICSID Implementation: An Effective Alternative to International Conflict," *The International Lawyer*, 1985, vol. 19, p. 521.

154 See generally, M.K. Young, "Dispute Resolution in the Uruguay Round: The Lawyers Triumph Over Diplomats," *The International Lawyer*, 1995, vol. 29, p. 389; and G.R. Schell, "Trade Legalism and International Relations Theory: An Analysis of the World Trade Organization," *Duke Law Journal*, 1995, vol. 44, p. 829.

Chapter 3

1 See J.V. Feinerman, "Legal Institution, Administrative Device or Foreign Import: The Roles of Contract in the People's Republic of China," in P.B. Potter (ed.), *Domestic Law Reforms in Post-Mao China*, Armonk, NY, and London: M.E. Sharpe, 1994, pp. 225–44.

2 See *Economic Contract Law of the PRC, 1981*, Articles 2 and 5. Citations for all laws, regulations and treaties are provided in Appendix A: Table of Laws, Regulations, and Treaties.

3 See P.B. Potter, *The Economic Contract Law of China: Legitimation and Contract Autonomy in the PRC*, Seattle and London: University of Washington Press, 1992. For a discussion of the concept of "economic law" see D.C. Clarke, "Regulation and Its Discontents: Understanding Economic Law in China," *Stanford Journal of International Law*, 1992, vol. 28, no. 2, pp. 283–322.

4 See generally, He Guanghui, "Continue to Deepen Reform by Centering on Economic Improvement and Rectification," *Zhongguo jingji tizhi gaige* (Reform of the Chinese Economic Structure), 1990, no. 2, in *FBIS Daily Report: China*, March 23, 1990, p. 21.

5 *Economic Contract Law of the PRC, 1981*, Articles 1, 4, and 7.

6 *Foreign Economic Contract Law of the PRC, 1985*, Article 7.

7 See generally, E.J. Epstein, "Evolution of China's General Principles of Civil Law," *American Journal of Comparative Law*, 1986, vol. 34, p. 705; and H.R. Zheng, *China's Civil and Commercial Law*, Singapore: Butterworth Asia, 1988.

8 See *General Principles of Civil Law, 1986*, Article 3 and Chap. III. For judicial decisions recognizing equality of the parties, see, e.g., "Nongcun chengbao jingying hu qianding de chengbao jingying hetong, shou falu baohu" (A Task Management Contract Signed by a Rural Contractor Receives Legal Safeguard), case no. 70, in Chen Youzun (ed.), *Minshi jingji jinan anli jiesi*, (Interpretation and Analysis of Difficult Civil and Economic Cases), Huhehaote: Inner Mongolia University Press, 1990, p. 119, and "Hetong dangshiren yi fang you guocuo, bing zaocheng dui fang jingji sunshi de, yingdang chengdan minshi zeren" (Where one contract party is at fault and also causes economic losses to the other party, it should bear civil liability), case no. 106, p. 187 in *ibid.*

9 See *General Principles of Civil Law, 1986*, Chaps I and II and Article 54. Also see E. Epstein, "Tortious Liability for Defective Products in the People's Republic of China,"*Journal of Chinese Law*, 1988, vol. 2, p. 285.

10 See *General Principles of Civil Law, 1986*, Article 6.

11 "Zhonghua renmin gongheguo jingji hetong fa tongze" (General Principles of the Economic Contract Law of the PRC), September 22, 1992 (draft on file with the author).

12 See "Amendments to Constitution Published," Beijing Xinhua Domestic Service, March 29, 1993, in *FBIS Daily Report: China* (FBIS-CHI-93–059), March 30, 1993, pp. 42–4.

13 See, e.g., Cai Yanmin and Zhu Tong, "Lun shichang jingji zhong hetong fa mianlin de ruogan wenti," (On Several Issues Confronting Contract Law in the Market Economy), *Zhongshan Daxue xuebao: She ke ban* (Zhongshan University Journal: Social Science Edition), 1993, no. 3, pp. 39–45.

14 See generally, "Cong «san zu dingli» zou xiang tongyi de hetong fa" (From the Three Legs of a Tripod to a Unified Contract Law), in Civil Law Office of the NPC Standing Committee Legal Affairs Committee (ed.), *«Zhonghua renmin gongheguo hetong fa» ji qi zhongyao caogao jieshao* (Introduction to the Contract Law of the PRC and Its Important Drafts), Beijing: Falu Chubanshe, 1999, pp. 1–14.

15 Liang Huixing, "Zhongguo hetong fa qicao guocheng zhong de zhenglun dian" (Points of Contention in the Process of Drafting China's Contract Law), *Faxue* (Jurisprudence), 1996, no. 2, pp. 13–15.

16 "Zhonghua renmin gongheguo hetong fa lifa fangan" (Legislative Proposal for the Contract Law of the PRC), 1995. Also see Pan Weida, "Zhonggong hetong fa zhi jiajiang ji qi weilai fazhan," in *Zhengda faxue pinglun*, 1995, no. 53, pp. 411–32.

17 See Chen Xiaojun and Gao Fei, "Zhiding tongyi hetong fa de ruogan fali wenti sikao" (Considerations of Several Jurisprudential Issues in Enacting a Unified Contract Law), *Faxue yanjiu* (Studies in Law), 1998, no. 1, pp. 53–9.

18 See Civil Law Office of the NPC Standing Committee Legal Affairs Committee (ed.), *«Zhonghua renmin gongheguo hetong fa» ji qi zhongyao caogao jieshao* (Introduction to the Contract Law of the PRC and Its Important Drafts), *op. cit.*, p. 101.

19 Specific proposals were made to link the form of contract to the needs of the economy – even to the extent of addressing issues of electronic commerce. See He Hongfeng and Chen Yaodong, "Dui woguo hetong xingshi lifa de fansi" (Reactions to Legislation of Our Country's Contract Form), *Falu kexue* (Law Science), 1997, no. 5, pp. 84–7.

20 See generally, Sun Weizhi, "Hetong ziyou de lifa quxiang" (Legislation of Freedom of Contract), *Faxue zazhi* (Law Science Magazine), 1998, no. 1, pp. 19–20.

21 Liang Huixing, "Guanyu Zhongguo tongyi hetong fa caoan di san gao" (Concerning the Third Draft of China's Unified Contract Law), *Faxue yuekan* (Law Science Monthly), 1998, no. 2, pp. 47–52.

22 See generally, Jiang P., "Drafting the Uniform Contract Law in China," *Columbia Journal of Asian Law*, 1996, vol. 10, no. 1, pp. 245–58; Liang Huixing, "Zhongguo hetong fa qicao guocheng zhong de zhenglun dian" (Points of Contention in the Process of Drafting China's Contract Law), *op. cit.*; Wang Liming, "Tongyi hetong fa zhiding zhong de ruogan yinan wenti tantao," (Inquiry into Various Thorny Questions in Enacting the Unified Contract Law), *Zhengfa luntan* (Forum on Politics and Law), 1996, no. 4, pp. 49–56, and no. 5, pp. 52–60.

23 See Yang Minglun, "Cong hetong fa shinigao dao zhenqiu yijian gao" (From the Provisional Draft of the Contract Law to the Draft for Soliciting Opinions), in Civil Law Office of the NPC Standing Committee Legal Affairs Committee (ed.), *«Zhonghua renmin gongheguo hetong fa» ji qi zhongyao caogao jieshao* (Introduction to the Contract Law of the PRC and Its Important Drafts), *op. cit.*, pp. 101–11.

24 See Du Tao, "Cong hetong fa zhengqiu yijian gao dao hetong fa cao an" (From the Contract Law Draft for Soliciting Opinions to the Draft Contract Law), *ibid.*, pp. 159–71.

25 See "Quanguo renda changweihui fabu tongzhi zhengqiu «Hetong fa (caoan)» yijian" (The NPC Standing Committee Issues a Circular Seeking Opinions on the "Contract Law (Draft)"), *Renmin ribao: haiwai ban* (People's Daily: Overseas Edition), September 5, 1998, p. 4; "China NPC Developing Unified Contract Code," Beijing Xinhua English Service, August 19, 1998, in *FBIS Daily Report: China* (FBIS-CHI-98–231), August 20, 1998. For reviews of the September draft by foreign specialists, see, e.g., H. Scogin and B. Braude, "New Contract Basics," *China Business Review*, January/February 1999, pp. 36–42; N. Wang, "The new PRC contract law," *China Law & Practice*, October 1998, pp. 42–6; and R. Peerenboom, "China's New Contract Law Fails to Address Concerns of Foreign Technology Providers," *East Asian Executive Reports*, September 15, 1998, pp. 9–15.

26 See "Guanyu hetong fa caoan de yijian" (Opinions on the Draft Contract Law) *Zhengzhi yu falu* (Politics and Law), 1999, no. 1, pp. 36–42; "Unified Contract Law Aids Orderly Economic Development," Beijing Xinhua English Service, March 13, 1999, in *FBIS Daily Report: China* (FBIS-CHI-1999–0313), March 16, 1999.

27 See "NPC Says Contract Law Should Be Expanded," Beijing Xinhua English Service, October 30, 1998, in *FBIS Daily Report: China* (FBIS-CHI-98–303), November 2, 1998; and "NPC Deputies Discuss Draft Contract Law," Beijing Xinhua Domestic Service, March 14, 1999, in *FBIS Daily Report: China* (FBIS-CHI-1999–0322), March 24, 1999.

28 See, e.g., Civil Law Research Office of Peking University Law Department, "Guanyu tongyi hetong fa caoan de xiugai jianyi" (Suggestions on Revising the Unified Contract Law Draft), *Zhong wai faxue* (Chinese and Foreign Jurisprudence), 1999 no. 1, pp. 91–101; and "Guanyu hetong fa caoan deyijian" (Opinions on the Draft Contract Law), *Zhengzhi yu falu* (Politics and Law), 1999, no. 1, pp. 36–42. Also see Civil Law Office of the NPC Standing Committee Legal Affairs Committee (ed.), *«Zhonghua renmin gongheguo hetong fa» lifa ziliao xuan* (Selected Legislative Materials on the Contract Law of the PRC), Beijing: Falu Chubanshe, 1999, pp. 189–282. Also see "Li Peng Solicits Public Opinion on Contract Law," Beijing Xinhua English Service, January 13, 1999, in *FBIS Daily Report: China* (FBIS-CHI-99–013), January 14, 1999; "Li Peng

Studies Contract Law Legislation," Beijing Xinhua Domestic Service, January 16, 1999, in *FBIS Daily Report: China* (FBIS-CHI-99–016), January 20, 1999.

29 See, e.g., Hu Jihua and Wang Zhaoying (eds), *Zhonghua renmin gongheguo hetong fa shiyi yu shiyong zhinan* (Guide to Interpretation and Application of the Contract Law of the PRC), Beijing: Red Flag Press, 1999, p. 6.

30 See Wang Jinlan and Li Jing, "Hetong fa guishu fanchou de sikao" (Reflecting on the Categorization of the New Contract Law), *Hebei shifan daxue xuebao* (Journal of Hebei Normal University), 1997, no. 4, pp. 31–2 and 74.

31 See generally, "Xin hetong fa bi tan" (Notes and Discussion on the New Contract Law), *Faxuejia* (Jurist), 1999, no. 3, pp. 69–82.

32 See, e.g., Economic Adjudication Chamber of the Supreme People's Court (ed.), *Hetong fa shijie yu shiyong* (Interpretation and application of contract law), Beijing: Xinhua Press, 1999, pp. 1670 *et seq.*, especially "Zhonghua renmin gongheguo cujin keji chengguo zhuanhua fa (jielu)" (Law of the PRC on promoting dissemination of the technical results – excerpts) *ibid.*, p. 1690 and Section 5.3 on adjudication of technology contract disputes in "Zuigao renmin fayuan guanyu quanguo jinji shenpan gongzuo zuotanhui jiyao (jielu)" (Outline of the Supreme People's Court work conference on economic adjudication – excerpts), *ibid.*, p. 1693.

33 See generally, Wang Liming, "An Effective Guarantee for a Socialist Market Economy – A Special Writing for the Contract Law Adopted," Beijing Xinhua Domestic Service, March 15, 1999, in *FBIS Daily Report: China* (FBIS-CHI-1999–0409), April 14, 1999; Zhong Min, "China's New Contract Law Meets the Demand of Market Economic Development," Hong Kong China News Agency, March 24, 1999, in *FBIS Daily Report: China* (FBIS-CHI-1999–0408), April 12, 1999; and Xiang Zhenhua and Wang Cheng, "Unify Contract Law," *Renmin ribao: haiwai ban* (People's Daily: Overseas Edition), March 26, 1999, in *FBIS Daily Report: China* (FBIS-CHI-1999–0407), April 8, 1999. For initial observations of foreign specialists, see E.A. Zaloom and H. Liu, "China's Contract Law Marks a New Stage in Commercial Law Drafting," in *China Law & Practice*, May 1999, pp. 15–18; and R. Peerenboom. "A Missed Opportunity? China's New Contract Law Fails to Address Foreign Technology Providers' Concerns," *China Law & Practice*, May 1999, pp. 83–7.

34 Li Peng had taken a highly visible approach to disseminating official views on the law in the months leading up to the NPC. See, e.g., "Li Peng dao Fengtai fayuan zuotan hetong fa caoan" (Li Peng goes to Fengtai court to discuss the draft contract law) *Renmin fayuan bao* (People's Court Gazette), January 14, 1999, p. 1.

35 See S.A. Harpole, "Supreme Court interpretation supports implementation of Contract Law," in CCH Australia Ltd (ed.), *China Law Update*, March 2000, pp. 3–7.

36 See W.C. Jones, "The Significance of the Opinion of the Supreme People's Court on Questions Concerning the Implementation of the General Principles of Civil Law of the People's Republic of China," in P.B. Potter (ed.), *op. cit.*, pp. 97–108.

37 See generally, R.C. Keith, *China's Struggle for the Rule of Law*, New York: St Martin's Press, 1994.

38 In reference to publication of the draft UCL in September 1998, the authoritative *People's Daily* noted that this is "the first civil law that was openly discussed by the public." See Xiang Z. and Wang Cheng, *op. cit.*

39 See P.B. Potter, "Foreign Investment Law in the PRC: Dilemmas of State Control," *The China Quarterly*, March 1995, no. 141, pp. 155–85.

40 See, e.g., Economic Tribunal of the Supreme People's Court (ed.), *Hetong fa shijie yu shiyong* (Interpretation and Application of Contract Law), Beijing: New China Press, 1999.

41 See "Supreme People's Court, Several Issues Concerning Application of the Contract Law of the PRC Interpretation (1)" (2000), Article 4. Also see Y. Chen, "Interpreting the PRC Contract Law" in *China Law & Practice*, March 2000, p. 42.

42 "Supreme People's Court Explanation of Several Questions Concerning the Application of the Foreign Economic Contract Law, 1988."

43 See Hu Jihua and Wang Zhaoying (eds), *Zhonghua renmin gongheguo hetong fa: Jie yong shouce* (Handbook on Interpretation and Application of the Contract Law of the PRC), Beijing: Red Flag Press, 1999, pp. 687–90.

44 See, e.g., *Secured Interests Law of the PRC, 1995*, Article 13; *Maritime Law of the PRC, 1992*, Articles 43 and 44. For discussion of written contract requirements in foreign trade and investment, see generally, Hu Jihua and Wang Zhaoying (eds), *Zhonghua renmin gongheguo hetong fa shiyi yu shiyong zhinan* (Guide to Interpretation and Application of the Contract Law of the PRC), *op. cit.*, p. 64.

45 Nothing is said about modifications that include additional as opposed to changed terms, an omission that will require clarification. See H. Scogin and B. Braude, "New Contract Basics," *China Business Review*, January/February 1999, pp. 36–42.

46 The approval requirements of prior law were often interpreted to deny legal effect to letters of intent. However, some courts in China were willing to give contract enforcement to letters of intent signed by foreign trade companies empowered to conduct import/export activities on their own. See Guo Yuyuan (ed.), *Renmin fayuan anli leibian pingxi: Jingji shen pan zhuan* (Evaluation of People's Court Cases by Category: Economic Adjudication Volume), Changchuan: Jilin People's Press, 1998, p. 392.

47 See "Supreme People's Court, Several Issues Concerning Application of the Contract Law of the PRC Interpretation (1)," (2000), Article 9. Also see S.A. Harpole, *op. cit.*, p. 4.

48 For an example of the difficulties with uncertain standards of agency law, see Guo Yuyuan (ed.), *op. cit.*, p. 400.

49 The term "full" (*wanquan*) was apparently added late in the drafting process to emphasize the duty of complete performance. See Xiang Z. and Wang Cheng, *op. cit.* Also see *Renmin ribao* (People's Daily), March 14, 1999.

50 For discussion of Li Peng's call for the UCL to address the "triangular debt" problem, see "Li Peng Solicits Public Opinion on Contract Law," *op. cit.*

51 April 11, 1980, UN Doc. A/Conf.97/18, Annex I (1980), *International Legal Materials (ILM)*, vol. 19, (came into force, January 1, 1988). For discussion of the CCISG's role in unifying private international law, see J. Honnold, *Uniform Law for International Sales under the 1980 United Nations Convention* (3rd edn), Deventer, Netherlands, and Boston, Kluwer: 1999. Also see J. Spanogle, "The Arrival of Private International Law," *George Washington Journal of International Law & Economics*, 1991, vol. 25, p. 477; and the collected articles on the CISG Convention in *Cornell International Law Journal*, 1988, vol. 21 and *Journal of Law and Commerce*, 1988, vol. 8.

52 E.A. Farnsworth, "Review of Standard Forms or Terms Under the Vienna Convention," *Cornell International Law Journal*, 1988, vol. 21, p. 446.

53 R.A. Hillman, "Article 29(2) of the United Nations Convention on Contracts for the International Sale of Goods: A New Effort at Clarifying the Legal Effect of 'No Oral Modification' Clauses," *Cornell International Law Journal*, 1988, vol. 21, p. 449.

54 See generally, P.B. Potter, *Chinese Foreign Business Law: Past Accomplishments, Future Challenges*, San Francisco: 1990 Institute, 1995.

55 See Liang Huixing, "Zichan jieji minfa zhong de hetong ziyou," (Freedom of Contract in Bourgeois Civil Law), *Xuexi yu tansuo* (Study and Inquiry), 1981, no.

6, pp. 39–43. Also see *ibid.*, "Lun wo guo hetong falu zhidu de jihua yuanze yu hetong ziyou yuanze," (On the Principles of Planning and Freedom of Contract in Our Country's Contract Law), *Faxue yanjiu* (Studies in Law), 1982, no. 4, pp. 44–9.

56 "Zhonghua renmin gongheguo jingji hetong fa tongze" (General Principles of the Economic Contract Law of the PRC), *op. cit.*

57 See Qu Guangming and Cai Xiao'e, "Shewai hetong falu shiyong yu guoji sifa de liang da jishi" (Two Cornerstones of the Application of Law in Foreign Contracts and International Private Law), *Fa shang yanjiu* (Studies in Law and Commerce), 1996, no. 4, pp. 51–6.

58 See generally, Civil Law Office of the NPC Standing Committee Legal Affairs Committee (ed.), «*Zhonghua renmin gongheguo hetong fa*» *lifa ziliao xuan* (Selected Legislative Materials on the Contract Law of the PRC), *op. cit.*, pp. 283 *et seq.*

59 See Zhang Guangxing, "Zhonghua renmin gongheguo hetong fa de qicao" (Drafting the Contract Law of the PRC), *Faxue yanjiu* (Studies in Law), 1995, no. 5, p. 12.

60 See, e.g., Wang Liming, "Lun hetong de xiangduixing," (On the Relationality of Contracts) *Zhongguo faxue* (Chinese Jurisprudence), 1996, no. 4, pp. 63–73; *ibid.*, "Hetong a de mubiao yu guli jiaoyi" (The Purpose of Contract Law and the Encouragement of Transactions), *Faxue yanjiu* (Studies in Law), 1996, no. 3, pp. 93–9; Liang Huixing, "Lun hetong wuxian zhidu; Lun woguo minfa hetong gainian" (On the Unlimited System of Contract; On the Concept of Civil Law Contract in Our Country), *Zhongguo faxue* (Chinese Jurisprudence), 1992, no. 1, pp. 52–7.

61 See, e.g., Zheng Li, "Lun heyi (xieyi) shi hetong lilun de jishi" (On Agreement as the Bedrock of Contract Theory), *Faxuejia* (Jurist), 1993, no. 4, pp. 9–16; Wang Tiejun, "Lun woguo de hetong jiechu zhidu" (On Our System of Termination of Contracts), *Faxue yanjiu* (Studies in Law), 1994, no. 4, pp. 25–31; Wang Weiguo, "Lun hetong wuxiao zhidu" (On the System for Invalidating Contracts), *Faxue yanjiu* (Studies in Law), 1994, no. 3, pp. 11–24; Cao Siquan and Zhu Gaungxin, "Hetong fa ding jiechu de shiyou tantao" (Inquiry on the Contract Law Setting the Particulars for Termination of Contract), *Zhongguo faxue* (Chinese Jurisprudence), 1998, no. 4, pp. 34–47; Li Yongjun, "Woguo hetong fa shi fou xuyao duli de yuqi weiyue zhidu" (Does Our Contract Law Need an Independent System for Anticipatory Breach), *Zhengfa luntan* (Forum on Politics and Law), 1998, no. 6, pp. 34–42; Ren Rongming, "Guoji shangshi hetong tongze dui wo guo hetong fa qishi" (The Influence of International Commercial Contract Principles on Our Contract Law), *Faxue* (Jurisprudence), 1998, no. 7, pp. 47–9; Gao Fuping and Wang Lianguo, "Weituo hetong yu shoutuo xingwei" (Agency Contracts and the Acceptance of Entrustment), *Faxue* (Jurisprudence), 1999, no. 4, pp. 38–42; Li Jing-shao, "EDI hetong de falu wenti" (Legal Issues of EDI Contracts), *Fa shang yanjiu* (Studies in Law and Commerce), 1999, no. 1, pp. 64–8; and Wang Xiaoneng, "«Zhonghua renmin gongheguo hetong fa» zhong de weiyue zeren zhidu" (The System for Liability for Breach in the Contract Law of the PRC), *Henan sheng zhengfa guanli ganbu xueyuan xuebao* (Journal of the Henan Provincial Institute for Political Legal Administrative Cadres), 1999, no. 3, pp. 10–20 and 28.

62 See generally, Jiang Ping, "Drafting the Uniform Contract Law in China," *op. cit.*; Liang Huixing, "Zhongguo hetong fa qicao guocheng zhong de zhenglun dian" (Points of Contention in the Process of Drafting China's Contract Law), *op. cit.*; and Wang Liming, "Tongyi hetong fa zhiding zhong de ruogan yinan wenti tantao," (Inquiry into Various Thorny Questions in Enacting a Unified Contract Law), *op. cit.*

63 See Yang Minglun, *op. cit.*, pp. 101–11 at p. 102.

64 See Du Tao, *op. cit.*

65 See, e.g., Shi Shaxia "Dui wo guo hetong lifa ruogan zhengyi wenti de tantao" (Inquiry on Various Controversial Issues in Our Contract Legislation), *Fazhi yu shehui fazhan* (The Legal System and Social Development), 1998, no. 2, pp. 20–5.

66 See "Difang, zhongyang youguan bumen he faxue jiaoxue yanjiu den danwei dui hetong fa zhengqiu yijian gao zongce de yijian" (General Opinions of Local and Central Level Relevant Departments and Legal, Teaching and Research Units on the General Principles of the Contract Law Draft for Soliciting Opinions), in Civil Law Office of the NPC Standing Committee Legal Affairs Committee (ed.), *«Zhonghua renmin gongheguo hetong fa» lifa ziliao xuan* (Selected Legislative Materials on the Contract Law of the PRC), *op. cit.*, pp. 75–6.

67 See "Faxue zhuanjia, youguan bumen he renmin fayuan de tongzhi tan hetong fa zhidao sixiang ji qi tiaozheng fanwei" (Legal Specialists and Comrades from Related Departments and People's Courts Speak on the Guiding Thought and Scope of Amendment of the Contract Law), in Civil Law Office of the NPC Standing Committee Legal Affairs Committee (ed.), *«Zhonghua renmin gongheguo hetong fa» lifa ziliao xuan* (Selected Legislative Materials on the Contract Law of the PRC), *op. cit.*, pp. 73–4.

68 See Du Tao, *op. cit.*

69 See generally, Li Kaiguo, "Dui «Hetong fa zhengqiu yijian gao» ruogan wenti de kanfa he xiugai jianyi" (Views and Suggestions for Revision on Several Issues of the Contract Law Draft for Soliciting Opinions), *Xiandai faxue* (Contemporary Jurisprudence) 1998, no. 6, pp. 17–26.

70 See, e.g., Jiang Ping, Cheng Hehong, and Shen Weixing, "Lun xin hetong fa zhong de hetong ziyou yuanze yu chengshi xinyong yuanze" (On the Principle of Freedom of Contract and the Principle of Good Faith on the New Contract Law), *Zhengfa luntan* (Politics and Law Forum), 1999, no. 1, pp. 2–11; Wang Liming, "Tongyi hetong da zhiding zhong de ruogan yinan wenti tantao" (Inquiry on Several Thorny Questions in the Course of Enacting the Unified Contract Law), *Zhengfa luntan*, *op. cit.*, no. 4, pp. 49–56.

71 See, e.g., Wang Yuanzhi and Feng Jingsheng, "Lun hetong zhengyi" (On Contract Justice), *Zhengfa luntan* (Politics and Law Forum), 1996, no. 6, pp. 60–4.

72 See Chen Ming, "Guanyu hetong xia shi gongping de rending" (Holding to Principle of Manifest Unfairness), *Xiandai faxue* (Contemporary Jurisprudence), 1998, no. 5, pp. 92–4; and Peng Zhenming and Ge Tongshan, "Lun hetong xian shi gongping yuanze" (On the Principle of Manifest Unfairness in Contract), *Faxue pinglun* (Legal Commentary), 1999, no. 1, pp. 62–8 and 105.

73 See Zhang Guangxing, *op. cit.*, p. 13.

74 See P.B. Potter, *The Economic Contract Law of China*, *op. cit.*

75 See "Difang, zhongyang youguan bumen he faxue jiaoxue yanjiu den danwei dui «hetong fa caoan de yijian»" (General Opinions of Local and Central Level Relevant Departments and Legal, Teaching and Research Units on the Contract Law Draft), *op. cit.*

76 See generally, A. Hagedorn, "Cultural Characteristics in the Chinese Contract Law: A Multidisciplinary Approach," Leiden–Beijing Legal Transformation Project Occasional Paper, 1996, C98/3.

77 A survey of 262 contract disputes in Tianjin in 1982 revealed that even among the contracts deemed valid, 88.35 percent of the agreements were incomplete or otherwise failed to comply with the requirements of the Economic Contract Law. See Han Tongzhen, "Cong jingji jiufen anjian kan dangqian Tianjin shi jingji tizhi gaige zhong ying zhuyi jiejue de jige wenti" (From Reviewing Cases of Economic Disputes in Tianjin, We Can See Several Issues of Economic

Structural Reform that Need to Be Resolved), *Zhongguo faxue* (Chinese Jurisprudence), 1986, no. 4, pp. 44–51.

78 See, e.g., cases at pp. 102, 109, 114, 118, 136, and 172, in An Conghua *et al.* (eds), *Renmin fayuan yinan panli pingxi: Jingji zhuan* (Evaluation of Difficult Cases of the People's Courts: Economic Volume), Changchun: Jilin Chubanshe, 1999. Also see Guo Yuyuan (ed.), *op. cit.*, p. 56 and case no. 33, in Supreme People's Court (ed.), *Renmin fayuan anli xuan* (Compilation of People's Court Cases), vol. 13, Beijing: People's Court Publishing, 1995, pp. 129–36.

79 The volumes of judicial decisions reviewed for this article include An Conghua *et al.* (eds), *Renmin fayuan yinan panli pingxi: Jingji zhuan* (Evaluation of difficult cases of the People's Courts: Economic Volume), *op. cit.*; Zhai J. *et al.* (eds), *Renmin fayuan yinan panli pingxi: Minshi zhuan* (Evaluation of Difficult Cases of the People's Courts: Civil Volume), Changchun: Jilin Chubanshe, 1999; Wang Guichen, *et al.* (eds), *Renmin fayuan yinan panli pingxi: Xingzheng zhuan* (Evaluation of Difficult Cases of the People's Courts: Administrative Volume), Changchun: Jilin Chubanshe, 1999; Zeng Xianyi, *Zhongguo minfa anli yu xueli yanjiu* (Studies in Chinese Civil Law Cases and Theory), (serial including volumes on General Principles of Civil Law; Tort and Inheritance, Obligations, and Property), Beijing: Law Publishing, 1998; volumes covering 1996–99 of the Shanghai fayuan anli jingxuan (Carefully Selected Cases of the Shanghai Courts), Shanghai: Shanghai People's Press, annual; Supreme People's Court (ed.), *Renmin fayuan anli xuan* (Compilation of People's Court Cases), nos 23–9, Beijing: Shishi Chubanshe, 1998–99; Civil Division of the Supreme People's Court (ed.), *Zuigao renmin fayuan minshi anjian jiexi* (Analysis of Civil Cases of the Supreme People's Court), nos 1 and 2, Beijing: Law Publishing, 1999, 2000; Liang Huaren and Zhang Jiyang (eds), *Changjian anjian guifanhua shenli zhinan* (Guide to the Standardization of Commonly Seen Cases) (3 vols), Beijing: Politics and Law University Press, 1992; Guo Yuyuan (ed.), *op. cit.*; *Jingji shenpan zhidao yu cankao* (Civil and Commercial Trial Review), Beijing: Law Publishing, periodical; and Chinese Academy of Social Sciences Intellectual Property Centre (ed.), *Zhishi chanquan yanjiu* (Intellectual Property Studies), Beijing: Zhongguo fangzhen chubanshe, periodical. Case reports also appear in the various periodicals cited throughout this volume.

80 See, e.g., case no. 111, in *Shanghai fayuan anli jingxuan: 1999* (Carefully Selected Cases of the Shanghai Courts: 1999), Shanghai: Shanghai People's Press, 2000, p. 564; housing loan case noted in Guo Yuyuan (ed.), *op. cit.*, p. 37; and case no. 5, in Liang Huaren and Zhang Jiyang (eds), *op. cit.*, p. 43.

81 See, e.g., case no. 19, in Supreme People's Court (ed.), *Renmin fayuan anli xuan* (Compilation of People's Court Cases), vol. 13, *op. cit.*

82 See, e.g., case no. 24, in *Shanghai fayuan anli jingxuan: 1999* (Carefully Selected Cases of the Shanghai Courts: 1999), *op. cit.*, p. 113; case no. 38 in case no. 27, *ibid.*, p. 141.

83 See, e.g., An Conghua *et al.* (eds), *Renmin fayuan yinan panli pingxi: Jingji zhuan* (Evaluation of Difficult Cases of the People's Courts: Economic Volume), *op. cit.*, p. 96.

84 See, e.g., case no. 18, in *Shanghai fayuan anli jingxuan: 1999* (Carefully Selected Cases of the Shanghai Courts: 1999), *op. cit.*, p. 85.

85 See, e.g., An Conghua *et al.* (eds), *Renmin fayuan yinan panli pingxi: Jingji zhuan* (Evaluation of Difficult Cases of the People's Courts: Economic Volume), *op. cit.*, p. 61; "Technology Transfer in Breach of Contract," *China Law & Practice*, February 25, 1993, p. 17.

86 See, e.g., An Conghua *et al.* (eds), *Renmin fayuan yinan panli pingxi: Jingji zhuan* (Evaluation of Difficult Cases of the People's Courts: Economic Volume), *op. cit.*, p. 9.

87 See, e.g., *ibid.*, p. 278.
88 See, e.g., case no. 27, in *Shanghai fayuan anli jingxuan: 1999* (Carefully Selected Cases of the Shanghai Courts: 1999), *op. cit.*, p. 128 (voluntary return of deposit in household refurbishment contract); case no. 88, in *Shanghai fayuan anli jingxuan: 1996* (Carefully Selected Cases of the Shanghai Courts: 1996) Shanghai: Shanghai People's Press, 1997, p. 302 (court managed settlement of dispute over commodities exchange contract); An Conghua *et al.* (eds), *Renmin fayuan yinan panli pingxi: Jingji zhuan* (Evaluation of Difficult Cases of the People's Courts: Economic Volume), *op. cit.*, p. 31 (unsuccessful negotiations to revise terms of swap contract for refrigerators); and case no. 54, in *Shanghai fayuan anli jingxuan: 1999* (Carefully Selected Cases of the Shanghai Courts: 1999), *op. cit.*, p. 275 (court managed mediation of dispute over steel supply contract).
89 See case compilations cited in note 79, supra.
90 See, e.g., Liang Huaren and Zhang Jiyang (eds), *Changjian anjian guifan hua sheli zhinan* (Guide to the Standardization of Commonly Seen Cases) (3 vols), Beijing: University of Politics and Law Press, 1992.
91 See case no. 9, in Supreme People's Court (ed.), *Renmin fayuan anli xuan* (Compilation of People's Court Cases), vol. 13, *op. cit.*
92 Despite recent efforts to increase their legal training, judges in China are still drawn mainly from the ranks of the military and have little formal legal education. See S.B. Lubman, *Bird in a Cage: Legal Reform in China After Mao*, Stanford, Calif.: Stanford University Press, 1999.
93 See Guo Yuyuan (ed.), *op. cit.* In this volume, cases from the late 1980s and early 1990s are cited with approval, where judgments are given based on issues of general fairness and subjectivity in the capacity of parties to predict market price changes or to respond to arbitrary changes in state-set prices.
94 See Guo Yuyuan (ed.), *op. cit.*, p. 3.
95 See Guo Yuyuan (ed.), *op. cit.*, p. 374.

Chapter 4

1 This chapter is adapted from P.B. Potter, "Globalization and Local Legal Culture: Dilemmas in China's Use of Liberal Ideas of Private Property Rights," *Asian Law*, 2000, vol. 2, pp. 1–33.
2 See generally, Liu Jingwei, "Cong woguo tudi zhidu zhi biange kan wuquanfa zhi feixing" (Viewing the Abandonment of Property Rights from the Transformation of the Land System), *Zhengzhi yu falu* (Politics and Law), 1996, no. 3, pp. 47–8.
3 For discussion of the liberal tradition in property rights see P.B. Potter, "Property: Questioning Efficiency, Liberty and Imperialism," in N. Mercuro and W.J. Samuels (eds), *The Fundamental Interrelationships Between Government and Property*, Stamford, Conn.: JAI Press, 1999.
4 See, e.g., Qian Mingxing, "Lun woguo wuquanfa de jiben yuance" (On the Basic Principles of Our Civil Law), *Beijing daxue xuebao* (Peking University Journal), 1998, no. 1, pp. 29–38; Zheng Chengsi, "Minfadian zhong de jige gainian xianyi" (Various Basic Ideas in the Civil Code), People's University Social Sciences Information Centre, *Minshang faxue* (Civil and Commercial Law), 1998, no. 7, pp. 14–15; Yu Nengwu and Wang Shenyi, "Lun wuquan fa de xiandaihua fazhan qushi" (The Development of Modern Property Law), *Minshang faxue* (Chinese Jurisprudence), 1998, no. 1, pp. 72–80; Zheng Ruikun, "Lun woguo de wuquan lifa" (Legislation of Our Country's Property Rights), *Faxue* (Jurisprudence), 1998, no. 3, pp. 16 and 18–19; Guo Mingrui, "Guanyu woguo

wuquan lifa de san dian sikao" (Three Perspectives on Our Country's Property Legislation), *Minshang faxue* (Chinese Jurisprudence), 1998, no. 2, pp. 21–6.

5 See, e.g., Liang Huixing, *Zhongguo wuquanfa caoan jianyi gao* (Outline of Opinion on a Draft Chinese Property Law), Beijing, Social Science Manuscripts Press, 2000; Sun Xianzhi, "Wuquan xingwei lilun tan yuan yiqi yiyi" (Exploring the Origins and Significance of Theories of Property Behavior), *Faxue yanjiu* (Studies in Law), 1996, no. 3, pp. 80–92; Wang Liming, "Wuquan xingwei ruogan wenti tantao" (Inquiry on Several Issues of Property Rights Behavior), *Minshang faxue* (Chinese Jurisprudence), 1997, no. 1, pp. 58–70. Also see E.J. Epstein, "The Theoretical System of Property Rights in China's General Principles of Civil Law: Theoretical Controversy in the Drafting Process and Beyond," *Law and Contemporary Problems*, 1989, vol. 52 no. 2/3, pp. 179–216.

6 See, e.g., Qian M., *Wuguan fa yuan li* (Principles of Property Law), Beijing: Peking University Press, 1994; Ji Yibao, "Lun wuquan gongshi de xingzhi he zhidu jiazhi" (On the Character and Systemic Value of Property Public Notice) *Zhong wai faxue* (Chinese and Foreign Jurisprudence), 1997, no. 3, pp. 47–51. Also see Wang Liming, "Wuquan xingwei ruogan wenti tantao" (Inquiry on Several Issues of Property Rights Behavior), *op. cit.*

7 See B. Bouckaert, "What is Property?" *Harvard Journal of Law & Public Policy*, 1990, vol. 13, no. 1, pp. 785, *et seq.*

8 See generally, H.J. Berman, *Law and Revolution: The Formation of the Western Legal Tradition*, Cambridge, Mass., and London: Harvard University Press, 1983; and M. Tigar and M. Levy, *Law and the Rise of Capitalism*, New York: Free Press, 1977.

9 See C. Rose, "Property as a Keystone Right?" *Notre Dame Law Review*, 1995/96, vol. 71, nos 1–3, pp. 329–65; S. Coval, J.C. Smith, and S. Coval, "The Foundations of Property and Property Law," *Cambridge Law Journal*, 1986, vol. 35, no. 3, pp. 457–75.

10 See "No. 10: Madison," *The Federalist Papers*, New York: New American Library, 1961, pp. 77–83; and C.A. Beard, *An Economic Interpretation of the Constitution of the United States*, New York: Free Press, 1941, p. 156. Also see L.S. Underkuffler, "On Property: An Essay," *Yale Law Journal*, 1990, vol. 100, nos 1–2, pp. 127–48.

11 See C.A. Beard, *op. cit.*, p. 176.

12 See P.G. Stillman, "Hegel's Analysis of Property in the Philosophy of Right," *Cardozo Law Review*, 1989, vol. 10, nos 5–6, pp. 1031–72.

13 For a discussion of the wide range of justifications for property rights, see C. Rose, "Property as a Keystone Right?" *op. cit.* Professor Rose identifies seven sources of property rights: (1) priority; (2) power-spreading; (3) independence; (4) symbolics; (5) civilizing; (6) distraction; and (7) pursuit of luxury.

14 R.A. Epstein, *Takings: Private Property and the Power of Eminent Domain*, Cambridge, Mass.: Harvard University Press, 1985.

15 R. Posner, *Economic Analysis of Law*, 3rd edn, Boston: Little, Brown, 1986.

16 See R.A. Epstein, "Property and Necessity," *Harvard Journal of Law & Public Policy*, 1990, vol. 13, no. 1, pp. 2–9.

17 See J.E. Krier, "The (Unlikely) Death of Property," *ibid.*, pp. 75–83.

18 See, e.g., C. Fried, "Protecting Property: Law and Politics," *ibid.*, pp. 44–66.

19 See, e.g., J. Rabkin, "Private Property and Public Office," *ibid.*, pp. 54–9.

20 See F. Schauer, "Property as Politics," *ibid.*, pp. 60–6.

21 See J. Stick, "Turning Rawls into Nozick and Back Again," *Northwestern University Law Review*, Spring 1987, vol. 81, no. 3, pp. 363–416.

22 Carol Rose's critique of Stick's analysis focuses on the perspective of the "rational utility maximizer" (RUM), who serves as an individuated expression of social

response to the alternatives presented by Rawls and Nozick, and who in Rose's view finds both somewhat wanting. See C. Rose, "'Enough, and as Good' Of What?" *ibid.*, pp. 417–42. Also see J. Stick, "Renegotiating a RUM Deal," *ibid.*, pp. 443–57.

23 See E.F. Paul, "Natural Rights and Property Rights," *Harvard Journal of Law & Public Policy*, 1990, vol. 13, no. 1, pp. 10–15.

24 See L.S. Underkuffler, *op. cit.*

25 C. Rose, "Property as a Keystone Right?" *op. cit.*, pp. 329–65.

26 A. Frame, "Property: Some Pacific Reflections," *New Zealand Law Journal*, January 1992, pp. 21–5.

27 See, e.g., W.M. Corden, *Trade Policy and Economic Welfare*, Oxford: Clarendon Press, 1974; and S.S. Silbey, "'Let Them Eat Cake': Globalization, Postmodern Colonialism, and the Possibilities of Justice," *Law & Society Review*, 1997, vol. 31, no. 2, pp. 207–35.

28 See R.H.A. Ashford, "The Binary Economics of Louis Kelso: The Promise of Universal Capitalism," *Rutgers Law Journal* 1990/91, vol. 22, no. 1, pp. 2–121.

29 See C.A. Reich, "The New Property After 25 Years," *University of San Francisco Law Review*, Winter 1990, vol. 24, no. 2, pp. 223–53.

30 *ibid.* Also see R.L. Rabin, "The Administrative State and Its Excesses: Reflections on The New Property," *ibid.*, pp. 273–9.

31 See W.M. Kunstler, "A 'Real World' Perspective on the New Property," *ibid.*, pp. 291–6.

32 J.S. Thomas and M.A. Meyer, *The New Rules of Global Trade: A Guide to the World Trade Organization*, Scarborough, Ontario: Carswell, 1998.

33 International Legal Materials (ILM), "Agreement on Trade-Related Intellectual Property Rights," *I.L.M.*, 1994, vol. 33, p. 1197; J.H. Reichman, "Universal Minimum Standards of Intellectual Property Protection under the TRIPs Component of the WTO Agreement," *The International Lawyer*, 1995, vol. 29(2), p. 345.

34 K. Aoki, "The Stakes of Intellectual Property Law" in D. Kairys (ed.) *The Politics of Law: A Progressive Critique* (3rd ed.), New York: Basic Books, 1998, pp. 259–78.

35 See generally, World Trade Organization, *Guide to the Uruguay Round Agreements*, The Hague: Kluwer International, 1999, pp. 77–80; ibid., *The Results of the Uruguay Round of Multilateral Trade Negotiations: The Legal Texts*, Cambridge: Cambridge University Press, 1999, pp. 143–6; J.S. Thomas and M.A. Meyer, *op. cit.*, pp. 196–202.

36 See generally, C. Arup, *The New World Trade Organization Agreements: Globalizing Law Through Services and Intellectual Property*, Cambridge: Cambridge University Press, 2000.

37 J.S. Thomas, "A First Look at the Multilateral Agreement on Investment," conference paper, University of British Columbia, 1997.

38 US Congress, "Bilateral Investment Treaties: Hearings before the Senate Foreign Relations Committee," 1998. US Presidential Documents, "United States Government Policy on International Investment," *Weekly Compilation of Presidential Documents*, 1983, vol. 19, p. 1214.

39 UNTS, 1966; I.F.I. Shihata, *Towards a Greater Depoliticization of Investment Disputes: The Roles of ICSID and MIGA*, Washington: International Center for the Settlement of Investment Disputes, 1993; T.L. Brewer, "International Investment Dispute Settlement Procedures: The Evolving Regime for Foreign Direct Investment," *Law & Politics in International Business*, 1995, vol. 26, p. 633.

40 See generally, H. Gibbons, "Justifying Law: An Explanation of the Deep Structure of American Law," *Law and Philosophy*, August 1984, vol. 3, no. 2, pp.

165–279. For discussion of the dilemmas attendant on challenging liberal private law regimes, see, e.g., A. Brudner, "Hegel and the Crisis of Private Law," K. Casebeer, "The Crisis of Private Law is not an Ideal Situation"; and C. Yablon, "Arguing from Necessity: A Comment on 'Hegel and the Crisis of Private Law'," *Cardozo Law Review*, 1989, vol. 10, nos 5–6, pp. 949–1000, 1001–18, and 1019–30, respectively.

41 See generally, Qian Mingxing, "Woguo minshi fazhi sishi nian de bianqian" (Changes in Forty Years of Our Civil Law System), *Zhongwai faxue* (Chinese and Foreign Law), 1989, no. 5, pp. 1–8.

42 See generally, A. Kent, *Between Freedom and Subsistence*, Hong Kong: Oxford University Press, 1993, pp. 30–2; D.E. Christensen, "Breaking the Deadlock: Toward a Socialist Confucianist Concept of Human Rights in China," *Michigan Journal of International Law*, 1992, vol. 13, p. 469. The importance of Confucianism as a basis for a collectivist legal order is the focus of many officially sanctioned studies of Chinese legal culture. See, e.g., Chinese Society for the Study of Confucianism and Legal Culture (ed.), *Confucianism and Legal Culture*, Shanghai: Fudan University Press, 1992.

43 See D.J. Munro, *The Concept of Man in Early China*, Stanford, Calif.: Stanford University Press, 1969, p. 17: "all people are equally deserving; all should be tolerated, none singled out for favor." While the Daoists did espouse a primitive solidarity within society, this was derived from a fundamental respect for the identity of the individual. See generally, J. Needham, *Science and Civilization in China*, Vol. II, Cambridge: Cambridge University Press, 1954, pp. 99 *et seq.* and pp. 139 *et seq.*

44 For discussion of individualism and its suppression by early Confucian orthodoxy, see E. Balazs, *Chinese Civilization and Bureaucracy*, A.F. Wright (ed.), H.M. Wright (trans.), New Haven, Conn.: Yale University Press, 1964, pp. 21–2 and 177. The emergence of activism and reformism in the "new text Confucianism" of the nineteenth century raised the possibility of increased tolerance for individualistic scholarship and research within the literati elite – a significant departure from the staid intellectual collectivism of prior years, although this too was ultimately unsuccessful. See B.A. Elman, *From Philosophy to Philology: Intellectual and Social Aspects of Change in Late Imperial China*, Cambridge, Mass.: Harvard University Press, 1984, pp. 26–36; and *ibid.*, *Classicism, Politics, and Kinship: The Ch'ang-chou School of New Text Confucianism in Late Imperial China*, Berkeley, Los Angeles, and London: University of California Press, 1990, chap. 9.

45 See, e.g., Lou Jingbo, "Ruhe kan dai dangjin nianqing sixiang guandian de xin bianhua?" (How to View and Handle New Changes in the Ideologies and Views of Youth Today?) *Neibu wengao* (Internal Manuscripts), 1991, no. 17, pp. 26–9.

46 See W.C. Jones, "The Significance of the Opinion of the Supreme People's Court for Civil Law in China," in P.B. Potter (ed.), *Domestic Law Reforms in Post-Mao China*, Armonk, NY: M.E. Sharpe, 1994, pp. 101–2.

47 See generally, W.T. Rowe, *Hankow: Commerce and Society in a Chinese City, 1796–1889*, Stanford, Calif.: Stanford University Press, 1984.

48 See generally, E. Friedman, Paul G. Pickowitcz, and Mark Selden, *Chinese Village, Socialist State*, New Haven, Conn.: Yale University Press, 1991.

49 See generally, He Guanghui, "Continue to Deepen Reform by Centering on Economic Improvement and Rectification," *Zhongguo jingji tizhi gaige* (Reform of the Chinese Economic Structure), 1990, no. 2, in *FBIS Daily Report: China*, March 23, 1990, p. 21.

50 See Wang Liming, "Guojia suoyouquan de falu tozheng yanjiu" (Research on the Legal Features of State Property Rights), *Falu kexue* (Legal Science), 1990, no. 6, pp. 29–35; Jiang Shan, "Shilun wuquan he qoguo de wuquan zhidu tixi"

(Tentative Theory on Property Rights and Out Country's Property Rights System), *Faxue yanjiu* (Studies in Law), 1988, no. 5, pp. 70–5.

51 See Constitution of the PRC, 1982, Article 13.

52 See ibid., Article 51.

53 See General Principles of Civil Law of the PRC, Article 6.

54 See, e.g., Liang Huixing, "Wo guo min fa de jiben yuanze" (Basic Principles of Our Civil Law), *Minshang faxue* (Chinese Jurisprudence), 1987, no. 4, pp. 3–10.

55 See, e.g., Meng Qinguo, "Jingji tizhi gaige shiqi de minshi lifa" (Civil Legislation in the Time of Economic Structural Reform), *Zhongguo shehui kexue* (Chinese Social Sciences), 1988 no. 6, pp. 77–90.

56 See Yang Lixin, *Renmin fayuan anli leibian pingxi: Minshi shenpan zhuan* (Critical Analysis of Types of People's Court Cases: Volume on Civil Judgments), Changchun: Jilin People's Press, 1998, pp. 19 and 168.

57 See Chui Xiuming et al., *Renmin fayuan yinan panli pingxi: Minshi zhuan* (Critical Analysis of Difficult Decisions by the People's Courts; Civil Volume), Changchun: Jilin People's Press, 1999, p. 45.

58 See Zhao Ziyang, "Advance Along the Road to Socialism With Chinese Characteristics," October 25, 1987, in *Documents of the Thirteenth National Congress of the Communist Party of China*, Beijing: Foreign Languages Press, 1987, pp. 3–77, esp. pp. 9 et seq. For discussion of the implications for civil law, see Yang Chenshan, "Shehui zhuyi chu jieduan lilun yu wo guo de minfa xue" (The Theory of the Primary Stage of Socialism and the Study of Our Civil Law), *Minshang faxue* (Chinese Jurisprudence), 1988, no. 5, pp. 3–9.

59 See Shi Zhuhua "Siying qiye lifa de lilun yiju he jiben yuanze" (Theoretical Basis and Basic Principles of Private Enterprise Law), *Zhengzhi yu falu* (Politics and Law), 1988, no. 4, pp. 35–6; Li Peizhuan, "Tan woguo siying qiye lifa wenti" (On Issues of Our Private Enterprise Legislation), *Minshang faxue* (Chinese Jurisprudence), 1988, no. 4, pp. 11–16; Xie Shisong, "Lun geti jingji de falu wenti" (On Legal Issues of the Individual Economy), *Zhengzhi yu falu* (Politics and Law), 1986, no. 2, pp. 28–30.

60 See Zhong Wenbin, "Woguo gongmin geren suoyouquan de xingzhi" (Characteristics of Our Citizens' Individual Property Rights), *Xiandai faxue* (Modern Law), 1989, no. 5, pp. 46–8.

61 See General Principles of Civil Law of the PRC, Article 82.

62 See Mu Xichuan and Zhang Lingyuan (eds), *Zhonghua renmin gongheguo quanmin suoyouzhi gongye qiye fa zhishi shouce* (Handbook of Knowledge on the Law of the PRC on Industrial Enterprises Owned by the Whole People), Beijing: Politics and Law University Press, 1988. For text and commentary, see China Economic Law Research Association, Beijing Branch and Beijing Municipal Government Electronic Industries Office (ed.), *Zen yang zhengque shishi «Qiye fa»* (How to Precisely Implement the "Enterprise Law"), Beijing: New Era Press, 1988.

63 See Wang Liming, "Lun shangpin suoyouquan" (On Commodity Ownership Rights), *Faxue yanjiu* (Studies in Law), 1986, no. 2, pp. 37–43 and ibid., "Suoyouquan minfa baohu de ruogan wenti" (Various Issues of Civil Law Protection of Property Rights), *Faxue xuexi yu yanjiu* (Study and Research in Jurisprudence), 1990, no. 4, pp. 57–62.

64 See Zhang Ling, "Jingyingquan chansheng genju xin tan" (New Inquiry on the Progeny of Managerial Rights), *Faxue yanjiu* (Studies in Law), 1988, no. 6, pp. 47–51; Ding Jimin, "Jingyingquan yu suoyouquan" (Managerial Rights and Ownership Rights), *Faxue yanjiu* (Studies in Law), 1987, no. 1, pp. 12–17; Li Yongfu, "Suoyouquan yu jingyingquan fenli wenti de bijiaofa sikao" (Comparative Law Perspectives on the Issue of Separating Ownership from

Management Rights), *Beijing shehui kexue* (Beijing Social Sciences), 1989, no. 1, pp. 153–7; Guo Shaodong, "Guanyu shehui zhuyi quanmin suoyouquan de xingzhi, tezheng he shixian wenti" (On the Issues of Character, Features and Implementation of Socialist Public Ownership Rights) *Faxue luncong* (Collected Theories on Legal Studies), 1989, no. 2, pp. 46–9; Wang Chong and Jiang Deyuan, "Lun guojia suoyouquan, xingzhengquan yu qiye jingyingquan de fenli" (On the Separation of State Ownership and Administrative Rights from Enterprise Management Rights), *Faxue yanjiu* (Studies in Law), 1988, no. 2, pp. 47–50.

65 See "Zhonghua renmin gongheguo siying qiye zanxing guiding" (Provisional Regulations of the PRC on Privately Managed Enterprises), in Law and Regulation Editorial Office of Law Publishing House (ed.), *Siying qiye changyong falu shouce* (Handbook of Commonly Used Laws on Private Enterprises), Beijing: Law Publishing House, 1988, pp. 1–9. For commentary see, e.g., Cheng Haoyi and Kian Gangsheng (eds), *op. cit.* For background discussion, see E.J. Epstein and Y. Lin, *op. cit.*

66 The Chinese Communist Party's authoritative journal *Qiushi* (Seeking Truth) specifically repudiated suggestions that the Constitution be revised yet again to accommodate expanded private property rights ideals. See Xiao Weiyun, "Woguo xianfa ji qi guiding de guojia genben zhidu bu rong fouding" (The Basic System of the State as Set Forth in the Constitution and Its Provisions Is not Easy to Deny), *Qiushi* (Seeking Truth), 1990, no. 22, pp. 25–31.

67 See, e.g., Li Yunhe, "Dui gongyouzhi we zhuti de yi dian kanfa" (A View on the Centrality of Public Ownership), *Zhongguo faxue* (Chinese Jurisprudence), 1993, no. 5, pp. 37–8; and Wang Shenyi, "Lun wuquan de shehuihua" (On the Socialization of Property Rights), *Faxue pinglun* (Legal Studies Commentary), 1999, no. 1, pp. 56–61.

68 See, e.g., Xie Zichang and Wang Xiujing, "Guanyu chanquan de ruogan lilun wenti" (Several Theoretical Questions about Property Rights), *Faxue yanjiu* (Studies in Law), 1994, no. 1, pp. 42–7.

69 See, e.g., forum comments in "Jiaqiang guoyou zichan guanli duse guoyou zichan liushi luodong" (Strengthen Management of State Property and Block the Runoff and Leakage of State Property), *Zhengzhi yu falu* (Law and Politics), 1996, no. 1, pp. 22–5 and 45; Wang Jueyu, "Ezhi guoyou zichan liushi de falu duixiang," (Legal Objectives of Halting the Losses of State-Owned Property), *Faxue* (Jurisprudence), 1995, no. 6, pp. 35–7.

70 See, e.g., Zou Xi and Shu Sheng, "Shichang jingji shehui zhong de guojia caichan suoyouquan" (State Property Ownership Rights in the Market Economy Society), *Minshang faxue* (Chinese Jurisprudence), 1996, no. 4, pp. 56–62.

71 See "Draft Amendments to Constitution Discussed," Beijing Xinhua English Service, March 22, 1993, in *FBIS Daily Report: China* (FBIS-CHI-93–054), March 23, 1993, pp. 13–14.

72 See Gong Xiangrui and Jiang Mingan, "Zai lun gongmin caichanquan de xianfa baohu" (Again, on Constitutional Protection for Citizens' Property Rights), *Minshang faxue* (Chinese Jurisprudence), 1992, no. 2, pp. 70–3.

73 See Property Law Research Program of CASS Law Institute, "Zhiding Zhongguo wuquanfa de jiben sikao" (Basic Perspectives on Enacting Chinese Property Law), *Faxue yanjiu* (Studies in Law), 1995, no. 3, pp. 3–10.

74 See Liang Huixing, *Zhongguo wuquanfa caoan jianyi gao* (Outline of Opinion on a Draft Chinese Property Law), *op. cit.*, pp. 93–5. Also see Qian Mingxing, "Lun woguo wuquanfa de jiben yuance" (On the Basic Principles of Our Civil Law), *op. cit.*, pp. 29–38. As applied to bills of lading for example, the property rights in the underlying goods remain independent of the documentation. See Guo

Yu, "Lun tidan de wuquanxing" (On the Property Rights Character of Bills of Lading), *Zhongguo faxue* (Chinese Jurisprudence), 1997, no. 4, pp. 69–77.

75 See Wang Liming, "Wuquan xingwei ruogan wenti tantao" (Inquiry on Several Issues of Property Rights Behavior), *op. cit.*

76 See Wang Yongxia, "Lun budongchan wuquan biandong zhong zhaiquan he wuquan de baohu" (Safeguarding Creditor and Property Rights in the Transfer of Immovable Property Rights), *Faxue pinglun* (Legal Studies Commentary), 1998, no. 2, pp. 121–5.

77 For examples of the debate, see Liang Huixing, "Wo guo minfa shi fou chengren wuquan xingwei?" (Does our Civil Law Recognize Actions in Property?), *Faxue yanjiu* (Studies in Law), 1989, no. 6, pp. 59–62 (arguing that the transactional requirements bring property rights within the purview of obligations, thus diminishing their autonomy); and Zhang Yumin and Tian Shaomei, "Wo guo minfa yingdang chengren wuquan xingwei" (Our Civil Law Ought to Recognize Actions in Property), *Xiandai faxue* (Modern Law), 1997, no. 6, pp. 27–30 (arguing that property rights are distinct from obligations and should be autonomous and protected).

78 See, e.g., Jiang Ping, "Zhiding minfadian de jidian xiongguan sikao" (Several macroscopic perspectives on drafting a civil code), *Zhengfa luntan* (Politics and Law Forum), 1997, no. 3, pp. 26–31.

79 See F.H. Foster, "Towards a Behavior-based Model of Inheritance?: The Chinese Experiment," *U.C. Davis Law Review*, 1998, vol. 32, no. 1, pp. 77–126; and *ibid.*, "Linking Support and Inheritance: A New Model From China," *Wisconsin Law Review*, 1999, no. 6, pp. 1199–258.

80 See, e.g., Guan Shouan, "Woguo gongsizhi qiye chanquan zhi yanjiu" (Research on the Property Rights System of Enterprises in Our Company System), *Zhengfa luntan* (Political Legal Forum), 1995, no. 6, pp. 55–9.

81 See Wang Geya, "Guanyu wanshan wo guo fuqi caichanzhi de jianyi" (Suggestions on Perfecting a System of Marital Property), *Zhongguo faxue* (Chinese Jurisprudence), 1997, no. 2, pp. 99–101; Yuan Minshu, "Fuqi caichanzhi tansuo" (Inquiry on the Marital Property System), *Zhengfa luntan* (Politics and Law Forum), 1996, no. 3, pp. 29–34.

82 See, e.g., Wang Jianrui, "Wanshen siyou caichan baohu zhidu de falu sizao" (Legal Perspectives on Perfecting the System of Protecting Private Property), *Faxue zazhi* (Legal Studies Magazine), 1999, no. 2, pp. 25–6 and *ibid.*, "Law on Private Economy Called For," *China Economic News*, August 23, 1999, pp. 1–2. Also see Hu Jingguang, "Shichang jingji huhuan dui gongmin caichan de xianfa baohu" (The Market Economy Cries out for Constitutional Protection for Citizens' Property Rights), *Zhongguo jingji ribao* (China Economic News), June 18, 1998, p. 4.

83 For examples of case decisions on property matters, see generally, Wang Liming (ed.), *Zhongguo minfa anli yu xueli yanjiu: Wuquan bian* (Studies in Chinese Civil Law Cases and Theory: Chapter on Property), Beijing: Law Publishing, 1998.

84 See Guo Mingrui, "Guanyu wo guo wuquan lifa de san dian sikao," (Three Perspectives on Chinese Property Legislation), *Zhongguo faxue* (Chinese Jurisprudence), 1998, no. 2, pp. 24–5.

85 See Zhao Shiyi, "Lun caichanquan de xianfa baohu yu zhiyue" (Constitutional Protection and Limitation of Property Rights), *Faxue pinglun* (Commentary on Legal Studies), 1999, no. 3, pp. 7–13 and 95.

86 See, e.g., Qu Maohui and Li Qiang, "Xianfa ying queren duozhong fenpei fangshi" (The Constitution Should Acknowledge Many Forms of Distribution), *Hunan shifan daxue shehui kexue xuebao* (Social Science Journal of Hunan Normal University), 1998, no. 5, pp. 22–5.

87 See Liu Shuilin, "Jingji fa yu minfa de shichang jingji guannian jichu yanjiu" (Basic Research on Concepts of the Market Economy of Economic Law and Civil Law), *Faxue yanjiu* (Studies in Law), 1997, no. 1, pp. 34–9.

88 See "Zhongguo wuquan fa (caoan)" (Chinese Property Law (draft)), Article 2, in Liang Huixing, *Zhongguo wuquanfa caoan jianyi gao* (Outline of Opinion on a Draft Chinese Property Law), *op. cit.*, p. 5.

89 See "Zhongguo wuquan fa (caoan)" (Chinese property law (draft)), Articles 1 and 5, *ibid.*

90 See *ibid.*, pp. 95–7.

91 See Huang Rutong, "Shi fou yiding yao ba «Siying caichan shensheng bu ke qinfan» xiejin woguo xianfa?" (Do We Definitely Want to Write "the Sanctity of Private Property is Inviolable" into our Constitution?), *Dangdai faxue* (Modern Law), 1998, no. 4, pp. 5–7.

92 See Qian Mingxing, "Woguo wuquanfa de tiaozheng fanwei, neirong tedian ji wuquan tixi" (The Scope of Adjustment, Special Contents and Property System in our Property Law), *Zhongwai faxue* (Chinese and Foreign Jurisprudence), 1997, no. 2, pp. 88–90.

93 See Guo Mingrui, "Guanyu woguo wuquan lifa de san dian sikao" (Three Perspectives on our Country's Property Legislation), *op. cit.*, pp. 23–4.

94 See, e.g., Yu Nengwu and Wang Shenyi, "Lun wuquan fa de xiandaihua fazhan qushi" (The Development of Modern Property Law), *op. cit.*, p. 73.

95 See generally, Wen Zhiyang, "Zhanlun Zhongguo minfa wuquan tixi" (Sketching China's Civil Law Property System), *Faxue* (Jurisprudence), 1997, no. 6, pp. 37–40. For a poignant example of a reformist scholar toeing the line in times of conservatism, see Wang Liming, "Lun guojia suoyouquan zhuti de quanminxing wenti" (On the Issue of the Mass Character of the Bulk of State Ownership Rights), *Zhongnan zhengfa xueyuan xuebao* (Journal of the Central South Political Legal Institute), 1990, no. 4, pp. 17–24.

96 See "Text of PRC Constitutional Amendment," Beijing Xinhua Domestic Service, March 16, 1999, in *FBIS Daily Report: China* (FBIS-CHI-1999–0316); "Tian Jiyun on Constitutional Amendments," Beijing Xinhua Domestic Service, March 13, 1999, in *FBIS Daily Report: China* (FBIS-CHI-1999–0316), March 13, 1999; "Li Peng Presides Over Closing of 9th NPC," Beijing Xinhua Domestic Service, March 15, 1999, in *FBIS Daily Report: China* (FBIS-CHI-1999–0326), March 15, 1999.

97 See "Constitution Amendment Gives Solid Legal Support to Private Business," *China Economic News: Special Supplement for the Second Plenary Session of the Ninth National People's Congress*, April 19, 1999, pp. 2–3; "Constitutional Amendments Propel China's Reform and Opening-up," Beijing Xinhua English Service, March 15, 1999, in *FBIS Daily Report: China* (FBIS-CHI-1999–0315), March 17, 1999.

98 See Contract Law of the PRC, Articles 1 and 52.

99 See Zhang Guangbo, "Lun caichan de shensheng bu ke qinfan" (On the Sanctity of Property is Inviolable), *Faxue zazhi* (Legal Studies Magazine), 1999, no. 4, pp. 10–11.

100 See, e.g., Dai Jiabing, "For Public Interest: Breaking the Law and Not Being Punished," *Beijing fazhi ribao* (Beijing Legal System Daily), February 23, 1998, p. 7, in *FBIS Daily Report: China* (FBIS-CHI-98–114), April 24, 1998.

101 See "More on NPC Third Plenary Meeting," Beijing Xinhua English Service, March 9, 1999, in *FBIS Daily Report: China* (FBIS-CHI-1999–0308), March 9, 1999.

102 See Yu Nengwu and Wang Shenyi, "Lun wuquan fa de xiandaihua fazhan qushi" (The Development of Modern Property Law), *op. cit.*, pp. 74 *et seq.*; J.

Alsen, "An Introduction to Chinese Property Law," *Maryland Journal of International Law and Trade*, 1996, vol. 20, pp. 1–60.

103 See Qian Mingxing, "Lun woguo wuquanfa de jiben yuance" (On the Basic Principles of Our Civil Law), *op. cit.*, pp. 29–38.

104 See "Shourangfang jieshou jishu fuzhu shishi, bu dei chaoyue ziji jing Gong Shang Xingzheng Guanli Bumen hezhun dengji de shengchan jingying fanwei" (The Transferee Receives Technical Input and Should not Overstep Its Own Registered Scope of Production Management Received Through Examination and Ratification by the Industrial and Commercial Administration Departments), in Dan You (ed.), *Jingji fa anli xuan xi* (Compilation and Analysis of Economic Law Cases), Beijing: Law Publishing, 1990, p. 236, where the court held invalid a contract that was deemed to be outside the registered scope of business of one of the parties. Formalistic approaches to enforcement that focus on capacity also reinforce doctrinal requirements that obligations not conflict with state policies. See Economic Contract Law of the PRC, Articles 4 and 7, and General Principles of Civil Law of the PRC, Articles 55 and 58.

105 See Sun Xianzhong, "Lun bu dongchan wuquan dengji" (On the Registration of Property Rights in Immovables), *Minshang faxue* (Chinese Jurisprudence), 1996, no. 5, pp. 51–62; Ji Yibao, *op. cit.*; Wang Shiwei and Wang Penglin, "Dui woguo «Caichan shenbao fa» de gouxiang" (Thoughts on our "Property Registration Law"), *Falu kexue* (Legal Science), 1998, no. 353–9.

106 See W.E. Butler, "The Chinese Soviet Republic in the Family of Socialist Legal Systems," in W.E. Butler (ed.), *The Legal System of the Chinese Soviet Republic 1931–34*, New York: Transnational, 1983; K. Hartford, "Step By Step: Reform, Resistance, and Revolution in Chin-Ch'a-Chi Border Region 1937–1945," Ph.D. dissertation, Stanford University, 1980.

107 R. MacFarquhar (ed.), *The Politics of China, 1949–1989*, Cambridge: Cambridge University Press, 1993.

108 See E.J. Perry, "Rural Collective Violence: The Fruits of Recent Reforms," in P. and C. Wong (eds), *The Political Economy of Reform in Post-Mao China*, Cambridge, Mass.: Harvard University Press, 1985, pp. 179 *et seq.*

109 See J.C. Oi, "The Fate of the Collective After the Commune," in D. Davis and E.F. Vogel (eds), *Chinese Society on the Eve of Tiananmen: The Impact of Reform*, Cambridge, Mass.: Harvard University Press, 1990, pp. 15–36.

110 See *Land Administration Law of the PRC* (1986, revised 1988, 1998). Also see "Nong mu yu bu fubuzhang Xiang Zhongyang xiang quanguo renda chang-weihui zuo guanyu tudi fa caoan de shuoming" (Vice Minister of Agriculture, Livestock and Fisheries Xiang Zhongyang Delivers an Explanation of the Draft Land Law to the NPC Standing Committee), *Zhongguo fazhi bao* (China Legal System Gazette), March 19, 1986, p. 2.

111 See D.C. Clarke and N.C. Howson, "Developing PRC Property and Real Estate Law: Revised Land Registration Rules," *East Asian Executive Reports*, April 15, 1996, pp. 9–17. Also see, Supreme People's Court Administrative Tribunal (ed.), *Xingzheng susong yu tudi guanlifa: Xin jie* (Administrative Litigation of Land Administration Law: New Interpretations), Beijing: Current Events Press, 1999.

112 P.B. Potter, "China's New Land Development Regulations," *China Business Review*, March/April 1991, pp. 12–14.

113 See generally, A. Walker, *Land Property and Construction in the People's Republic of China*, Hong Kong: Hong Kong University Press, 1991.

114 See cases discussed in An Conghua *et al.* (eds), *Renmin fayuan yinan panli pingxi: Minshi zhuan* (Evaluation of Difficult Cases of the People's Courts: Civil

Volume), Changchun: Jilin Chubanshe, 1999, pp. 201, 205, 211, 217, and 226.

115 See "People's Republic of China, Administration of Urban Real Property Law," *China Law & Practice*, October 3, 1994, pp. 23–38. Also see generally, W.D. Soileau, "Past is Present: Urban Real Property Rights and Housing Reform in the People's Republic of China," *Pacific Rim Law & Policy Journal*, 1995, vol. 3, pp. 299–387.

116 See, e.g., "Shanghai Municipality, PRC Land Administration Law Implementing Measures," *China Law & Practice*, December 15, 1994, pp. 32–49.

117 See Cao Fengying, "Fangdichan lifa ruogan wenti sikao" (Perspectives on Several Questions of Real Estate Legislation), *Zhengzhi yu falu* (Law and Politics), 1994, no. 3, pp. 50–2.

118 See, e.g., Case no. 15, in Li Changdao (ed.), *Shanghai fayuan anli jingxuan: 1997* (Carefully Selected Cases from the Shanghai Courts: 1997), Shanghai: Shanghai People's Press, 1997, p. 50.

119 See, e.g., Case no. 17, in Qiao Xianzhi (ed.), *Shanghai fayuan anli jingxuan: 1999* (Carefully Selected Cases from the Shanghai Courts: 1999), Shanghai: Shanghai People's Press, 2000, p. 81.

120 See, e.g., Case no. 6, in Li Changdao (ed.), *Shanghai fayuan anli jingxuan: 1997* (Carefully Selected Cases from the Shanghai Courts: 1997), *op. cit.*, p. 16.

121 See, e.g., Case no. 9, in Qiao Xianzhi (ed.), *op. cit.*, p. 44.

122 See, e.g., Case no. 6, in Li Changdao (ed.), *Shanghai fayuan anli jingxuan: 1997* (Carefully Selected Cases from the Shanghai Courts: 1997), *op. cit.*, p. 43.

123 See, e.g., Qian Weiqing and Guo Yuyuan, "Pochan qiye fangdichan chuli yi ji youguan wenti de tantao" (Inquiry on Resolution of Real Estate of Bankrupt Enterprises and Related Questions), *Zhengzhi yu falu* (Politics and Law), 1995, no. 1, pp. 51–3.

124 See "The Law of Land Administration of the People's Republic of China," Articles 1, 2, and 8, *China Economic News*, October 26, 1998, pp. 8–12, and November 2, 1998, pp. 8–11. Also see Supreme People's Court Administrative Tribunal (ed.), *op. cit.*, pp. 108–9.

125 See Cui Jianyuan, "Tudi shang de quanliqun lungang" (Theoretical Outline of the Cluster of Rights in Land), *Zhongguo faxue* (Chinese Jurisprudence), 1998, no. 2, pp. 14–20. Also see Wen Zhiyang, "Zhanlun Zhongguo minfa wuquan tixi" (Sketching China's Civil Law Property System) *Faxue* (Jurisprudence), 1997, no. 6, pp. 37–40.

126 See generally, Qian Mingxing, "Woguo wuquanfa de tiaozheng fanwei, neirong tedian ji wuquan tixi" (The Scope of Adjustment, Special Contents, and Property System in Our Property Law), *Zhong wai faxue* (Chinese and Foreign Jurisprudence), 1997, no. 2, pp. 88–90. Also see Wang Yongxia, "Lun budongchan wuquan biandong zhong zhaiquan he wuquan de baohu" (Safeguarding Creditor and Property Rights in the Transfer of Immovable Property Rights), *op. cit.*

127 See Zhang Suanggen and Zhang Xuezhe, "Lun woguo tudi wuquan zhidu" (On Our Land Property Rights System), *Zhongguo tudi kexue* (China Land Science), 1997, no. 3, pp. 6 and 7–10.

128 See Wang Lanping, "Lun woguo tudi shiyongquan yu yongyi wuquan" (On Rights of Use and Property Rights in Usage of Land in China), *Shandong shida xuebao* (Journal of Shandong Normal University), 1997, no. 2, pp. 28–30.

129 See, e.g., Zhang Shaopeng, "Guanyu fangdichan diya falu zhidu ruogan wenti de yanjiu" (Research on Various Questions in the Legal System for Real Estate Mortgages), *Zhongguo faxue* (Chinese Jurisprudence), 1997, no. 2, pp. 71–8; Shi Diao, Wang Jin, and Du Xuexi, "Wanshan woguo diya zhidu de ji dian lifa sikao"

(Considerations on Perfecting Various Items of Legislation in our Mortgage System), *Zhongguo faxue* (Chinese Jurisprudence), 1997, no. 4, pp. 45–9.

130 See Ji Yibao, *op. cit.*; and Sun Xianzhi, "Lun budongchan quan dengji" (On the Registration of Rights to Immovable Property), *op. cit.*

131 See generally, G. Butterton, "Norms and Property in the Middle Kingdom," *Wisconsin International Law Journal*, 1997, vol. 15, pp. 281–97.

132 See, e.g., Zhang Chengsi, "Zhishi chanquan ruogan wenti zaixi" (Re-analysis of Various Issues of Intellectual Property Rights), *Zhongguo faxue* (Chinese Jurisprudence), 1996, no. 6, pp. 48–62.

133 See generally, Zheng Chengsi, "Zhishi chanquan ruogan wenti bianxi" (Differential Analysis of Various Issues in Intellectual Property Rights), *Zhongguo Shehuikexueyuan Yanjiushengyuan xuebao* (Journal of the CASS Graduate School), 1993, no. 2, pp. 1–9; A. Han, "Technology Licensing to China: The Influence of Culture," *Hastings Internal and Comparative Law Review*, 1996, vol. 19, no. 4, pp. 629–43; L. Wang, "Political and Cultural Perspectives of the Patent Law of the PRC: The Role of Article 14," *Wisconsin International Law Journal*, 1988, vol. 6, no. 1, p. 193.

134 See "China: PRC to Adopt New IPR Measures," Beijing Xinhua English Service, April 3, 1997, in *FBIS Daily Report: China* (FBIS-CHI-97–093), April 4, 1997; and Wang Chunfa, "Development of Knowledge Economy an Choice for Our Economic Policies," *Qiushi* (Truth), August 16, 1998, pp. 20–4, in *FBIS Daily Report: China* (FBIS-CHI-98–257).

135 See generally, D. Dressler, "China's Intellectual Property Protection: Prospects for Achieving International Standards," (Comment), *Fordham International Law Journal*, 1995, vol. 19, no. 1, pp. 181–246.

136 See generally, E. Chien-Hale, "Asserting U.S. Intellectual Property Rights in China: Expansion of Extraterritorial Jurisdiction?" *Journal of the Copyright Society of the USA*, 1997, vol. 44, no. 3, pp. 198–230.

137 Indeed, the PRC "White Paper on Intellectual Property Rights" (1994) makes little effort to articulate specific proposals to improve China's intellectual property protection system. See "White Paper in Intellectual Property Protection." Also see "China Defends Copyright System Ahead of U.S. Sanction Threat," Agence France Presse English Wire, June 16, 1994, *China News Digest* (electronic media), June 16, 1994.

138 See "Memorandum of Understanding between the Government of the People's Republic of China and the Government of the United States of America on the Protection of Intellectual Property, 1992," Article 3 (author's copy).

139 See "Implementing International Copyright Treaties Provisions," 1992, *China Law & Practice*, January 14, 1993, p. 36. Also see Berne Convention on the Protection of Literary and Artistic Works, 1886, 1971, Article 18(1), WIPO Doc. 287(E).

140 See generally, M. Oksenberg, P.B. Potter, and W.B. Abnett, *Advancing Intellectual Property Rights: Information Technologies and the Course of Economic Development in China*, Seattle: National Bureau of Asian Research, 1996.

141 See, e.g., General Office of the State Council Working Conference on Intellectual Property (ed.), "Report of Chinese Enforcement Actions Under the 1995 IPR Agreement," June 17, 1996 (author's copy); "Status Report of the Enforcement of IPR Laws in China, 1996," May 1997 (author's copy); and "1999 White Paper on Intellectual Property Rights Enforcement," 2000 (author's copy). See "Main Points on Strengthening Current Implementation of Intellectual Rights Protection," in "Intellectual Property Rights Protection Document Issued," Beijing Xinhua Domestic Service, January 21, 1998, in *FBIS Daily Report: China* (FBIS-CHI-98–026), January 29, 1998.

142 See P.B. Potter, "Comment on International and Bilateral Treaties," Asia Law & Practice (ed.), *Intellectual Property Protection in China: The Law* (2nd ed.), Hong Kong, Asia Law & Practice, 1998, pp. 414–28.

143 See International Legal Materials (ILM), *op. cit.*, pp. 1197 and 1994. For discussion of Chinese compliance with TRIPS, see M. Schlesinger, "Intellectual Property Protection in China," *East Asian Executive Reports*, January 15, 1997; Zheng Chengsi, "TRIPS and Intellectual Property Protection in China," *European Intellectual Property Review*, 1997, no. 5, pp. 243–6. For discussion of GATT requirements, see *ibid.*, "Guanmao zongxieding yu zhishichanquan" (GATT and Intellectual Property Protection), *Zhongguo faxue* (Chinese Jurisprudence), 1993, no. 3, pp. 72–80; and Li Yongming, "Guanmao zongxieding yu woguo zhishi chanquan baohu zhidu" (GATT and Our System of Intellectual Property Protection), *Hangzhou daxue xuebao* (Journal of Hangzhou University), 1994, no. 2, pp. 53–9.

144 See, e.g., Zheng Chengsi, *Zhishi chanquanfa tonglun* (General Theories on Intellectual Property Law), Beijing: Law Publishing, 1986, pp. 148–292; Liu Chuntian (ed.), Zhishi chanquan fa jiaocheng (Course on Intellectual Property Law), Beijing: People's University Press, 1995, pp. 434–64; Yang Dongxu, *Zhishi chanquan shiyong shouce* (Practical Handbook on Intellectual Property Rights), Beijing: Economic Daily Press, 1991, pp. 326–73.

145 See, e.g., Ma Qingchun, *Guoji banquan falu zhidu* (The International Copyright Law System), Shanghai, 1994; Bai Yingfu and Huang Rui, *Guoji jishu zhuanrang fa* (International Technology Transfer Law), Wuhan: Wuhan University Press, 1995; and Wu Handong, *Zhishi chanquan falu zhishi shouce* (Handbook of Knowledge on Intellectual Property Law), Hubei: People's Press, 1990.

146 See "Jiang Zemin Stresses Cooperation with WIPO," Beijing Xinhua English Service, January 27, 1999, in *FBIS Daily Report: China* (FBIS-CHI-99–027); "Jiang Ying Addresses World IPR Organization Meeting," Beijing Xinhua Domestic Service, September 8, 1998, in *FBIS Daily Report: China* (FBIS-CHI-98–257), September 15, 1998.

147 For a useful compilations of laws and regulations, see *Zhishi chanquan shenpan shouce* (Handbook on Intellectual Property Adjudication), Beijing: People's Courts Press, periodical; and Peking University Intellectual Property Institute (ed.), *Zhishichanquan fagui huibian* (Compilation of Laws and Regulations on Intellectual Property), Beijing, mimeo, 1997. For discussion, see Asia Law & Practice (ed.), *Intellectual Property Protection in China: The Law, op. cit.*; Zhang Naigen, "Intellectual Property Law in China: Basic Policy and New Developments," *Annual Survey of International and Comparative Law*, 1997, vol. 4, pp. 1–17; Zheng Chengsi, "Zhongguo zhishi chanquan fa: Tedian, youdian yu quedian" (Chinese Intellectual Property Law: Special Features, Advantages and Problems) *Zhongguo shehuike xueyuan yanjiuyuan xuebao* (Journal of CASS Graduate School), 1994, no. 1, pp. 64–74.

148 See *Trademark Law of the PRC* (as amended, 1993), in CCH Australia (ed.), *China Laws for Foreign Business*, paras 11–500. For a Chinese-language text of the 1963 regulations, see "Shangbiao guanli tiaoli" (Administrative Regulations for Trademarks), in Trademark Office of the State Administration for Industry and Commerce, *Shangbiao fagui ziliao xuanbian* (Selected Laws and Regulations and Materials on Trademarks), Beijing: Law Publishing, 1985, p. 52.

149 See J.T. Chang and C. Conroy, "Trademark in the People's Republic of China," in M.J. Moser, *Foreign Trade, Investment and the Law in the People's Republic of China*, Hong Kong, Oxford, and New York: Oxford University Press, 1984, p. 269.

150 See "Detailed Rules for the Implementation of the Trademark Law of the People's Republic of China" (1983, revised 1988), in CCH (ed.), *op. cit.*, paras 11–510.

151 See "Trademark Law Implementing Regulations" (as amended), Article 9.

152 In some cases, the application for trademark protection was submitted to the local Patent Bureau, reflecting an interim solution used pending the establishment of local trademark offices. See Case no. 53 in Li Changdao (ed.), *Shanghai fayuan anli jingxuan: 1997* (Carefully Selected Cases from the Shanghai Courts: 1997), *op. cit.*, p. 183.

153 See Trademark Law of the PRC, *op. cit.*, Article 8. The prohibited marks follow broadly those listed in the Paris Convention for the Protection of Industrial Property; however, note subparagraphs (g) and (h) disallowing marks having "exaggeration and deceit in advertising," or that are "detrimental to socialist morals or customs, or having another unhealthy influence."

154 See *Administrative Litigation Law of the PRC, 1989*, in CCH (ed.), *op. cit.*, paras 19–558.

155 See *Trademark Law of the PRC*, *op. cit.*, Articles 6 and 31.

156 See *ibid.*, Article 38.

157 See Case no. 34, in Li Changdao (ed.), *Shanghai fayuan anli jingxuan: 1997* (Carefully Selected Cases from the Shanghai Courts: 1997), *op. cit.*, p. 102.

158 See Case no. 35, *ibid.*, p. 106.

159 See Case nos 35 and 53, *ibid.*, pp. 106 and 183, respectively.

160 See *Trademark Law of the PRC*, *op. cit.* Also see "Standing Committee of the National People's Congress, Amendment of the Trademark Law Decision," *China Law & Practice*, April 29, 1993, p. 42.

161 See "MOFTEC and SAIC, Administration of Trademarks in Foreign Trade Provisions," *China Law & Practice*, February 1996, pp. 34–7. Also see M.L. Donnan, "Administration of Trademarks in Foreign Trade Provisions," *ibid.*, pp. 32–3.

162 Paris Convention for the Protection of Industrial Property, *International Legal Materials*, 1968, vol. 6.

163 See Patent Law of the PRC (1985, revised 1993), in CCH (ed.), *op. cit.*, paras 11–600; and "Implementation Regulations of the Patent Law of the PRC," *ibid.*, paras 11–603. The *Patent Law of the PRC* was promulgated on March 12, 1984, but it did not become effective until April 1, 1985, when the implementing regulations also came into effect.

164 For recent reviews, see J.A. Collins, "China's Patent Paradox," *Law and Technology*, 1997, vol. 30, no. 1, pp. 1–26; Y. Ou, "The Practice of Patent Law of the PRC in China: Some Firsthand Observations," *Wisconsin International Law Journal*, 1997, vol. 15, no. 2, pp. 313–19.

165 See "Ren Jianxin at Forum on Implementation of Patent Law of the PRC," Beijing Xinhua Hong Kong Service, April 6, 2000, in *FBIS Daily Report: China* (FBIS-CHI-2000–0406), April 25, 2000.

166 See Patent Law of the PRC, *op. cit.*, Articles 2 and 22.

167 For example, the Joint Venture Law, 1990, makes specific reference to promoting international economic cooperation and technological exchange. Also see generally, Guo Shoukang, *op. cit.*

168 See *Patent Law of the PRC*, *op. cit.*, Article 24.

169 See *ibid.*, Articles 34–45.

170 See *ibid.*, Articles 51–2.

171 See, e.g., Case nos 40 and 41, in Li Changdao (ed.), *Shanghai fayuan anli jingxuan: 1997* (Carefully Selected Cases from the Shanghai Courts: 1997), *op. cit.*, pp. 153 and 157.

172 See *Patent Law of the PRC*, *op. cit.*, Article 62.

173 See, e.g., Case no. 52, in Li Changdao (ed.), *Shanghai fayuan anli jingxuan: 1996* (Carefully Selected Cases from the Shanghai Courts: 1996), Shanghai: Shanghai People's Press, 1997, p. 180.

174 See "Beijing Municipality Patent Dispute Mediation Procedures" (1988), *China Law & Practice*, August 21, 1989, p. 54; "Shanghai Patent Dispute Mediation Tentative Procedures" (1988), *ibid.*, p. 59. These were followed by national regulations. See "Patent Administrative Authority Adjudicating Patent Disputes Procedures" (1989), *China Law & Practice*, May 7, 1990. p. 40.

175 See *ibid.*, pp. 40–8.

176 See Patent Law of the PRC, *op. cit.*, Article 45.

177 See "Administrative Protection of Pharmaceutical Regulations, 1993," *China Law & Practice*, March 25, 1993, p. 37.

178 See "China's NPC to Amend *Patent Law of the PRC*," Beijing Xinhua English Service, April 28, 2000, in *FBIS Daily Report: China* (FBIS-CHI-2000–0428), May 2, 2000.

179 See "RMRB Commentator on Promulgation of Amended *Patent Law of the PRC*," *Renmin ribao* (People's Daily), August 28, 2000, in *FBIS Daily Report: China* (FBIS-CHI-2000–0830), August 31, 2000. This has been a much-contested issue under previous Patent Law of the PRC provisions. See, e.g., case involving employee of Beijing Boiler Works JV discussed in *Supreme People's Court Bulletin*, 1995, no. 3 and Hu Jihua and Wang Chaoying (eds), *Zhonghua renmin gongheguo hetong fa: Jie yong shouce* (Handbook on Interpretation and Application of the Contract Law of the PRC), Beijing: Red Flag Press, 1999, pp. 711–17.

180 See "Copyright Law of the PRC, 1990," in CCH (ed.), *op. cit.*, paras 11–700; "Detailed Rules for the Implementation of the Copyright Law of the PRC" (1991), *ibid.*, paras 11–702. For a useful statutory compilation, see Copyright Manuscript Center of State Council Copyright Office (ed.), *Zhonghua renmin gongheguo zhuzuoquan fa* (Authorship Rights Law of the PRC), Beijing: Sanlian Press, 1993. For discussion, see Shen Rengan *et al.*, *Zhonghua renmin gongheguo zhuzuoquan fa jianghua* (Lectures on the Authorship Rights Law of the PRC), Beijing: Law Publishing, 1991; K. Kenckes, "Protection of Foreign Copyrights in China: The Intellectual Property Courts and Alternative Avenues of Protection," *Southern California Interdisciplinary Law Journal*, 1997, vol. 5, pp. 551–71; J.C. Lazar, "Protecting Ideas and Ideals: Copyright Law in the People's Republic of China," *Law & Policy in International Business*, 1996, vol. 27, no. 4, pp. 1185–211; W. Fei "Copyright Practice in the Two Regimes of One Country: A Prospective Harmonization Process in Hong Kong and the PRC," *European Intellectual Property Review*, 1997, no. 7, pp. 30–366; Shi Wenqing and Mei Shenshi, *Zhuzuo quan zhe wenti yanjiu* (Study of Author's Rights), Shanghai: Fudan University Press, 1992.

181 "Official Says PRC Committed to Protect Copyright Owners," Beijing Xinhua English Service, July 23, 1998, in *FBIS Daily Report: China* (FBIS-CHI-98–204); "Sources Say PRC Ready to Revise Copyright Law," Beijing Xinhua English Service, September 22, 1998, in *FBIS Daily Report: China* (FBIS-CHI-98–265).

182 See Zheng Chengsi, "The Development of Intellectual Property in China in 1998," *Zhishi chanquan yanjiu* (Intellectual Property Studies), May 1999, no. 7, pp. 317–32; and Shen Rengan, "Guanyu xiugai xianxing zhuzuoquan fa de sikao" (Perspectives on Revising the Authorship Rights Law), *Zhishi chanquan yanjiu*, (Intellectual Property Studies), November 1999, no. 8, pp. 34–53.

183 See *Copyright Law of the PRC, 1990, op. cit.*, Article 22.

184 See Case no. 64, in Qiao Xianzhi (ed.), *op. cit.*, p. 324.

185 See "Copyright Implementing Rules," Article 25.

186 See "Memorandum of Understanding Between the Government of the People's Republic of China and the Government of the United States of America on the Protection of Intellectual Property, 1992," Article 3.
187 See Berne Convention on the Protection of Literary and Artistic Works, 1886, 1971, Article 18(1), *op. cit.*
188 See "Implementing International Treaties Provisions," *China Law & Practice*, January 14, 1993, p. 36.
189 See "Quanguo renmin daibiao dahui changwu weiyuanhui gunyu chengzhi qinfan zhuzuoquan de fanzui de jueding (caoan)" (Decision (Draft) of the NPC Standing Committee on Punishing Crimes of Violating Copyright), February 4, 1994 (author's copy).
190 See Copyright Law of the PRC, 1990, *op. cit.*, Article 53.
191 See "Computer Software Protection Regulations of the PRC, 1991," in CCH (ed.), *op. cit.*, paras 11–704. For discussion, see R.A. Declet Jr, "Protecting American Intellectual Property in China: The Persistent Problem of Software Piracy," *New York International Law Review*, 1997, vol. 10, no. 2, pp. 57–76.
192 See "Landmark judgment against Juren Computer Co.," *IP Asia*, June 1996, p. 26.
193 See Case no. 43, in Li Changdao (ed.), *Shanghai fayuan anli jingxuan: 1996* (Carefully Selected Cases from the Shanghai Courts: 1996), *op. cit.*, p. 166.
194 See Lu G., "Advances in the Protection of Intellectual Property Rights in China," *Harvard China Review*, vol. 1, no. 17, pp. 71–4.
195 See "Supreme People's Court on Strengthening IPR Protection," *Renmin ribao* (People's Daily), July 19, 1997, in *FBIS Daily Report: China* (FBIS-CHI-97–217), August 6, 1997.
196 "Yearender: PRC Protector of Intellectual Property," Beijing Xinhua English Service, December 30, 1998, in *FBIS Daily Report: China* (FBIS-CHI-98–364).
197 See "Zuigao renmin fayuan zhishi chanquan jiufen an shouan tongji" (Statistics of the Supreme People's Court on Acceptance of Intellectual Property Dispute Cases), *Zhishi chanquan yanuiu* (Intellectual Property Studies), May 1999, no. 7, p. 240.
198 See, e.g., "PRC Court Sentences 7 for Audio, Video Piracy," Beijing Xinhua English Service, April 15, 1997, in *FBIS Daily Report: China* (FBIS-CHI-97–105). Despite revisions to the Criminal Law expanding criminal penalties for IP violations, only a small minority of IP case decisions (128 of 3,953 in 1998) involve criminal matters. See "Zuigao renmin fayuan zhishi chanquan jiufen an shouan tongji" (Statistics of the Supreme People's Court on Acceptance of Intellectual Property Dispute Cases), *op. cit.*
199 See C. Borg-Marks and M.B. Lao, "Artist wins China's first painting case," *China Law & Practice*, December 1996/January 1997, pp. 53–4; C.B. Marks and K. Yung, "Landmark damages awarded for software infringement," *China Law & Practice*, May 1996, pp. 50–2; "Beijing Court Rules in Favor of Microsoft," Beijing Xinhua English Service, February 13, 1999, in *FBIS Daily Report: China* (FBIS-CHI-1999–0213), February 16, 1999.
200 See "Guanxi Zhuang Region Destroys Illegal Publications," Beijing Xinhua English Service, January 18, 1999, in *FBIS Daily Report: China* (FBIS-CHI-99–018), January 20, 1999; "Liaoning Cracks Down on Pirated Audio-Video Products," Beijing Xinhua English Service, January 14, 1999, in *FBIS Daily Report: China* (FBIS-CHI-99–014), January 20, 1999; "Guangdong Joins Hong Kong in Expanded Anti-Piracy Efforts," Xinhua English Language Service, January 8, 1999, in *FBIS Daily Report: China* (FBIS-CHI-99–008), January 11, 1999; "Pirated Disc Production Line Closed in Fujian," Beijing Xinhua English Service, September 28, 1998, in *FBIS Daily Report: China* (FBIS-CHI-8–271), September 30, 1998.

201 See, e.g., "RMRB Article on Fighting Porn, Illegal Publications," *Beijing Renmin ribao*, June 15, 2000, in *FBIS Daily Report: China* (FBIS-CHI-2000–0621), July 5, 2000; "Beijing Closes More CD Production Lines," Beijing Xinhua English Service, January 8, 1997, in *FBIS Daily Report: China* (FBIS-CHI-97–005); "Beijing To Crack Down on Illegal Cultural Activities," Beijing Xinhua English Service, January 8, 1998, in *FBIS Daily Report: China* (FBIS-CHI-98–008), January 11, 1998; "Report on Beijing's Crackdown in Pornography," Beijing Xinhua English Service, January 7, 1997, in *FBIS Daily Report: China* (FBIS-CHI-97–004), January 8, 1997; "State Council Issues New Rules on Control of Publications," Beijing Xinhua English Service, January 15, 1997, in *FBIS Daily Report: China* (FBIS-CHI-97–011), January 17, 1997.

202 See S. Tiefenbrun, "Piracy of Intellectual Property in China and the Former Soviet Union and its Effects Upon International Trade: A Comparison," *Buffalo Law Review*, 1998, vol. 86, no. 1, pp. 1–69. Also see International Intellectual Property Alliance, "1997 Special 301 Recommendations," February 24, 1997 and "1999 Special 301 Recommendations," February 15, 1999.

203 See, e.g., R.A. Declet Jr, *op. cit.*, A. Simpson, "Copyright Law and Software Regulations in the People's Republic of China: Have the Chinese Pirates Affected International Trade?" (comment) *North Carolina Journal of International Law and Commercial Regulation*, 1995, vol. 20, no. 3, pp. 575–628.

204 See D.E. Long, "China's IP Reforms Show Little Success," *IP Worldwide*, November/December 1998. Also see International Intellectual Property Alliance, "1999 Special 301 Recommendations," February 16, 1999.

205 See, e.g., S. Faison, "China Turns Blind Eye to Pirated Disks," *New York Times*, March 28, 1998, p. 1.

206 See "Directive Will Eliminate Software Piracy in Chinese Government Agencies," *Business Wire*, April 8, 1999.

207 See "Testimony of Stuart Eizenstat, Undersecretary of State for Economic Business and Agricultural Affairs, before Senate Foreign Relations Committee," Federal News Service, April 29, 1999.

208 For discussion of structural and behavioral issues, see D. Shannon and T. Loke-Khoon, "Intellectual Property Developments and Enforcement Challenges in Hong Kong and the People's Republic of China," *California International Practitioner*, 1997, vol. 8, pp. 13–27. In this respect, it is worth noting that Taiwan dramatically improved its record of IPR enforcement in 1996–97, sufficient to be removed from the US Trade Representative's Watch List, only to see piracy rise dramatically in 1998, resulting in Taiwan being relisted on the USTR's Watch List. See International Intellectual Property Alliance, "1999 Special 301 Recommendations," February 15, 1999.

209 See "PRC Firms Promote Legal S/W Use," *Keji ribao* (Science and Technology Daily), April 1, 1998, in *FBIS Daily Report: China* (FBIS-CHI-98–230), August 19, 1998.

210 See generally, W.P. Alford, *To Steal a Book is an Elegant Offense*, Stanford, Calif.: Stanford University Press, 1995. Also see Li Fang, "Difficulties and Hardships of Copyright Protection," *Renmin ribao* (People's Daily), October 16, 1998, in *FBIS Daily Report: China* (FBIS-CHI-98–307), November 5, 1998.

211 For example, the imperial examination system was based on rote memorization of Confucian classics. See Ho P., *The Ladder of Success in Imperial China*, New York: John Wiley and Sons, 1962. The training of artists and calligraphers, on the other hand, involved the ritual copying of old masters. See M. Sze (ed.), *The Mustard Seed Garden of Painting*, Princeton, NJ: Princeton University Press, 1963; S.Y.C. Fu, *Challenging the Past: The Paintings of Chang Dai-chien*, Washington: Smithsonian Institution, 1991.

212 See generally, J.A. Cohen, "China's Changing Constitution," *The China Quarterly*, 1978, vol. 76.

213 See *Constitution of the PRC 1982*, Article 13.

214 For example, the Joint Venture Law, 1990 makes specific reference to promoting international economic cooperation and technological exchange. Also see generally, Guo Shoukang, "Technology Transfer," in Rui M. and Wang G. (eds) *Chinese Foreign Economic Law*, Washington: International Law Institute, 1994, section 4, pp. 1–21.

215 See Patent Law of the PRC (as amended), *op. cit.*, Chap. VI.

216 See "Memorandum of Understanding Between the Government of the People's Republic of China and the Government of the United States of America on the Protection of Intellectual Property, 1992," Article 1 (i) (d).

217 See generally, Asia Law & Practice (ed.), *Intellectual Property Protection in China: Practical Strategies* (2nd edn), Hong Kong: Asia Law & Practice, 1998. Also see Comment, "China's Intellectual Property Protection: Prospects for Achieving International Standards," *Fordham International Law Journal*, 1995, vol. 19, p. 181.

218 See, e.g., "Regulations of Beijing and Shanghai Municipalities on Resolving Patent Disputes," which make extensive use of administrative measures.

219 See Patent Law of the PRC, *op. cit.*, Article 60; Trademark Law of the PRC, *op. cit.*, Article 39; and Copyright Law of the PRC, 1990, *op. cit.*, Article 46.

220 See, e.g., Dai Jianzhi and Chen Xu, *Zhishi chanquan sunhai peichang* (Compensation for Loss in Intellectual Property), Beijing: Law Publishing, 1997.

221 See General Office of the State Council Working Conference on Intellectual Property (ed.), *op. cit.*; "Status Report of the Enforcement of IPR Laws in China 1996," *op. cit.*; "1999 White Paper on Intellectual Property Rights Enforcement," *op. cit.* Also see "China Defends Copyright System Ahead of U.S. Sanction Threat," *op. cit.* Also see "Marked Progress Seen in Patent Law of the PRC's Use," *Xinhua*, May 6, 1995, in *FBIS Daily Report: China*, May 8, 1995, p. 26; and "NPC Copyright Law Team Inspects Hainan," in *FBIS Daily Report: China*, June 21, 1995, p. 58.

222 For an extensive collection of articles offering a variety of opinions on the ideological and operations aspects of the issue of stock holding in China, see Wang Mengkui and Xing Junfang (eds) *Guanyu gufen zhi wenti* (Questions about the Stock System), Beijing: Economy Publishing House, 1987.

223 See generally P.B. Potter, "The Legal Framework for Securities Markets in China: The Challenge of Maintaining State Control, and Inducing Investor Confidence," *China Law Reporter*, 1992, vol. 7, p. 61. Also see Hu Y., *China's Capital Market*, Hong Kong: Chinese University Press, 1993.

224 See "Shanghai shi zhengquan jiaoyi guanli banfa ben yue qi zhixing" (The Shanghai Municipal Regulations on Administration of the Securities Exchange Come into Effect This Month), *Shanghai fazhi bao* (Shanghai Legal System Gazette), December 10, 1990; and "Shanghai zhengquan jiaoyi guanli banfa shixing" (The Administrative Methods for the Shanghai Securities Exchange Come into Effect), *Jinrong shibao* (Financial Times), December 13, 1990. Subsequently, regulations were issued concerning the issuance of bonds. See "Rules Issued to Regulate Bond Mart," *China Daily Business Weekly*, January 1, 1991. State Council regulations on enterprise stock issues were also issued in early 1991, providing a model for later Shanghai enactments. See "Guowuyuan zuijin fabu qiye gupiao faxing guanli guiding" (State Council Recently Issues Regulations on Administration of Enterprise Stock Issues), *Chengshi jinrong* (Municipal Finance), January 1991, p. 2.

225 See "Shenzhen zhengquan jiaoyi suo zhangcheng" (Articles of Association for the Shenzhen Securities Exchange); "Shenzhen shi gupiao faxing yu jiaoyi guanli zanxing banfa" (Provisional Methods of Shenzhen Municipality for the Issue and Transferring of Shares), May 15, 1991 (hereafter, the "Shenzhen Stock Transaction Regulations"); and "Shenzhen shi zhengquan jigou guanli zanxing guiding" (Provisional Regulations of Shenzhen Municipality for the Administration of Securities Organs), June 25, 1991. For a useful collection of securities regulations in the early 1990s, see Pan Jinsheng, Liu Hongbie, and Zhang Xue (eds) *Zhong wai zhengquan fagui ziliao huibian* (Compilation of Chinese and Foreign Securities Laws and Regulations and Materials), Beijing: Finance Press, 1993.

226 See "Shanghai zhengquan jiaoyi suo jiaoyi shichang yewu shixing guize" (Trial Regulations of the Shanghai Securities Exchange on the Activities of the Exchange Market), November 26, 1990, Shanghai: Shanghai Securities Exchange Board of Directors, 1990.

227 See "Shanghai shi zhengquan jiaoyi guanli banfa" (Methods of Shanghai Municipality for Administration of Securities Transactions), *Jiefang ribao* (Liberation Daily), December 12, 1990, p. 3. An English translation appears as "Shanghai Securities Transaction Regulations," *FBIS Daily Report: China*, December 20, 1990, p. 46.

228 Article 5 of the Shanghai Exchange Regulations provides that the department in charge (*zhuguan jiguan*) is PBOC/Shanghai, whose approval and supervisory authority is reiterated throughout.

229 See "Shanghai shi zhengquan jiaoyi guanli banfa" (Methods of Shanghai Municipality for Administration of Securities Transactions), *op. cit.*

230 See "Shanghai Transaction Regulations," Article 3, which provides, in addition to the types of securities listed in the Shanghai Exchange Regulations, that other approved securities may be traded as well. Although Article 3 of the Shanghai Exchange Rules defines security by reference to the provisions of the Shanghai Transaction Regulations, Article 27 of the Exchange Rules limits the securities approved for issuance on the SSE to state bonds, construction bonds, finance bonds, and enterprise stocks, bonds, and debentures.

231 For example, the standard information required to be disclosed for issuance of stocks and bonds is more nearly equal than under the Shanghai Exchange Regulations, requiring a prospectus, underwriting contract, documents of approval, and financial reports for the past two years. See Shanghai Transaction Regulations, Articles 9–11. Compare with Shanghai Exchange Regulations, Articles 30 and 31.

232 See T.T. Xia, "The Shanghai Exchange Scandal and Chinese Bonds Law," *Columbia Journal of Asian Law*, 1996, vol. 10, no. 1, pp. 281–303.

233 See "Zhongguo Renmin Yinhang Shanghai Shi Fenhang guanyu faxing gupiao de zanxing guanli fangfa" (Provisional Methods of the Shanghai Municipal Branch of the People's Bank of China Concerning the Issuance of Stock), in Guo Zhenying (ed.), *Zhongguo shehui zhuyi gufen jingji wen da* (Questions and Answers on China's Socialist Share Economy), Beijing: Aeronautics Academy Press, 1986, p. 361. These regulations are described as "approved by the Shanghai Municipal People's Government" and the term used for "methods" is *banfa*, not *fangfa*, in "Guanyu faxing gupiao de zanxing guanli banfa" (Provisional Methods for Issuing Stock), August 10, 1984, in Shanghai Shi Renmin Zhengfu Bangongting (General Office of the Shanghai Municipal Government) and Shanghai Renmin Zhengfu Jingji Fagui Yanjiu Zhongxin (Economic Laws and Regulations Research Center of the Shanghai Municipal Government) (eds), *Shanghai shifagui guizhang huibian: 1949–1985* (Compilation of Statutes and Regulations and Rules of Shanghai

Municipality), Shanghai: Shanghai People's Press, 1986, although otherwise the content is the same.

234 Compare "Guanyu faxing gupiao de zanxing guanli fangfa"/"Guanyu faxing gupiao de zanxing guanli banfa," supra with "Shanghai zhengquan jiaoyi suo jiaoyi shichang yewu shixing guize," supra, Articles 7, 27, and 29; and "Shanghai Securities Transaction Regulations," Articles 45 and 50.

235 The emergence of "B" Shares was predicated on the non-convertibility of the renminbi. Despite the restrictions on their offerings and trading, "B" shares were for a time the only way to introduce foreign currency investment into Chinese domestic companies on a portfolio basis. However, with the introduction of "H" shares in 1993 and the American Depository Receipts (ADRs) listed by Chinese companies on the NYSE, alternative avenues have made the "B" share market less attractive. (See, e.g., Liu Weiling, "Experts Call for Moves to Revive B-Share Markets," *China Daily*, April 15, 1994, p. 3; also D. Whittall, "Heavy Hitting H Shares," *China Business Review*, May/June 1994, p. 44.) With the reform of the Chinese foreign exchange system in December 1993, non-convertibility is on the way out, and with it the premise for limits on "B" share markets. (See "Announcement of the People's Bank of China on Further Reforming the Foreign Exchange Management System," December 28, 1993, *China Economic News*, January 10, 1994, p. 9.) Recent proposals on expanding the availability of "B" shares may help make these securities more attractive.

236 "Measures of Shanghai Municipality for Administration of Special Renminbi-Denominated Shares" (Shanghai B Share Administrative Measures), November 22, 1991, enacted by the People's Bank of China and the Shanghai Municipal Government, translation by Baker and McKenzie.

237 "Detailed Implementing Rules for the Measures of Shanghai Municipality for the Administration of Special Renminbi-Denominated Shares" (Shanghai B Share Implementing Rules), November 5, 1991, enacted by Shanghai Branch of the People's Bank of China, translation by Baker and McKenzie.

238 "Supplementary Operating Rules for the Trading Market (Special Renminbi-Denominated Shares) of the Shanghai Securities Exchange" (Shanghai B Share Operating Rules), February 18, 1992, enacted by the Shanghai Securities Exchange, translation by Baker and McKenzie.

239 See *Shenzhen Zhengquan Shichang Nianbao: 1990* (Annual Report on Shenzhen Securities Market: 1990), p. 69 *et seq.* For discussion of the bank's 1988 issues, see "Roundup: A Glimpse of China's Securities Market," Beijing Xinhua English Service, February 11, 1991, in *FBIS Daily Report: China*, February 11, 1991, p. 49.

240 See, e.g., K. McParland, "The Phantom Exchange: Why China's Shenzhen Bourse is Kept under Wraps," *The Financial Post*, March 18, 1991, p. 35.

241 See "Guangdong sheng gupiao zhaiquan guanli zanxing banfa" (Provisional Methods of Guangdong Province for the Administration of Stocks and Bonds), September 30, 1986, in Zhonghua renmin gongheguo sifabu falu zhengce yanjiu shi (Laws and Policy Research Office of the PRC Ministry of Justice), *Hengxiang jingji lianhe falu fa gui zhengce huibian* (Compilation of Laws and Statutes and Regulations on Horizontal Economic Linkages), Beijing, 1987, pp. 353–7.

242 See "Shenzhen shi renmin zhengfu «Guanyu chengli Shenzhen shi zhengquan shichang Lingdao Xiaozu» de tongzhi" (Notice of the Shenzhen Municipal People's Government Concerning the Establishment of the Leading Small Group for the Shenzhen Securities Market), *Shenzhen Zhengquan Shichang Nianbao: 1990* (Annual Report on Shenzhen Securities Market, 1990), p. 229. Also see statement by the Shenzhen Municipal People's Government dated

July 2, 1990, *ibid.*, p. 222. Also see "Zhengquan shichang lingdao xiaozu huiyi jiyao" (Summary of Minutes of the Small Leading Group for the Shenzhen Securities Market), *ibid.*, pp. 210–15.

243 For discussion of provisions for issuance and marketing of securities by the leading small group, see "Zhengquan shichang lingdao xiaozu huiyi jiyao (xuandeng san)" (Summary of Minutes of the Leading Small Group of the Shenzhen Securities Market: Selection Three), *ibid.*, p. 113. During these drafting meetings, reference was made to the "Shenzhen zhengquan guanli zanxing banfa" (Provisional Regulations for Administration of the Shenzhen Securities Market), which were described in October 1990 as already having undergone preliminary consideration and final drafting ("yi jing chubu shenyi dinggao"). Much of the text was incorporated in the Shenzhen Stock Transaction Regulations, *op. cit.* Compare Section 4 of "Zhengquan shichang lingdao xiaozu huiyi jiyao (xuandeng san)" (Summary of Minutes of the Leading Small Group of the Shenzhen Securities Market: Selection Three), *op. cit.*, with Articles 15 and 36 of the "Shenzhen Transaction Regulations."

244 See "Shenzhen zhengquan jiaoyi suo zhangcheng" (Articles of Association for the Shenzhen Securities Exchange) and Shenzhen Stock Transaction Regulations, *op. cit.* Also see "Guanyu [Shenzhen shi gupiao faxing yu jiaoyi guanli zanxing banfa] he [Shenzhen zhengquan jiaoyi suo zhangcheng] de pifu" (Official Reply Concerning the Provisional Methods of Shenzhen Municipality for the Issue and Transferring of Shares and the Articles of Association for the Shenzhen Securities Exchange), Document Yin Fu [1991] No. 154, April 11, 1991, addressed to PBOC – Shenzhen branch. Also see "Shenzhen shi fa gui jin chutai" (Statutes and Regulations of Shenzhen Municipality are Tabled Today), *Wenhui bao* (Literary Daily), May 15, 1991.

245 "Interim Procedures on Control of Shenzhen Special (B-Type) RMB Stocks" ("Shenzhen B Share Interim Procedures"), *China Economic News*, January 27, 1992. p. 7.

246 "Rules for the Implementation of the Interim Procedures on Control of Shenzhen Special (B-Type) RMB Stocks" (Shenzhen B Share Implementing Rules), *China Economic News*, February 3, 1992, p. 7.

247 See Tao Da and Wu Dakun, "Dui Shanghai zhengquan shichang yi gufenzhi de jidian yijian he jianyi" (Several opinions and suggestions on the Shanghai securities market and stock system), *Neibu wengao* (Internal Manuscripts), 1992, no. 7, pp. 5–8.

248 See Zhang Qizuo, "Gufenzhi bu hui gaibian shehui zhuyi qiye de xingzhi" (The Stock System Will not Change the Character of Socialist Enterprises), *Neibu wengao* (Internal Manuscripts), 1992, no. 6, pp. 3–7. Also see Qian A., "Riding Two Horses: Corporatizing Enterprises and the Emerging Securities Regulatory Regime in China," *UCLA Pacific Basin Law Journal*, 1993, vol. 12, p. 62; X. Gao, "Developments in Securities and Investment Law in China," *Australian Journal of Corporate Law*, 1996, vol. 6, pp. 228–47.

249 See, e.g., Peng Zhenming, "Touze jijian lifa ruogan wenti sikao" (Considering Various Issues in Legislation on Investment Funds), *Zhengzhi yu falu* (Politics and Law), 1996 no. 1, pp. 8–10.

250 See "Company Law of the People's Republic of China," *China Economic News*, Supplement No. 2, March 7, 1994.

251 See "The Securities Law of the People's Republic of China," *China Economic News*, Supplement No. 3, March 15, 1999, pp. 1–18. For discussions of the contentious drafting process, see "Analysts Say NPC Plans Securities Laws," *South China Morning Post*, August 6, 1993, p. 9, in *FBIS Daily Report: China*, August 6, 1993, p. 33; "Economist Li Yining Says Securities Law Scheduled," Beijing Xinhua English Service, March 11, 1994, in *FBIS Daily Report: China*,

March 11, 1994; "'Ideological Debates' Block Passage of Securities Law," *Eastern Express* (Hong Kong), March 8, 1994, in *FBIS Daily Report: China*, March 9, 1994; Mei Shengshi, "Wo guo zhengzhuan li fa de que he luan ji qi zhili" (The Deficiencies and Disorder in our Securities Legislation and their Resolution), *Zhongguo zhengquan bao* (China Securities Reporter), January 25, 1994, p. 7.

252 See "Company Law of the PRC," *op. cit.* A number of preliminary analyses have emerged addressing this legislation, including P. Torbert, "Broadening the Scope of Investment," *China Business Review*, May/June 1994, p. 48; D. Ho, "China's New Company Law: Something Concrete to Go By," *East Asian Executive Reports*, February 1994, p. 9; R.C. Art and M. Gu, "China Incorporated: The First Corporation Law of the People's Republic of China," *Yale Journal of International Law*, 1995, vol. 20, pp. 273–308; M.I. Nikkel, "'Chinese Characteristics' in Corporate Clothing: Questions About Fiduciary Duty in China's Company Law" (Note), *Minnesota Law Review*, 1995, vol. 80, no. 2, pp. 503–42; C.R. Peng, "Limited Liability in China: A Partial Reading of China's Company Law of 1994," *Columbia Journal of Asian Law*, 1996, vol. 10, no. 1, pp. 263–80. The *Company Law* was amended in December 1999 to allow more flexibility in the membership of boards of directors for state-owned companies and to permit government support for new technology companies. See "NPC Amends Corporate Law," Beijing Xinhua Domestic Service, December 6, 1999, in *FBIS Daily Report: China* (FBIS-CHI-1999–1229), December 30, 1999.

253 See "Draft Corporate Law Submitted," *FBIS Daily Report: China*, February 16, 1993, p. 29; and "Speech by Qiao Shi at Closing of NPC," *FBIS Daily Report: China*, April 1, 1993, p. 22. One source from which many of the Company Law's provision were drawn is the "Provisional Regulations of Shenzhen Municipality on Companies Limited by Shares," March 17, 1992, reprinted in *China Law & Practice*, May 7, 1992, p. 12.

254 See, e.g., "Gufen you xian gongsi guifan yijian" (Opinion on Standards for Limited Liability Stock Companies), *Renmin ribao* (People's Daily), June 19, 1992.

255 See note 235 supra, and accompanying text.

256 See Company Law of the PRC, *op. cit.*, Article 155.

257 See *ibid.*, Articles 130 and 131.

258 See *ibid.*, Article 89.

259 See *ibid.*, Article 152.

260 These include (1) the issuing company's total share capital must be no less than RMB500 million; (2) the company must have been in business for at least three years and have been profitable for the past three years; (3) the number of shareholders who each hold shares at a par value of at least RMB1,000 shall not be less than one thousand, and the shares already issued to the public account for more than 25 percent of the total shares (or 15 percent if the total share capital exceeds RMB400 million); (4) there have been no significant violations of law and no false reporting over the past three years; and (5) such other requirements as may be prescribed by the State Council. See Company Law of the PRC, *op. cit.*, Article 152.

261 See *ibid.*, Article 153.

262 See *ibid.*, Article 159.

263 See *ibid.*, Article 163.

264 See *ibid.*, Article 161.

265 See *ibid.*, Article 162.

266 See Kan Ren, "Fairness the Key to Securities Law," *China Daily*, November 25, 1993, in *FBIS Daily Report: China* (FBIS-CHI-93–227), November 29, 1993, p. 42.

267 See, e.g., Li Zhe, "Guoying qiye gufenzhi shi shenhua gaige de xinlu" (The Securities System for State-Owned Enterprises is a New Route to Deepening Reform), *Neibu wengao* (Internal Manuscripts), 1992, no. 7, pp. 3–4.

268 Much of this discussion is drawn from the author's "China's Regulation of Securities: A National System Begins to Emerge" and "PRC State Council Issues National Stock Regulations," *East Asian Executive Reports*, May 15, 1993, p. 9 and July 15, 1993, p. 9, respectively.

269 These included (1) "Regulations on Enterprises' Shareholding System Experiment," May 15, 1992; (2) "Temporary Provisions on Several Issues Concerning Financial Management in Experimental Shareholding Enterprises," June 27, 1992; (3) "Temporary Provisions on Issues Concerning Tax Revenue of Experimental Shareholding Enterprises," June 12, 1992; (4) "Interim Procedures Governing the Supply and Marketing of Goods and Materials by Experimental Shareholding Enterprises," June 30, 1992; (5) "Provisional Regulations on the Macroeconomic Control of Experimental Joint-Stock Enterprises," July 6, 1992; (6) "Interim Regulations Governing Labor and Wages in Enterprises Experimenting with Share-Holding Systems," June 1, 1992; (7) "Provisional Regulations on Auditing at Experimental Shareholding Enterprises," July 19, 1992; and (8) "Interim Provisions on Administering Land Assets of Experimental Shareholding Enterprises," July 9, 1992.

270 See "State Regulations on Shareholding Experiment," *FBIS Daily Report: China*, June 22, 1992, p. 31.

271 See "Temporary Provisions on Several Issues Concerning Financial Management in Experimental Shareholding Enterprises" in "Provisions on Financial Management of Stock Firms," *FBIS Daily Report: China*, July 6, 1992, p. 52. Also see "Provisional Regulations on Auditing at Experimental Shareholding Enterprises," in "Regulations on Shareholding Enterprise Auditing," *ibid.*, p. 37.

272 See "Temporary Provisions on Issues Concerning Tax Revenue of Experimental Shareholding Enterprises," in "Rules on Taxing Experimental Shareholding Firms," *ibid.*, p. 57.

273 See "Interim Procedures Governing the Supply and Marketing of Goods and Materials by Experimental Shareholding Enterprises" in "Rules on Marketing by Pilot Shareholding Firms," *ibid.*, p. 58.

274 See "Provisional Regulations on the Macroeconomic Control of Experimental Joint-Stock Enterprises" in Regulations on Forming Joint-Stock Enterprises, *FBIS Daily Report: China*, July 14, 1992, p. 37.

275 See "Interim Provisions on the Management of the Issuing and Trading of Stocks," *China Economic News*, June 7, 1993, p. 7 and June 14, 1993, p. 7. Also see *South China Morning Post*, 8 June 1993, p. B4.

276 See "State Council Circular on Securities Markets," *FBIS Daily Report: China*, January 25, 1993, p. 24.

277 See "Interim Procedures on the Management of Stock Exchanges," July 7, 1993, *China Economic News*, August 9, 1993, no. 30, pp. 6–9 and August 16, 1993, no. 31, pp. 6–8.

278 Following enactment of the State Council measures, the Hong Kong Stock Exchange's listing rules were amended to permit Chinese domestic firms to list on the Hong Kong Stock Exchange. See "New rules governing mainland listings in HK," *South China Morning Post*, June 20, 1993, p. Money 9. The Qingdao Brewery became the first Chinese entity to list on the Hong Kong

Stock Exchange. For discussion of the volatile "H" share market in Hong Kong, see D. Whittall, *op. cit.*

279 Under the January Circular, the chief organ was labeled the Securities Committee of the State Council (SCOSC), while the executive organ was the China Securities Supervision and Control Committee (CSSACC). See P.B. Potter, "China's Regulation of Securities: A National System Begins to Emerge," *op. cit.*

280 See "Overseer for share issues established," *South China Morning Post*, June 25, 1993, p. B1.

281 See "China Puts More Rules on Stock Market," *China News Digest* (electronic media), January 22, 1997. A useful compilation appears in Cheng Gong *et al.* (eds), *Zhongguo zhengquan fagui huibian* (Compilation of Chinese Securities Laws and Regulations) (2nd edn), Beijing: People's University Press, 1998.

282 See "Stock Exchange Administration Procedures," *China Law & Practice*, 1996 no. 7, p. 9.

283 See "Procedures for Checking of Listed Companies," *China Economic News*, February 17, 1997, no. 6, pp. 7–8.

284 See "Provisional Regulations on the Process of New Stock Issuances and Subscriptions," *China Economic News*, March 17, 1997, no. 10, pp. 6–10.

285 See "Interim Procedures on Administration of Securities and Futures Investment Consultancy," *China Economic News*, May 4, 1998, no. 16, pp. 7–12; "Provisional Regulations on License Control of Securities and Futures-Related Business Carried Out by Certified Public Accountants," *China Economic News*, March 23, 1998, no. 11, pp. 6–8 and March 30, 1998, no. 12, pp. 8–10. Also see "CSRC circular regulates futures brokerage companies," *China Law & Practice*, February 1997, p. 17.

286 See "Interim Procedures Concerning Capital Accretion Through Additional Issues of B-Shares by Domestically Listed Companies," *China Economic News*, June 15, 1998, no. 22, pp. 8–10.

287 See "Procedures on the Administration of Issuance and Transfer of Enterprise Bonds," *China Economic News*, Supplement No. 6, June 22, 1998, pp. 1–10.

288 See "Zhonghua renmin gongheguo zhengquan fa" (Securities Law of the PRC), *Fazhi ribao* (Legal System Daily), December 30, 1998, pp. 2–3.

289 Securities Law of the PRC, 1999, *op. cit.*, Articles 1 and 7.

290 *Ibid.*, Article 211. On the issue of unification of securities regimes, see J. Lo, "New PRC Securities Law Fails to Fully Unify Regulation of Securities Issues in China," *China Law & Practice*, February 1999, pp. 21–4.

291 Securities Law of the PRC, 1999, *op. cit.*, Article 1.

292 See "Zhou on Enforcement of Securities Law," Beijing Xinhua Domestic Service, June 29, 1999, in *FBIS Daily Report: China* (FBIS-CHI-1999–0715), September 9, 1999.

293 Securities Law of the PRC, 1999, *op. cit.*, Article 3.

294 *Ibid.*, Article 4.

295 See "PRC Amends Law on Securities, Futures-Related Crimes," Beijing Xinhua English Service, December 25, 1999, in *FBIS Daily Report: China* (FBIS-CHI-1999–1225), December 27, 1999.

296 See Liu Junhai *et al.*, *Zhengquan fa shishi wenda* (Questions and Answers on Knowledge of the Securities Law), Beijing: Law Publishing, 1999, p. 1.

297 Securities Law of the PRC, 1999, *op. cit.*, Article 5.

298 *Ibid.*, Articles 58 *et seq.*

299 See "Regulation on Stock Issuance Approval Commission," Beijing Xinhua Domestic Service, October 13, 1999, in *FBIS Daily Report: China* (FBIS-CHI-1999–1206), December 8, 1999.

300 Securities Law of the PRC, 1999, *op. cit.*, Articles 78 *et seq.*

301 *Ibid.*, Articles 96, 109.
302 *Ibid.*, Chaps VI–IX.
303 *Ibid.*, Chap. X.
304 See, e.g., Mei Shengshi, "Wo guo zhengzhuan li fa de que he luan ji qi zhili" (The Deficiencies and Disorder in Our Securities Legislation and their Resolution), *op. cit.*; and Peng Zhenming, *op. cit.*
305 Gao Xiqing, former general counsel for the Chinese Administration for Securities Exchanges, was educated at Duke University, and Gao Peiji, former general counsel for the Shenzhen Securities Exchange, was trained at Berkeley. Other influential Chinese officials received US training under the auspices of the Committee on Legal Education Exchanges with China, and US and Canadian law schools continue to benefit from the contributions of law students and scholars from China writing on securities law. See, e.g., T.T. Xia, *op. cit.*; J.Z. Zhang, "Comment: Securities Markets and Securities Regulation in China," *North Carolina Journal of International Law and Commercial Regulation*, 1997, vol. 22, pp. 558–630.
306 With regard to information disclosure, see "Shenzhen Stock Transaction Regulations," *op. cit.*, Article 18 and "Shanghai Transaction Regulations," Article 16. Both sets of regulations require the prospectus to contain *inter alia* the following information: name and address of issuer; scope of business; purpose, method and objective of issuing shares; assets and liabilities; and status of the issuer's development or lack thereof, main business, financial circumstances, total value and composition of production. With regard to insider dealing, see "Shanghai Transaction Regulations," Articles 39 and 40, and "Shenzhen Stock Transaction Regulations," Articles 29, 43, and 62, and Chap. VII. Compare with discussion of US securities law models in J. Seligman, "The Reformulation of Federal Securities Law Concerning Non-Public Information," *Georgetown Law Journal*, vol. 73, pp. 1115 *et seq.*; and D.L. Johnston, *Canadian Securities Regulation*, Toronto: Butterworth, 1977, pp. 1–36.
307 See, e.g., Policy and Law Office of the State Council's State Owned Enterprise Administration (ed.), *Zhong wai gufen zhi fagui huibian* (Compilation of Chinese and Foreign Laws and Regulations on the Stock System), Beijing: Politics and Law University Press, 1992.
308 See, e.g., Jin Jiandong *et al.* (eds), *Gudong zhaiquan quanshu* (Encyclopedia of Stocks and Bonds) (2 vols), Beijing: Physics University Press, 1992.
309 Securities Law of the PRC, 1999, *op. cit.*, Article 62.
310 For discussion of the dominant role of the state in Chinese securities market regulation and behavior, see E. Hertz, *The Trading Crowd: An Ethnography of the Shanghai Stock Market*, Cambridge: Cambridge University Press, 1998.
311 See, e.g., Mei Shengshi, "Ying an shichang jingji guilu wanshan «Gongsi fa»" (We Should Perfect the Company Law According to the Rules of the Market Economy), *Zhongguo zhengquan bao* (China Securities Reporter), February 26, 1994, p. 5.
312 See, e.g., M.I. Nikkel, *op. cit.*
313 See Jiang Yifan, "State Enterprise Problems Worsen Despite Reform," *Zhenli de zhuiqiu* (Seeking Truth), April 11, 1998, in *FBIS Daily Report: China* (FBIS-CHI-98–154), June 3, 1998; "Reform of SOEs a Tough Nut to Crack," *Jingji ribao* (Economy Daily), February 13, 1999, in *FBIS Daily Report: China* (FBIS-CHI-1999–0301), February 13, 1999.
314 See Li Zibin, "Boldly Explore Public Ownership Forms: Shenzhen's Successful State Enterprises Reform Practice and Exploration," *Renmin ribao* (People's Daily), December 27, 1997, in *FBIS Daily Report: China* (FBIS-CHI-98–024), January 24, 1998.

315 See, e.g., Company Law of the PRC, *op. cit.*, Article 84's requirement that applications for approval of public stock issues must include (1) documents approving the formation of the company; (2) company charter; (3) management appraisal (*jingying guxuan shu*); (4) issuer's name, stock holdings, investments and assessed capital; (5) prospectus; (6) name and address of collecting bank for payment of shares; and (7) name and address of underwriter. Compare with Securities Law of the PRC, *op. cit.*, Article 45's requirements that applications for listing of stock include (1) listing report; (2) board of directors decision on listing; (3) company charter; (4) company business license; (5) certified financial accounting for the previous three years or since company formation; (6) legal opinion; and (7) most recent prospectus.

316 See Liu Junhai *et al.*, *op. cit.*, pp. 7–8.

317 See, e.g., Supreme People's Court Case (involving non-performance on bond issue), in Hu Jihua and Wang Chaoying (eds), *op. cit.*, pp. 705–7; Case no. 8 (involving a dispute over assignment of rights to income from state bonds), in Qiao Xianzhi (ed.), *op. cit.*, p. 38; Case no. 32 (involving a dispute over stock losses), in Li Changdao (ed.), *Shanghai fayuan anli jingxuan: 1996* (Carefully Selected Cases from the Shanghai Courts: 1996), *op. cit.*, p. 96; Case no. 33, *ibid.*, p. 99 and Case no. 31 (involving disputes over authorization to deal in securities), in Li Changdao (ed.), *Shanghai fayuan anli jingxuan: 1997* (Carefully Selected Cases from the Shanghai Courts: 1997), *op. cit.*, p. 112; Case nos 28 and 30 (involving disputes over stock transaction orders), *ibid.*, pp. 99 and 108.

Chapter 5

1 Portions of this chapter are adapted from P.B. Potter, "The Right to Development: Philosophical Differences and Political Implications," in E.P. Mendes and A.-M. Traeholt (eds), *Human Rights: Chinese and Canadian Perspectives*, Ottawa: Human Rights Research and Education Centre, 1997.

2 See, e.g., Wang J., Liu H., and Li L. (eds), *Renquan yu 21 shijie* (Human Rights and the Twenty-first Century), Beijing: China Law Publishing, 2000; and Xia Yong (ed.), *Zuoxiang quanli de shidai: Zhongguo gongmin quanli fazhan yanjiu* (Proceeding Toward an Era of Rights: A Study of the Development of Citizens' Rights in China), Beijing: University of Politics and Law Press, 1995; *ibid.*, *Renquan gainian qiyuan* (Origins of Human Rights Concepts), Beijing: University of Politics and Law Press, 1992.

3 See, e.g., CASS Law Institute (ed.), *Guoji renquan wenjian yu Guoji renquan jigou* (International Human Rights Documents and International Human Rights Institutions), Beijing, Chinese Academy of Social Sciences Press, 1993.

4 Results of an exchange program with Denmark are published in Liu H. *et al.* (eds), *Renquan yu sifa* (Human Rights and Administration of Justice), Beijing: Legal System Press, 1999. Results of an exchange between Canada and China appear in E.P. Mendes and A.-M. Traeholt (eds), *Human Rights: Chinese and Canadian Perspectives*, Ottawa: Human Rights Research and Education Centre, 1997. Results of an exchange between the Netherlands and China appear in P.R. Baehr *et al.* (eds), *Human Rights: Chinese and Dutch Perspectives*, Kluwer, 1996.

5 See generally, Asia Watch, "Punishment Season: Human Rights in China After Martial Law," 1990.

6 See "14 Year Prison Term," Beijing Xinhua Domestic Service, December 13, 1995, in *FBIS Daily Report: China*, (FBIS-CHI-95–239), December 13, 1995, p. 9. Ultimately, Wei was permitted to go into exile in the United States.

"Wei Jingsheng has been released," *China News Digest* (electronic media), November 16, 1997.

7 See "Spokesman Says China to Mark UN Human Rights Declaration Anniversary," Xinhua News Agency, December 13, 1997; Gu Ping, "A Logical Development," *Renmin ribao* (People's Daily), October 9, 1998, in *FBIS Daily Report: China* (FBIS-CHI-98–288), October 15, 1998. Compare with E. Eckholm, "After Signing Rights Pact, China Launches Crackdown," *New York Times*, October 28, 1998.

8 See US Department of State, "China Country Report on Human Rights Practices for 1996," January 30, 1997.

9 See Human Rights Watch, *HRW World Report 2000: China*, February 2000; Human Rights Watch, "China Uses 'Rule of Law' to Justify Falun Gong Crackdown," November 9, 1999; and S. Mufson, "China Uses Arrests, Threat to Silence Domestic Critics," *New York Times*, December 29, 1995, p. 1.

10 See "Zhonghua renmin gongheguo baoshou guojia mimi fa" (Law of the PRC on Protecting State Secrets) (1989). Citations for all laws, regulations and treaties are provided in Appendix A: Table of Laws, Regulations, and Treaties. Also see "Zhonghua renmin gongheguo baoshou guojia mimi fa shishi banfa" (Implementing Methods for Law of the PRC on Protecting State Secrets), 1990.

11 See "State Secrecy Protection Regulations for Computer Information Systems on the Internet," 2000; "Zhonghua renmin gongheguo jixuanji xinxi wangluo guoji lianwang guanli zanxing guiding" (Provisional Regulations of the PRC on Administration of Computer Information Systems and the International Internet), 1996. Also see "State Council Directive to Control Flow of Information in China Sparks International Criticism," *China News Digest* (electronic format), January 18, 1996.

12 See Human Rights Watch – Asia, "China: Enforced Exile of Dissidents: Government 'Re-Entry Blacklist' Revealed," 1994; M. Farley, "China Dissident to Stay in Hong Kong," *Los Angeles Times*, June 6, 1997.

13 See T. Shakya, *The Dragon in the Land of Snows: A History of Modern Tibet Since 1947*, New York: Columbia University Press, 1999; International Rehabilitation Council for Torture Victims (ed.), *Torture in Tibet 1949–1999*, Copenhagen: IRCT, 1999; P. Wing, L. and J. Sims, "Human Rights in Tibet: An Emerging Foreign Policy Issue," *Harvard Human Rights Journal*, 1992, vol. 5, pp. 193–203. *Cf.* A. Rosett, "Legal Structures for Special Treatment of Minorities in the People's Republic of China," *Notre Dame Law Review*, 1991, vol. 66, no. 5, pp. 1503–28.

14 See Human Rights in China *et al.*, *Report on the Implementation of CEDAW in the People's Republic of China*, 1998; J. Mirsky, "The Bottom of the Well," *New York Review of Books*, October 6, 1994, pp. 24–8.

15 See, e.g., US Department of State annual "China Country Reports" on human rights practices.

16 See "EU Critical of PRC Human Rights, Capital Punishment," AFP – Hong Kong, December 21, 1999, in *FBIS Daily Report: China*, (FBIS-CHI-1999–1221), December 22, 1999. Contrast with "EU Abandons US over human rights in China," AFP – Brussels, February 23, 1998.

17 See generally, Human Rights in China (ed.), "From Principle to Pragmatism: Can 'Dialogue' Improve China's Human Rights Situation?" 1998.

18 See, e.g., "Attempt to block rights resolution, Beijing expected to counter Geneva offensive," *South China Morning Post*, April 15, 1997, p. 8; "Disappointed, Not Discouraged on China," *International Herald–Tribune*, April 17, 1997, p. 4.

19 See Office of the High Commissioner for Human Rights, "Mission Report on China," 1999; A. Kent, "China and the International Human Rights Regime: A Case Study of Multilateral Monitoring: 1989–1994," Human Rights Quarterly, 1995, vol. 17, no. 1, pp. 1–47.

20 For discussion of the dilemma as applied in other Asian states, see A. Woodiwiss, *Globalisation, Human Rights and Labour Law in Pacific Asia*, Cambridge: Cambridge University Press, 1998.

21 For discussion of application of international standards to human rights protection in China and other countries, see Lawyers Committee on Human Rights, "Shackling the Defenders: Legal Restrictions on Independent Human Advocacy Worldwide," 1994.

22 See "Final Declaration of the Regional Meeting for Asia of the World Conference on Human Rights" (1993).

23 See, e.g., D. Kelly and A. Reid (eds), *Asian Freedoms: The Idea of Freedom in East and Southeast Asia*, Cambridge: Cambridge University Press, 1998.

24 See generally, P. Van Ness (ed.), *Debating Human Rights: Critical Essays from the United States and Asia*, London: Routledge, 1999.

25 See "Text of Human Rights White Paper," *FBIS Daily Report: China* (Supplement), November 21, 1991.

26 See "Interview with Zhu Muzhi, Director of the State Council Information Office," *Xinhua*, November 2, 1991, in *FBIS Daily Report: China*, November 4, 1991, p. 16.

27 See, e.g., "Statistical Communiqué of the State Statistical Bureau of the People's Republic of China on the 1993 National Economic and Social Development," (February 28, 1994), *China Economic News*, Supp. No. 3, March 14, 1994, in which nearly six pages of the seven-page report are devoted to economic growth statistics. This pattern was repeated in the 1994 communiqué. See "Statistical Communiqué of the State Statistical Bureau of the People's Republic of China on the 1994 National Economic and Social Development," *China Economic News*, Supp. No. 1, March 27, 1995.

28 See "The Progress of Human Rights in China," Xinhua Domestic Service, December 27, 1995, in *FBIS Daily Report: China*, December 28, 1996, pp. 8–26.

29 See "Quarterly Chronicle and Documentation (April/June 1997)," *The China Quarterly*, September 1997, vol. 151, p. 698.

30 See State Council Information Office, "White Paper: Fifty Years of Progress in China's Human Rights," February 2000.

31 See, e.g., J. Donnelly, "In Search of the Unicorn: The Jurisprudence and Politics of the Right to Development," *California Western International Law Journal*, 1985, vol. 15, p. 473; Bai G., "Are There Any Hierarchies of Human Rights in International Law?" in P.R. Baehr, *et al.* (eds), *op. cit.*, pp. 133–42.

32 See "The Progress of Human Rights in China," *op. cit.*, p. 25.

33 See "Human rights accusations refuted," *China Daily*, March 29, 1995, p. 4.

34 See "Freedom loser when democracy wins," *China Daily*, December 6, 1995, p. 4.

35 See generally J. Murphy and J.L. Coleman, *The Philosophy of Law: An Introduction to Jurisprudence*, Totowa, NJ: Rowman & Allanheld, 1990; R. Dworkin, *Taking Rights Seriously*, Cambridge, Mass.:, Harvard University Press, 1978; S. Lukes, *Individualism*, 1973; J. Raz, "Rights and Individualism," in *The Morality of Freedom*, New York: Oxford University Press, 1986 and *ibid.*, "On the Nature of Rights," *Mind*, 1984, vol. 93, p. 194; and J. Waldron, *Theories of Rights*, New York: Oxford University Press, 1984.

36 See Constitution of the PRC, 1982, Articles 33 and 34.

37 See "The Progress of Human Rights in China," Xinhua Domestic Service, 27 December, 1995, in *FBIS Daily Report,* 28 December, 1995, pp. 8–26.

38 See, e.g., "Damming Debate," in *China Rights Forum,* Spring 1993, pp. 14–16. For indications of the dilemmas involved in Chinese environmental law and regulation, see W.P. Alford and Y. Shen, "Limits of the Law in Addressing China's Environmental Dilemma," in *Stanford Environmental Law Journal,* vol. 16, no. 1 (January 1997), pp. 125–48.

39 See P.B. Potter and Li J., "Regulating Labour Relations in China: The Challenge of Adapting to the Socialist Market Economy," *Université Laval Law Review,* 1996.

40 See generally, H. Harding, *China's Second Revolution: Reform After Mao,* Washington: Brookings Institution, 1987.

41 See "Communiqué of the Third Plenum of the 11th Central Committee," *Hongqi* (Red Flag), 1979, no. 1, p. 14.

42 For a review of Chinese economic policies and conditions in the 1980s, see Joint Economic Committee of US Congress, *China's Economy Looks Toward the Year 2000,* Washington: US Government Printing Office, 1986.

43 *Zhonghua renmin gongheguo quanmin suo you zhi gongye qiye fa* (Law of the PRC on Enterprises Owned by the Whole People), 1988.

44 *Guoying qiye shixing laodong hetong zanxing guiding* (Provisional Regulations for Implementation of Labor Contracts by State Enterprises). Also see generally, H.K. Josephs, *Labour Law in China,* Butterworth, 1990.

45 See J. Howell, *China Opens its Doors: The Politics of Economic Transition,* Boulder, Colo., Lynne Rienner, 1993, pp. 209–43.

46 For a general review of the late stages of reform and many of the attendant consequences, see Joint Economic Committee of US Congress, *China's Economic Dilemmas in the 1990s: The Problems of Reforms, Modernization, and Interdependence,* Washington: US Government Printing Office, 1991.

47 See K. Hartford, "The Political Economy Behind Beijing Spring," in T. Saich (ed.), *The Chinese People's Movement: Perspectives on Spring 1989,* Armonk, NY: M.E. Sharpe, 1990, pp. 50–82.

48 See A.G. Walder, "China's Transitional Economy: Interpreting its Significance," in *The China Quarterly Special Issue: China's Transitional Economy,* December 1995, pp. 963–79.

49 For a collection of insightful articles on the latest stages of the reform process, see *The China Quarterly Special Issue: China's Transitional Economy,* December 1995.

50 See generally, A. Chan, "Labor Standards and Human Rights: The Case of Chinese Workers Under Market Socialism," *Human Rights Quarterly,* 1998; M.C.F. Gao, "On the sharp end of China's economic boom – migrant workers," *China Rights Forum,* Spring 1994, pp. 12–13 and 27, Liu P., "Dying for Development," *China Rights Forum,* Fall 1994, pp. 14–15 and 27. For discussion of privatization policies, see A.G. Walder, *op. cit.*

51 See, e.g., "Qiye zhi gong shangwang shigu baogao he chuli guiding" (Regulations on the Reporting and Resolution of Injuries and Accidents Involving Enterprise Workers and Staff), 1991.

52 See "Labor Minister: Strikes 'Inevitable' with Reform," AFP – Hong Kong, July 15, 1994, in *FBIS Daily Report: China,* July 15, 1994, pp. 12–13.

53 See *ibid.*

54 See Shaanxi Provincial and Municipal Social and Economic Investigation Team, "«Huise shouru» touxi" (Penetrating Analysis of 'Gray Income'), *Neibu wengao* (Internal Manuscripts), 1992, no. 5, pp. 25–9.

55 See M. Forney, "We Want to Eat," *Far Eastern Economic Review,* June 26, 1997.

56 See "China dissidents call on workers to form unions," Reuters, December 23, 1997.
57 See "China: New Arrests Linked to Worker Rights," in Human Rights Watch – Asia, March 11, 1994; B. Gilley, "Shen Yuan Escapes 27 July," *Eastern Express* (Hong Kong), August 9, 1994, in *FBIS Daily Report: China*, August 9, 1994, pp. 18–19; *ibid.*, "Further on Labor Activist," *ibid.*, p. 19. In one recent example, the Shenzhen Municipal High Court sentenced two labor union activists to three-and-a-half-year prison terms on the charge of conspiring to subvert the government. See Human Rights Watch – Asia, press release, June 3, 1997.
58 See, e.g., Wang Liming, "Guojia suoyouquan yu jingji minzhu" (State Ownership Rights and Economic Democracy), *Zhengfa luntan* (Politics and Law Forum), 1989, no. 1, pp. 51–8.
59 See Wang Yantian and Fu Gang, "A Channel Begins to Open up as the Tide of Reform Surges Forward – A Commentary on the Passage of the Labor Law of the PRC," Beijing Xinhua Domestic Service, July 28, 1994, in *FBIS Daily Report: China*, August 3, 1994, pp. 17–18.
60 See "Labor Law 'Should be adopted soon'," Xinhua Domestic Service, June 30, 1994, in *FBIS Daily Report: China*, July 1, 1994, p. 21.
61 See Zhang Xia, "Foreign-funded Ventures in China Told to Unionize," *China Daily*, July 15, 1994, p. 4, in *FBIS Daily Report: China*, July 15, 1994, pp. 20–1, wherein labor abuses by foreign investment enterprises (usually Hong Kong owned or managed) are cited as the reason for increased attention to labor conditions. Also see "Labor Law 'Should be Adopted Soon'," *op. cit.*, and Guo Xiang, "Laodong fa: Weihu zhigong hefa quanyi de jiben fa" (The Labor Law: a basic law for protecting the lawful rights of staff and workers), *Gongren ribao* (Workers Daily), January 5, 1995, p. 5.
62 See "Offenders of labor regulations exposed," Xinhua English Service, July 28, 1994, in *FBIS Daily Report: China*, July 28, 1994, p. 34.
63 See, e.g., "Jiji anpai chengshi daiye qingnian" (Positively Arrange Urban Employment for Youth), in *Renmin ribao* (People's Daily), June 7, 1979, p. 3; "Ben shi quanmin qiye shou ci zhijie zhao shou hetong gong" (This City's Public Enterprises Accept Recruitment Through the Contract Labor for the First Time), *Jiefang ribao* (Liberation Daily) (Shanghai), August 16, 1980, p. 1.
64 See Ministry of Labor *et al.*, *Laodong fa shouce* (Labor Law Handbook), Beijing: Economic Management Press, 1988, p. 288.
65 *Ibid.*, p. 290.
66 See Zhao Lukuan, "Lun laodong hetong zhi" (On the Labor Contract System), *Renmin ribao* (People's Daily), September 7, 1983, p. 5.
67 See Chen Wenyuan, "Guanyu laodong hetong de jige jiben wenti" (Some Basic Issues Concerning Labor Contracts), *Zhongguo fazhi bao* (Chinese Legal System Gazette), August 25, 1986, p. 3.
68 Guoying qiye shixing laodong hetong zhi zanxing guiding (1986).
69 Zhonghua renmin gongheguo siying qiye zanxing tiaoli (1988).
70 Siying qiye laodong guanli zanxing guiding (1989).
71 Quanmin suoyouzhi gongye qiye zhuanhuan jingying ji zhi tiaoli (1992).
72 See R. Weir, "Foreign enterprises bend under labor contract pressure," *China Law & Practice*, March 1996, pp. 21–2.
73 See Li Boyong, "Speech at the National Meeting on Labor Work: Implementation of the Labor Code" *People's Daily* (overseas edition), December 14, 1994. Li Boyong is PRC Minister of Labor.
74 See "Jiechu laodong hetong, gai bu gai fa jingji buchangjin?" (In Case of Cancellation of a Labor Contract, Must the Compensation Fee Still be Paid?), *Gongren ribao* (Workers Daily), January 5, 1995.

75 See Guangdong Provincial Labor Office Document, "Yue Labor and Salary," 1997, no. 115 (copy on file with the author).
76 See generally, S. Biddulph and S. Cooney, "Regulation of Trade Unions in the People's Republic of China," *Melbourne University Law Review*, December 1993, vol. 19, pp. 255–92.
77 See, e.g., "Fayuan cuo jiang huifei di zizuo susong fei" (The Court Improperly Takes Union Dues to Pay Litigation Fee), *Laodong ribao* (Workers Daily), October 10, 1995, p. 5.
78 See "Qiye yao zijue weihu laodong zhe hefa quanyi" (The Enterprise Should Take the Initiative to Safeguard the Legitimate Rights and Interests of Workers), *Gongren ribao* (Workers Daily), February 28, 1995.
79 See "Zheiyang jiechu hetong dui ma?" (Is this Kind of Cancellation of Contract Proper?), *Gongren ribao* (Workers Daily), January 9, 1995, p. 6.
80 See, e.g., "«Laodong fa» shi jingying zhe you fa ke yi" (The "Labor Law" Will Cause Managers to Have a Law to Follow), *Gongren ribao* (Workers Daily), January 5, 1995.
81 See D. Hunter, "Chinese Labor Dispute Arbitration Procedures: An Early Review in Zhejiang Province," *Comparative Labor Law Journal*, Spring 1990, vol. 11, pp. 340–51.
82 Guoying qiye laodong zhengyi chuli zanxing guiding (1987).
83 See "Answers to Questions About the Policy of Handling Labor Disputes," Ministry of Labor, *Zhongguo laodong fa zhengce fagui quanshu* (Encyclopedia of China's Labor Laws and Policies), Jilin: Science and Technology Press, 1994, p. 648.
84 See, e.g., Yu Min, "Laodong hetong jiufen zhong weiyue shoushan ren bujiu zhi yanjiu" (Study of the Remedies Available to Persons Harmed by Breach of Contract in Labor Contract Disputes), *Faxue yanjiu* (Studies in Law), 1997, no. 5, pp. 135–43.
85 See "Fayuan cuo jiang huifei di zizuo susong fei" (The Court Improperly Takes Union Dues to Pay Litigation Fee), *op. cit.*, in which the court handling a dispute over investment funds improperly deducted litigation fees from the union membership fund.
86 See China Labor Law Research Association (ed.), *Xin bian laodong zhengyi zhongcai anli* (New Edition of Labor Dispute Arbitration Cases), Beijing: Law Publishing, 2000.
87 Guo Xiang, *op. cit.*
88 "Laodong fa zhi jianshe de lichengbei" (The Milestone Established by the Labor Law System), *Gongren ribao* (Workers Daily), January 9, 1995, p. 1; "Qixin xieli tuijin laodong fa zhi jianshe" (Make Consolidated Efforts to Promote the Establishment of the Labor Law System), *Gongren ribao* (Workers Daily), January 27, 1995, p. 1; Cao Min, "State vows to protect interests of laborers," *China Daily*, July 8, 1994, p. 1, in *FBIS Daily Report: China*, July 8, 1994, pp. 17–18.
89 See, e.g., Ji Yanxiang, "Weihu laodongzhe hefa quanyi de jiben falu" (A Basic Law for Safeguarding the Legitimate Rights and Interests of Workers), *Jingji jingwei* (Economic Transit) (Zhengzhou), June 1994, pp. 30–2 and 69.
90 *Ibid.* While China claims adherence to international treaties on the rights of workers, it claims as a developing country that some international labor standards are inapplicable to China. See Zhang Zuoyi, "Zhongguo laodong lifa" (China's Labor Legislation), *Zhengfa luntan* (Theory and Discussion on Politics and Law), 1994, no. 6, pp. 1 and 4.
91 See Zhang Shuqing, "The employees in the joint-venture, cooperative, and foreigners' invested enterprises ask for the protection for their rights and interests," *Minzhu yu fazhi* (Democracy and Legal System), 1995, no. 20, pp. 24–5.

92 See Chen Wenyuan, "Guanyu laodong fa de jige jiben wenti chusuo" (Preliminary Inquiry on Several Basic Issues of the *Labor Law*), *Zhengfa luntan* (Theory and Discussion on Politics and Law), June 1994, pp. 55–9 and 62.

93 See Article 6 of the Trade Union Law promulgated by ACFTU, June 1950.

94 See PRC Supreme People's Court, *Laodong zhengyi shenpan shouce* (Judicial Handbook on Labor Disputes), Beijing: Law Publishing, 1994, p. 216.

95 See "«Laodong fa» jiaqiangle gonghui de weihu zhineng" (The "Labor Law" Has Strengthened the Safeguarding Capacity of the Unions), *Gongren ribao* (Workers Daily), January 5, 1995, p. 4; "Jiaqiang gonghui gaige he jianshe de qiaoji" (A Useful Scheme for Strengthening Reform and Construction of the Unions), *Gongren ribao* (Workers Daily), January 23, 1995, p. 1; Guo Xiang, *op. cit.*

96 See L.L. To, *Trade Unions in China*, Singapore: Singapore University Press, 1986, p. 71.

97 See A. Chan, "The Emerging Patterns of Industrial Relations in China and the Rise of Two New Labor Movements," *China Information*, 1995, vol. IX, no. 4, pp. 36–59.

98 See Li Tian, "Population flow into big cities," *Beijing Review*, July 18–24, 1994, pp. 15–19, in *FBIS Daily Report: China*, July 20, 1994, pp. 20–1.

99 For a discussion of corporatism in Chinese reforms, see K. Parris, "Local Initiative and National Reform: The Wenzhou Model of Development," *The China Quarterly*, 1993, vol. 134, p. 242.

100 See, e.g., "Wei han bu zhixing Gonghui fa," (Nonsensically Failing to Enforce Trade Union Law), *Gongren ribao* (Workers Daily), October 10, 1995, p. 5.

101 See generally, J.P. Burns and J.-P. Cabestan, "Provisional Chinese Civil Service Regulations," *Chinese Law and Government*, Winter 1990–91.

102 See generally, J.A. Cohen, *The Criminal Process in the People's Republic of China*, Cambridge, Mass.: Harvard University Press, 1968; S. Leng and H. Chiu, *Criminal Justice in Post-Mao China*, Albany: State University of New York Press, 1985; V.H. Li, "The Evolution and Development of the Chinese Legal System," in J.M.H. Lindbeck, *China: Management of a Revolutionary Society*, Seattle and London: University of Washington Press, 1971.

103 See generally, M.R. Dutton, *Policing and Punishment in China: From Patriarch to "the People"*, Cambridge: Cambridge University Press, 1992.

104 For general discussion of criminal justice in China under the 1980 legislation, see D.C. Clarke and J.V. Feinerman, "Antagonistic Contradictions: Criminal Law and Human Rights," *The China Quarterly*, 1995, vol. 141, p. 135.

105 See generally, Xie Baogui and Zhang Qiong, *Jingji fanzui de dingzui yu liangxing* (The Determination of Crime and the Measurement of Penalty for Economic Crimes), Beijing: Law Publishing, 1988; and D.E. Townsend, "The Concept of Law in Post-Mao China: A Case Study of Economic Crime," *Stanford Journal of International Law*, 1987, vol. 24, no. 1, pp. 227–58. For a compilation of regulations on economic crime, see *Cha chu guandao anjian shiyong fagui shouce* (Handbook on Investigation and Handling of Profiteering Cases), Beijing: Law Publishing, 1989.

106 See generally, C.W. Lo, *China's Legal Awakening: Legal Theory and Criminal Justice in Deng's Era*, Hong Kong: Hong Kong University Press, 1995.

107 See Legal Department of the Public Security Ministry (ed.), *Gongan fagui huibian* (Compilation of Laws and Regulations on Public Security), Beijing: Masses Publishing, 1988.

108 Amnesty International, "China – Punishment Without Trial: Administrative Detention," 1981.

109 "Decision of the State Council on Questions of Re-education and Rehabilitation Through Labor" (1957); "Supplementary Provisions on Re-

education and Rehabilitation Through Labor" (1979). These measures were consolidated and formalized in the authority. Incarceration of those committing "minor" crimes was also provided in the 1982 "Provisional Measures on Re-Education and Rehabilitation Through Labor." See T.Hsia and W.I. Zeldin, "Sheltering for Examination (*Shourong Shencha*) in the Legal System of the People's Republic of China," *China Law Reporter*, 1992, vol. 7, p. 97. Also see J.D. Seymour and R. Anderson, *New Ghosts, Old Ghosts: Prisons and Labor Reform Camps in China*, Armonk, NY: M.E. Sharpe, 1998.

110 See "Provisional Measures for Dealing with the Release of Reform through Labor Criminals at the Expiration of their Term of Imprisonment and for Placing Them and Getting Them Employed." Also see CPC General Political Committee, "Suggestions Concerning Strengthening Resettlement and Training Work for Released Labor Reform and Labor Re-education Prisoners" (1995), in J.D. Seymour and R. Anderson, *op. cit.* Subsequent State Council regulations on the handling of reform through labor criminals provided that those who "have not reformed" could be detained under imprisonment at the place of reform. See National People's Congress Standing Committee, "Decision Regarding the Handling of Offenders Undergoing Reform through Labor and Persons Undergoing Rehabilitation through Labor who Escape or Commit New Crimes," 1981.

111 Prison Law of the PRC, 1994.

112 See T. Hsia and W.I. Zeldin, *op. cit.*; Kam C. Wong, "Police Powers and Control in the People's Republic of China: The History of *Shoushen*," *Columbia Journal of Asian Law*, 1996, vol. 10, p. 367.

113 See Lawyers' Committee on Human Rights, "Opening to Reform? An Analysis of China's Revised Criminal Procedure Law," 1996, pp. 22 *et seq.*

114 See *ibid.*, p. 27.

115 See Human Rights in China, "Note Welcome at the Party: Behind the 'Clean-Up' of China's Cities – A Report on Administrative Detention Under 'Custody and Repatriation'," September 1999.

116 See generally, *Zhonghua renmin gongheguo xingshi susong fa* (Criminal Procedure Law of the PRC, 1996). Also see "Commentary: Law Amendments for Better Checks and Balances," Xinhua English Service, March 14, 1996, in *FBIS Daily Report: China*, March 14, 1996, p. 13 and Lawyers' Committee for Human Rights (ed.), *op. cit.*

117 See Criminal Law of the PRC, 1997.

118 For discussion, see Y. Situ and W. Liu, "Comprehensive Treatment to Social Order: A Chinese Approach against Crime," *International Journal of Comparative and Applied Criminal Justice*, 1996, vol. 20, no. 1, pp. 95–115.

119 See, e.g., Yang Chunxi, *Fanzui yu xingfa xinlun* (New Theories of Crime and Criminal Punishment), Beijing: Peking University Press, 1991.

120 See, e.g., He J. and J.R. Waltz, *Criminal Prosecution in the People's Republic of China and the United States of America: A Comparative Study*, Beijing: China Procuratorial Press, 1995; Yang Chunxi, *Zhong mei xuezhe lun qingshao nian fanzui* (Chinese and American Scholars on Juvenile Delinquency), Yantai: Yantai University Press, 1989.

121 See Chen Guanzhong and D. Prefontaine (eds), *Lianheguo xingshi sifa zhunce yu Zhongguo xingshi fazhi* (United Nations Standards of Criminal Justice and the Chinese Criminal Law System), Beijing: Law Publishing, 1998.

122 See, e.g., CASS Law Institute (ed.), *Zhong ri gongwuyuan huilu fanzui yanjiu* (Chinese and Japanese Research on Crimes of Bribery), Beijing: Chinese Academy of Social Sciences Press, 1995.

123 See, e.g., "PRC: Commentary Views NPC Criminal Law Draft Amendments," Beijing Xinhua English Service, March 14, 1996, in *FBIS Daily Report: China*

(FBIS-CHI-96–051), March 14, 1996, p. 13. Also see Chen Weidong, *Zhongguo xingshi susong fa* (Chinese Criminal Procedure Law), Hong Kong: Joint Publishing, 1997.

124 See, e.g., Cui Min, "Xingshi susong fa shishi zhong de wenti yu jianyi" (Questions and Suggestions in the Implementation of the Criminal Procedure Law), in *Xiandai faxue* (Modern Legal Studies), 1998, no. 1, pp. 18–22.

125 See generally, D. Buxbaum *et al.*, "Criminal Law Regime Sees Progress after 17 Years," *China Law & Practice*, May 1996, pp. 54–5.

126 See "Zuigao renmin fayuan gu anyu zhixing «Zhonghua renmin gongheguo xingshi susong fa» ruogan wenti to jieshi" (Interpretation by the Supreme People's Court on Certain Issues Related to the Implementation of the "Criminal Procedure Law of the PRC") (1998). For a discussion of the evolution of this interpretation over the course of two drafts and a joint regulation by the Supreme People's Court and six other central-level departments, see "Zuifao fayuan fabu xingshi susong fa sifa jieshi" (Supreme People's Court Issues Judicial Interpretation of the Criminal Procedure Law), *Zhongguo fazhi bao* (China Legal System Gazette), September 8, 1998, p. 1. For discussion of the "presumption of innocence" prior to the revisions, see T.A. Gelatt, "The People's Republic of China and the Presumption of Innocence," *Journal of Criminal Law and Criminology*, 1982, vol. 73 no. 1, pp. 260–316.

127 See Zhao B. and Xiao Z., "Lun Zhongguo xing fa de zuixin gaige" (On the Most Recent Reforms in China's Criminal Law), *Xiandai faxue* (Modern Legal Studies), 1998, no. 2, pp. 21–6.

128 See, e.g., "National Meeting Reveals Law Violations by Cadres, Policy," Beijing Xinhua Domestic Service, May 15, 2000, in *FBIS Daily Report: China* (FBIS-CHI-2000–0515), May 15, 2000.

129 See "Zuigao renmin fayuan guanyu zhixing «Zhonghua renmin gongheguo xingshi susong fa» ruogan wenti to jieshi" (Interpretation by the Supreme People's Court on Certain Issues Related to the Implementation of the "Criminal Procedure Law of the PRC"), p. 1.

130 See Zuigao renmin fayuan, "Guanyu renzhen xuexi xuanchuan chanche xiuding de «Zhonghua renmin gongheguo xingfa» de tongzhi" (Notice on Serious Studying, Propagandizing and Fully Implementing the Revised "Criminal Law of the PRC"), 1997.

131 See S. Finder *et al.*, "Tightening up Chinese Courts' 'Bags' – The Amended PRC Criminal Law," *China Law & Practice*, June 1997, pp. 35–8.

132 See "Zhonghua renmin gonghe guo baoshou guojia mimi fa" (Law of the PRC on Protecting State Secrets), 1989; "Zhonghua renmin gong heguo baoshou guojia mimi fa shishi banfa" (Implementing Methods for Law of the PRC on Protecting State Secrets), 1990; "Zhonghua renmin gongheguo guojia anquan fa" (National Security Law of the PRC) (1993). For discussion, see Amnesty International, "China: Law Reform and Human Rights – Not Far Enough," February 28, 1997 and Lawyers Committee on Human Rights, "Shackling the Defenders: Legal Restrictions on Independent Human Advocacy Worldwide," 1994.

133 See, e.g., "Notice on Strictly Preventing Reactionary Publications from Using our Execution of Criminals to Engage in Rumor-Mongering and Slander," 1984; "Directive Concerning the Strict Prohibition on Parading on the Streets in front of the Masses Criminals who are about to be Executed," 1986; and Supreme People's Court, Supreme People's Procuracy, and Ministry of Public Security, "Notice on Resolutely Putting a Stop to [the Practice of] Parading through the Street and Exhibiting to the Public Convicted and Not-Yet-Convicted Criminals," 1988. Thanks to Donald C. Clarke for these references.

Chapter 6

1 The content of the legal regime governing foreign trade and investment in China is identified by reference to the texts of applicable laws and regulations, as well as formal interpretations of law, official policy statements, and other less formal rules. These materials were taken from a variety of Chinese- and English-language sources. Chinese-language sources include *Zhonghua renmin gongheguo fagui huibian* (Compilation of Current Laws and Regulations of the PRC), Beijing: Law Publishing, annual; *Zhonghua renmin gonghegua xin fagui huibian* (Compilation of New Laws and Regulations of the PRC), Beijing: Legal System Publishing, periodical; *Zhonghua renmin gongheguo duiwai jingji fagui huibian: 1945–1985* (Compilation of Economic Laws and Regulations Pertaining to Foreign Matters), Beijing: People's Press, 1986; *Zhongguo jingji tequ kaifaqu falu fagui xuanbian* (Compilation of Laws and Regulations for China's Special Economic Zones and Open Areas), Beijing, 1987; *Renmin ribao* (People's Daily); *Fazhi ribao* (Legal System Daily); and *Guoji shang bao* (Journal of International Commerce). English-language sources include CCH Australia Ltd (ed.), *China Laws for Foreign Business*; V. Nee (ed.), *China Commercial Laws and Regulations*, New York: Oceana; *China Economic News*; *China Law & Practice*; *China Business Review* and *East Asian Executive Reports*.

2 For a discussion of China's experience with Western capital that adopts a dependency perspective, see generally, F.V. Moulder, *Japan, China and the Modern World Economy: Toward a Reinterpretation of East Asian Development ca. 1600 to ca. 1918*, Cambridge: Cambridge University Press, 1977. For an alternative view, see S. Cochran, *Big Business in China: Sino-Foreign Rivalry in the Cigarette Industry, 1890–1930*, Cambridge, Mass.: Harvard University Press, 1980. Although Cochran's nuanced analysis of ability of the Chinese-owned Nanyang Brothers Tobacco Company to compete effectively during the early twentieth century with the multinational British-American Tobacco Company has been viewed as a repudiation of the dependency argument as applied to China, Cochran's work also supports a contrary conclusion: the economic imperialism of BAT distorted the Chinese market by retarding the emergence of small local firms other than Nanyang and that the presence of BAT in China was a positive barrier to local development and acquisition of technology as Nanyang itself was forced to go abroad for technical training and expertise.

3 For a discussion of the contrast between neoclassical and dependency approaches to economic development in East Asia, see S. Haggard, *Pathways from the Periphery: The Politics of Growth in the Newly Industrialized Countries*, Ithaca, NY, and London: Cornell University Press, 1990.

4 The "self-reliance" policies of Maoist China, while grounded in part in expediency born of China's isolation from both the Soviet Union and the United States, were viewed as an alternative to the Stalinist and capitalist approaches to economic growth. See generally A. Eckstein, *China's Economic Revolution*, Cambridge: Cambridge University Press, 1977, pp. 123 *et seq.* And while the "open door policy" established in 1978 expressed the Chinese leadership's recognition of the failures of self-reliance and its commitment to harnessing foreign investment in pursuit of economic growth, the new policies also express the view that China can find an alternative route. See generally, R.F. Dernberger, "The Chinese Search for the Path of Self-Sustained Growth in the 1980s," in Joint Economic Committee of US Congress, *China under the Four Modernizations*, Washington: US Government Printing Office, 1982, pp. 19–76; H. Harding, "The Problematic Future of China's Economic Reforms," in Joint Economic Committee of US Congress, *China's Economic Dilemmas in the 1990s: The Problems of Reforms, Modernization, and Interdependence*, Washington: US Government Printing Office, 1991, pp. 78–88.

5 There is a rich and wide-ranging literature on the problems of dependency. Among the most useful works are P.A. Baran, *The Political Economy of Growth*, New York: Monthly Review Press, 1968; A.G. Frank, *Capitalism and Underdevelopment in Latin America*, New York: Monthly Review Press, 1967; C. Furtado, *Development and Underdevelopment: A Structural View of the Problems of Developed and Underdeveloped Countries*, Berkeley: University of California Press, 1964; J. Galtung, "An Economic Theory of Imperialism," *Journal of Peace Research*, 1971, vol. 2, pp. 81–117; A. Portes, "The Sociology of National Development, *American Journal of Sociology*, 1976, vol. 82, no. 1, pp. 55–85; I. Wallerstein, "The Rise and Future Demise of the World Capitalist System: Concepts for Comparative Analysis," *Comparative Studies in Society and History*, 1974, vol. 14, no. 4, pp. 1–26; and C.K. Wilber (ed.), *The Political Economy of Development and Underdevelopment* (2nd edn), New York: Random House, 1979. For a critical survey of the dependency literature, see R.A. Packenham, *The Dependency Movement: Scholarship and Politics in Development Studies*, Cambridge, Mass., and London: Harvard University Press, 1992.

6 See S. Haggard, *op. cit.*, pp. 19–22.

7 See R.A. Packenham, *The Dependency Movement, op. cit.*, esp. p. 315.

8 See S. Haggard, *op. cit.*

9 See generally, F.H. Cardoso and E. Faletto, *Dependency and Development in Latin America*, Berkeley: University of California Press, 1979. For a critique, see R.A. Packenham, *The Dependency Movement, op. cit.*, pp. 93–4.

10 See P.A. Baran, "On the Political Economy of Backwardness," in C.K. Wilber (ed.), *op. cit.*, pp. 91–113. Also see C.K. Wilber and J.H. Weaver, "Patterns of Dependency: Income Distribution and the History of Underdevelopment," in C.K. Wilber (ed.), *op. cit.*, pp. 114–29.

11 See generally, M. Singer, *Weak States in a World of Power: The Dynamics of International Relationships*, New York: Free Press, 1972; and R. Muller, "The Multinational Corporation and the Underdevelopment of the Third World," in C.K. Wilber (ed.), *op. cit.*, pp. 151–78.

12 See J.A. Gardner, *Legal Imperialism: American Lawyers and Foreign Aid in Latin America*, Madison: University of Wisconsin Press, 1980, pp. 187 *et seq.*

13 While it may come as a surprise to many in the United States who equate liberalism with government intervention, classic liberal economic policies are generally considered to be ones that minimize state involvement and instead rely on largely unregulated market forces to determine supply and demand dynamics. See generally, R.A. Packenham, *Liberal America and the Third World*, Princeton, NJ: Princeton University Press, 1973, esp. pp. 112–29.

14 See generally, J.A. Gardner, *op. cit.*

15 See generally, M. Weber, *Economy and Society*, Roth and Wittich (eds), Berkeley and Los Angeles: University of California Press, 1978. Links between law and development were the focus of a group of Yale University legal scholars, of whom perhaps Professor David Trubek is best known. See, e.g., "Toward a Social Theory of Law: An Essay on the Study of Law and Development," *Yale Law Journal*, 1972, vol. 82, p. 1. For application to economic growth models, see generally, W.W. Rostow, *The Economics of the Take Off into Sustained Economic Growth*, New York, St Martins Press, 1963. While Professor Trubek has come to question the link between law and economic development, preferring instead to focus on the political economy of legal change, assumptions about the linkage are still held dear by many international development agencies.

16 For a particularly useful critical survey, see, e.g., F.G. Snyder, "Law and Development in the Light of Dependency Theory," *Law & Society Review*, 1980, vol. 14, p. 722.

17 See generally, R.O. Keohane and V.D. Ooms, "The Multinational Firm and International Regulation," *International Organization*, 1975, vol. 29, no. 1, pp. 186–206. Also see F.O. Vicun, "The Control of Multinational Enterprises" and F.B. Weinstein, "Underdevelopment and Efforts to Control Multinational Corporations," both in G. Modelski (ed.), *Transnational Corporations and World Order: Readings in International Political Economy*, San Francisco, W.H. Freeman, 1979, pp. 296–308 and 338–46; S. Hymer, "The Multinational Corporation and the Law of Uneven Development," in J.N. Bhagwati (ed.), *Economics and World Order*, New York: Macmillan, 1972, pp. 113–35; R. Muller, "Poverty is the Product," *Foreign Policy*, Winter 1973/74, vol. 13, pp. 71–102; and United Nations, *Multinational Corporations in World Development*, New York: United Nations, 1973.

18 See, e.g., Y.G.R. Luckham and F.G. Snyder (eds), *The Political Economy of Law: A Third World Reader*, New Delhi: Oxford University Press, 1987. *Cf.* A. Stone, "The Place of Law in the Marxian Structure–Superstructure Archetype," *Law & Society Review*, 1985, vol. 19, no. 1, pp. 40–67; M. Kelman, *A Guide to Critical Legal Studies*, Cambridge, Mass.: Harvard University Press, 1987, pp. 249 *et seq.* In the international trade context, see D. Kennedy, "Turning to Market Democracy: A Tale of Two Architectures," *Harvard Journal of International Law*, 1991, vol. 32, no. 2, pp. 373–96.

19 For discussion concerning the East Asian development experience, see generally, R.A. Scalapino, S. Sato, and J. Wanandi (eds), *Asian Economic Development: Past and Future*, Berkeley, Calif.: Institute of East Asian Studies, 1985; J. Woo, *Race to the Swift: State and Finance in Korean Industrialization*, New York: Columbia University Press, 1991; Economist Intelligence Unit, *China, Japan, and the Asian NICs: Economic Structure and Analysis*, London: The Economist, 1988.

20 See, e.g., E. Chen and G. Hamilton, "Business Groups and Economic Development," in G. Hamilton (ed.), *Business Networks and Economic Development in East and Southeast Asia*, Centre of Asian Studies, University of Hong Kong, 1991, p. 3. Also see G.S. Redding, *The Spirit of Chinese Capitalism*, Berlin: Walter de Gruyter, 1990. The importance of regional business networks is also seen as crucial in one interpretation of Japan's economic development experience. See D. Friedman, *The Misunderstood Miracle: Industrial Development and Political Change in Japan*, Ithaca, NY, and London: Cornell University Press, 1988, esp. chap. 5.

21 See, e.g., E. Vogel, *The Four Little Dragons*, Cambridge, Mass.: Harvard University Press, 1991.

22 See, e.g., C. Johnson, *MITI and the Japanese Miracle: The Growth of Japanese Industrial Policy 1925–1975*, Stanford, Calif.: Stanford University Press, 1982. For an analysis questioning the effectiveness of state management of economic growth, see D. Friedman, *The Misunderstood Miracle, op. cit.*

23 See J. Woo, *op. cit.* While she suggests that recent efforts at financial liberalization signal the end of an era of state patronage of heavy industry, the author provides considerable evidence of the central role of the state in developing South Korea's industrialized economy.

24 See T.B. Gold, "Entrepreneurs, Multinationals and the State," in E.A. Winckler and S. Greenhalgh (eds), *Contending Approaches to the Political Economy of Taiwan*, Armonk, NY, and London: M.E. Sharpe, 1990, pp. 175–205; and *ibid..*, *State and Society in the Taiwan Miracle*, Armonk, NY, and London: M.E. Sharpe, 1986.

25 See C. Johnson, "Political Institutions and Economic Performance: The Government–Business Relationship in Japan, South Korea, and Taiwan," in R.A. Scalapino *et al.* (eds), *op. cit.*, pp. 63–89. Also see P. Regnier, *Singapore: City-State in South-East Asia*, Christopher Hurst (trans.), Kuala Lumpur: S. Abdul Majeed & Co., 1993; L.S. Ann, *Industrialization in Singapore*, Melbourne:

Longman 1973,; and L.C. Yah, *Economic Restructuring in Singapore*, Singapore: Federal Publications, 1984. Also see generally, United States International Trade Commission, *East Asia: Regional Economic Integration and Implications for the United States*, Washington: USITC, 1993, pp. 12 *et seq.* and 19 *et seq.*; E.K.Y. Chen, "The Newly Industrialized Countries in Asia: Growth Experience and Prospects," in R.A. Scalapino *et al.* (eds), *op. cit.*, pp. 131–60.

26 See generally, S. Haggard, *op. cit.*

27 *Ibid.* Also see T.B. Gold, *op. cit.*

28 See generally, P.B. Potter, *Foreign Business Law in China*, Ann Arbor: University of Michigan Press and San Francisco: 1990 Institute, 1995.

29 For examples of this trend, see Case no. 86 in Li C. (ed.), *Shanghai fayuan anli jingxuan: 1997* (Carefully Selected Cases from the Shanghai Courts: 1997), Shanghai: Shanghai People's Press, 1997, p. 322 (defendant company's shares in a joint-venture company transferred to the plaintiff Chinese company as compensation for damages caused by the defendant's breach of a sales contract); and Case no. 109 in Qiao X. (ed.), *Shanghai fayuan anli jingxuan: 1999* (Carefully Selected Cases from the Shanghai Courts: 1999), Shanghai: Shanghai People's Press, 2000, p. 551 (shares for debt arrangement under court-mediated solution to dispute over non-payment on import contract).

30 See "Foreign Trade Law of the PRC, 1994," *China Economic News*, May 23, 1994, p. 8 and May 30, 1994, p. 7.

31 See *ibid.*

32 See generally, Zhang Yuejiao, "All Below Heaven are Divided Three Ways Like Three Legs of a Tripod: Legal Problems in the Chinese-Style Foreign Trade Agency System," *Guoji maoyi* (International Trade), no. 182, p. 407, in *FBIS Daily Report: China* (FBIS-CHI-97–094), May 16, 1997.

33 See generally, J.P. Horsley, "The Regulation of China's Foreign Trade," supra.

34 These NFTCs include (1) China National Tobacco Import and Export Corporation; (2) China National Electronics Import and Export Corporation; (3) China National Auto Import and Export Corporation; (4) China Iron and Steel Manufacturing and Trading Group Corporation; (5) China Petrochemical International Company; and (6) China National Nonferrous Metals Import and Export Corporation.

35 See generally, World Bank, *China: Foreign Trade Reform*, Washington: World Bank, 1994. Also see Hong Kong Trade Development Council, *China's Foreign Trade System*, 1991.

36 See *China Economic News*, June 24, 1996, no. 23, pp. 5–8 and July 1, 1996, no. 24, pp. 6–8.

37 See, e.g., "China Adjusts Catalogue of Import Licensing," *China Economic News*, Supplement No. 7, August 19, 1996.

38 While the State Planning Commission recognized as early as 1994 the need for state foreign trade plans to reflect market conditions, planning remains an important mechanism for ensuring state control over foreign trade. See "Zhongyang yu difang de waimao guanli quanxian guanxi" (Relations Between Central and Local Jurisdiction over Foreign Trade), in PRC State Planning Commission Research Office, "Wo guo zhongyang yu difang jingji guanli quan xian yanjiu" (A Study of Central and Local Jurisdiction over Economic Administration), *Jingji yanjiu cankao* (Reference Materials on Economic Research), March 1, 1994, pp. 44–9.

39 See "Implementing Measures of the Ministry of Foreign Economic Relations and Trade Concerning Application for Import and Export Licenses by Foreign Investment Enterprises" (1987).

40 See "Anti-dumping and Anti-subsidy Regulations of the People's Republic of China, 1997," *China Economic News*, June 2, 1997, no. 20 and July 9, 1997, no.

21. Also see J. Shen, "A Critical Analysis of China's First Regulation on Foreign Dumping and Subsidies and Its Consistency with WTO Agreements," *Berkeley Journal of International Law*, 1997, vol. 15, p. 295; M. Zheng, "Regulations on Antidumping, Countervailing Duties Adopted," *East Asian Economic Reports*, February 15, 1997, pp. 9–13.

41 See, e.g., L. Wang, "China's Difficulties and Concerns as a Respondent in Antidumping Proceedings," *World Competition Law and Economic Review*, 1996, vol. 19, no. 3, pp. 55–8.

42 "Anti-Dumping and Anti-Subsidy Regulations of the PRC, 1997," *op. cit.*, Article 3. For discussion, see Ministry of Foreign Trade and Economic Cooperation, "Announcement No. 2 1998: Preliminary Ruling in the Anti-Dumping Investigation of Newsprint Imported from Canada, Korea and the United States," *Guoji shangbao* (International Trade), July 10, 1998, in *FBIS Daily Report: China* (FBIS-CHI-98–259), September 18, 1998.

43 "Anti-Dumping and Anti-Subsidy Regulations of the PRC, 1997," *op. cit.*, Article 4.

44 See P.M. Norton and K.W. Almstedt, "Defending Dumping Claims: Exporters to China Beware," *China Law & Practice*, June 2000, pp. 32–9. Also see Han G., "China Learns how to Deal with Dumping Charges," *Beijing Review*, August 3–9, 1998, pp. 12–14.

45 For discussion, see "China's Inspection of Foreign Trade Goods is Growing More Efficient," Beijing Xinhua Domestic Service, July 31, 1998, in *FBIS Daily Report: China* (FBIS-CHI-98–222), August 12, 1998. Also see Tu Yangchun *et al.*, *Jin chu kou shangpin jianyan fagui yu shixian* (Regulation and Practice of Import and Export Commodity Inspection), Beijing: Law Publishing, 1989.

46 See, e.g., "Procedures Governing Inspections Over Imported Automobiles," in *China Economic News*, March 6, 2000, no. 9, pp. 10–11.

47 See Chen Jiaqin, "A Relationship Between Tariff and Non-Tariff Barriers and their Use," *Guoji maoyi wenti* (Issues in International Trade), December 6, 1997, pp. 6–9, in *FBIS Daily Report: China* (FBIS-CHI-98–057), May 3, 1998.

48 See "Customs Law of the PRC, 1987", in CCH Australia (ed.), *op. cit.*, paras 50–300.

49 See, e.g., Zou Chunyi and Fan Wenxin, "Barshefsky Welcomes PRC Tariff-Cut Plan," Beijing Xinhua Hong Kong Service, April 24, 1998, in *FBIS Daily Report: China* (FBIS-CHI-98–114), April 28, 1998, "China to cut industrial tariffs to 10 percent by 2005," Agence France Presse, November 26, 1997; G. Hewitt, "China Slashes Customs Tariffs by 26 Percent," Agence France Presse, September 14, 1997; "China to Adjust Policy on Tariffs," *China Economic News*, January 8, 1996, no. 2, p. 2.

50 This section is adapted from P.B. Potter, "Foreign Investment Law in the PRC: Dilemmas of State Control," *The China Quarterly*, 1995, vol. 141, pp. 155–185.

51 While the official communiqué made scant reference to the "open-door policy" directly, the Plenum has come to be seen as the watershed event giving rise to the introduction of foreign investment in China. See "Zhongguo gongchandang di shi yi jie zhongyang weiyuanhui di san ci quanti huiyi gongbao" (Communiqué 9 of the Third Plenum of the Eleventh CCP Central Committee), *Hongqi* (Red Flag), 1979, no. 1, pp. 14–21; Peng Zhen, "Explanation on the seven draft laws made at the second session of the fifth NPC on 26th June, 1979," *NCNA, in Selections from World Broadcasts*, July 4, 1979, p. FE/6158/C/1; Liu Xiangdong (ed.), *Liyong wai zi zhishi shouce* (Handbook of Knowledge on the Use of Foreign Capital), Beijing: World Knowledge (shijie zhishi) Publishing, 1989, pp. 2–3; Yu H. (ed.), *Dui wai jing mao yu falu shoyong shouce* (Practical

Handbook on Finance and Law Related to Foreign Matters), Beijing: Law Publishing, 1992, pp. 5–7.

52 See "Law of the PRC on Joint Ventures Using Chinese and Foreign Investment" (1979, as amended 1990) ("Joint Venture Law"), in CCH Australia (ed.), *op. cit.*, paras 6–500.

53 See "Implementing Regulations for the Law of the PRC on Joint Ventures Using Chinese and Foreign Investment" (1983, as amended 1986) ("Joint Venture Implementing Regulations"), *ibid.*, paras 6–550.

54 See "Economic Contract Law of the PRC, 1981" and "Foreign Economic Contract Law of the PRC, 1985," *ibid.*, paras 5–500 and 5–50, respectively.

55 See, e.g., "Income Tax Law of the PRC Concerning Joint Ventures with Chinese and Foreign Investment, 1980"; "Detailed Rules for the Implementation of the Income Tax Law of the PRC for Joint Ventures with Chinese and Foreign Investment" (1980); and "Foreign Enterprise Income Tax Law of the PRC, 1981," all in *China's Foreign Economic Legislation, Vol. I*, Beijing: Foreign Languages Press, 1982, pp. 36–44, 45–55, and 55–63, respectively; "Detailed Rules for the Implementation of the Foreign Enterprise Income Tax Law of the PRC" (1982), Article 24, in *China's Foreign Economic Legislation Vol. II*, Beijing: Foreign Languages Press, 1982, pp. 64–74; and "Income Tax Law of the PRC for Foreign Investment Enterprises and Foreign Enterprises, 1991"; in CCH Australia (ed.), *op. cit.*, paras 32–505.

56 See, e.g., "Provisional Regulations of the People's Republic of China Governing Foreign Exchange Control" (1980) and "Rules for the Implementation of Foreign Exchange Controls Relating to Enterprises with Overseas Chinese Capital, Enterprises with Foreign Capital, and Chinese/Foreign Equity Joint Ventures" (1983), in CCH Australia (ed.), *op. cit.*, paras 8–550 and 8–670, respectively. Also see P.D. McKenzie, "Foreign Exchange and Joint Ventures with China: Short-Term Strategies and Long-Term Prospects," *Canadian Business Law Journal*, 1990, vol. 17, pp. 114–49.

57 See "Law of the PRC on Sino-Foreign Cooperative Enterprises, 1988" and "Law of the PRC on Wholly Foreign-Owned Enterprises 1986" ("WFOE Law"), in CCH Australia (ed.), *op. cit.*, paras 6–100 and 13–506, respectively.

58 For discussion of the links between investment tax preference regimes and international liberal norms, see R.A. Avi-Yonah, "Globalization, Tax Competition, and the Fiscal Crisis of the Welfare State," *Harvard Law Review*, May 2000, vol. 113, no. 7, pp. 1573–676.

59 See "Quan guo renmin daibiao dahui chang wu weiyuan hui guanyu shouquan Guangdong sheng, Fujian sheng renmin daibiao hui ji qita chang wu weiyuanhui zhiding suo shu jingji tequ de ge xiang danxing jingji fagui de jueyi" (Decision of the Standing Committee of the National People's Congress Authorizing the People's Congresses of Guangdong and Fujian Provinces and their Standing Committees to Enact Various Specific Laws and Regulations for the Special Economic Zones under their Jurisdiction) (1981) and "Guangdong sheng jingji tequ tiaoli" (Regulations of Guangdong Province for Special Economic Zones) (1985), both in *Zhongguo jingji tequ kaifa qu falu fagui xuanbian* (Selection of Laws and Regulations for China's Special Economic Zones and Development Zones), Beijing: Zhanlan Publishing, 1987, pp. 1 and 2. Also see generally, V.C. Falkenheim, "China's Special Economic Zones," in Joint Economic Committee of US Congress, *China's Economy Looks to the Year 2000*, Washington: US Government Printing Office, 1986, pp. 348–70.

60 Under the "Provisions of the State Council of the People's Republic of China for the Encouragement of Foreign Investment" (1986) (*China Business Review*, January/February 1987, pp. 14–15), special preferences were given to enter-

prises denoted as "export-oriented enterprises" and "advanced technology enterprises."

61 China's individual income tax was amended to bring within its scope Chinese taxpayers who had been effectively excluded previously. See "Individual Income Tax Law of the PRC" (1980, as amended 1993), in CCH Australia (ed.), *op. cit.*, paras 30–500(4); "Detailed Rules for the Implementation of the Individual Income Tax Law of the PRC" (1980), *ibid.*, paras 300–520(4); also P.B. Potter, "Taxation of Foreign Individuals" in W.P. Streng and A.D. Wilcox, *Doing Business in China*, Irvington-on-Hudson, NY: Transnational Juris, looseleaf, chap. 19.

62 While the Unified Foreign Enterprise Tax Law continues to tax the income of foreign businesses in China differently from Chinese business incomes, other taxes have recently been enacted that strive to tax foreign and Chinese businesses alike on turnover proceeds. See "Decision on the Use of Interim Regulations Concerning Value-Added Taxes, Consumption Taxes and Business Taxes on FFEs and Foreign Enterprises" (1993), *China Economic News*, January 31, 1994, p. 7. One recent report suggests that foreign investment incentives themselves will be abolished in favor of an incentive system applicable to Chinese and foreign investors alike. See "Foreigners May Lose Investment Privileges," *Hong Kong Standard*, June 6, 1994.

63 See "Announcement of the People's Bank of China on Further Reforming the Foreign Exchange Management System" (December 28, 1993), *China Economic News*, January 10, 1994, p. 9.

64 See "Company Law of the PRC, 1993," *China Economic News*, Supplement No. 2, March 7, 1994.

65 See "Foreign Investment in China: Changing Trends and Policies," *East Asian Executive Reports*, vol. 20, no. 4, p. 8.

66 See, e.g., K. Lieberthal and M. Oksenberg, *Policy Making in China: Leaders, Structures, and Processes*, Princeton, NJ: Princeton University Press, 1988.

67 See, e.g., L. Pye, *The Mandarin and the Cadre*, Ann Arbor: University of Michigan Press, 1988.

68 See, e.g., S.L. Shirk, *The Political Logic of Economic Reform in China*, Berkeley, Los Angeles and Oxford: University of California Press, 1993.

69 A working definition of foreign investment enterprises, which distinguishes them from other foreign business forms, emerged belatedly and was formalized only in 1986 with the State Council Measures for Encouraging Foreign Investment. See P.B. Potter, "Seeking Special Status," *China Business Review*, March/April 1989, pp. 36–9. The term "foreign investment enterprises" means equity and contractual joint ventures and wholly foreign-owned enterprises. The term "foreign enterprises" means foreign companies, enterprises, and other economic organizations either having establishments or sites in China engaged in production or business operations, or having no establishments or sites but deriving income from sources in China. Foreign representative offices fall within the definition of foreign enterprises.

70 The basic provisions governing equity joint ventures are set forth in the Joint Venture Law and the Joint Venture Implementing Regulations, *op. cit.* Also see generally, L. Chu and C.T. Randt Jr, "Foreign Investment Vehicles," in W.P. Streng and A.D. Wilcox (eds), *Doing Business in China*, Irvington-on-Hudson, NY: Transnational Juris Publishers, 1993, pp. 6-1–6-33.

71 See T. Gelatt and M. Rong, "Taxation of Business Enterprises," *ibid.*, pp. 17-1–17-39.

72 See R. Pomfret, *Investing in China: Ten Years of the Open Door Policy*, Ames: Iowa University Press, 1991, p. 26.

73 See generally, M.J. Moser, "Legal Aspects of Offshore Oil and Gas Exploration and Development in China," in M.J. Moser (ed.), *Foreign Trade, Investment, and the Law in the People's Republic of China* (2nd edn), Hong Kong: Oxford University Press, 1987, p. 270.

74 See "WFOE Law", *op. cit.*; and "Implementing Rules for China's Law on Wholly Foreign-Owned Enterprises" (1990), in *East Asian Executive Reports*, February 1991, p. 25.

75 See R. Pomfret, *op. cit.*, p. 65.

76 See "Interim Regulations Concerning the Control of Resident Offices of Foreign Enterprises" (1980), in CCH Australia (ed.), *op. cit.*, paras 7–500(4). Also see Price Waterhouse, *Doing Business in the People's Republic of China*, 1988, pp. 20 and 48.

77 See "Procedures of the People's Bank of China for the Establishment of Representative Offices in China by Overseas and Foreign Financial Institutions" (1983), in CCH Australia (ed.), *op. cit.*, paras 7–540(4).

78 See "Administrative Measures of the People's Bank of China on Establishment in China of Resident Representative Offices by Foreign Financial Institutions" (1991), *ibid.*, paras 7–542.

79 See "Several Questions Concerning the Establishment of Foreign Investment Companies Limited by Shares Tentative Provisions" (January 10, 1995), *China Law & Practice*, August 11, 1995, p. 52. Also see P.B. Potter, "Foreign Participation in Chinese Securities Markets," in W.P. Streng and A.D. Wilcox (eds) *Doing Business in China*, New York: Matthew Bender, 1993.

80 See generally P.B. Potter, "MOFTEC'S New Regulations on Holding Companies," *East Asian Executive Reports*, May 15, 1995, vol. 17, no. 5, pp. 7–12. See "Several Questions Concerning the Establishment of Foreign Investment Companies Limited by Shares Tentative Provisions" (January 10, 1995), *op. cit.* Also see P.B. Potter, "Foreign Participation in Chinese Securities Markets," *op. cit.*

81 See generally, L. Chu and C.T. Randt Jr, *op. cit.*

82 For the 1998 catalog, see *China Economic News*, 1998 Supplement No. 1, March 2, 1998.

83 For discussion of the problems of uncertainty with government policies and directives, see "The Council's Investment Initiative," *China Business Review*, September/October 1992, pp. 6–10. Also see J.B. Stepanek, "China's Enduring State Factories: Why Ten Years of Reform has Left China's Big State Factories Unchanged," in Joint Economic Committee of US Congress (ed.), *China's Economic Dilemmas in the 1990s: The Problems of Reforms, Modernization, and Interdependence, op. cit.*, p. 440.

84 For discussion of these frustrations, see "The Council's Investment Initiative," *op. cit.*

85 Arbitral decisions by CIETAC are available in Cheng Dejun (ed.), *Shewai zhongcai yu falu* (Foreign-related Arbitration and Law), Beijing: Chinese People's University Press, 1992; and Civil Law Office of the NPC Standing Committee, Committee on Legal Affairs and CCPIT Secretariat (eds), *Zhonghua renmin gongheguo zhongcai fa quanshu* (Encyclopedia of Arbitration Law of the PRC), Beijing: Law Publishing, 1995. Case decisions by Chinese courts and arbitral agencies appear in Li Ziping (ed.), *Shewai jingji fa anli* (Cases in Foreign Economic Law), Nanchang: Jiangxi Higher Education Press, 1997; Qi Tianchang (ed.), *Hetong an li pingxi* (Discussion of Contract Cases), Beijing: Chinese University of Politics and Law Press, 1991; Wang Cunxue, *Zhongguo jingji zhongcai he susong shiyong shouce* (Practical Handbook of Chinese Economic Arbitration and Litigation), Beijing: Development Press, 1993; Zhang Huilong, *She wai jingji fa anli jiexi* (Analysis of Sino-foreign Economic Law

Cases), Beijing: Youth Publishers, 1990; and *New Selections of the Foreign-related Economic Cases in China*, Shanghai: Economic Information Agency, 1992.

86 See generally, F.L. Lavin, "Negotiating with the Chinese, or How Not to Kowtow," *Foreign Affairs*, July/August 1994, pp. 16–22; R.F. Grow, "Resolving Commercial Disputes in China: Foreign Firms and the Role of Contract Law," *Northwestern Journal of International Law and Business*, 1993, vol. 14, pp. 161–83. For general discussion of cultural aspects of negotiations with Chinese counterparts, see, e.g., R.A. Kapp (ed.), *Communicating with China*, Chicago: Intercultural Press, 1983; B. Purves, *Barefoot in the Boardroom: Venture and Misadventure in the People's Republic of China*, Toronto: NC Press, 1991; and L. Pye, *Chinese Negotiating Style: Commercial Approaches and Cultural Approaches*, New York: Quorum Books, 1992.

87 "Recommendations on Asia of the President's Advisory Committee for Trade Policy and Negotiations," 1995.

88 For a penetrating analysis of conflicts in contemporary Chinese culture in the face of resurgent and foreign-driven capitalism, see T. Brook, "Commercial Economy and Cultural Doubt in China," Joint Centre for Asia Pacific Studies, 1994.

89 For discussion of the problem of agency in the context of a dispute between Lehman Brothers and the Shanghai Division of CITIC (China International Trust and Investment Corporation), see N. Page, "Lehman Brothers' Chinese Puzzle," *International Commercial Arbitration*, 1995, vol. 8(5), p. 7. For discussion of the problem of enforcing a personal handshake agreement in a textile production/procurement deal that was not later ratified through a written contract, see "How Was CNY 13,000 as Business Introduction Commission Returned," in *New Selections of the Foreign-related Economic Cases in China*, p. 49.

90 See "Zhong wai heying qiye wei huo pijun, heying hetong ying guan wei wuxiao" (The Chinese–Foreign Joint Venture Contract is not Approved, the Joint Venture Contract should be Considered Void), in Qi Tianchang (ed.), *op. cit.*, p. 408.

91 See Cheng Dejun (ed.), *op. cit.*, Case no. 1.

92 See *ibid.*, Case no. 2.

93 See Wang Cunxue, *op. cit.*, Case no. 3.

94 See generally, L. Chu, "The Chimera of the China Market," *Atlantic Monthly*, October 1990, p. 56.

95 See Li Ziping (ed.), *op. cit.*, Case no. 15, in which amendments were requested in a contract for the sale of flour, due to changes in the international market price.

96 See, e.g., *Zhonghua renmin gongheguo zhongcai fa quanshu* (Encyclopedia of Arbitration Law of the PRC), *op. cit.*, Case no. 3. Also see Si X., "CIETAC Arbitration: Joint Venture Case Studies No. 1," China Law & Practice (ed.), *Dispute Resolution in the PRC: A Practical Guide to Litigation and Arbitration in China*, Hong Kong, China Law & Practice, 1995, p. 139; and Wang Cunxue, *op. cit.*, Case no. 6.

97 For discussion of this concern in the context of the Sino-Japanese Fujian Television JV, see "Zhong wai hezi jingying qiye ruhe 'hezi'?" in Zhang Huilong, *op. cit.*, p. 239.

98 See *Zhonghua renmin gongheguo zhongcai fa quanshu* (Encyclopedia of Arbitration Law of the PRC), *op. cit.*, Case no. 5.

99 See "Wai shang yong zuo chu zi de shebei bixu fuhe hetong he wo guo falu de yaoqiu" (The Equipment Used by the Foreign Investor as Capital Contribution must Conform to the Contract and Our Country's Laws), in Qi Tianchang (ed.), *op. cit.*, p. 422.

100 See *Zhonghua renmin gongheguo zhongcai fa quanshu* (Encyclopedia of Arbitration Law of the PRC), *op. cit.*, Case no. 7.

101 See *ibid.*, Case no. 10.

102 See *ibid.*, Case no. 12.

103 See, e.g., J. Trappe, "Conciliation in the Far East," *Journal of International Arbitration*, 1989, vol. 5(2), p. 173; G. Vickery, "International Commercial Arbitration in China," *Australian Dispute Resolution Journal*, 1994, vol. 5, p. 75; and A.J. Farina, "'Talking Disputes into Harmony;' China Approaches International Commercial Arbitration," *American University Journal of International Law and Policy*, 1989, vol. 4, p. 137.

104 See Cheng Dejun (ed.), *op. cit.*, Case no. 7. Also see *Zhonghua renmin gongheguo zhongcai fa quanshu* (Encyclopedia of Arbitration Law of the PRC), *op. cit.*, Case no. 8.

105 See generally, J.G. Castel, A.L.C. de Mestral, and W.C. Graham, *The Canadian Law and Practice of International Trade*, Toronto: Edmond Montgomery, 1991, pp. 263–5.

106 See *Zhonghua renmin gongheguo zhongcai fa quanshu* (Encyclopedia of Arbitration Law of the PRC), *op. cit.*, Case no. 11.

107 See *ibid.* Case nos 12 (sale of fax machine packing materials and equipment) and 13 (sale of parts and equipment for use on Jacquard looms).

108 See generally, M.A. Groombridge and C.E. Barfield, *Tiger by the Tail: China and the World Trade Organization*, Washington: AEI Press, 1999; S. MacCormac, "Eyeing the GATT," *China Business Review*, March/April, 1993, p. 34; and M. Oksenberg (ed.), *China's Participation in the IMF, the World Bank and GATT: Toward a Global Economic Order*, Ann Arbor: University of Michigan Press, 1990. For discussion of implications for Taiwan, see J.V. Feinerman, "Taiwan and the GATT," *Columbia Business Law Review*, 1992, vol. 1, p. 39.

109 See generally, M. Goldman and R. MacFarquhar (eds), *The Paradox of China's Post-Mao Reforms*, Cambridge, Mass.: Harvard University Press, 1999; and E.J. Perry and M. Selden (eds), *Chinese Society: Change Conflict and Resistance*, London: Routledge 2000.

110 See generally, F. Wu and S.P. Kheng, "China's WTO Membership: Implications for Macroeconomic Outlook and Financial Sector," *DBS Asia Economic Briefing*, December 4, 2000.

111 For a recent discussion, see G. Barme, *In the Red: On Contemporary Chinese Culture*, New York: Columbia University Press, 1999, chap. 10.

112 See generally, D. Burstein and A. deKeijzer, *Big Dragon: The Future of China, What it Means for Business, the Economy and the Global Order*, New York: Simon & Schuster, 1998.

113 See generally, D. Wank, "Producing Property Rights: Strategies, Networks, and Efficiency in Urban China's Non-State Firms," in J.C. Oi and A.G. Walder (eds), *Property Rights and Economic Reform in China*, Stanford, Calif.: Stanford University Press, 1999, pp. 248–72; J.T.G. Arias, "A Relationship Marketing Approach to *Guanxi*," *European Journal of Marketing*, 1998, vol. 32, no. 1/2, p. 145; and H. Chin and G. Graen, "*Guanxi* and Professional Leadership in Contemporary Sino-American Joint Ventures in Mainland China," *Leadership Quarterly*, Winter 1997, vol. 8, no. 4, pp. 451–65.

114 See generally, Zheng J., "Various Forms of Tax Evasion by the Three Kinds of Foreign-Invested Enterprises," *Jingji cankao bao* (Economic Reference Report), August 16, 1997, in *FBIS Daily Report: China* (FBIS-CHI-97–318), November 18, 1997.

115 See, e.g., Chen Xiaojun and Gao Fei, "Zhiding tongyi hetong fa de ruogan fali wenti sikao" (Considerations of Several Jurisprudential Issues in Enacting a Unified Contract Law), *Faxue yanjiu* (Studies in Law), 1998, no. 1, pp. 53–9.

116 "Announcement of the People's Bank of China on Further Reforming the Foreign Exchange Management System" (1993), *China Economic News*, January 10, 1994.

117 *China News Digest* (electronic media), December 20, 1995.

118 See, e.g., L. Wang, *op. cit.*

119 See, e.g., Yang Guohua, "Respond to Anti-Dumping Complaints Vigorously," *Guoji maoyi* (International Trade), January 20, 1998, in *FBIS Daily Report: China* (FBIS-CHI-98–077), March 20, 1998.

120 For discussion of the nationalist consensus in China, see P. Heer, "A House Divided," *Foreign Affairs*, vol. 79, no. 4, July/August 2000, pp. 18–24.

121 See Yi Xiaozhun, "Sharpening the Sword for Ten Years: How to Look at the Problem of China's Entry into the WTO," *Guoji maoyi* (International Trade), January 29, 1988, in *FBIS Daily Report: China* (FBIS-CHI 98–061), March 2, 1998. This article by the deputy director of MOFTEC's Treaty and Law Department appeared in anticipation of the resumption of negotiations between China and the GATT Working Party in April 1998.

122 Influential reformist economic scholar Cao Siyuan, for example, suggested that China's accession would have beneficial effects in the areas of trade and investment liberalization, market competition, promotion of all-round reform, and improvement of living standards. See "Scholar on Changes in China's Economy after Joining WTO," Beijing Zhongguo Xinwen She (Beijing China News Agency), February 18, 2000, in *FBIS Daily Report: China* (FBIS-CHI-2000–0218), February 22, 2000. For further discussion, see, e.g., "The Great Policy Decision on Opening up to the World," *Qiushi* (Truth), February 16, 2000, in *FBIS Daily Report: China* (FBIS-CHI-2000–0216), February 18, 2000; "An Inevitable Choice in the Development of a Socialist Market Economy," *Guangming ribao* (Guangming Daily), January 28, 2000, in *FBIS Daily Report: China* (FBIS-CHI-2000–0130), January 31, 2000; "Meaning of Membership in WTO Discussed," *Jingji ribao* (Economy Daily), May 6, 1999, in *FBIS Daily Report: China* (FBIS-CHI-1999–0523), May 28, 1999; "Impact on Chinese Economy of Accession to WTO," *Cankao bao* (Reference News), May 5, 1999, in *FBIS Daily Report: China* (FBIS-CHI-1999–0527), May 28, 1999; "WTO's Impact on China's Modern Enterprise System," Beijing Xinhua Domestic Service, January 4, 2000, in *FBIS Daily Report: China* (FBIS-CHI-2000–0121), January 24, 2000; "Impact of WTO on China Discussed," *Ta Kung Pao* (Hong Kong), January 20, 2000, in *FBIS Daily Report: China* (FBIS-CHI-2000–0121), January 24, 2000.

123 See, e.g., "China Sets Deadline for GATT Re-entry, Slams US 'Road Blocks'," Agence France Presse English Wire, July 10, 1994, in *China News Digest* (electronic media); "Foot-stomping Helps China in GATT Bid," *South China Morning Post*, August 1, 1994, in *China News Digest* (electronic media); "China Vows not to Beg for WTO Membership," *China News Digest* (electronic media), September 23, 1995.

124 See generally, Lung Hua, "The Challenge of China Joining the WTO: China Will Pay a High Price for Joining the WTO," *Hsin Bao* (Hong Kong), May 27, 1999, in *FBIS Daily Report: China* (FBIS-CHI-1999–0528), June 1, 1999.

125 See, e.g., "China Prepared to Make Concessions to Join WTO," Kyodo News Service, March 15, 1999; Yao Hsin-pao, "China's WTO Entry does not Mean Fully Opening Market," *Wen Wei Po* (Hong Kong), July 12, 1999, in *FBIS Daily Report: China* (FBIS-CHI-1999–0712), July 13, 1999; Peng Kai-lei, "Long Yongtu Clarifies Misunderstandings about China's WTO Entry," *Wen Wei Po* (Hong Kong), July 12, 1999, in *FBIS Daily Report: China* (FBIS-CHI-1999–0712), July 13, 1999. Criticism of Long has apparently intensified to the point of him being compared to Li Hongzhang, the Qing official blamed

for making concessions to the West. See P. Pan, "Beijing Slaps Gag on WTO Talks Report," *Hong Kong Standard*, July 2, 1999, in *FBIS Daily Report: China* (FBIS-CHI-1999–0702), July 6, 1999.

126 See, e.g., Yu Nanping, "China's Listed Companies Will be Deeply Impacted by China Joining the WTO," *Guoji shangbao* (International Commerce), April 19, 1999, in *FBIS Daily Report: China* (FBIS-CHI-1999–0510), May 12, 1999.

127 See, e.g., Li Zhijun, "China's Accession to the WTO: Opportunities and Challenges Co-Exist," *Wen Wei Bao* (Hong Kong), May 6, 1999, in *FBIS Daily Report: China* (FBIS-CHI-1999–0517), May 18, 1999.

128 See, e.g., Hsia Wen-szu, "Jiang Zemin is Unhappy with Zhu Rongji's US Visit," *Kai Fang* (Hong Kong), May 4, 1999, in *FBIS Daily Report: China* (FBIS-CHI-1999–0518), May 19, 1999; Lo Bing, "Li Peng Sets Off a High Tide for Zhu Rongji's Downfall," *Cheng Ming* (Hong Kong), June 1, 1999, in *FBIS Daily Report: China* (FBIS-CHI-1999–0624), June 25, 1999; "AFP Cites Ma Xiuhong: No Compromise for WTO Entry," *FBIS Daily Report: China* (FBIS-CHI-1999–0610), June 11, 1999.

129 See Kung Wen, "Does China's Accession to WTO Suddenly Become Uncertain?" *Kuang Chiao Ching* (Hong Kong), June 16, 1999, in *FBIS Daily Report: China* (FBIS-CHI-1999–0625), June 28, 1999.

130 See Department of Foreign Affairs and International Trade Canada, "Canada and China Sign Historic Bilateral WTO Agreement," press release no. 256, November 26, 1999; "EU–China Agreement on WTO," European Union news release, May 19, 2000; "Agreement on Market Access between the People's Republic of China and the United States of America," USTR, November 15, 1999.

131 See *ibid.*, also see J. Fewsmith, "China and the WTO: The Politics behind the Agreement," *NBR Report*, November 1999; "The Bilateral Agreement and the United States," *China Business Review* (electronic media); US–China Business Council, "Copy of the US–China Bilateral Market Access Agreement as Released by USTR on 14 March 2000"; and H.C.H. Lee and J.M. Brazzil, "The Sino-US WTO Agreement: sectoral summary," *China Law & Practice*, December 1999/January 2000, pp. 30–4.

132 See, e.g., J. Zhang, "U.S.–China Trade Issues after the WTO and the PNTR Deal: A Chinese Perspective," *Hoover Institution Essays in Public Policy*, No. 103, 2000.

133 See Department of Foreign Affairs and International Trade Canada, *op. cit.*

134 See "EU–China Agreement on WTO," *op. cit.*; "The Sino–EU Agreement on China's Accession to the WTO: Results of the Bilateral Negotiations," EU website.

135 For discussion of the WTO agreements permitting exceptions to GATT disciplines for developing countries, see World Trade Organization (ed.), *Guide to the Uruguay Round Agreements*, The Hague: Kluwer, 1999, pp. 223–46.

136 See generally, P.B. Potter, "Commentary: China the WTO and Taiwan" in *ASEAN and Asian Trade*, 2000; A.S. Alexandroff, "The WTO's China Problem," *Policy Options*, May 2000, pp. 61–6; P.B. Potter, "China and the WTO: Tensions Between Globalized Liberalism and Local Culture," *Canadian Business Law Journal*, 1999, vol. 32, no. 3; R. Steinberg, "Institutional Implications of WTO Accession for China," working paper 110 delivered at the Third Meeting of the Trilateral Forum, November 11–12, 1997.

137 For an excellent treatise on the World Trade Organization, see J.S. Thomas and M.A. Meyer, *The New Rules of Global Trade: A Guide to the World Trade Organization*, Scarborough, Ontario: Carswell, 1998. Also see J.H. Bello and M.E. Footer, "Preface to Symposium: Uruguay Round GATT/WTO," *The*

International Lawyer, 1995, vol. 29, p. 335. For documentation and commentary, also see *International Legal Materials (ILM)*, 1994, vol. 33, pp. 1125 *et seq.*

138 For text of the General Agreement on Tariffs and Trade, see Basic Instruments and Selected Documents (BISD). Also see World Trade Organization (ed.), *The Results of the Uruguay Round of Multilateral Trade Negotiations*, Cambridge: Cambridge University Press, 1999, pp. 423 *et seq.* The many useful treatises on the GATT include J.H. Jackson, *World Trade and the Law of GATT*, Indianapolis: Bobbs-Merrill, 1969; and F. Stone, *Canada, the GATT and the International Trade System*, Montreal: Institute for Research on Public Policy, 1984.

139 For a skeptical review, see generally B.S. Brown, "Developing Countries in the International Trade Order," *Northern Illinois University Law Review*, 1994, vol. 14, p. 347. For discussion of the role of governments in directing foreign trade policy, see B.J. Cohen, *Crossing Frontiers: Explorations in International Political Economy*, Boulder, Colo.: Westview, 1991.

140 See E.M. Fox and J.A. Ordover, "Internationalizing Competition Law to Limit Parochial State and Private Action: Moving Towards a Vision of World Welfare," *International Business Lawyer*, 1996, vol. 24, p. 453.

141 See generally, D.C. Clarke, "China and the World Trade Organization," in Freshfields (ed.), *Doing Business in China*, looseleaf; W. Van Der Geest, "Bringing China into the Concert of Nations: An Analysis of its Accession to the WTO," *Journal of World Trade*, 1998, vol. 32, no. 4, pp. 99–115; T. Benson, "Will this Year's Financial Reforms Qualify China for the WTO?" *China Law & Practice*, October 1996, p. 19.

142 For discussion, see J.H. Jackson, *World Trade and the Law of GATT, op. cit.*, pp. 110–17.

143 See ILM, *op. cit.*, p. 1161.

144 See *ibid.*, p. 1226.

145 See Constitution of the PRC, 1982, 1993, Article 3. Also see K. Lieberthal, *Governing China: From Revolution Through Reform*, New York: W.W. Norton, 1995, chap. 6; and A.H.Y. Chen, *An Introduction to the Legal System of the People's Republic of China*, Singapore: Butterworth, 1992, chap. 4.

146 See State Statistical Bureau, *China Statistics Yearbook*, annual. Also see generally, D.S.G. Goodman and G. Segal (eds), *China Deconstructs*, London: Routledge, 1994.

147 See generally, essays by R. Dernberger, J.C. Oi, and D. Solinger at "Conference on the PRC at Fifty," organized by the Universidade de Aveiro and the China Quarterly, January 28–31, 1999. Also see B. Naughton, *Growing Out of the Plan*, New York: Cambridge University Press, 1995.

148 See Xinhua reporting on PRC Supreme People's Court President Ren Jianxin's reports to the First Session of the Eighth National People's Congress, March 22, 1993, in "Court President Ren Jianxin Reports to Session," *FBIS Daily Report: China*, March 23, 1993, pp. 40–2. Also see generally, J. Kohut, "Going to War on Corruption," *South China Morning Post*, April 17, 1994, p. 5.

149 See generally, Chen Feng, "Dalu [Wu gua feng] meng gua bu zhi" (The Wind of Corrupt Reporting in the Mainland is Blowing Unceasingly), *Zhengming* (Hong Kong), April 1994, no. 198, p. 19.

150 See J.H. Jackson,*World Trade and the Law of GATT, op. cit.*, p. 463.

151 See *ibid.*, pp. 273 *et seq.*

152 See C. Arup, *The New World Trade Organization Agreements: Globalizing Law Through Services and Intellectual Property*, Cambridge: Cambridge University Press, 2000, pp. 57–62, 114–17, and 184–6. Also see J. Braithwaite and P. Drahos, *Global Business Regulation*, Cambridge: Cambridge University Press, 2000, pp. 78–82, 126–7, 212–15, 512–15, and 571–2.

153 See, e.g., Xin Yi, "Wo guo canjia guanmao zong xieding hou de falu jiegui wenti" (Issues of Legal Convergence after our Entry to the GATT," *Jianghai xuekan* (Jianghai Journal), 1993 no. 1, pp. 90–2.

Conclusion

1 For discussion of the continued role of the Party, see S.B. Lubman, *Bird in a Cage: Legal Reform in China After Mao*, Stanford, Calif.: Stanford University Press, 1999; K. Lieberthal, *Governing China*, New York: W.W. Norton, 1995. These authors' conclusions are reinforced by my personal observation of documents from Party organs directing MOFTEC decisions on such matters as the registration and licensing of joint ventures.

2 See J.S. Thomas and M.A. Meyer, *The New Rules of Global Trade: A Guide to the World Trade Organization*, Scarborough, Ontario: Carswell, 1998, p. 200.

3 See generally, J. H. Jackson, *World Trade and the Law of GATT*, Indianapolis: Bobbs-Merrill, 1969, chap. 14.

4 This legislation has been discussed at length in China but has not yet been enshrined in legislation. See Yang Haikun and Huang Xuejian, *Zhongguo xingzheng chengxu fadianhua: Cong bijiao jiaodu yanjiu* (Codification of Chinese Administrative Procedure: Studied from a Comparative Perspective), Beijing: Law Publishing, 1999.

5 See C. Arup, *The New World Trade Organization Agreements: Globalizing Law Through Services and Intellectual Property*, Cambridge: Cambridge University Press, 2000, pp. 158–61. Also see World Trade Organization (ed.), *Guide to the Uruguay Round Agreements*, The Hague: Kluwer, 1999, pp. 161–205.

6 See "Civil Case Trial System Reformed for WTO Entry," Xinhua News Agency, March 30, 2000.

7 See, e.g., R. A. Aronson, testimony before the House Ways and Means Trade Subcommittee, May 23, 1995, Federal Information Systems, 1995; M. Bersani, "Enforcement of Arbitration Awards in China," *China Business Review*, May/June 1992, p. 6 and "Enforcement of Arbitration Awards in China," *International Arbitration*, 1993, vol. 10, no. 2, p. 47; and A. Mora, "The Revpower Dispute: China's Breach of the New York Convention?" in China Law & Practice (ed.), *Dispute Resolution in the PRC: A Practical Guide to Litigation and Arbitration in China*, Hong Kong: China Law & Practice, 1995, at 151.

8 See C. Arup, *op. cit.*, pp. 183–7 and 199–201.

9 See generally, World Trade Organization (ed.), *Guide to the Uruguay Round Agreements*, *op. cit.*, pp. 217–19.

10 See generally, "Enterprise Reforms: Too Early Yet to Invest?" *China Economic Review*, May 1998, p. 18.

11 See generally, J.C. Oi and A. G. Walder (eds), *Property Rights and Economic Reform in China*, Stanford, Calif.: Stanford University Press, 1999.

12 See generally, W.D. Holmes, "Capital Reforms in the Global Market," *Law and Policy in International Business*, 1997, vol. 28, no. 3, pp. 715–77.

13 See "Dai Xianglong on WTO Entry's Impact on Local Banks," Hong Kong Zhongguo Tongxun She (Hong Kong China News Agency), January 21, 2000, in *FBIS Daily Report: China* (FBIS-CHI-20000122), January 24, 2000.

14 See Administrative Measures on Foreign Investment Financial Institutions (1994) and Implementing Regulations Administrative Measures on Foreign Investment Financial Institutions (1996).

15 Citations for all laws, regulations, and treaties are provided in Appendix A: Table of Laws, Regulations, and Treaties.

16 See M. Silk and L. Ross, "The Powers and Supervision of Commercial Banks in China," *China Law & Practice*, February 1996, pp. 44 *et seq.*

17 See cases cited in An C. *et al.* (eds), *Renmin fayuan yinan panli pingxi: Jingji zhuan* (Evaluation of Difficult Cases of the People's Courts: Economic Volume), Changchun: Jilin Chubanshe, 1999, p. 43; and Guo Y. (ed.), *Renmin fayuan anli leibian pingxi: Jingji shen pan zhuan*, (Evaluation of People's Court Cases by Category: Economic Adjudication Volume), Changchun: Jilin People's Press, 1998, p. 379.

18 See generally, M.E. Burke IV's "Stock Markets and the World Trade Organization," *Law and Policy in International Business*, 1999, vol. 30, no. 2, p. 321.

19 See, e.g., H. Gao, "What Should the Government Do in the Face of the WTO?" *Ta Kung Pao* (Hong Kong), June 26, 2000, in *FBIS Daily Report: China* (FBIS-CHI-20000626), July 10, 2000.

20 For an unfortunate example of both the potential for and the dangers of such expansion, see A. Blass, "Lehman Discovers Derivative Debt Has Chinese Characteristics," *China Law & Practice*, February 1996, pp. 40–2.

21 See, e.g., Measures for the Administration of Foreign Securities-based Organizations Representative Offices in China (1999).

22 See R. Cai, "Bargaining Powers of Chinese Employees Set to Rise," *China Law & Practice*, November 1997, pp. 23–4.

23 See generally, World Trade Organization (ed.), *Guide to the Uruguay Round Agreements*, *op. cit.*, pp. 71–4. For background on non-tariff barriers, see J.H. Jackson, *World Trade and the Law of GATT*, *op. cit.*, pp. 517–22; A.E. Scaperlanda (ed.), *Prospects for Eliminating Non-Tariff Distortions*, Leiden: Sijthoff, 1973.

24 See World Trade Organization (ed.), *Guide to the Uruguay Round Agreements*, *op. cit.*, pp. 77–80; and J.S. Thomas and M.A. Meyer, *op. cit.*, pp. 196–202.

25 See C. Arup, *op. cit.*, pp. 95 *et seq.*

26 For general discussion, see J.S. Thomas and M.A. Meyer, *op. cit.*, pp. 307–27.

27 See R.E. Hudec, *The GATT Legal System and World Trade Diplomacy*, Salem, NH: Butterworth Legal Publishers, 1990.

28 For an early discussion on this subject, see J.H. Jackson, *The World Trading System*, Cambridge, Mass.: MIT Press, 1989, pp. 287–9.

29 See World Trade Organization (ed.), *Guide to the Uruguay Round Agreements*, *op. cit.*, pp. 31–6.

30 For an early discussion on this subject, see J.H. Jackson, *The World Trading System*, Cambridge, Mass.: MIT Press, 1989, pp. 287–9.

Bibliography

English-language books

Alford, W.P. and L. Fang (1994) "Legal Training and Education in the 1990s: An Overview and Assessment of China's Needs," (unpublished manuscript) UADP.

Alford, W.P. (1995) *To Steal a Book is an Elegant Offense*, Stanford, Calif.: Stanford University Press.

—— (forthcoming) *To Steal a Book is an Elegant Offense: Intellectual Property in Traditional China*, Stanford, Calif.: Stanford University Press.

Amnesty International (1981) "China – Punishment Without Trial: Administrative Detention."

Ann, L.S. (1973) *Industrialization in Singapore*, Melbourne, Longman.

Apter, D.E. (ed.) (1964) *Ideology and Discontent*, New York: Free Press; London: Collier-Macmillan.

Arup, C. (2000) *The New World Trade Organization Agreements: Globalizing Law Through Services and Intellectual Property*, Cambridge: Cambridge University Press.

Asia Law & Practice (ed.) (1995) *Dispute Resolution in the PRC*, Hong Kong: Asia Law & Practice.

—— (1998) *Intellectual Property Protection in China: The Law* (2nd edn), Hong Kong: Asia Law & Practice.

—— (1998) *Intellectual Property Protection in China: Practical Strategies* (2nd edn), Hong Kong: Asia Law & Practice.

Baehr, P.R., *et al.* (eds) (1996) *Human Rights: Chinese and Dutch Perspectives*, Kluwer.

Balazs, E. (1964) *Chinese Civilization and Bureaucracy*, A.F. Wright (ed.), H.M. Wright (trans.), New Haven, Conn.: Yale University Press.

Baran, P.A. (1968) *The Political Economy of Growth*, New York: Monthly Review Press.

Barme, G. (1999) *In the Red: On Contemporary Chinese Culture*, New York: Columbia University Press.

Barry, D. and R.C. Keith (1999) *Regionalism, Multilateralism and the Politics of Global Trade*, Vancouver: University of British Columbia Press.

Baum, R. (1994) *Burying Mao: Chinese Politics in the Age of Deng Xiaoping*, Princeton: Princeton University Press.

Beard, C.A. (1941) *An Economic Interpretation of the Constitution of the United States*, New York: Free Press.

Berman, H.J. (1983) *Law and Revolution: The Formation of the Western Legal Tradition*, Cambridge, Mass., and London: Harvard University Press.

Bhagwati, J.N. (ed.) (1972) *Economics and World Order*, New York: Macmillan.

Black, D. and M. Mileski (eds) (1973) *The Social Organization of Law*, New York and London: Seminar Press.

Bodde, D. and C. Morris (1967) *Law in Imperial China*, Philadelphia: University of Pennsylvania Press.

Braithwaite, J. and P. Drahos (2000) *Global Business Regulation*, Cambridge: Cambridge University Press.

Brosseau, M., S. Pepper and S.K. Tsang (eds) (1996) *China Review 1996*, Hong Kong: Chinese University Press.

Brown, A. (ed.) (1984) *Political Culture and Communist Studies*, Hampshire and London: Macmillan.

Brzezinski, Z. (1970) *Between Two Ages: America's Role in the Technetronic Era*, New York: Viking.

Burstein, D. and A. de Keijzer (1998) *Big Dragon: The Future of China, What it Means for Business, the Economy and the Global Order*, New York: Simon & Schuster.

Butler, W.E. (ed.) (1983) *The Legal System of the Chinese Soviet Republic 1931–34*, New York: Transnational.

Cardoso, F.H. and E. Faletto, (1979) *Dependency and Development in Latin America*, Berkeley: University of California Press.

Castel, J.G., A.L.C. de Mestral and W.C. Graham (1991) *The Canadian Law and Practice of International Trade*, Toronto: Edmond Montgomery.

CCH Australia Ltd (ed.) *China Laws for Foreign Business*.

—— *China Law Update*, March 2000.

Chen, A.H.Y. (1992) *An Introduction to the Legal System of the People's Republic of China*, Singapore: Butterworth.

Chin, P. (1960) *The Adventurous History of Hsi Men and His Six Wives*, New York: Capricorn Books.

—— (1968) *The Dream of the Red Chamber: A Chinese Novel of the Early Ch'ing Period*, New York, Grosset & Dunlap.

China Law & Practice (ed.) (1995) *Dispute Resolution in the PRC: A Practical Guide to Litigation and Arbitration in China*, Hong Kong: China Law & Practice.

China's Foreign Economic Legislation, Vol. I (1982) Beijing: Foreign Languages Press.

China's Foreign Economic Legislation Vol. II (1982) Beijing: Foreign Languages Press.

Chinese Society for the Study of Confucianism and Legal Culture (ed.) (1992) *Confucianism and Legal Culture*, Shanghai: Fudan University Press.

Chu, G.C. and Y. Ju (1993) *The Great Wall in Ruins: Communication and Cultural Change in China*, Albany: State University of New York Press.

Ch'u T. (1961) *Law and Society in Traditional China*, Paris: Mouton Press.

Coates, A. (1976) *Myself a Mandarin*, London, Frederick Muller, 1968; and R. Van Gulik, *Celebrated Cases of Judge Dee*, New York: Dover Publications.

Cochran, S. (1980) *Big Business in China: Sino–Foreign Rivalry in the Cigarette Industry, 1890–1930*, Cambridge, Mass.: Harvard University Press.

Cohen, B.J. (1991) *Crossing Frontiers: Explorations in International Political Economy*, Boulder, Colo.: Westview.

Cohen, J.A. (1968) *The Criminal Process in the People's Republic of China*, Cambridge, Mass.: Harvard University Press.

—— (ed.) (1970) *Contemporary Chinese Law: Research Problems and Perspectives*, Cambridge, Mass.: Harvard University Press.

Cohen, J.A., R.R. Edwards and F. Chen (eds) (1980) *Essays on China's Legal Tradition*, Princeton: Princeton University Press.

Corden, W.M. (1974) *Trade Policy and Economic Welfare*, Oxford: Clarendon Press.

Corne, P.H. (1997) *Foreign Investment in China: The Administrative Legal System*, Hong Kong: Hong Kong University Press.

Cover, R.M. and O.M. Fiss (1979) *The Structure of Procedure*, Mineola, NY: Foundation Press.

Davis, D. and E.F. Vogel (eds) (1990) *Chinese Society on the Eve of Tiananmen: The Impact of Reform*, Cambridge, Mass.: Harvard University Press.

Diamond, A.S. (1971) *Primitive Law, Past and Present*, London: Methuen.

Dutton, M. (1992) *Policing and Punishment in China: From Patriarchy to "The People,"* Hong Kong: Oxford University Press.

Dworkin, R. (1978) *Taking Rights Seriously*, Cambridge, Mass.: Harvard University Press.

Eckstein, A. (1977) *China's Economic Revolution*, Cambridge: Cambridge University Press.

Economist Intelligence Unit (1988) *China, Japan, and the Asian NICs: Economic Structure and Analysis*, London: The Economist.

Ehrmann, H.W. (1976) *Comparative Legal Cultures*, Englewood Cliffs, NJ: Prentice Hall.

Eisenstadt, S.W. and L. Roniger (1984) *Patrons, Clients and Friends: Interpersonal Relations and the Structure of Trust in Society*, Cambridge: Cambridge University Press.

Elman, B.A. (1984) *From Philosophy to Philology: Intellectual and Social Aspects of Change in Late Imperial China*, Cambridge, Mass.: Harvard University Press.

—— (1990) *Classicism, Politics, and Kinship: The Ch'ang-chou School of New Text Confucianism in Late Imperial China*, Berkeley, Los Angeles and London: University of California Press.

Epstein, E.J. (1985) *Takings: Private Property and the Power of Eminent Domain*, Cambridge, Mass.: Harvard University Press.

Fairbank, J.K. (ed.) (1957) *Chinese Thought and Institutions*, Chicago and London: University of Chicago Press.

Frank, A.G. (1967) *Capitalism and Underdevelopment in Latin America*, New York: Monthly Review Press.

Fried, M.H. (1953) *The Fabric of Chinese Society*, New York: Praeger.

Friedman, D. (1988) *The Misunderstood Miracle: Industrial Development and Political Change in Japan*, Ithaca, NY, and London: Cornell University Press.

Friedman, E., P.G. Pickowitcz and M. Selden (1991) *Chinese Village, Socialist State*, New Haven, Conn.: Yale University Press.

Friedman, L.M. (1975) *The Legal System: A Social Science Perspective*, Englewood Cliffs, NJ: Prentice Hall.

Fu, S.Y.C. (1991) *Challenging the Past: The Paintings of Chang Dai-chien*, Washington: Smithsonian Institution.

Furtado, C. (1964) *Development and Underdevelopment: A Structural View of the Problems of Developed and Underdeveloped Countries*, Berkeley: University of California Press.

Gardner, J.A. (1980) *Legal Imperialism: American Lawyers and Foreign Aid in Latin America*, Madison: University of Wisconsin Press.

Gates, H. (1987) *Chinese Working Class Lives: Getting by in Taiwan*, Ithaca, NY, and London: Cornell University Press.

Ghai, Y., R. Luckham and F.G. Snyder (eds) (1987) *The Political Economy of Law: A Third World Reader*, New Delhi: Oxford University Press.

Glendon, M.A. (1985) *Comparative Legal Systems*, St Paul, Minn.: West.

Goldman, M. and R. MacFarquhar (eds) (1999) *The Paradox of China's Post-Mao Reforms*, Cambridge, Mass.: Harvard University Press.

Goodman, D.S.G. (ed.) (1984) *Groups and Politics in the People's Republic of China*, Cardiff, UK: University College Cardiff Press.

Goodman, D.S.G. and G. Segal (eds) (1994) *China Deconstructs*, London: Routledge.

Groombridge, M.A. and C.E. Barfield (1999) *Tiger by the Tail: China and the World Trade Organization*, Washington: AEI Press.

Guo X. (1996) *Case Studies of China International Economic and Trade Arbitration*, Hong Kong: Sweet & Maxwell.

Haggard, S. (1990) *Pathways from the Periphery: The Politics of Growth in the Newly Industrialized Countries*, Ithaca, NY, and London: Cornell University Press.

Haggard, S. and C.H. Lee (1995) *Financial Systems and Economic Policy in Developing Countries*, Ithaca, NY: Cornell University Press.

Haggard, S., C.H. Lee and S. Maxfield (eds) (1993) *The Politics of Finance in Developing Countries*, Ithaca, NY: Cornell University Press.

Hamilton, G. (ed.) (1991) *Business Networks and Economic Development in East and Southeast Asia*, Hong Kong: Centre of Asian Studies, University of Hong Kong.

Harding, H. (1981) *Organizing China: The Problem of Bureaucracy*, Stanford, Calif.: Stanford University Press.

—— (1987) *China's Second Revolution: Reform After Mao*, Washington: Brookings Institution.

Hartford, K. (1980) "Step By Step: Reform, Resistance, and Revolution in Chin-Ch'a-Chi Border Region 1937–1945," Ph.D. dissertation, Stanford University.

He, J. and J.R. Waltz (1995) *Criminal Prosecution in the People's Republic of China and the United States of America: A Comparative Study*, Beijing: China Procuratorial Press.

Herman, M. (ed.) (1986) *Political Psychology*, San Francisco and London: Jossey-Bass.

Hertz, E. (1998) *The Trading Crowd: An Ethnography of the Shanghai Stock Market*, Cambridge: Cambridge University Press.

Ho, P. (1962) *The Ladder of Success in Imperial China*, New York.

Ho, P. and T. Tsou (1968) *China in Crisis*, Chicago: University of Chicago Press.

Hong Kong Trade Development Council (1991) *China's Foreign Trade System.*

Honnold, J. (1999) *Uniform Law for International Sales under the 1980 United Nations Convention* (3rd edn), Deventer, Netherlands, and Boston: Kluwer.

Howell, J. (1993) *China Opens Its Doors: The Politics of Economic Transition*, Boulder, Colo.: Lynne Rienner.

Hsia, C.T. (1968) *The Classic Chinese Novel: A Critical Introduction*, New York and London: Columbia University Press.

Hu Y. (1993) *China's Capital Market*, Hong Kong: Chinese University Press.

Hudec, R.E. (1990) *The GATT Legal System and World Trade Diplomacy*, Salem, NH: Butterworth Legal Publishers.

Human Rights in China *et al.* (1998) *Report on the Implementation of CEDAW in the People's Republic of China.*

—— (2000) *HRW World Report 2000: China*, February.

International Rehabilitation Council for Torture Victims (ed.) (1999) *Torture in Tibet 1949–1999*, Copenhagen: IRCT.

Jackson, J.H. (1969) *World Trade and the Law of GATT*, Indianapolis: Bobbs-Merrill.

—— (1989) *The World Trading System*, Cambridge, Mass.: MIT Press.

Jameson, F. and M. Miyoshi (eds) (1998) *The Cultures of Globalization*, Durham, NC: Duke University Press.

Jayasuriya, K. (ed.) (1999) *Law, Capitalism and Power in Asia*, London: Routledge.

Johnson, C. (1982) *MITI and the Japanese Miracle: The Growth of Japanese Industrial Policy 1925–1975*, Stanford: Stanford University Press.

Johnston, D.L. (1977) *Canadian Securities Regulation*, Toronto: Butterworth.

Joint Economic Committee of US Congress (ed.) (1982) *China Under the Four Modernizations*, Washington: US Government Printing Office.

—— (1986) *China's Economy Looks Toward the Year 2000*, Washington: US Government Printing Office.

—— (1991) *China's Economic Dilemmas in the 1990s: The Problems of Reforms, Modernization, and Interdependence*, Washington: US Government Printing Office.

Jones, W.C. (ed.) (1989) *Basic Principles of Civil Law in China*, Armonk, NY: M.E. Sharpe.

Josephs, H.K. (1990) *Labour Law in China*, Butterworth.

Kairys, D. (1998) *The Politics of Law: A Progressive Critique* (3rd ed.), New York: Basic Books.

Kaplan, N., J. Spruce and M.J. Moser (1994) *Hong Kong and China Arbitration Cases and Materials*, Singapore: Butterworth.

Kapp, R.A. (ed.) (1983) *Communicating with China*, Chicago: Intercultural Press.

Keith, R.C. (1994) *China's Struggle for the Rule of Law*, New York: St Martin's Press.

Kelly, D. and A. Reid (ed.) (1998) *Asian Freedoms: The Idea of Freedom in East and Southeast Asia*, Cambridge: Cambridge University Press.

Kelman, M. (1987) *A Guide to Critical Legal Studies*, Cambridge, Mass.: Harvard University Press.

Kent, A. (1993) *Between Freedom and Subsistence: China and Human Rights*, Hong Kong: Oxford University Press.

Ladany, L. (1992) *Law and Legality in China: The Testament of a China-watcher*, M. Nath (ed.), London, Hurst & Co.

Lechner, F.J. and J. Boli (eds) (2000) *The Globalization Reader*, Malden, Mass.: Blackwell.

Legal Research Institute of the PRC Supreme People's Court (ed.) (1992) *New Selections of the Foreign-Related Economic Cases in China*, Shanghai: Economic Information Agency.

Leng, S. and H. Chiu (1985) *Criminal Justice in Post-Mao China*, Albany, NY: State University of New York Press.

Levenson, J. (1958) *Confucian China and Its Modern Fate*, Berkeley: University of California Press.

Li, V.H. (1977) *Law and Politics in China's Foreign Trade*, Seattle: University of Washington Press.

Lieberthal, K. and M. Oksenberg (1988) *Policy Making in China*, Princeton: Princeton University Press.

—— (1995) *Governing China: From Revolution through Reform*, New York and London: W.W. Norton.

Lin, S., *China's Decentralization and Provincial Economic Legislation, 1980–89*, Ph.D. thesis, University of Calgary.

Lindbeck, J. (1970) *China: Management of a Revolutionary Society*, Seattle and London: University of Washington Press.

Lo, C.W. (1995) *China's Legal Awakening: Legal Theory and Criminal Justice in Deng's Era*, Hong Kong: Hong Kong University Press.

Lubman, S.B. (1999) *Bird in a Cage: Legal Reform in China After Mao*, Stanford: Stanford University Press.

Ma Xiaoying and Leonard Ortolano (2000) *Environmental Regulation in China: Institutions, Enforcement and Compliance*, New York: Rowman & Littlefield.

MacFarquhar, R. (ed.) (1993) *The Politics of China, 1949–1989*, Cambridge: Cambridge University Press.

Madison, J., *et al.* (1961) *The Federalist Papers*, New York: New American Library.

Maine, H.S., *Ancient Law*, London: Oxford University Press (reprinted 1959, copyright 1861).

Mendes, E.P. and A.-M. Traeholt (eds) (1997) *Human Rights: Chinese and Canadian Perspectives*, Ottawa: Human Rights Research and Education Centre.

Mercuro, N. and W.J. Samuels (eds) (1999) *The Fundamental Interrelationships Between Government and Property*, Stamford, Conn.: JAI Press.

Merton, R.K. (1965) *Social Theory and Social Structure* (revised and enlarged edition), New York: Free Press.

Modelski, G. (ed.) (1979) *Transnational Corporations and World Order: Readings in International Political Economy*, San Francisco, W.H. Freeman & Co.

Moore, B. (1978) *Injustice: The Social Bases of Obedience and Revolt*, White Plains, NY: M.E. Sharpe.

Moser, M.J. (ed.) (1987) *Foreign Trade, Investment, and the Law in the People's Republic of China* (2nd edn), Hong Kong: Oxford University Press.

Moulder, F.V. (1977) *Japan, China and the Modern World Economy: Toward a Reinterpretation of East Asian Development ca. 1600 to ca. 1918*, Cambridge: Cambridge University Press.

Munro, D.J. (1969) *The Concept of Man in Early China*, Stanford, Calif.: Stanford University Press.

Murphy, J., and J.L. Coleman (1990) *The Philosophy of Law: An Introduction to Jurisprudence*, Totowa, NJ: Rowman & Allanheld.

Nader, L. (1969) *Law in Culture and Society*, Chicago: Aldine Press.

Nathan, A.J. (1985) *Chinese Democracy*, Berkeley and Los Angeles: University of California Press.

Naughton, B. (1995) *Growing Out of the Plan*, New York: Cambridge University Press.

Nee, V. (ed.) *China Commercial Laws and Regulations*, New York: Oceana.

Needham, J. (1954) *Science and Civilization in China, Vol. II*, Cambridge: Cambridge University Press.

Noble, G.W. and J. Ravenhill (eds) (2000) *The Asian Financial Crisis and the Architecture of Global Finance*, Cambridge: Cambridge University Press.

O'Brien, K.J. (1990) *Reform Without Liberalization: The National People's Congress and the Politics of Institutional Change*, New York: Cambridge University Press.

Oi, J.C. and A.G. Walder (eds) (1999) *Property Rights and Economic Reform in China*, Stanford: Stanford University Press.

Oksenberg, M. (ed.) (1990) *China's Participation in the IMF, the World Bank and GATT: Toward a Global Economic Order*, Ann Arbor: University of Michigan Press.

Oksenberg, M. and E. Economy (1999) *China Joins the World: Progress and Prospects*, New York: Council on Foreign Relations Press.

Oksenberg, M., P.B. Potter and W.B. Abnett (1996) *Advancing Intellectual Property Rights: Information Technologies and the Course of Economic Development in China*, Seattle: National Bureau of Asian Research.

Packenham, R.A. (1973) *Liberal America and the Third World*, Princeton: Princeton University Press.

—— (1992) *The Dependency Movement: Scholarship and Politics in Development Studies*, Cambridge, Mass., and London: Harvard University Press.

Perry, E.J. and C. Wong (1985) *The Political Economy of Reform in Post-Mao China*, Cambridge, Mass.: Harvard University Press.

Perry, E.J., C. Wong and M. Selden (eds) (2000) *Chinese Society: Change, Conflict and Resistance*, London and New York: Routledge.

Pomfret, R. (1991) *Investing in China: Ten Years of the Open Door Policy*, Ames: Iowa University Press.

Posner, R. (1986) *Economic Analysis of Law* (3rd edn), Boston: Little, Brown.

Potter, P.B. (1992) *The Economic Contract Law of China: Legitimation and Contract Autonomy in the PRC*, Seattle and London: University of Washington Press.

—— (ed.) (1994) *Domestic Law Reforms in Post-Mao China*, Armonk, NY, and London: M.E. Sharpe.

—— (1995) *Chinese Foreign Business Law: Past Accomplishments, Future Challenges*, San Francisco: 1990 Institute.

Price Waterhouse (1988) *Doing Business in the People's Republic of China*.

Purves, B. (1991) *Barefoot in the Boardroom: Venture and Misadventure in the People's Republic of China*, Toronto: NC Press.

Pye, L. (1981) *The Dynamics of Chinese Politics*, Cambridge: Oelgeschlager, Gunn & Hain.

—— (1988) *The Mandarin and the Cadre*, Ann Arbor: University of Michigan Press.

—— (1992) *Chinese Negotiating Style: Commercial Approaches and Cultural Approaches*, New York: Quorum Books.

Qian, M. (1994) *Law and Contemporary Problems* (Principles of Property Law), Beijing: Peking University Press.

Rajaee, F. (2000) *Globalization on Trial: The Human Condition and the Information Civilization*, Ottawa: International Development Research Centre.

Raz, J. (1986) "Rights and Individualism," in *The Morality of Freedom*, New York: Oxford University Press.

Redding, G.S. (1990) *The Spirit of Chinese Capitalism*, Berlin: Walter de Gruyter.

Regnier, P. (1993) *Singapore: City-State in South-East Asia*, Christopher Hurst (trans.), Kuala Lumpur: S. Abdul Majeed & Co.

Rostow, W.W. (1963) *The Economics of the Take Off into Sustained Economic Growth*, New York: St Martins Press.

Rowe, W.T. (1984) *Hankow: Commerce and Society in a Chinese City, 1796–1889*, Stanford, Calif.: Stanford University Press.

Rui, M. and Wang, G. (eds) (1994) *Chinese Foreign Economic Law*, Washington: International Law Institute.

Saich, T. (ed.) (1990) *The Chinese People's Movement: Perspectives on Spring 1989*, Armonk, NY: M.E. Sharpe.

Scalapino, R.A., S. Sato and J. Wanandi (eds) (1985) *Asian Economic Development: Past and Future*, Berkeley, Calif.: Institute of East Asian Studies.

Scaperlanda, A.E. (ed.) (1973) *Prospects for Eliminating Non-Tariff Distortions*, Leiden: Sijthoff.

Schurmann, F. (1968) *Ideology and Organization in Communist China* (2nd edn), Berkeley: University of California Press.

Segal, G. and D.S.G. Goodman (eds) (2000) *Towards Recovery in Pacific Asia*, London: Routledge.

Seidman, A., R. Seidman and J. Payne (eds) (1997) *Legislative Drafting for Market Reform: Some Lessons from China*, New York: St Martin's Press.

Selected Works of China International Economic and Trade Arbitration Commission (periodical), Hong Kong: Sweet & Maxwell.

Seymour, J.D. and R. Anderson (1998) *New Ghosts, Old Ghosts: Prisons and Labor Reform Camps in China*, Armonk, NY: M.E. Sharpe.

Shakya, T. (1999) *The Dragon in the Land of Snows: A History of Modern Tibet Since 1947*, New York: Columbia University Press.

Shih, C. (1972) *Injustice to Tou O (Tou O Yuan): A Study and Translation*, Cambridge: Cambridge University Press.

Shihata, I.F.I. (1993) *Towards a Greater Depoliticization of Investment Disputes: The Roles of ICSID and MIGA*, Washington: International Center for the Settlement of Investment Disputes.

Shirk, S.L. (1993) *The Political Logic of Economic Reform in China*, Berkeley: University of California Press.

Shue, V. (1988) *The Reach of the State: Sketches of the Chinese Body Politic*, Stanford, Calif.: Stanford University Press.

Singer, M. (1972) *Weak States in a World of Power: The Dynamics of International Relationships*, New York: Free Press.

Smith, J.C. and D.N. Weisstub (1983) *The Western Idea of Law*, London and Toronto: Butterworth.

Stone, F. (1984) *Canada, the GATT and the International Trade System*, Montreal: Institute for Research on Public Policy.

Streng, W.P. and A.D. Wilcox (eds) *Doing Business in China*, looseleaf, Interjura.

—— (eds) (1993) *Doing Business in China*, Irvington-on-Hudson: Transnational Juris Publishers.

—— (1993) *Doing Business in China*, New York: Matthew Bender.

Sze, M. (ed.) (1963) *The Mustard Seed Garden of Painting*, Princeton: Princeton University Press.

Tang, W. and W.L. Parish (2000) *Chinese Urban Life Under Reform*, Cambridge: Cambridge University Press.

Thomas, J.S. and M.A. Meyer (1998) *The New Rules of Global Trade: A Guide to the World Trade Organization*, Scarborough, Ontario: Carswell.

Tigar, M. and M. Levy (1977) *Law and the Rise of Capitalism*, New York: Free Press.

To, L.L. (1986) *Trade Unions in China*, Singapore: Singapore University Press.

Tomlinson, J. (1999) *Globalization and Culture*, Chicago: University of Chicago Press.

Trubek, D., *et al.* (1993) "Global Restructuring and the Law: The Internationalization of Legal Fields and the Creation of Transnational Arenas," working paper, University of Wisconsin, Madison.

US Department of State, *China Country Reports* (annual).

United Nations (1966) *United Nations Treaty Series (UNTS)*, New York: United Nations.

—— (1973) *Multinational Corporations in World Development*, New York: United Nations.

United States International Trade Commission (1993) *East Asia: Regional Economic Integration and Implications for the United States*, Washington: USITC.

Van Der Sprenkel, S. (1962) *Legal Institutions in Manchu China*, New York: Athlone Press.

Van Ness, P. (ed.) (1999) *Debating Human Rights: Critical Essays from the United States and Asia*, London: Routledge.

Varga, C. (ed.) (1992) *Comparative Legal Cultures*, Aldershot: Dartmouth.

Vogel, E. (1991) *The Four Little Dragons*, Cambridge, Mass.: Harvard University Press.

Waldron, J. (1984) *Theories of Rights*, New York: Oxford University Press.

Walker, A. (1991) *Land Property and Construction in the People's Republic of China*, Hong Kong: Hong Kong University Press.

Wang, S. (1996) *Resolving Disputes in the PRC: A Practical Guide to Arbitration and Conciliation in China*, Hong Kong: Sweet & Maxwell Asia.

Weber, M. (1978) *Economy and Society*, Roth and Wittich (eds), Berkeley and Los Angeles: University of California Press.

Wilber, C.K., (ed.) (1979) *The Political Economy of Development and Underdevelopment* (2nd edn), New York: Random House.

Wilson, R.W., S.L. Greenblatt and A.A. Wilson (eds) (1981) *Moral Behavior in Chinese Society*, New York: Praeger.

Winckler, E.A. and S. Greenhalgh (eds) (1986) *State and Society in the Taiwan Miracle*, Armonk, NY, and London: M.E. Sharpe.

—— (eds) (1990) *Contending Approaches to the Political Economy of Taiwan*, Armonk, NY, and London: M.E. Sharpe.

Woo, J. (1991) *Race to the Swift: State and Finance in Korean Industrialization*, New York: Columbia University Press.

Woodiwiss, A. (1998) *Globalisation, Human Rights and Labour Law in Pacific Asia*, Cambridge: Cambridge University Press.

World Bank (1994) *China: Foreign Trade Reform*, Washington: World Bank.

World Trade Organization (ed.) (1999) *Guide to the Uruguay Round Agreements*, The Hague: Kluwer.

—— (1999) *The Results of the Uruguay Round of Multilateral Trade Negotiations*, Cambridge: Cambridge University Press.

Yah, L.C. (1984) *Economic Restructuring in Singapore*, Singapore: Federal Publications.

Yang, B. (1992) *The Ugly Chinaman and the Crisis of Chinese Culture*, D.J. Cohn and J. Qing (trans.), St Leonards, New South Wales: Allen & Unwin.

Yang, M. (1994) *Gifts, Favors, and Banquets: The Art of Social Relationships in China*, Ithaca, NY: Cornell University Press.

Zheng, C. (with M. Pendleton) (1987) *Chinese Intellectual Property and Technology Transfer Law*, London: Sweet & Maxwell.

Zheng, H.R. (1988) *China's Civil and Commercial Law*, Singapore: Butterworth Asia.

English-language periodicals

Academy of Management Journal
Administrative Law Review
AFP – Brussels
AFP – Hong Kong

Agence France Presse
Agence France Presse English Wire
American Anthropologist
American Journal of Comparative Law
American Journal of Sociology
American University Journal of International Law and Policy
Annual Survey of International and Comparative Law
ASEAN and Asian Trade
Asia Week
Asian Law
Atlantic Monthly
Australian Journal of Corporate Law
Beijing Review
Berkeley Journal of International Law
Buffalo Law Review
Business Wire
California International Practitioner
California Western International Law Journal
Cambridge Law Journal
Canadian Business Law Journal
Canadian Journal of Law and Society
Cardozo Law Review
Case Western Reserve Law Review
China Business Review
China Business Review (electronic media)
China Daily
China Daily Business Weekly
China Economic News
China Economic Review
China Exchange News Special Issue: Law and Legal Studies in the People's Republic of China (1994)
China Focus
China Information
China Joint Venturer
China Law Reporter
China News Digest (electronic media)
China Online
China Perspectives
China Report: Political, Social, Military
China Rights Forum
Chinalaw.net (electronic service)
Chinese Law & Practice
Chinese Law and Government
Columbia Business Law Review
Columbia Journal of Asian Law
Comparative Labor Law Journal
Comparative Studies in Society and History
Connecticut Journal of International Law
Cornell International Law Journal

Cultural Anthropology
Current History
DBS Asia Economic Briefing
Dispute Resolution Journal
Duke Law Journal
East Asian Executive Reports
Eastern Express (Hong Kong)
EU website (www.eurunion.org)
European Intellectual Property Review
European Journal of Marketing
Far Eastern Economic Review
FBIS Daily Report: China
Federal News Service
Fordham International Law Journal
Foreign Affairs
Foreign Policy
George Washington Journal of International Law & Economics
Georgetown Law Journal
Harvard China Review
Harvard Human Rights Journal
Harvard Journal of International Law
Harvard Journal of Law & Public Policy
Harvard Law Review
Hastings Internal and Comparative Law Review
Hong Kong China News Agency
Hong Kong Standard
Hoover Institution Essays in Public Policy
Human Rights in China
Human Rights Law Journal
Human Rights Quarterly
Human Rights Watch – Asia
Information Systems
International Business Lawyer
International Commercial Arbitration
International Herald-Tribune
International Journal of Comparative and Applied Criminal Justice
International Legal Materials (I.L.M.)
International Organization
IP Asia
IP Worldwide
JCI Arbitration
John Marshall Law Review
Journal of Chinese Law
Journal of Criminal Law and Criminology
Journal of International Arbitration
Journal of Peace Research
Journal of the Copyright Society of the USA
Journal of World Trade
Kyodo News Service

Law & Policy in International Business
Law & Politics in International Business
Law & Society Review
Law and Contemporary Problems
Law and Philosophy
Leadership Quarterly
Legislative Studies Quarterly
Leiden–Beijing Legal Transformation Project Occasional Papers
National People's Congress Reports
Los Angeles Times
Maryland Journal of International Law and Trade
Melbourne University Law Review
Michigan Journal of International Law
Mind
Minnesota Law Review
NCNA, in *Selections From World Broadcasts*
New York International Law Review
New York Review of Books
New York Times
New Zealand Law Journal
North Carolina Journal of International Law and Commercial Regulation
Northern Illinois University Law Review
Northwestern Journal of International Law and Business
Northwestern University Law Review
Notre Dame Law Review
Osgoode Hall Law Journal
Pacific Rim Law & Policy Journal
People's Daily (overseas edition)
Options
Problems of Communism
Reuters Wire Service
Rutgers Law Journal
South China Morning Post
Southern California Interdisciplinary Law Journal
Stanford Environmental Law Journal
Stanford Journal of Environmental Law
Stanford Journal of International Law
The China Quarterly
The Financial Post
The International Lawyer
U.C. Davis Law Review
UCLA Pacific Basin Law Journal
Université Laval Law Review
University of British Columbia Law Review
University of Pittsburgh Law Review
University of San Francisco Law Review
Washington University Law Quarterly
Wisconsin International Law Journal
World Competition Law and Economic Review

Yale Journal of International Law
Yale Law Journal

Chinese-language books

Administrative Adjudication Chamber of the Supreme People's Court (ed.) *Xingzheng susong yu tudi guanli fa* (Administrative Litigation and the Land Administration Law), Beijing: Times Press (1999).

An Conghua *et al.* (eds) (1999) *Renmin fayuan yinan panli pingxi: Minshi zhuan* (Evaluation of Difficult Cases of the People's Courts: Civil Volume), Changchun: Jilin Chubanshe.

—— (1999) *Renmin fayuan yinan panli pingxi: Xingzheng zhuan* (Evaluation of Difficult Cases of the People's Courts: Administrative Volume) Changchun: Jilin Chubanshe.

—— (1999) *Renmin fayuan yinan panli pingxi: Jingji zhuan* (Evaluation of Difficult Cases of the People's Courts: Economic Volume), Changchun: Jilin Chubanshe.

Bai Yingfu and Huang Rui (1995) *Guoji jishu zhuanrang fa* (International Technology Transfer Law), Wuhan: Wuhan University Press.

Bi Yuquian (1999) *Minshi zhengju fa panli shiwu yanjiu* (Practical Study of Adjudication in Civil Evidence Law), Beijing: Law Publishing.

CASS Law Institute (ed.) (1993) *Guoji renquan wenjian yu Guoji renquan jigou* (International Human Rights Documents and International Human Rights Institutions), Beijing: Chinese Academy of Social Sciences Press.

—— (1995) *Zhong ri gongwuyuan huilu fanzui yanjiu* (Chinese and Japanese Research on Crimes of Bribery), Beijing: Chinese Academy of Social Sciences Press.

Cha chu guandao anjian shiyong fagui shouce (Handbook on Investigation and Handling of Profiteering Cases), Beijing: Law Publishers (1989).

Chen Guanzhong and D. Prefontaine (eds) (1998) *Lianheguo xingshi sifa zhunce yu Zhongguo xingshi fazhi* (United Nations Standards of Criminal Justice and the Chinese Criminal Law System), Beijing: Law Publishers.

Chen Weidong (1997) *Zhongguo xingshi susong fa* (Chinese Criminal Procedure Law), Hong Kong: Joint Publishing.

Chen Youzun (ed.) (1990) *Minshi jingji jinan anli jiesi* (Interpretation and Analysis of Difficult Civil and Economic Cases), Huhehaote: Inner Mongolia University Press.

Cheng Dejun (ed.) (1992) *Shewai zhongcai yu falu* (Foreign-Related Arbitration and Law), Beijing: Chinese People's University Press.

Cheng Gong *et al.* (eds) (1998) *Zhongguo zhengquan fagui huibian* (Compilation of Chinese Securities Laws and Regulations, 2nd edn), Beijing: People's University Press.

Cheng Haoyi and Kian Gangsheng (eds) (1988) *Jiti qiye xiang zhen qiye geti gong-shanghu bibei* (Musts for Collective Enterprises, Village and Township Enterprises, and Individual Commercial and Industrial Merchants), Beijing: Social Science Manuscripts Press.

China Economic Law Research Association, Beijing Branch and Beijing Municipal Government Electronic Industries Office (eds) (1988) *Zen yang zhengque shishi «Qiye fa»* (How to Precisely Implement the "Enterprise Law"), Beijing: New Era Press.

China Labour Law Research Association (ed.) (2000) *Xin bian laodong zhengyi zhongcai anli* (New Edition of Labour Dispute Arbitration Cases), Beijing: Law Publishers.

China Senior Judges Training Centre and Chinese People's University Law Faculty (ed.) *Zhongguo shenpan anli yaolan* (Compendium of Chinese Case Decisions, periodical), Beijing: Public Security University Press.

Chui Xiuming *et al.* (1999) *Renmin fayuan yinan panli pingxi: Minshi zhuan* (Critical Analysis of Difficult Decisions by the People's Courts: Civil Volume), Changchun: Jilin People's Press.

Civil Division of the Supreme People's Court (ed.) (1999, 2000) *Zuigao renmin fayuan minshi anjian jiexi* (Analysis of Civil Cases of the Supreme People's Court), nos 1 and 2, Beijing: Law Publishers.

Civil Law Office of the NPC Standing Committee Legal Affairs Committee (ed.) (1999) *«Zhonghua renmin gongheguo hetong fa» ji qi zhongyao caogao jieshao* (Introduction to the Contract Law of the PRC and Its Important Drafts), Beijing: Falu Chubanshe.

—— (1999) *«Zhonghua renmin gongheguo hetong fa» lifa ziliao xuan* (Selected Legislative Materials on the Contract Law of the PRC), Beijing: Falu Chubanshe.

Civil Law Office of the NPC Standing Committee on Legal Affairs and CCPIT Secretariat (ed.) (1995) *Zhonghua renmin gongheguo zhongcai fa quanshu* (Encyclopedia of Arbitration Law of the PRC), Beijing: Law Publishers.

Copyright Manuscript Center of State Council Copyright Office (ed.) (1993) *Zhonghua renmin gongheguo zhuzuoquan fa* (Authorship Rights Law of the PRC), Beijing: Sanlian Press.

Dai Jianzhi and Chen Xu (1997) *Zhishi chanquan sunhai peichang* (Compensation for Loss in Intellectual Property), Beijing: Law Publishers.

Dan You (ed.) (1990) *Jingji fa anli xuan xi* (Compilation and Analysis of Economic Law Cases), Beijing: Law Publishers.

Documents of the Thirteenth National Congress of the Communist Party of China, Beijing, Foreign Languages Press (1987).

Economic Tribunal of the Supreme People's Court (ed.) (1999) *Hetong fa shijie yu shiyong* (Interpretation and Application of Contract Law), Beijing: New China Press.

Gonghui fa shouce (Handbook of Trade Union Law), Beijing: Democracy and Legal System Press (1994).

Guo Yuyuan (ed.) (1998) *Renmin fayuan anli leibian pingxi: Jingji shen pan zhuan* (Evaluation of People's Court Cases by Category: Economic Adjudication Volume), Changchun: Jilin People's Press.

Guo Zhenying (ed.) (1986) *Zhongguo shehui zhuyi gufen jingji wen da* (Questions and Answers on China's Socialist Share Economy), Beijing: Aeronautics Academy Press.

Guowuyuan jingji fa gui yanjiu zhongxin bangong shi (Administrative Office of the State Council Economic Laws and Regulations Research Center) (1982) *Zhonghua renmin gongheguo jingji hetong fa tiaowen shiyi* (Explanation of Articles of the Economic Contract Law of the PRC), Beijing.

Hu Jihua and Wang Chaoying (eds) (1999) *Zhonghua renmin gongheguo hetong fa: Jie yong shouce* (Handbook on Interpretation and Application of the Contract Law of the PRC), Beijing: Red Flag Press.

Huang S. (1989) *Xingzheng susong fa 100 wen* (100 Questions on the Administrative Litigation Law), Beijing.

Jiang Bixin (ed.) (1999) *Xingzheng susong yu tudi guanlifa: Xin jie* (Administrative Litigation of Land Administration Law: New Interpretations), Beijing: Current Events Press.

Jiang Mingan (1998) *Zhongguo xingzheng fazhi fazhan jingcheng diaocha baogao* (Report on Investigation of the Development and Progress of China's Administrative Rule of Law), Beijing: Law Publishers.

Jiang Yong (ed.) (1999) *Dianxing xingzheng anli pingxi* (Analysis of Representative Administrative Cases), Beijing: Law Publishers.

Jin Jiandong *et al.* (eds) (1992) *Gudong zhaiquan quanshu* (Encyclopedia of Stocks and Bonds) (2 vols), Beijing: Physics University Press.

Jingji sifa gongzuo shouce (Handbook for Economic Adjudication Work), Kunming (1984).

Laodong fa yu laodong zhengyi shiyong shouce (Practical Handbook on Labor Law and Labor Disputes), Beijing: Chian Economy Press (1994).

Law and Regulation Editorial Office of Law Publishing House (ed.) (1988) *Siying qiye changyong falu shouce* (Handbook of Commonly Used Laws on Private Enterprises), Beijing: Law Publishing House.

Legal Department of the Public Security Ministry (ed.) (1988) *Gongan fagui huibian* (Compilation of Laws and Regulations on Public Security), Beijing: Masses Publishing.

Legal Research Institute of the PRC Supreme People's Court (ed.) *Renmin fayuan anli xuan* (Compilation of Court Cases, periodical), Beijing: Public Security University Press.

Li Buyun (1998) *Zouxiang fazhi* (Proceeding Toward Rule of Law), Changsha: Hunan People's Press.

—— (ed.) (1999) *Lifa fa yanjiu* (Study of Legislation Law), Changsha, Hunan People's Press.

Li Changdao (ed.) (1997) *Shanghai fayuan anli jingxuan: 1996* (Carefully Selected Cases from the Shanghai Courts: 1996), Shanghai: Shanghai People's Press.

—— (ed.) (1997) *Shanghai fayuan anli jingxuan: 1997* (Carefully Selected Cases from the Shanghai Courts: 1997), Shanghai: Shanghai People's Press.

Li Peizhuan (1991) *Zhongguo shehui zhuyi lifa de lilun yu shixian* (Theory and Practice of Socialist Legislation in China), Beijing: China Legal System Press.

Li Ziping (ed.) (1997) *Shewai jingji fa anli* (Cases in Foreign Economic Law), Nanchang: Jiangxi Higher Education Press.

Liang Huaren and Zhang Jiyang (eds) (1992) *Changjian anjian guifanhua shenli zhinan* (Guide to the Standardization of Commonly Seen Cases) (3 vols), Beijing: University of Law and Politics Press.

Liang Huixing (2000) *Zhongguo wuquanfa caoan jianyi gao* (Outline of Opinion on a Draft Chinese Property Law), Beijing: Social Science Manuscripts Press.

Lin Zhe (1997) *Quanli fubai yu quanli zhiyue* (Corruption of Authority and Limitations on Authority), Beijing: Law Publishers.

Liu Chuntian (ed.) (1995) *Zhishi chanquan fa jiaocheng* (Course on Intellectual Property Law), Beijing: People's University Press.

Liu Hainian *et al.* (eds) (1999) *Renquan yu sifa* (Human Rights and Administration of Justice), Beijing: Legal System Press.

Liu Junhai *et al.* (1999) *Zhengquan fa shishi wenda* (Questions and Answers on Knowledge of the Securities Law), Beijing: Law Publishers.

Liu Ruifu (ed.) (1995) *Zhonghua renmin gongheguo falu panli fenxi quanshu* (Compendium of Analysis of Legal Decisions), Beijing: International Culture Press.

Liu Wenhua (ed.) (1997) *Shewai jingji jiufen jingjie* (Introduction to Foreign Economic Disputes), Beijing: China Economy Press.

Liu Xiangdong (ed.) (1989) *Liyong wai zi zhishi shouce* (Handbook of Knowledge on the Use of Foreign Capital), Beijing: World Knowledge (*shijie zhishi*) Publishing.

Ma Qingchun (1994) *Guoji banquan falu zhidu* (The International Copyright Law System), Shanghai.

Ma Yuan (ed.) (1992) *Minshi shenpan de lilun yu shiwu* (Theory and Application of Civil Adjudication), Beijing: People's Court Publishers.

Mao Duanzhi and Yu Lei (eds) (1999) *Xin leixing jingji jiefen anjian shenli* (Trials of New Types of Economic Dispute Cases), Beijing: People's Court Press.

Ministry of Labour *et al.* (1988) *Laodong fa shouce* (Labour Law Handbook), Beijing: Economic Management Press.

—— (1994) *Zhongguo laodong fa zhengce fagui quanshu* (Encyclopedia of China's Labor Laws and Policies), Jilin: Science and Technology Press.

Minshi falu shiyong daquan (Practical Compendium on Civil Law), Beijing: People's University Press (1990).

Mu Xichuan and Zhang Lingyuan (eds) (1988) *Zhonghua renmin gongheguo quanmin suoyouzhi gongye qiye fa zhishi shouce* (Handbook of Knowledge on the Law of the PRC on Industrial Enterprises Owned by the Whole People), Beijing: Politics and Law University Press.

Pan Jinsheng, Liu Hongbie, and Zhang Xue (eds) (1993) *Zhong wai zhengquan fagui ziliao huibian* (Compilation of Chinese and Foreign Securities Laws and Regulations and Materials), Beijing: Finance Press.

Peking University Intellectual Property Institute (ed.) (1997) *Zhishichanquan fagui huibian* (Compilation of Laws and Regulations on Intellectual Property, mimeo), Beijing.

Peng Zhen (1989) *Lun xin shiqi de shehui zhu minzhu yu fazhi jianshe* (On the Establishment of Socialist Democracy and Legal System in the New Period), Beijing: Central Digest Publishers.

Peng Zhen wenxuan (Collected works of Peng Zhen), Beijing: People's Press (1991).

Policy and Law Office of the State Council's State Owned Enterprise Administration (ed.) (1992) *Zhong wai gufen zhi fagui huibian* (Compilation of Chinese and Foreign Laws and Regulations on the Stock System), Beijing: Politics and Law University Press.

PRC Supreme People's Court Economic Adjudication Chamber (ed.) (1994) *Zuigao renmin fayuan sheli de er shen zai shen jingji jiufen anli xuanbian* (Compilation of Second and Revisited Economic Case Decisions by the Supreme People's Court), Beijing: People's Court Press.

PRC Supreme People's Court (1994) *Laodong zhengyi shenpan shouce* (Judicial Handbook on Labour Disputes), Beijing: Law Publishers.

Qi Tianchang (ed.) (1991) *Hetong an li pingxi* (Discussion of Contract Cases), Beijing: Chinese University of Politics and Law Press.

Qiao Xianzhi (ed.) (2000) *Shanghai fayuan anli jingxuan: 1999* (Carefully Selected Cases from the Shanghai Courts: 1999), Shanghai: Shanghai People's Press.

Renmin fayuan yinan panli pingxi (Critical Analysis of Difficult Decisions by the People's Courts), Changchun: Jilin People's Press (1999).

Shanghai High People's Court (ed.) *Shanghai fayuan anli jingxuan* (Carefully Selected Cases of the Shanghai Courts, annual), Shanghai: Shanghai People's Press.

Shanghai Shi Renmin Zhengfu Bangongting (General Office of the Shanghai Municipal Government) and Shanghai Renmin Zhengfu Jingji Fagui Yanjiu Zhongxin (Economic Laws and Regulations Research Centre of the Shanghai Municipal Government) (eds) (1986) *Shanghai shi fagui guizhang huibian: 1949–1985* (Compilation of Statutes and Regulations and Rules of Shanghai Municipality: 1949–1985), Shanghai: Shanghai People's Press.

Shao Chongzhu (ed.) (1998) *Zhong gong fan tan da an zhong an* (Big Cases and Serious Cases on the Chinese Communists Fight Against Corruption), Hong Kong: So Far (*Xiafeier*) Publishers.

Shen Rengan *et al.* (1991) *Zhonghua renmin gongheguo zhuzuoquan fa jianghua* (Lectures on the Authorship Rights Law of the PRC), Beijing: Law Publishers.

Shen Zongling (ed.) (1999) *Lifaxue yu bijiaofa lunji* (Theoretical Compilation on Jurisprudence and Comparative Law), Beijing: Peking University Press.

Shenzhen Zhengquan Shichang Nianbao: 1990 (Annual Report on Shenzhen Securities Market: 1990).

Shi Wenqing and Mei Shenshi (1992) *Zhuzuo quan zhe wenti yanjiu* (Study of Authors' Rights), Shanghai: Fudan University Press.

Siying qiye changyong falu shouce (Handbook of Commonly Used Laws for Private Enterprises), Beijing: Law Publishers (1988).

Song Xiangguan (ed.) (1989) *Shiyong laodong fa daquan* (Encyclopedia on the Use of Labour Law), Changchun: Jilin Documentary History Press.

State Council Legal Affairs Bureau (ed.) (1988) *Zhonghua renmin gongheguo xin fagui huibian* (New Compilation of Laws and Regulations of the PRC).

State Statistical Bureau *China Statistics Yearbook* (annual).

Supreme People's Court (ed.) (1990) *Minshi falu shiyong daquan* (Practical Compendium on Civil Law), Beijing: People's University Press.

—— (ed.) (1995) *Renmin fayuan anli xuan* (Compilation of People's Court Cases), Vol. 13, Beijing: People's Court Publishing.

—— (ed.) *Renmin fayuan anli xuan* (Compilation of Cases from the People's Courts, quarterly).

Supreme People's Court Administrative Tribunal (ed.) (1999) *Xingzheng susong yu tudi guanlifa: Xin jie* (Administrative Litigation of Land Administration Law: New Interpretations), Beijing: Current Events Press.

Trademark Office of the State Administration for Industry and Commerce (1985) *Shangbiao fagui ziliao xuanbian* (Selected Laws and Regulations and Materials on Trademark), Beijing: Law Publishers.

Tu Yangchun *et al.* (1989) *Jin chu kou shangpin jianyan fagui yu shixian* (Regulation and Practice of Import and Export Commodity Inspection), Beijing: Law Publishers.

Wang Cunxue (ed.) (1993) *Zhongguo jingji zhongcai he susong shiyong shouce* (Practical Handbook on China's Economic Arbitration and Litigation), Beijing: China Development Press.

Wang Farong *et al.* (1992) *Zhongguo minshi shenpan xue* (The Study of China's Civil Litigation), Beijing: Law Publishers.

Wang Guichen *et al.* (eds) (1999) *Renmin fayuan yinan panli pingxi: xingzheng juan* (Analysis of Difficult Judgments of the People's Courts: Administrative Volume), Changchun: Jilin Publishers.

Wang Jiafu, Liu Hainian, and Li Lin (eds) (2000) *Renquan yu 21 shijie* (Human Rights and the 21st Century), Beijing: China Law Publishing.

Wang Lianchang (1988) *Dangdai zhongguo xingzheng fa* (Modern Chinese Administrative Law), Chongqing.

Wang Liming, Zhang Huarguang, and Hu Jianmiao, (1988) *Xingzheng guan si mantan* (Informal Discussion of Administrative Suits), Beijing.

Wang Liming (ed.) (1998) *Minshang fa yanjiu* (Studies in Civil and Commercial Law), Beijing: Law Publishers.

—— (1998) *Zhongguo minfa anli yu xueli yanjiu: Wuquan bian* (Studies in Chinese Civil Law Cases and Theory: Chapter on Property), Beijing: Law Publishers.

Wang Mengkui and Xing Junfang (eds) (1987) *Guanyu gufen zhi wenti* (Questions About the Stock System), Beijing: Economy Publishing House.

Wang Mincan (1983) *Xingzheng fa gaiyao* (Introductory Outline to Administrative Law), Beijing.

Wang Ruoshui (ed.) (1986) *Wei rendao zhuyi bianhu* (In Defense of Humanism), Beijing: United Press.

Wang Zhaoying (ed.) (1999) *Guoji jingji fa jiaoxue anli* (Teaching Cases on International Economic Law), Beijing: China University of Politics and Law Press.

Wu, D., *et al.* (1981) *Lifa zhidu bijian yanjiu* (Comparative Study of the Legislative System), Beijing: Law Publishers.

Wu Handong (1990) *Zhishi chanquan falu zhishi shouce* (Handbook of Knowledge on Intellectual Property Law), Hubei: People's Press.

Xia Yong (1992) *Renquan gainian qiyuan* (Origins of Human Rights Concepts), Beijing: University of Politics and Law Press.

—— (ed.) (1995) *Zuoxiang quanli de shidai: Zhongguo gongmin quanli fazhan yanjiu* (Proceeding Toward an Era of Rights: A Study of the Development of Citizens' Rights in China), Beijing: University of Politics and Law Press.

Xie Baogui and Zhang Qiong (1988) *Jingji fanzui de dingzui yu liangxing* (The Determination of Crime and the Measurement of Penalty for Economic Crimes), Beijing: Law Publishers.

Xie Pengcheng (2000) *Jieben falu jiazhi* (Basic Legal Values), Jinan: Shandong People's Press.

Xin Shanyin and Ye Xiaoli (eds) (1993) *Xinbian changzhang jingli shiyong jinji falu quanshu* (Newly Compiled Compendium of Practical Economic Laws for Factory Directors and Managers), Beijing: Procuracy Press.

Xingzheng shenpan shouce (Handbook on Administrative Adjudication), Beijing (1987).

«Xingzheng susong fa» tong shi bian xie zu (Group for Editing and Drafting General Interpretation of the "Administrative Litigation Law"); *Xingzheng susong fa tong shi* (General Interpretation of the Administrative Litigation Law), Beijing (1989).

Yang Chunxi (1989) *Zhong mei xuezhe lun qingshao nian fanzui* (Chinese and American Scholars on Juvenile Delinquency), Yantai: Yantai University Press.

—— (1991) *Fanzui yu xingfa xinlun* (New Theories of Crime and Criminal Punishment), Beijing: Peking University Press.

Yang Dongxu (1991) *Zhishi chanquan shiyong shouce* (Practical Handbook on Intellectual Property Rights), Beijing: Economic Daily Press.

Yang Haikun and Huang Xuexian (1999) *Zhongguo xingzheng chengxu fadianhua: Cong bijiao jiaodu yanjiu* (Codification of Chinese Administrative Procedure: Studied from a Comparative Perspective), Beijing: Law Publishers.

Yang Lixin (1998) *Renmin fayuan anli leibian pingxi: Minshi shenpan zhuan* (Critical Analysis of Types of People's Court Cases: Volume on Civil Judgments), Changchun: Jilin People's Press.

Ying Songnian (1988) *Xingzheng susong zhishi shouce* (Handbook of Knowledge on Administrative Litigation), Beijing.

Yu Hansheng (ed.) (1992) *Dui wai jing mao yu falu shiyong shouce* (Practical Handbook on Finance and Law Related to Foreign Matters), Beijing: Law Publishing.

Zeng Xianyi (1998) *Zhongguo minfa anli yu xueli yanjiu* (Studies in Chinese Civil Law Cases and Theory, serial, including volumes on General Principles of Civil Law; Tort and Inheritance; Obligations; and Property), Beijing: Law Publishers.

Zhang Huilong (1990) *She wai jingji fa anli jiexi* (Analysis of Sino–Foreign Economic Law Cases), Beijing: Youth Publishers.

Zhang Lingyuan and Du Xichuan (1989) *«Zhonghua renmin gongheguo xingzheng susong fa» shiyi* (Explanation of the "Administrative Litigation Act of the PRC"), Beijing.

Zheng Chengsi (1986) *Zhishi chanquanfa tonglun* (General Theories on Intellectual Property Law), Beijing: Law Publishers.

Zhishi chanquan shenpan shouce (Handbook on Intellectual Property Adjudication, periodical), Beijing: People's Courts Press.

Zhongguo jingji tequ kaifa qu falu fagui xuanbian (Selection of Laws and Regulations for China's Special Economic Zones and Development Zones), Beijing: Zhanlan Publishing (1987).

Zhongguo jingji tequ kaifaqu falu fagui xuanbian (Compilation of Laws and Regulations for China's Special Economic Zones and Open Areas), Beijing (1987).

Zhonghua renmin gonghegua xin fagui huibian (Compilation of New Laws and Regulations of the PRC, periodical), Beijing: Legal System Publishers.

Zhonghua renmin gongheguo duiwai jingji fagui huibian: 1945–1985 (Compilation of Economic Laws and Regulations Pertaining to Foreign Matters), Beijing: People's Press (1986).

Zhonghua renmin gongheguo fagui huibian (Compilation of Current Laws and Regulations of the PRC, annual), Beijing: Law Publishers.

Zhonghua renmin gongheguo sifabu falu zhengce yanjiu shi (Laws and Policy Research Office of the PRC Ministry of Justice), *Hengxiang jingji lianhe falu fa gui zhengce huibian* (Compilation of Laws and Statutes and Regulations on Horizontal Economic Linkages), Beijing (1987).

Zhonghua shiyong faxue da cidian (Dictionary of Chinese Jurisprudence), Changchun: Jilin University Press (1988).

Zhou Wangsheng (1988) *Lifa xue* (Legislation), Beijing: Peking University Press.

—— (1994) *Lifa lun* (Theory of Legislation), Beijing: Peking University Press.

Zui gao renmin fayuan yanjiu shi (Research Office of the Supreme People's Court) (1988) *Xingzheng shenpan shouce* (Handbook on Administrative Adjudication), Beijing.

Chinese-language periodicals

Bai ke zhishi (Encyclopedia of Knowledge)
Beijing daxue xuebao (Peking University Journal)
Beijing ribao
Beijing shehui kexue (Beijing Social Sciences)
Beijing Xinhua
Beijing Zhongwen xinwenshe
Cankao bao (Reference News)
Cheng Ming (Hong Kong)
Chengshi jinrong (Municipal Finance)
Dangdai faxue (Modern Law)
Fa shang yanjiu (Studies in Law and Commerce)
Fa zhi jianshe (Building the Legal System)
Falu kexue (Law Science)
Faxue (Jurisprudence)
Faxue jianshe (Building the Legal System)
Faxue luncong (Collected Theories on Legal Studies)
Faxue pinglun (Commentary on Legal Studies)
Faxue ribao (Legal System Daily)
Faxue xuexi yu yanjiu (Study and Research in Jurisprudence)
Faxue yanjiu (Studies in Law)
Faxue yuekan (Law Science Monthly)
Faxue zazhi (Legal Studies Magazine)
Faxuejia (Jurist)
Fazhi ribao (Legal System Daily)
Fazhi yu shehui fazhan (The Legal System and Social Development)
Gongren ribao (Worker's Daily)
Guangming ribao (Guangming Daily)
Guoji maoyi (International Trade)
Guoji maoyi wenti (Issues in International Trade)
Guoji shang bao (Journal of International Commerce)
Guowuyuan gongbao (State Council Bulletin)
Hangzhou daxue xuebao (Journal of Hangzhou University)
Hebei shifan daxue xuebao (Journal of Hebei Normal University)
Henan sheng zhengfa guanli ganbu xueyuan xuebao (Journal of the Henan Provincial
    Institute for Political Legal Administrative Cadres)
Hong Kong Zhongguo Tongxun She (HK China News Agency)
Hongqi (Red Flag)
Hsin Bao (Hong Kong)
Hunan shifan daxue shehui kexue xuebao (Social Science Journal of Hunan Normal
    University)
Jianghai xuekan (Jianghai Journal)
Jiefang ribao (Liberation Daily)
Jingji cankao bao (Economic Reference Report)
Jingji yanjiu cankao (Reference Materials on Economic Research)
Jingji fazhi (Economic Legal System)
Jingji jingwei (Economic Transit) (Zhengzhou)
Jingji ribao (Economy Daily)
Jingji shenpan zhidao yu cankao (Civil and Commercial Trial Review)

Jinrong shibao (Financial Times)
Kai Fang (Hong Kong)
Keji ribao (Science and Technology Daily)
Kuang Chiao Ching (Hong Kong)
Laodong ribao (Worker's Daily)
Liaoning daxue xuebao (Liaoning University Journal)
Liaowang (Outlook)
Lilun yuetan (Theory Monthly)
Minshang faxue (Civil and Commercial Law)
Minzhu yu fazhi (Democracy and the Legal System)
Neibu wengao (Internal Manuscripts)
Qiushi (Truth)
Renmin fayuan anli xuan (Compilation of cases from the People's Courts)
Renmin fayuan bao (People's Court Gazette)
Renmin ribao (People's Daily)
Renmin ribao – hai wai ban (People's Daily – overseas edition)
Shandong shida xuebao (Journal of Shandong Normal University)
Shanghai fazhi bao (Shanghai Legal System Gazette)
Shanghai Legal System
Ta Kung Pao (Hong Kong)
Tansuo yu zhengming (Inquiry and Debate)
Tianjin shehui kexue (Tianjin Social Sciences)
Wen Wei Po (Hong Kong)
Wenhui bao (Literary Daily)
Xiandai faxue (Modern Legal Studies)
Xinhua Domestic Service
Xinhua English Service
Xinhua Hong Kong Service
Xinhua News Agency
Xuexi yu tansuo (Study and Inquiry)
Zhengda faxue pinglun (Chengchi University Jurisprudence and Discussion)
Zhengfa luntan: Zhongguo zheng fa daxue xuebao (Politics and Law Forum: Journal of the Chinese University of Politics and Law)
Zhengming (Hong Kong)
Zhengzhi yu falu (Politics and Law)
Zhishi chanquan yanjiu (Intellectual Property Studies)
Zhong wai faxue (Chinese and Foreign Jurisprudence)
Zhongguo faxue (Chinese Legal Studies)
Zhongguo fazhi bao (Chinese Legal System Gazette)
Zhongguo jingji tizhi gaige (Reform of the Chinese Economic Structure)
Zhongguo renmin daxue xuebao (Journal of Chinese People's University)
Zhongguo shehui kexue (Chinese Social Science)
Zhongguo Shehuikexueyuan Yanjiushengyuan xuebao (Journal of the CASS Graduate School)
Zhongguo tudi kexue (China Land Science)
Zhongguo zhengquan bao (China Securities Reporter)
Zhongguo zhi chun (China Spring)
Zhonghua renmin gongheguo zui gao renmin fayuan gongbao (PRC Supreme Court Bulletin)

Zhongguo Xinwen She (Beijing China News Agency)

Zhongnan zhengfa xueyuan xuebao (Journal of the Central South Political Legal Institute)

Zhongshan Daxue xuebao: She ke ban (Zhongshan University Journal: Social Science Edition)

Zhongwai faxue (Chinese and Foreign Legal Studies)

Index